# STRANGE WONDER

INSURRECTIONS: CRITICAL STUDIES IN RELIGION, POLITICS, AND CULTURE

INSURRECTIONS: CRITICAL STUDIES IN RELIGION,
POLITICS, AND CULTURE
Slavoj Žižek, Clayton Crockett, Creston Davis, Jeffrey W. Robbins, editors

The intersection of religion, politics, and culture is one of the most discussed areas in theory today. It also has the deepest and most wide-ranging impact on the world. Insurrections: Critical Studies in Religion, Politics, and Culture will bring the tools of philosophy and critical theory to the political implications of the religious turn. The series will address a range of religious traditions and political viewpoints in the United States, Europe, and other parts of the world. Without advocating any specific religious or theological stance, the series aims nonetheless to be faithful to the radical emancipatory potential of religion.

# STRANGE
# WONDER

## THE CLOSURE OF METAPHYSICS

## AND THE OPENING OF AWE

*Mary-Jane Rubenstein*

COLUMBIA UNIVERSITY PRESS   NEW YORK

COLUMBIA UNIVERSITY PRESS

*Publishers Since 1893*

New York   Chichester, West Sussex

Copyright © 2008 Columbia University Press

Paperback edition, 2011

Library of Congress Cataloging-in-Publication Data

Rubenstein, Mary-Jane.

Strange wonder: the closure of metaphysics and the opening of awe / Mary-Jane Rubenstein.

p. cm. — (Insurrections: critical studies in religion, politics, and culture)

Includes bibliographical references and index.

ISBN 978-0-231-14632-6 (cloth: alk. paper) — ISBN 978-0-231-14633-3 (pbk.: alk. paper) —
ISBN 978-0-231-51859-8 (e-book)

1. Wonder (Philosophy) 2. Philosophy. I. Title. II. Series.

B105.W65R83   2008

190—dc22                                        2008032131

Casebound editions of Columbia University Press books are printed
on permanent and durable acid-free paper.

Printed in the United States of America

c 10 9 8 7 6 5 4 3

p 10 9 8 7 6 5 4 3 2

References to Internet Web Sites (URLs) were accurate at the time
of writing. Neither the author nor Columbia University Press is
responsible for Web sites that may have expired or changed since
the book was prepared.

Horatio: O day and night, but this is wondrous strange.
Hamlet: And therefore as a stranger give it welcome.
There are more things in heaven and earth, Horatio,
Than are dreamt of in your philosophy.

    —William Shakespeare, *Hamlet*

## FOR MY TEACHERS

For my part I have already, thanks to you, given utterance to more than I had in me.

  —Plato, *Theaetetus*

# CONTENTS

## ACKNOWLEDGMENTS

I would like here to acknowledge just some of the numerous people upon whom my research, thinking, and sanity have relied in the course of writing this book. Thanks are due first of all to my doctoral adviser, Wayne Proudfoot, whose careful critique and thoughtful suggestions throughout this process have been invaluable. I am also grateful to Elizabeth Castelli for her help with the Platonic material, her eye for the political landscape, her ear for metaphor, and her tireless encouragement. Mark C. Taylor first pointed me toward Jean-Luc Nancy in relation to this study, and I have appreciated his intellectual generosity and interpretation of modern philosophy ever since I worked with him as an undergraduate at Williams College.

Much of the initial impetus to undertake this project emerged from a seminar co-taught by Avital Ronell and Jacques Derrida at New York University, which I attended from 2001 to 2003. With her characteristic combination of grace and incisiveness, Professor Ronell has taught me to become a much more attentive reader, and I will forever remember Professor Derrida's painstaking, courageous, and, above all, caring approach to the task of thinking. I also thank my friend and colleague Elizabeth Loeb, who understood what I was trying to do with Derrida and wonder before I did.

Perhaps not surprisingly, this topic has provoked a vast range of conversations with a vast range of colleagues, friends, and mentors. For thoughts that have haunted my writing to the extent that I would not know how to go about footnoting them, I thank Storm Swain, Randall Styers, Denys Turner, Celia Deutsch, Jack Hawley, Catherine Keller, Simon Oliver, John Milbank, Cate Williamson, Patti Welch, Cláudio Carvalhaes, Raffaele Timarchi, Chloe Breyer, Ephraim Rubenstein, and Jenna Tiitsman. Jenna also read—more closely than it probably deserved—an early version of the introduction. Many thanks to Taylor Carman for his insight into the Heidegger material, Jeff Rider for his thoughtful reading of parts of the draft, Jodi Eichler-Levine for her help with the Greek material, Will Blomquist for the last-minute editing, and Wendy Lochner and Christine Mortlock at Columbia University Press. I am especially grateful to Susan Pensak for the extraordinary care she has taken in editing the manuscript. I also thank Thomas Ashley for the Keats, Michael Ashley for the solidarity, Elizabeth Salzer for taking my farthest-flung thoughts seriously, Vanessa Morris-Burke for keeping me on my feet, my students for keeping me on my toes, and my colleagues in the Religion Department at Wesleyan University for their careful engagement of this work.

My research has been generously supported by the Jacob K. Javits Foundation; the Episcopal Church Foundation; the Center for Comparative Literature and Society at Columbia University; and the Cathedral Church of St. John the Divine, the Very Reverend James A. Kowalski, dean. The project has also relied heavily upon the unflagging encouragement—not to mention the paper products and leftovers—of all my parents: Veronica and Thomas Warren, Joshua and Jennifer Rubenstein, and Marta Johnson. My siblings do their best to keep me honest and amazed: Isaac, Marlena, Rebecca, and certainly Kenan, without whom I doubt I would be able to think through anything at all. And literally boundless thanks are due to Helen Ashley, whose patience, creativity, and compassion are themselves nothing short of miraculous.

Lastly, I thank H. Ganse Little Jr., Bill Darrow, and Catherine Pickstock, for getting so much of this going in the first place.

# STRANGE WONDER

To say philosophy originates in wonder means philosophy is wondrous in its essence and becomes more wondrous the more it becomes what it really is.

—Martin Heidegger

Do not all charms fly at the mere touch of cold philosophy?

—John Keats

## INTRODUCTION: Wonder and the Births of Philosophy

### Socrates' Small Difficulty

One day in Athens, sensing he is nearing the end of his life, Socrates asks Theodorus whether there are any extraordinary students at the gymnasium. The wise old geometer names one Theaetetus, extolling the boy's "amazing" nature and his "astonishing" mind, not to mention his remarkable resemblance to Socrates.[1] Just then, the object of their fascination appears on the horizon. As he approaches, Socrates decides to "examine" Theaetetus, telling the wide-eyed, snub-nosed boy, "I want to see for myself what kind of face I have" (144d). The conversation that ensues between the Master and the Wunderkind is nothing short of a reflection upon the nature—and future—of philosophy itself.

"I have a small difficulty," Socrates tells his mirror image, "which I think ought to be investigated" (145d). Socrates confesses that while he continues to gain knowledge of geometry and astronomy and music, he "can't get a proper grasp of what on earth *knowledge* really is" (145e; emphasis added). Presumably, he ventures, one seeks knowledge in order to gain wisdom, but, in this very pursuit, knowledge and wisdom themselves remain a mystery. So the "small difficulty" haunting this dialogue is quite simply that Socrates does not know what it is to know; the father of Western philosophy does not know what he loves when he loves *sophia*.[2]

If Socrates cannot get a grip on knowledge, however, he also cannot leave it alone; he can neither resolve nor ignore the problem of the what it means to know. Theaetetus echoes this dilemma: "I have often tried to think this out. . . . But I can never persuade myself that anything I say will really do. . . . I can't even stop worrying about it" (148a). And, in fact, nothing Theaetetus says about knowledge will suffice. Even after an extensive conversation with Western philosophy's greatest teacher, knowledge remains both inscrutable and insurmountable for Theaetetus; that is, the problem of knowledge persists throughout the dialogue *as a problem*. Perhaps the problem with this particular problem is that that which stands under every investigation is precisely what investigation cannot understand. Knowledge is presupposed by every philosophical examination, yet, as Socrates and his pseudodouble repeatedly discover, it recedes like a ghost when confronted directly. Like all that truly calls for thought, knowledge itself cannot be thought—and yet it must be thought.

As usual, Socrates himself offers no opinions or theories during the course of this dialogue, concentrating instead on his interlocutor's own ideas about the nature of knowledge. Claiming to be "barren of wisdom," Socrates announces himself as a midwife of the soul called to deliver ideas from wise young men like Theaetetus (150b–c). The first step in this process will determine that Theaetetus is, in fact, pregnant and in labor with a philosophical viewpoint. The next will use dialogic drugs and incantations either to "bring about the birth" or to "promote a miscarriage" (149d), depending on whether the brain child is a genuine (*alêthes*) idea or whether it is just an image (*eidolon*), or phantom, of an idea.[3] Discerning these two is, for Socrates, "the midwife's greatest and most noble function" (150b), and so Socrates spends most of the dialogue examining each one of Theaetetus's views on knowledge, trying to ascertain whether it is "really fertile or a mere wind-egg" (151e). Before Theaetetus gives birth, however, Socrates warns him that he must not attempt to cling to a view if it turns out to be insubstantial: "when I examine what you say, I may perhaps think it is a phantom and not truth, and proceed to take it quietly from you and abandon it. Now if this happens, you mustn't get savage with me, like a mother over her first-born child. Do you know, people have often before now got into such a state with me as to be literally ready to bite when I take away some nonsense or other from them" (151c).

But Theaetetus is not just any interlocutor. Theodorus has already distinguished him from the other young men at the gymnasium by saying he is neither rash and impetuous nor heavy and "sluggish," but rather so "good-tempered," particularly for his age, that "it is astonishing" (144b). During the course of his conversation with Socrates, this awe-inspiring pupil gives birth to three potential definitions of the essence of knowledge: perception, true judgment, and true judgment plus a reason or account. And, true to his reputation, Theaetetus does not "get into a rage" (161a) when Socrates shows each one of them to be a phantom and takes them all away from him. Rather, his reaction to this noetic divestment is one of wonder: "By the gods, Socrates, I am lost in wonder when I think of all these things, and sometimes when I regard them it really makes my head swim."[4] Socrates responds, "It seems that Theodorus was not far from the truth when he guessed what kind of person you are. For this is an experience which is characteristic of a philosopher, this wondering [*thaumazein*]: this is where philosophy begins and nowhere else" (155d).[5]

What does it mean to locate the origin of philosophy in wonder? What does it mean to distinguish the philosopher as one who experiences wonder—or to say that a protophilosopher is right on track when he is lost in it? *What is wonder* that it marks the origin of thinking and thinkers themselves? Interrogating wonder in this fashion, one is immediately thrown back upon Socrates' eternally recurring "small difficulty," that is, the necessity of thinking the condition of thinking's own possibility. How is philosophy to go about seeking the very wonder that sets it in motion?

To make matters more complicated, this is precisely the sort of dilemma that gives rise to wonder in the first place. *Thaumazein* arises when the understanding cannot master that which lies closest to it—when, surrounded by utterly ordinary concepts and things, the philosopher suddenly finds himself surrounded on all sides by aporia. Theaetetus's exclamation, for example, is provoked during the course of the examination of his first wind-egg: that knowledge is perception. Socrates begins from the self-evident premise that nothing can be anything other than what it is, but then goes on to demonstrate that a group of six dice can at once be described as *more* in relation to a group of four dice and *less* in relation to a group of twelve. Similarly, Socrates, who now is *bigger* than Theaetetus, will in a year's time be described as *smaller* than Theaetetus, without undergoing any change in substance. It is at this moment that Theaetetus exclaims that he is "lost in wonder." It might seem, as some scholars have suggested, that wonder in the Platonic dialogues is therefore provoked by the "mixing-up of opposites" (less/more, bigger/smaller).[6] This hypothesis seems to be confirmed in the *Parmenides*, where Socrates tells his interlocutor that if the form of the "one" and the form of the "many" were shown to be both distinct and the same, "that would call for astonishment."[7] I would argue, however, that the coincidence of opposites is not the source of Socratic wonder, but is rather a particular instance of a broader phenomenon.

After having taken Theaetetus's first phantom child away from him, Socrates asks the boy to account for what has just taken place—to describe what happens when he examines the everyday opinion that knowledge is perception. Theaetetus answers, "I draw a conclusion that contradicts my original suppositions." Socrates responds, "and that is the kind of thing that might have happened to you more than once, you wonderful fellow" (165d). Theaetetus, then, is wonder-struck not at the coincidence of opposites in particular, but rather at the sudden insubstantiality of something he had held to be self-evident. So it is not the coincidence of "bigger and smaller" in the same body that leaves Theaetetus wondering, but rather the collapse of the perfectly sensible premise that nothing can be anything other than what it is. What is astonishing is that an everyday assumption has suddenly become untenable: the familiar has become strange, throwing even the unquestionable into question.

Wonder, then, comes on the scene neither as a tranquilizing force nor as a kind of will-toward-epistemological domination, but rather as a profoundly unsettling pathos. Rather than setting him on some sure course toward the Forms, the philosopher's wonder marks his inability to ground himself in the ordinary as he reaches toward the extraordinary; it indicates, in fact, that the skyward reach has rendered uncanny the very ground on which the philosopher stands. And because it leaves thinking thus ungrounded, thaumazein is not merely uncomfortable; it is downright *dangerous*. Standing in thaumazein, the philosopher stands exposed to that which he cannot master; that which, in turn, threatens to disable the sort of mastery one expects of philosophers.

Socrates introduces the perilous nature of thaumazein during his evaluation of Protagoras's infamous statement of relativism. When Protagoras proclaims that "Man is the measure of all things," his audience is "astounded at his wisdom as though he were a god" (161c).[8] Starting with such a commonsensical precept, Protagoras cannot but gain the unquestioning assent of those who hear him. And yet, Socrates reflects, if Protagoras is just trying to say that all perceptions are equally valid, then he would have been more responsible to announce, "'Pig is the measure of all things,' or 'Baboon' or some yet more out-of-the-way creature with the power of perception" (161c). Had he begun with *anything* other than "Man," his formula would at least have provoked a modicum of critical reflection among his students. "Come, Theaetetus," Socrates asks his young doppelganger, "tell me if you are not yourself astonished at suddenly finding that you are the equal in wisdom of any man or even a god?" Theaetetus responds that he is "very much astonished," for while he and Socrates were initially discussing Protagoras's theorem, "it appeared to me a very sound one. But now, all in a minute, it is quite the other way around" (162c–d). This, as we have seen, is the way wonder strikes: it arises when something that seemed reasonable and self-evident becomes strange and insupportable. But here Socrates introduces another problematic layer to the experience of thaumazein: if wonder wonders at the way the unquestionable opens onto the incomprehensible, then wonder is also susceptible to a kind of dumb or misplaced reverence. Socrates ventures that if Protagoras *had* called Baboon or Pig the measure of all things, then "it would have made it clear to us at once that, while we were standing astounded at his wisdom as though he were a god, he was in reality no better authority than a tadpole—let alone any other man" (161d). As it stands, though, Protagoras's theory draws people in by means of what seems a perfectly reasonable presupposition and then leaves them dumbstruck at his conclusions, revering him as the source of all wisdom.

Socrates thus draws an implicit distinction between the wonder that opens up inquiry (Theaetetus's astonishment at the incoherence of the Protagorean theorem) and the wonder that closes it down (the astonishment of Protagoras's dazzled disciples). So the thaumazein that opens philosophy can lead either to tireless critical inquiry or to unquestioning discipleship. For this reason, the very tendency toward wondering that makes Theaetetus a philosopher also leaves him vulnerable to manipulation by false teachers. If one of these teachers were to get his hands on Theaetetus, Socrates cautions, "he would keep on refuting you and not let you go till you had been struck with wonder at his wisdom . . . and had got yourself thoroughly tied up by him. Then, when he had you tamed and bound, he would set you free for a ransom—whatever price seemed appropriate to the two of you" (165d–e).[9] This is how founders of schools and political parties go about making disciples: by beginning from commonsensical principles, divesting their pupils of all they thought they knew, and then filling in that wondrous openness with unquestionable doctrines and dicta. It seems, then, that there are two kinds of wonder: wonder that keeps the philosopher questioning and giving birth (if only to wind-eggs) and wonder that keeps him chained in stupefied assent to the very "self-evident" positions that Socratic thaumazein dispels. Yet it will become clear that this latter "wonder" is not really wonder at all. Rather, such uncritical discipleship clings to inviolable theories in order to take *refuge* from wonder's open sea of endless questioning, strangeness, and impossibility. There is wonder, then, and there is the retreat from wonder. Wonder either keeps itself open, exposing itself to the raging elements, or it shuts itself down, shielding itself against all uncertainty within the comfortable confines of the certain, the familiar, and the possible. It must be said, however, that the opening of wonder conditions the possibility of its own closure and that such closure can lead to intellectual complacency at best, philo-sociopolitical manipulation at worst. Either way, this wondering is a dangerous game.

As such, thaumazein is exceedingly difficult to sustain. Socrates himself attests to this problem at one remarkable juncture of his conversation with Theaetetus. The young man has offered his second position up to Socratic examination: knowledge, he ventures, is true opinion or judgment (*alêthes doxa*). In order to determine what this true opinion might mean, Socrates says it will be necessary to examine its opposite: false opinion (*pseudês doxa*).

Unfortunately, the pseudês doxa is a phenomenon whose philosophical possibility Socrates has never quite been able to secure. "I have something on my mind," Socrates cautions Theaetetus, "which has often bothered me before, and got me into great difficulty, both in my own thought and in discussion with other people—I mean, I can't say what it is, this experience we have, and how it arises in us" (187d). And yet, for some reason, Socrates maintains that this pseudês doxa must be understood before the alêthes doxa can be evaluated as a candidate for the essence of knowledge.

After a good deal of stalling, Socrates begins to examine the bothersome phenomenon of false opinion, beginning from the perfectly reasonable proposition that a person either knows something or he does not know it (188a). And immediately, Socrates loses his grasp on the pseudês doxa. Following the logic of his own presupposition, Socrates posits three situations that might produce a false opinion: either a person mistakes a thing he knows for another thing he knows, or he mistakes a thing he does not know for another thing he does not know, *or* he mistakes something he knows (or does not know) for something he does not know (or knows). None of these, Socrates realizes, is a possible source of false opinion, for if a person truly knows something, he will not mistake it for something else, nor will he mistake something else for it. Nor, if a person does *not* know something, will he know it well enough to mistake something else he does not know for it. So, after numerous thwarted attempts to reconfigure and secure these three situations, Socrates admits that the only remaining possibility is that his presupposition was wrong—that somehow it must be possible both to know something and not to know it.

With the demise of Socrates' seemingly watertight thesis, Martin Heidegger will tell us that philosophy itself is unmoored,[10] and indeed, the ancient mariner himself confesses to feeling nauseous now that his grounding principle has become ungrounded. Surrounded by wondrous impossibility, Socrates and Theaetetus have sailed into dangerous (a-)philosophical waters that just might overpower them completely: "If we can't find any way of extricating ourselves, then I suppose we shall be laid low, like sea-sick passengers, and give ourselves into the hands of the argument and let it trample all over us and do what it likes with us. . . . We are in such an extremity that we need to turn every argument over and over and test it from all sides" (191a–c). But rather than getting on with the argument-inverting he needs to do, Socrates attempts something utterly un-Socratic. He sets forth a *theory* of the pseudês doxa. Perhaps, he suggests, a false opinion is formed when perception and knowledge are improperly matched to one another, like two misaligned wax imprints. But this definition is no help at all, for the simple reason that Socrates still does not know what knowledge is. Why on earth would he call upon knowledge to define false opinion, when the reason he is calling on false opinion in the first place is to define knowledge?

Socrates, it seems, is driven to this desperate act because the scene in which he finds himself is entirely aporetic. Obviously, false judgments are made all the time. Yet, philosophically examined, it looks as though a false judgment cannot occur. The pseudês doxa, perhaps the most common type of doxa in the world, is somehow utterly impossible. Things are so slippery that even Socrates needs something to grab onto, and so he proceeds to fashion a philosophical climbing rope that might haul him out of the abyss into which he has been thrown. Once Socrates realizes what he has done, he is almost completely unhinged: "I'm annoyed at my own stupidity. . . . I am not only annoyed; I am alarmed/afraid [dedoika]" (195c–d). Socrates' effort to nail down the possibility of true and false opinion is misguided, not only because he has unwittingly called upon an unknown "knowledge" to stabilize him, but also because, as he stated at the outset, the gods have prohibited him from forming any positive doctrine. Socrates' "stupidity," which astonishingly enacts the very pseudês doxa that so stubbornly eludes him, is that he has tried to form an opinion too soon—that he could not withstand the frightening indeterminacy of wonder.

Finally regaining his groundless ground, Socrates returns to the business of midwifery, demonstrating the untenability of every one of Theaetetus's remaining views on the nature of knowledge. Having shown that Theaetetus's progeny were all mere "wind-eggs and not worth bringing up" (210b), Socrates tells him that, should Theaetetus happen to concoct any more theories, they will be better off as a result of these phantom births. But, Socrates adds, "if you remain barren, your companions will find you gentler and less tiresome; you will be modest and not think you know what you don't know." Then, by telling Theaetetus, "this is all my art can achieve—nothing more" (210c), Socrates reveals that Theaetetus's children could never have grown into full-fledged adults. Under Socrates' maieutic scrutiny, all theories turn out to be phantoms and wind-eggs; all doxai pseudês doxai. The only "real child," as it turns out, is Theaetetus himself. Having been made Socratically barren, Theaetetus has been made into a truer image of Socrates[11]—a snub-nosed, wide-eyed thinker who stands astonished, not at the abilities of his teacher, but rather at the groundlessness of things.[12] In freeing the young philosopher from his own fledgling doctrines, Socrates has freed him for the aporetic vertigo of wonder.

## The Wound of Wonder

As Socrates and Theaetetus describe it, thaumazein wonders at the stubborn inscrutability of the everyday. Unlike curiosity or puzzlement, then, wonder does not vanish when the cause of a surprising phenomenon is discovered, nor does it relentlessly seek out new marvels to calculate, comprehend, or possess. Rather, wonder wonders at that which conditions—and for that reason ultimately eludes—the mechanisms of calculation, comprehension, and possession themselves. This is not to say that wonder precludes all calculation, representation, and opining; to the contrary, it will be argued, particularly in chapter 4, that wonder is the condition of possibility for all of these (after all, Theaetetus goes on to become a mathematician). I am trying, rather, to mark as inimical to wonder a particular kind of mastery that proceeds by means of *certainty* and exceptionless appropriation. There is an irreducible difference between a rigorous, investigative thinking that sustains wonder's strangeness and a rigorous, investigative thinking that endeavors to assimilate that strangeness.[13] To the extent that thinking remains with wonder, it is not inimical to all propositions, but rather keeps propositions provisional, open-ended, and incomplete. This is because wonder wonders at the strangeness of the most familiar: at that which, *within the possibilities of determinate thinking*, still remains indeterminate, unthinkable, and impossible. Wonder wonders, therefore, at the opening in which all determinate thinking takes place. And insofar as Socrates tells us that wonder opens the possibility of thinking itself, we can risk the tautology: wonder wonders at wonder.

The critical usefulness of such a declaration is admittedly questionable. "Wonder wonders at wonder" still leaves one wondering what wonder *is*. As John Sallis has pointed out, however, the problem with asking what wonder is, is that "the question comes too late. For when one comes to ask the philosophical question 'What is . . . ?' ('*ti esti* . . . ?'), one moves already within the opening [of metaphysics]; and wonder has already come into play in prompting that opening."[14] If, as Aristotle claimed and Wayne Proudfoot has demonstrated, any pathos without an explicitly conceptual structure "cannot be identified" as such, then what is one to do with the pathos of thaumazein that conditions the structuring of concepts in the first place?[15] Wonder leaves one, it seems, with the character in Beckett's *Happy Days* who mumbles to herself, "I can do no more. (Pause.) Say no more. (Pause.) But I must say more. (Pause.) Problem here. (Pause.)"[16] Again: opening the question about wonder opens the question of opening itself. What gives thinking pause when it goes about thinking wonder is that "one will never be able to interrogate wonder philosophically except by way of a questioning that the operation of wonder will already have determined."[17] Impossible as the task may be, however, one cannot *not* interrogate the uninterrogable condition of interrogation—at least not without closing thinking off to that which inspires it in the first place. Any thinking of wonder is destined to miss its mark, and yet thinking cannot *not* think wonder. One hopes, therefore, that even if the difference between the thinkable and the unthinkable will never be closed, attempting to think the unthinkable *as such* will at the very least expand the limits of thought before collapsing back into them. Therefore, ever bearing in mind its inescapable determination by the stuff it seeks to elucidate, this analysis will begin its strategic evasion of the "what is" by traveling straight *through* it.

The word *wonder* derives from the Old English *wundor*, which some etymologists suggest might be cognate not only with the German *Wunder*, but also with *Wunde*: cut, gash, *wound*.[18] While the *Oxford English Dictionary* does not recognize this derivation of *wonder* (appropriately, its origin is said to be "unknown"), the OED does support a possible shared ancestry between wonder and wounding in the entry's "obsolete" listings. Among these, one finds definitions ranging from "omen or portent" to "an evil or shameful action," "evil or horrible deeds," "destruction, disaster"; "great distress or grief." "Phraseological" uses of the word include both the familiar "marvelously, wonderfully" and the more surprising "dreadfully, horribly, terribly." Antiquated uses of the word include a transitive, almost violent function: "to affect or strike with wonder; to cause to marvel, amaze, astound."[19]

Wonder, then, is inherently ambivalent. The coincidence in this word of marvel and dread, amazement and terror, will find resonance with a Heideggerian mood that we will explore at length in the next chapter: *Verhaltenheit*. Usually translated as "restraint" or "reservedness," Heidegger claims that this mood comprises both terror and awe without reducing either to the other. And the duplicity of wonder is hardly limited to English usage and Heideggerian philosophy. In *The Sublime and the Beautiful*, Edmund Burke notes that "several languages bear a strong testimony" to a profound ambivalence between terror and awe in his analysis of the ruling emotion of the sublime. He writes,

> *Thambos* is in Greek, either fear or wonder; *deinos* is terrible or respectable; *aideo*, to reverence or to fear. *Vereor* in Latin, is what *aideo* is in Greek. The Romans used the verb *stupeo*, a term which strongly marks the state of an astonished mind, to express the effect either of simple fear, or of astonishment; the word *attonitus* (thunderstruck) is equally expressive of the alliance of these ideas; and do not the French *éttonement* [sic.], and the English *astonishment* and *amazement*, point out as clearly the kindred emotions which attend fear and wonder? They who have a more general knowledge of languages, could produce, I make no doubt, many other and equally striking examples.[20]

While I do not pretend to have anything approaching the linguistic knowledge Burke is looking for here, perhaps the most noticeable absence in this list is the mood of "fear" as it takes shape in the Hebrew Bible. The Hebrew *yir'ah* designates that particular combination of awe, dread, and reverence proper to those who have witnessed the signs, wonders, and portents of God's works in the world. Hence Psalm 33 entreats, "Let all the earth fear the Lord: let all the inhabitants of the world stand in awe/dread of him."[21] Psalm 139 proclaims, "I will praise thee; for I am fearfully and wonderfully made: marvelous are thy works; and that my soul knoweth right well."[22] Of course, God's "works" in the biblical world are often "marvelous" in the sense of being downright *terrifying*: one might think, for example, of the "signs," "wonders," "war," and "great terrors" that God performs to deliver the Israelites out of Egypt.[23] God turns the Nile to blood; sends frogs, gnats, flies, boils, hail; and finally kills the Egyptians' first-born sons, all in order to teach the Israelites to "fear" God. Unfortunately for the Egyptians, it is only after the ten plagues, the parting of the Red Sea, and the drowning of the Pharaoh's army that Exodus tells us, for the first time, "and the people feared the Lord."[24]

Another of God's infamous "great terrors" is his fiery obliteration of Sodom and Gomorrah, which Augustine of Hippo recounts as a "wondrous transformation": "The land of Sodom was certainly not always as it is now . . . in the Divine Scriptures it is compared to the Paradise of God. But after it was touched by heaven, it became a place of wondrous, blackened horror."[25] For Augustine as for the Psalms, these "wondrous" divine acts demand the human response of *admiratio*. In the face of "The Fear of Isaac,"[26] the appropriate response is, to put it bluntly, fear. The terrified awe of *yir'ah* can therefore be said to be the theological mood par excellence. This origin in wonder is perhaps not surprising, considering Western theology's near-identity with philosophy until the early modern separation of the disciplines. Socrates tells Theaetetus that wonder is the origin of all philo-sophy. And the Psalms, Proverbs, and Job all name *yir'ah* as "the beginning of wisdom."[27]

If we follow the traces of its forgotten and repressed meanings, then, wonder loses much of the sugarcoating it has acquired in contemporary usage. As we saw with Socrates' reaction to the *pseudês doxa*, wonder in the biblical and classical worlds responds to a destabilizing and unassimilable interruption in the ordinary course of things, an uncanny opening, rift, or wound in the everyday. Like the parting of a sea, the destruction of a city, the incoherence of the self-evident. Yet wonder's capacity to arouse and inflict terror, worship, and grief is utterly decimated—or, more precisely, fervently repressed—by the modern brand of wonder that connotes white bread, lunchbox superheroes, and fifties sitcoms. As will become clear, metaphysics performs a similar set of repressions: something about wonder provokes its domestication and declawing at the hands of its offspring.

Insofar as wonder can function as a kind of wound in the everyday (and here I resist such grating coinages as *wounder* or *wo/(u)nd(er)*), it must again be emphasized: just as a wound ceases to be itself when it heals, wonder is only wonder when it remains open. Wonder opens an originary rift in thought, an unsuturable gash that both constitutes and deconstitutes thinking as such. To open the question of wonder, then, is to open thought not only to the fantastic and amazing but also to the dreadful and the threatening. As we try to follow the traces of this wondrous primordiality, we therefore find ourselves in the ambivalent nether regions of Burke's (and Kant's) sublime—as well as Blaise Pascal's abysmal awe, Rudolf Otto's numinous, Maurice Blanchot's disaster, Jacques Lacan's real, Julia Kristeva's abject, and Søren Kierkegaard's *horror religiosus*.[28] Opening the question of wonder, thinking opens the fascinating/repulsive, creative/ruinous, astounding/horrifying, heirophanic/monstrous excess against which, as we will see, more "proper" philosophy takes pains to secure itself.

To the extent that it tries to resolve wonder into certainty, formulas, and clear and distinct ideas, I will argue that the philosophy that begins in thaumazein short-circuits its own genealogy. And, in fact, philosophy's tendency to prune its family tree can already be seen in the *Theaetetus*. "This is an experience which is characteristic of a philosopher, this wondering," Socrates tells Theaetetus, "this is where philosophy begins and nowhere else." He continues: "And the man who made Iris the child of Thaumas was perhaps no bad genealogist—But aren't you beginning to see now what is the explanation of these puzzles, according to the theory which we are attributing to Protagoras?" (155d). The strange gap here between the lineage of thaumazein and the game theory of Protagoras—marked in the Levett and Burnyeat translation by a dash—seems to indicate that Socrates is leaving something out of his genealogy. And in fact, he is.

According to Hesiod's *Theogony*, the sea god Thaumas (wonder) is the son of Gaia (earth) and Oceanus (sea). Thaumas marries Electra, and their union produces Iris (rainbow), the breathtaking messenger of the gods. As it is in the biblical tradition, then, the "Greek" rainbow is what Onians has called "the supreme wonder, a miracle linking heaven and earth."[29] What Socrates does not say here, interrupting himself suddenly to return to a tangential point about Protagoras, is that Iris, the "supreme wonder," is not the only child of Thaumas and Electra. The passage in Hesiod reads as follows: "And Thaumas married deep-flowing Ocean's / Daughter, Elektra, who bore swift Iris and / The rich-haired Harpies, Aello and Oypetes, / Who keep pace with stormwinds and birds / Flying their missions on wings swift as time."[30] For some reason, Socrates neglects to tell Theaetetus that Wonder's *other* daughters are the Harpies. Like their sister, these winged creatures were also employed as intercosmic messengers, frequently charged with the frightful task of carrying humans off to the underworld. Hesiod (c. 800 BCE) does not convey any particularly repellent characteristics in relation to the Harpies, and, in fact, the earliest myths portrayed them as quite beautiful. But by Plato's time (427–347 bce) the Harpies were thought of as "ugly bird-like monsters with large claws. They always stank, were perpetually hungry and Zeus sent them continually to take the food away from Phineus."[31] Even as Socrates claims wonder as the origin of all philosophy, then, he only avows *half* of its progeny, excluding the ravenous and noisome for the sake of the properly wondrous. If thinking were truly to keep wonder open, however, it would have to give up all efforts to purify itself of the ugly and the monstrous; to open itself to rainbows and Harpies, the awesome and the terrifying alike.

### The Death and Resurrection of Thaumazein

As Socrates himself demonstrates through his selective genealogy and his performative attempt to define the pseudês doxa, the openness of wonder is nearly impossible to sustain. To be sure, this is partly because the particularly fearful, anxious, or terrifying aspects of wonder are often highly unpleasant: to put it crudely, it is *nicer* to think about rainbows than Harpies. As far as Western philosophy is concerned, however, every aspect of wonder becomes susceptible to erasure, because, whether it responds to that which is fascinating or repugnant, thaumazein keeps problems unresolved. It renders the thinker incapable of doing the kind of simple calculating, sure representing, or remainderless opining that might secure himself and his knowledge against the storm of indeterminacy. For this reason, wonder becomes an increasingly problematic ancestor for the increasingly "scientific" Western philosophical heritage. As the tradition progresses, wonder is progressively relegated to something like a temporary irritant: a discomfort not to be endured, but rather to be cured—or at least tranquilized.

It is Aristotle who first proposes a remedy for wonder in the knowledge of cause and effect. He explains that while philosophy begins in thaumazein, "it must in a sense end in something which is the opposite of our original inquiries."[32] As distinct from Socrates, for whom wonder keeps inquiry unresolved, Aristotle values wonder because it prompts the learner to find the causes of that which confounds him. As soon as the philosopher discovers each cause, he moves his attention to the next puzzling phenomenon, wondering at higher and higher things until he has worked his way back to the moon, the sun, the stars, and finally, the First Cause.[33] It is important to note that in the course of this progression, wonder's function is not to expand its scope infinitely, but rather to eliminate itself. Wonder for Aristotle serves as a temporary goad, provoking the philosopher to inquiry, but then dissipating as it leads him into a "better state, as is the case in these instances when men learn the cause."[34] Aristotelian thaumazein, one might say, seeks the very resolution that Socratic thaumazein struggles to resist; for, all the way up the ontological chain, causal knowledge gradually replaces the very wonder that sets it in motion. In the words of the early seventeenth-century mechanician Simon Stevinus, "*Wonder en is gheen wonder*"—(the) wonder is no longer (a) wonder.[35]

As the dominant strand of the Western philotheological tradition progresses, Socratic thaumazein becomes increasingly overshadowed by the Aristotelian variant that eliminates itself through the knowledge of causes. If, as Aristotle tells us, ignorance provokes wonder, then persistent wonder comes to be seen as a sign of persistent ignorance. Wonder ought to be a fleeting experience, lest it leave the wonderer stranded in intellectual complacency, immaturity, or worse, femininity. This was the opinion of the twelfth-century philosopher Adelard of Bath, who told his awestruck nephew that when he had learned the cause of thunder and lightning, his childish wonder at them would cease.[36] Similarly, Albert the Great thought that wonder was appropriate for beginning students and old women, but not for mature philosophers: "wonder is the movement of the man who does not know on his way to finding out, to get at the bottom of that at which he wonders and to determine its cause . . . such is the origin of philosophy."[37] Albert's star pupil Thomas Aquinas, for his part, went on to distinguish this preliminary wonder, which responds to natural phenomena, from a more permanent wonder at divine phenomena.[38] For Thomas, as for Aristotle, wonder (*admiratio*) is provoked by an ignorance of causes,[39] but whereas most causes can eventually be apprehended, the Cause of all causes cannot. This prompts Thomas to distinguish "miracles" from "wonders," attributing the latter to unknown (but knowable) natural causation and the former to unknown (and unknowable) divine causation.[40] While the philosopher should therefore be astonished at genuine miracles, he should not be astonished by the "wonders" that far outnumber them, since wonders are only astonishing to those who have no understanding of causes. Thomas thus entreats his readers to work their way out of as much *admiratio* as they can, that is, out of ignorance and into the knowledge of causes. To dwell in wonder is, for the most part, nothing short of sloth: "just as laziness shrinks from the toil of external work, so amazement and stupor shrink from the difficulty of considering a great and unaccustomed thing, whether good or evil."[41] A surprising reversal thus begins to show itself: wonder, which was for Socrates and Theaetetus the most strenuous of intellectual states, becomes for mainline medieval philosophy and theology a sign of intellectual torpor. In other words, the "stupidity" that arose with Socrates' premature *foreclosure* of wonder becomes for subsequent thinking *a mark of wonder itself.*

It could perhaps be argued at this juncture that many of these thinkers—perhaps Aquinas in particular—were not looking to eliminate wonder so much as they were looking to refine it, to reserve it for the highest and first of all causes.[42] And, one might claim, it is the elimination of ordinary wonder (at natural causes) that allows the soul to attain wonder at the truly Wondrous. I am not arguing, however, that wonder somehow goes away with the onslaught of Aristotelianism; nor, at the risk of redundancy, do I hold wonder and determinate thinking to be inimical to one another. What I *am* claiming is that, with increasing intensity as Western philosophy approaches modernity, wonder becomes the source of great ambivalence. It is both the height of intellectual attainment and the depth of stupidity, depending on when it strikes. So wonder becomes something to ration, to rein in, to delimit—something whose entrances and exits are ultimately subject to the knowing self. Wonder, in other words, is both avowed and disavowed at the same time—so that it gradually becomes subject to the philosophical subject itself.

This internalization of wonder might have been of no concern to anyone, were it not for the profound cultural and economic shifts that attended modernity's philosophical dawn. The end of the middle ages saw the accelerated opening of trade routes into Asia, Africa, and the Americas, which provoked a "tremendous influx to Europe of exotic objects, both natural and man-made."[43] The physical presence of objective "wonders" in Europe prompted a desire among the political and intellectual elite alike to *possess* the marvelous—both materially and epistemologically—and the early-modern age of wonders was born. As early as the late fourteenth-century, the European royalty began maintaining "cabinets of curiosities" (*Wunderkammern*). Forerunners of the modern natural history museum, these cabinets housed every natural and mechanical marvel their owners could get their hands on.[44] As John Onians explains it, "If you put a large number of strange objects into the cage of any monkey it will, as Darwin noted, greet them with astonishment and curiosity, and that is what happened in the palaces of Europe."[45]

What distinguished early European princes from monkeys, however, were the political ends to which they put their cabinets of curiosity. As Lorraine Daston and Katharine Park have demonstrated, "mirabilia corresponded to liquidity and represented the wealth and power of the prince" in the early modern period.[46] Daston and Park go on to describe the highly alcoholic banquets at the court of Burgundy, for example, which would culminate in a lavish display of the duke's "collections of exotica." Particularly renowned for such wonder banquets was Philip the Good (1396–1467), the would-be crusader and captor of Joan of Arc. Particularly when he was in need of support for a military initiative, Philip displayed his impressive collection to his inebriated guests. As Daston and Park explain it, the guests would be "softened," come to see Philip himself as a wonder, "give up their will to the duke and follow him on his Crusade."[47]

In terms of the trajectory we have been tracing, these cabinets of curiosities are a material expression of the increasing philosophical attempt to neutralize wonder by comprehending every object that might provoke it. Perhaps the most exhaustive philo-scientific exhauster of wonders was Francis Bacon, who called upon his colleagues to collect every strange object and to record each inexplicable event from the four corners of the earth. He was hoping to compile every last marvel into a complete scientific *Wunderkammer* of sorts, convinced that a total catalogue of all "preternatural" phenomena would give rise to new laws that would account for every seeming irregularity. Wonder, in other words, would serve its own demise, giving way to an exceptionless knowledge of causes. Bacon therefore called wonder "broken knowledge," a signal of the incompletion of the inquiry it provokes. *Admiratio*, he believed, must be overcome systematically for sake of the advancement of learning.[48] *Wonder en is gheen wonder.*

But the foregoing philosophical roundup begs the question, why would thinking seek to put an end to that which gives rise to it in the first place? What is it about wonder that provokes such parricidal tendencies in its philo-sophical offspring? René Descartes gives us a way to begin to think through wonder's gradual demise in his treatise *The Passions of the Soul* (1649). Like his scientific forebears, Descartes exhibits a profound filial ambivalence toward wonder (*l'admiration*). On the one hand, Descartes privileges wonder as "the first of all the passions" because it precedes all emotive bifurcation into good and evil, love and hatred, delight and sadness, etc. Free from all judgment of value, wonder simply prompts us to focus our attention on what-ever has taken us by surprise. But herein lies its danger. Since this "sudden surprise of the soul" precedes our ability to tell whether that which provokes wonder is helpful or harmful to us, Descartes values *l'admiration* only as a means toward a more determinate knowledge of things. A bit of wonder is "useful" insofar as it causes us to "learn and retain in our memory things we have previously been ignorant of," and, in fact, Descartes admits that those who are not at all disposed toward wonder "are ordinarily very ignorant."[49] Yet he goes on to say that it is less often the case that people wonder too little than that they wonder too much, ending up in a state of astonishment (*l'estonnement*). And astonishment, Descartes writes, "is an excess of wonder which can never be anything but bad."[50] Stuck in astonishment, a person will be disinclined to investigate the causes of astonishing things, incapable of making his way to clear and distinct ideas. Descartes therefore suggests that, after we are prodded by wonder, "we should . . . try afterwards to emancipate ourselves from it as much as possible," recommending scientific cataloguing as the most effective defense against wonder's attack on reason.[51]

For Descartes as for Bacon, causal knowledge of wonderful things disci-plines and eradicates the ur-passion of wonder. Descartes goes so far as to promise that once his method replaces all wonder with comprehension, "we" philosophers and scientists will become "masters of ourselves . . . like God in a way."[52] Similarly, and perhaps with Philip the Good in mind, a young Francis Bacon once told a hypothetical prince that the best way to gain mastery over himself and his people was to possess and understand as many wondrous objects as possible, so that "when all other miracles and wonders cease by reason that you should have discovered their natural causes, yourself shall be left the only miracle and wonder of the world."[53] The progressive eclipse of wonder is therefore related to a certain will toward mastery, even toward divinity: by *comprehending* the source of the wondrous, the thinking self in effect *becomes* the source of the wondrous—or at the very least, it appears that way to the uneducated masses, who "stand astounded at his wisdom as though he were a god" (*Theaetetus* 161d).

Twelve centuries before Descartes' and Bacon's reflections on the appropriation of wonder(s), Augustine of Hippo had warned against a kind of self-deification he saw at work in the contemporary sciences. Augustine directed his theological ire primarily against astronomers and astrologers who, unwilling just to marvel at the celestial bodies, set out to chart planetary positions and predict their courses. Augustine admits that it is God who has given them this ability in the first place. The problem is that they themselves cannot concede as much and imagine themselves to be the sources of their own wisdom. So, while their knowledge may *work* (eclipses happen when and as they are predicted to happen), it is improperly referred: "About the creation they say many things that are true; but . . . they become lost in their own ideas and claim to be wise, *attributing to themselves things which belong to you.*"[54] By mastering the most mysterious realm of creation, those who examine the stars make themselves into gods—not only in their own estimation but also in the eyes of the common people, who "are amazed and stupefied" by the astronomers' foresight and proceed to direct toward human beings the wonder (*admiratio*) of which God alone should be the object.[55]

One might say, then, that modern philosophy's call to do away with wonder is a call to wipe away the whole horizon—to drink up the open sea onto which thinking has been released. If wonder continually ungrounds the philosopher, preventing his solipsistic return from secured object to securing subject, then wonder's comprehensive eradication promises not only the certainty forbidden to the awestruck but also the self-mastery (and, by extension, the mastery of others) that characterizes the thinker of clear and distinct ideas. Reflecting on modernity's fervor to classify, codify, and record all knowledge of all of its objects, John Onians goes so far as to say that "in a sense the age of wonder of the sixteenth and seventeenth centuries brought wonder to an end."[56] In another sense, though, it could be argued that the Western philosophical tradition does not so much do away with wonder as it does *internalize* it, presenting itself as the agent, rather than the patient, of wonder. Philosophy, I would suggest, has endeavored to make itself its own god by swallowing the very condition of its possibility, making theories of its wind-eggs and denying the phantoms beneath each purported substance. Like everything thinking represses, however, the ghost of thaumazein has haunted this progressively masterful tradition, returning now and again at the bidding of some poet, mystic, or misfit: Hildegard, Eckhart, Kierkegaard, Goethe. But it could be argued that the one such conjurer who finally got Western thought to listen to and for the ghost of thaumazein was a latter-day Theaetetus named Martin Heidegger.

It was Heidegger who first revealed the parricidal tendencies of the Western philotheological tradition, which he ties together under the name of *metaphysics*. For Heidegger, the house of metaphysics is built upon the oblivion of its own foundation: grounded in being (*Sein*), metaphysics is unable to think being itself.[57] Metaphysics *thinks* it thinks being, but really only thinks in terms of beings. Even when it proclaims itself to be "ontological," metaphysics is merely "ontic." For Heidegger, the result of this confinement to the being of beings is that philosophy from Plato onward becomes increasingly *objectifying*. That is, metaphysics only confers the status of a "being" upon something that can be represented by a human subject—something that can be calculated "in advance." Western philosophy thereby elevates representer and represented, or subject and object, over the *occurrence* of being that constitutes them in the first place, and then leaves that occurrence uninterrogated. Attentive only to what is representable, metaphysics is incapable of thinking the unrepresentable event that sets representation in motion. This steady fall into "calculative-representational thought" eventually gives rise to the curse and blessing of modern technology.

Especially for the "later" Heidegger, however, this capitulation to an objectifying thinking is not so much a failure on the part of humanity as it is an event in the history of being itself. Unlike original sin, metaphysics' persistent inability to access the truth of being is not a function of beings' having turned away from being and toward themselves. It is rather a sign that being has turned away from beings, leaving them open to all manner of technical manipulation. To signify this shift in his thinking, Heidegger replaces *Sein*, which he fears remains an ontotheological category, with the more arcane *Seyn*, which gives itself to beings precisely by withdrawing from them: "*Abandonment of beyng* means that beyng abandons beings and leaves beings to themselves and thus lets beings become objects of machination."[58] Thinking beyng would thus be a matter of somehow being drawn into being's withdrawal. Blocking the way, however, is a particularly violent kind of modern thinking that insists there *is* nothing that can't be calculated. Heidegger calls this era of thought *Gestell*, which has no real English equivalent (it is usually translated as "enframing"). Under the sway of *Gestell*, the call of being is heard as a perverse injunction to *frame* everything that is, in other words, to put representational boundaries around the whole world. In the age of *Gestell*, being lets beings appear as calculable, and humanity responds by calculating them. Gradually, the whole world is transformed into a "stand-ing-reserve" for a manic technological advancement that eventually instru-mentalizes humanity itself. Called by *Gestell*, "man" begins to think himself "lord of the earth." But this, for Heidegger, is the "final delusion." When the modern will to calculate everything has truly overcome every indeterminacy, securing the subjectivity of man through the objectivity of the world he has created, "it seems as though man everywhere and always encounters only himself. . . . *In truth, however, precisely nowhere does man today any longer encounter himself; i.e., his essence.*"[59] Trying to master the cosmos by making of it a technological stockpile, "man" ends up becoming *part* of the stockpile, one effect of "scientific" manipulation among others.

Unlike Bacon, Descartes, and most of the dominant figures of the modern West, the task of thinking for Heidegger is not to make the thinker "mas-ter" of himself or of others, but rather to return to the ground of being that ungrounds the thinking self. Since being remains unthinkable from the standpoint of metaphysics, however, this "way back into the ground of meta-physics," if such a path is even possible, will eventually open onto a way *beyond* metaphysics.[60] Precisely in thinking the unthought "first beginning," thinking prepares to leap into "another beginning." Heidegger is insistent, however, that one cannot simply choose to make this leap. Just as "man" did not "cause" being to withdraw, he also cannot grab it by means of some superhuman representational reach and drag it back to himself. To the contrary, all thinking can do is to *prepare* the leap by facing and enduring being's withdrawal. Between the first and the other beginning, thinking must relinquish the will toward domination that fuels the orphaned metaphysical machine, attuning itself to the incalculable and unrepresentable and finally letting being *be* (*Gelassenheit*).

For Heidegger, the two primary characteristics of the metaphysics that does *not* let being be are 1. its privilege of beings over being and 2. its pre-sumption that being is simply self-evident. "Overcoming" metaphysics, then, would mean first of all acknowledging that *we do not know what being is*. Not knowing what being is, we cannot possibly know what beings genuinely are. To be sure, this offends the understanding. Every time one goes about the business of thinking anything, one relies upon some fuzzily contoured notion of being: I am, you are, this table is: how could thinking fail to know what it is to be? And yet, as Socrates and Theaetetus discover as they seek to know the essence of knowledge, it is nearly impossible to think what thinking itself presupposes: "our relation to the obvious is always dull and dumb. The path to what lies under our nose is always the fullest and hence the most diffi-cult path for us humans."[61] A thinking that thinks the being that metaphysics misses must therefore find a way to take what is most familiar of all—and make it strange. This is Heidegger's primary concern in *Being and Time*: to demonstrate that we don't know what we think we know about being.

And so the text opens by invoking Socrates: "For manifestly you have long been aware of what you mean when you use the expression '*being.*' We, however, who used to think we understood it, have now become perplexed."[62] Awakening the perplexing at the heart of the everyday, Heidegger is effectively rousing the monsters of indeterminacy under the house of philosophy. Like Socrates, he insists that thinking does not understand that which it deems self-evident and calls thinking to endure the sea-sickness of being-in-the-wake-of-being: "all through his life and right into his death," Heidegger writes, "Socrates did nothing else than place himself into this draft, this current, and maintain himself in it."[63] Thinking in the wake of being would amount, for Heidegger, to a thinking that could finally *think*, rather than objectify and calculate. And it is the suggestion of this study, because it attends to the strangeness of the most familiar, that such wakeful thinking might finally endure, rather than close down, the perilous openness of wonder.

### The Thales Dilemma

What would it mean, however, to sustain the duplicitous, abyssal origin that philosophy has fled for so long? Exactly what sort of thinker would emerge in and through persistent wonder? The Socrates of the *Theaetetus* does give us some hints, not all of which are entirely encouraging. As we have already seen, Theaetetus's own predisposition to wonder could turn him either into a Socrates or a sophist pawn. While the possibility of the former makes a philosophical retrieval of thaumazein look quite promising, the possibility of the latter requires us to stop and think before proclaiming the arrival or necessity of anything like a "philosophy of wonder." One might call this particular difficulty the "Thales dilemma."

During one of the *Theaetetus*'s long and winding detours, Socrates describes the average philosopher in much the same way that a contemporary comic novelist might characterize a scholar of the humanities. The philosopher, says Socrates, displays a "helpless ignorance in matters of daily life": he has no idea how to get to the marketplace, or where the courts are, or who is running for public office, or how to make a bed (173c–175e). He stutters incomprehensibly when asked about everyday matters, knowing nothing that might be described as practical, public, or political. Moreover, Socrates adds,

in all these matters, he knows not even that he knows not; for he does not hold himself aloof from them in order to get a reputation, but because it is in reality only his body that lives and sleeps in the city. His mind, having come to the conclusion that all these things are of little or no account, spurns them and pursues its wingèd way, as Pindar says, throughout the universe, "in the deeps below the earth" and "in the heights above the heaven"; geometrizing upon earth, measuring its surfaces, astronomising in the heavens; tracking down by every path the entire nature of each whole among the things that are, and never condescending to what lies near at hand. (173c–174a)

This stereotypical philosopher, who shuns everything particular, material, and everyday in favor of the universal, spiritual, and transcendent, is embodied for Socrates in the figure of Thales, the father of natural philosophy. According to legend, Thales was in such a habit of fixing his vision on the stars above him that, one day, he fell into a well below him. A passing Thracian maid was bemused by the brilliant man's stupidity, remarking that "he was wild to know about what was up in the sky but failed to see what was in front of him and under his feet." Socrates tells Theodorus that "the same joke applies to all who spend their lives in philosophy" (174a–b).[64] And, two thousand years later, Hannah Arendt applies it to Martin Heidegger.

In an essay written for Heidegger's eightieth birthday, Arendt ranks Heidegger with the greatest philosophical giants of all time, even likening him to Plato.[65] She goes on to say that those of us who would like to follow such powerful thinkers hit a formidable stumbling block when we realize that philosophers often make utterly disastrous political decisions. Akin to, but infinitely more devastating than, Plato's attempt to teach philosophy to Dionysus the tyrant of Syracuse in 362 BC was Heidegger's commitment in 1933 to National Socialism, when he assumed the rectorship of the nazified Freiburg University. And Arendt attributes this formidable error to, of all things, an excess of wonder. In keeping with Aristotle, Arendt argues that wonder is merely supposed to be a temporary goad, disorienting the thinker momentarily before setting her on a course to surer knowledge. Arendt herself, however, locates the momentary thaumazein she commends not in Aristotle but in Plato, identifying wonder with the "leaping spark" that consummates the process of instruction in his Seventh Letter.[66] This is a questionable move indeed, considering Plato does not mention wonder at all in relation to this "leaping spark," nor, when the matter of wonder or astonishment does arise (e.g., in the Theaetetus, Parmenides, or Timaeus)[67] does he characterize it as fleeting. Regardless, Arendt ventures that Heidegger's mistake was not his appealing to Plato's "faculty of wondering at the simple," rather, it was his "taking up and accepting this faculty of wondering as [his] abode."[68] Had he only come down from the philosophical clouds, Arendt suggests, Heidegger would have seen the dangers beneath his all-too-human feet. But he was too hell-bent on the coming of some metaphysical revolution to notice the deportations, the storefronts, the yellow stars, the burning of the temples.

Arendt's suspicion of excessive wonder can be grouped into four main concerns. First, wonder seems to offer what Arendt calls an "escape from reality," relieving the wonderer of any sense of obligation to the messy, sociopolitical state of things or, worse, clouding his vision of the everyday world so that he thinks he is fulfilling said obligation precisely at the moment he defaults on it. Cut off from what in common parlance one might call "the real world," the philosopher is vulnerable to being carried along by any particularly strong current—ethereal or otherwise. This uncritical openness to the wondrous constitutes the second of Arendt's reservations with respect to thaumazein, and it is the reason, she argues, that so many brilliant philosophers have been swept away by dictators. Holding herself apart from the very wonder dwellers to whom she nonetheless pays tribute, Arendt writes, "we who wish to honor the thinkers, even if our own residence lies in the midst of the world, can hardly help finding it striking and perhaps exasperating that Plato and Heidegger, when they entered into human affairs, turned to tyrants and Führers."[69] As for the starstruck Heidegger, she laments, "he was served somewhat worse than Plato, because the tyrant and his victims were not located beyond the sea but in his own country."[70] The third of Arendt's reservations about wonder is its purported tendency to alienate the philosopher from the world around him. "Philosophical shock strikes man in his singularity," she argues, destroying any possibility of genuine relation to others. Hiding away in "speechless wonder," the Thales figure concerns himself exclusively with that which is "too general for words," which is also to say too particular for generality. Eventually, he becomes unable to account for himself within the relational structure of language (a bit like Søren Kierkegaard's knight of faith).[71] In holy silence, this Single Individual floats along in a rarefied realm above the public sphere, shunning all relations to particularity and effectively abandoning the whole world for some "other" one. Finally, because it stands exposed to oncoming storms, dwells outside all language, dismantles all interpersonal relations, and neglects particularity, wonder allegedly renders the philosopher incapable of forming opinions or making decisions. This is the most pressing problem with thaumazein for Arendt: it obstructs *doxazein*, making people unable to think for themselves. Arendt's deepest suspicion of wonder lies therefore in its seemingly inexorable tendency to slip into terror. Like Theaetetus, the persistent wonderer is exposed to manipulation by irresistible forces that dismantle all its relations to reality. By disabling decision making, Arendt concludes, wonder serves the strategic ends of totalitarian "education" initiatives, the aim of which "has never been to instill convictions but to destroy the capacity to form any."[72]

Against the terrifying logic of totalitarianism, Arendt appeals to Socrates, saying that the ancient teacher's function was not to tell his interlocutors what to believe, but rather to draw their own opinions out of them by means of specific questions. A sign that he understood how "the world opens up differently to every man," Arendt claims that Socrates' function qua midwife was to help each student to find his own doxa.[73] She thus sets Socrates apart from those philosophers who dwell in thaumazein—the ones who provoke their students into a perpetual "experience of not-knowing." Because wonder can only contemplate "ultimate questions" that have no answer, it only prevents the formation of concrete opinions. Arendt thus compares the philosopher who chooses to stay in the realm of wonder to the soul who, liberated from Plato's cave, refuses to reenter the cave after he has seen the sun—or to the one who returns but has forgotten how to see in the darkness.[74] When he speaks, he speaks ironically, incomprehensibly, upside down, and when he tries to make a decision, he is unable to tell the good from the bad or the helpful from the harmful. It was this awe-full blindness, Arendt suggests, that conditioned in 1933 what Heidegger later referred to—or perhaps did not refer to—as "the greatest stupidity" of his life.[75]

We, however, who thought we understood wonder, have now become perplexed. Socrates, whom the *Theaetetus* seems to put squarely on the side of thaumazein, is aligned in Arendt's work *against* it. Arendt argues that, unlike those mercenary ideologues who shout the party line as a means of drowning out individual voices, Socrates delivers each young man of his proper doxa, helping him to solidify his own opinion to shield him against ideological manipulation. To be sure, as we saw in the *Theaetetus*, Socrates' labor is dedicated to drawing his interlocutors' opinions from him. But then again, all of these opinions turn out to be wind-eggs—ultimately vaporous doxai that would form weak bulwarks indeed. As Socrates reveals when he tells Theaetetus that delivering phantoms is "all [his] art can do," Socrates is therefore much closer to the wonder dwellers with whom Arendt contrasts him—the ones for whom all premises become untenable and all incontestable logic gives way to contestation. Is Socrates, then, just another Sophist? Or worse, a totalitarian foot soldier?

Perhaps it is best to examine this conflict from a brief point of convergence. For both Arendt and the Socrates of the *Theaetetus*, the philosopher who tarries too long with thaumazein cannot form a reliable opinion. For Arendt, this inability makes the philosopher susceptible to manipulation by dictators and tyrants, and we will recall that Socrates also warned his younger image that his capacity for wonder could become enslaved to charismatic, mercenary teachers. Yet here a crucial distinction emerges. For Arendt, dwelling in thaumazein led Heidegger to make a dumb mistake—to adhere to what one might call a "false opinion"—while for Socrates, it was not dwelling in but *stepping out of* thaumazein that led to his stupid enactment of the pseudês doxa.

As we have seen, the experience of wonder also opens out the possibility of its closure. The groundless awe upon which thinking "rests" can either be inquisitively endured or it can be covered over with unquestionable premises and conclusions that obstruct further inquiry. For this reason, just as one must not be too quick to separate wonder from terror, one should also not rush simply to equate the two. The ideologies driving regimes of "total terror," far from encouraging the kind of relentless questioning that Socrates nurtures in Theaetetus, leave no room for indeterminacy. They do indeed prey upon thaumazein, but they then resolve it into unquestioning obedience. In fact, Arendt herself refutes the alignment of wonder and totalitarian obedience in her analysis of the logic of the latter. Regimes of "total terror," she demonstrates, rely upon a "stone-cold" process of reasoning that begins from a "self-evident" premise and marches steadily on, from if/then to if/then, so that "you can't say A without saying B and C and so on, down to the end of the murderous alphabet."[76] A whole world of experience might directly contradict the conclusions of this runaway sophistry, but the "irresistible force" of totalitarian a priorism runs over any pesky actuality that might throw itself onto its tracks: "once it has established its premise, its point of departure, experiences no longer interfere with ideological thinking, nor can it be taught by reality."[77] If this is indeed the case, then thaumazein would presumably work *against* the enforced complacency of totalitarian regimes—not by solidifying theories but by dismantling them—by revealing "self-evident" premises as insubstantial and thereby preventing the forward march of the murderous alphabet.

I would therefore suggest that any unquestioning capitulation to ideology, Heidegger's included, is a matter not of too much wonder, but rather of too little. Throughout this study, I will be asking what it might mean to *stay with* the perilous wonder that resists final resolution, simple identity, and sure teleology. As a means of attempting to dwell in the dizzying terrain of thaumazein, this book will explore four interresonant problems that surface in the wake of Heidegger's aweful retrieval: repetition, openness, relation, and decision. While these themes can only truly be discerned as echoes of one another, each of the following chapters will focus on one of them. The first chapter will trace Heidegger's shifting interpretation of thaumazein, focusing particularly on its role in propelling thinking into "another beginning." Ultimately, this chapter will establish Heideggerian wonder as a double movement. A certain shock or terror recoils at the sudden impossibility of the everyday, while awe goes on to marvel that the impossible nonetheless *is*. Because of wonder's attunement to the strangeness of the everyday, this chapter will seek to demonstrate its irreducible this-worldliness, contra Hannah Arendt's first objection *and* Heidegger's own tendency to contradict himself on the matter.

Following this preliminary sketch of wonder's "what," the next three chapters will go on to examine the "how" and "why" of thaumazein, responding

to Arendt's three remaining arguments against it. Each will do so by engaging a thinker who maintains a kind of near-farness to Heidegger. And so the
second chapter will consider the state of vulnerability into which wonder's
double movement undoubtedly throws thinking, charting its dangers as well
as its possibilities through the radical passivity of Emmanuel Levinas. The
third chapter will interrogate wonder's alleged suspension of relationality by
means of Jean-Luc Nancy's (anti-)ontology of "being-with." And the fourth
will address the crisis of indeterminacy that wonder issues in, arguing with
Jacques Derrida that if decision is only truly possible where it is impossible,
then thaumazein's obstruction of decision actually enables its emergence
from the thick of undecidability. In close critical conversation with Heidegger
and one another, these three authors will therefore allow us gradually to consider more clearly the perils and promises of "tak[ing] up this wonder as
one's abode." As we will notice, however, even these resolute thinkers of the
unthinkable are susceptible to shutting wonder down from time to time, taking refuge either in a theory of the autonomous subject or in a rift between
"this," ordinary world and some wonderful "other" one. Therefore, much of
the (un)work of this book will be merely to mark wonder's various openings
and closures and to try to remain as long as it can with the discomfort of the
inessential and the shock of the everyday. Neither taking flight above the
clouds nor resting complacently in itself, a thinking of wonder would look for
the extraordinary in and through the ordinary, the awe-full truth in the midst
of the cave.

Dawn points, and another day
Prepares for heat and silence. Out at sea the dawn wind
Wrinkles and slides. I am here
Or there, or elsewhere. In my beginning.

—T.S. Eliot, "East Coker"

# 1. REPETITION: Martin Heidegger

## Metaphysics' Small Difficulty

If, as Heidegger maintains, metaphysics cannot think the "being" that gets it going, then "overcoming" metaphysics will be a matter of going back to its roots. The attempt to propel thought into "another beginning" is, in other words, *always* inextricably bound up with the attempt to think the unthinkable "first beginning." This is the reason, despite numerous efforts to the contrary, that post-Heideggerian philosophy or theology cannot simply proclaim itself unmetaphysical by listing the ontotheological tenets to which it no longer adheres (essentialism, Cartesianism, theism, atheism, etc.). "Metaphysics cannot be abolished like an opinion," Heidegger tells us; "one can by no means leave it behind as a doctrine no longer believed in and represented."[1] Thinking must, to the contrary, continually *retrieve* metaphysics in its very essence, and only in beginning again from its beginning can it open the possibility of beginning differently. For this reason, even as he proclaims the "end" of the tradition they began, Heidegger hits the philosophical ground and returns to "the Greeks."[2]

As opposed to Hegel, Heidegger claims it is his task not to think the totality of thought as the self-unfolding of being, but rather to think that which has *not* been thought as the self-*withholding* of being. As philosophy has "progressed," he insists, it has not moved dialectically closer to its ur-condition; rather, it has fallen ever farther from it. Even more disturbingly, philosophy cannot simply elect to return to "being-itself," for being is no object that sits where it "was" at the beginning of things, waiting for thinking to come around to it. In an age when beings can only be recognized insofar as they can be objectified, the unobjectifiable event of being itself has become absolutely unthinkable. Far from lying in wait for us, much less from being progressively realized in history, being is no longer accessible to the very beings it brings into being. In fact, it has fled from them. What keeps Heidegger closer to Hegel than he might like to imagine, however, is his conviction, haunted by Hölderlin, that thought's greatest *distance* from the truth of being might ultimately give onto its greatest *nearness* to it: "But where danger is, grows / That which saves also."[3] At its most abandoned, Heidegger ventures, thinking might finally be able to confront its own being-abandoned, and by extension, might be projected into a thinking of the event of being itself. Holding itself in the most extreme danger, thinking might be delivered *through* this danger into the truth of being's self-withholding donation.

Insofar as this inscrutable event of being constitutes not only the truth of being but also truth itself, it is not surprising that philosophy's inability to think being is accompanied by a truth-obstructing concept of truth. The Greek word for truth is *alêtheia*, a word we have already seen in the *alêthes doxa*, or true opinion, of the *Theaetetus*. Heidegger translates *alêtheia* as *Unverborgenheit*, or "unconcealment." In its most original form (which is to say, in accordance with his often creative readings of Heraclitus and Parmenides), truth for Heidegger means emergence from hiddenness. Truth as unconcealment designates the revealing *of* the concealed, which means both the revealing of that which is concealed and the revealing that concealment does. Beginning with Plato, however, Heidegger claims that this movement of unconcealment has been slowly overtaken by an understanding of truth as the static correspondence between a "subjective" representation and an "objective" thing. The early modern philosopher Gottfried Leibniz (1646–1716) consolidated this idea of truth, which would come to be encompassed under the doctrine of the "adequation of reality and thought" (*adequatio rei ad intellectum*). To say that truth is adequation means that truth is truth only insofar as it presents itself to the human, representing subject. This representing subject, or "monad" for Leibniz, thus becomes the fundamental unit of being—as Protagoras would say, the measure of all things. Other beings come into being only insofar as they can be represented by autonomous human subjects.[4]

Heidegger reads this Leibnizian monadology as the culmination of the gradual eclipse of being at the hands of beings. By taking being into their own hands, beings stage an ontic revolt that, Heidegger claims, is as complete as it is self-defeating. With escalating fervor, the Western philosophical tradition has codified its "objective truths" at the expense of truth itself, covering over every absence with presence and every mystery with the certainty of full representation. By attempting to incorporate everything in its path, however, philosophy has only pushed the unassimilable event of being and/ as truth farther away, thereby severing from being the very epistemological subjects and objects it purports to secure. Of course, it must be granted that calculative-representational thinking "works": it gets airplanes into the sky, medicine into our veins, and food on the table—at least for those who have access to the mechanisms of calculation and representation. And Heidegger concedes as much. Sounding like Augustine in his fourth-century critique of the astronomers, Heidegger does not deny the effectiveness of calculation. He affirms that "the unconcealment in accordance with which nature presents itself as a calculable complex of the effects of forces can indeed permit correct determinations."[5] But just as Augustine's astronomers fail to acknowledge the source of their wisdom, calculative-representative thought forgets that "adequation" is only one kind of truth—one particular form of unconcealment. But because calculation cannot calculate unconcealment, it risks shutting itself off from truth itself: "the danger may remain that in the midst of all that is correct the true may withdraw."[6]

Again echoing Augustine, Heidegger partially attributes the simultaneously self-aggrandizing and self-defeating ascent of the representational subject to *curiosity*.[7] Provoking a desire to know all the wonders of the world, curiosity constitutes for Heidegger "the origin of all scientific investigation of beings."[8] Curiosity is responsible for humanity's technological advancement because it encourages beings to reveal themselves as potential objects of scientific observation and experimentation and then seeks to calculate them as quickly as possible.[9] The benefits of this curiosity, from modern medicine to information technologies, are clear. The limitation of this sort of curiosity, however, is that it necessarily misses everything that cannot be understood by means of a formula, which is to say "in advance." It is not curiosity per se that is at issue here, but rather curiosity to the extent that it seeks to understand *everything* by objectifying everything. In this case, curiosity only moves faster and faster away from the unobjectifiable truth of being. In *Being and Time*, Heidegger characterizes curiosity's frantic self-sabotage as a persistent "not-staying": a state of ontic dispersion resulting from the attempt to conquer all difficulties.[10] Rather than dwell with the incalculable, curiosity at its most irresponsible skips from one marvelous phenomenon to the next, "resolving" each puzzle as quickly as possible in order to possess it—materially or epistemologically—and move on to something newer and more bizarre. Accelerating toward a state of perpetual distraction and departure, curiosity eventually becomes "*the inability to stay at all*."[11]

This representational (ego-)mania is perhaps most clearly instantiated in the early modern European cabinets of curiosities. The not-staying to which such collections attest is almost parodically expressed in one of Leibniz's essays entitled "An Odd Thought Concerning a New Sort of Exhibition." Very odd indeed, this stream-of-consciousness musing sketches a hypothetical academy in which absolutely everything in the universe would be displayed. Leibniz imagined that such an academy would be a fiscal magnet for wealthy men and society ladies who, in the spirit of Descartes, Bacon, and Philip the Good, would become marvels themselves by virtue of their possession—or at least financial backing—of such wonderful things. Leibniz therefore compiles a haphazard catalogue of all the wonder-bestowing wonders this institute would possess, including "fire-eaters, horse ballerinas, Hindu comedies, Magic Lanterns . . . artificial meteors, all sorts of optical wonders; a representation of the heavens and stars and of comets; a globe like that of Gottorp at Jena; fire-works, water fountains, strangely shaped boats; Madragoras and other rare plants . . . naval combats in miniature on a canal. Extraordinary Concerts. Rare instruments of music. Speaking trumpets. Counterfeit gems and jewelry."[12]

As one might learn from actually trying to walk through a collection of *everything*, however, and as one senses even trying to make one's way through Leibniz's syntactical riot, the sort of totalizing curiosity that flits from wonder to wonder does not illuminate any of them as such, but rather eclipses them all, rendering them mere elements in a long list of weird things. Here one sees enacted the tragic flaw of metaphysics: its tendency to push away the truth it seeks by encapsulating it within collectible objects of representation. Always looking to add more "truths" to its ontic cabinet, a calculative curiosity can only prevent thinking from staying with the truth itself, which cannot be physically or conceptually secured. To think beyond and before the ascendancy of truth-as-adequation, thinking must therefore find another mood—one that resists the flightiness of curiosity by remaining in the uncertainty and irresolution of what reveals itself. To attune itself to unconcealment, in other words, thinking will have to go back—and forward—to something like wonder.

## Wonder and the "First Beginning"

In *Being and Time* (1927) Heidegger briefly distinguishes the curiosity driving modern thought from the wonder with which it is frequently conflated: "curiosity has nothing to do with the contemplation that wonders at being, thaumazein, it has no interest in wondering to the point of not understanding. Rather, it makes sure of knowing, but just in order to have known."[13] For Heidegger, then, insofar as it can withstand uncertainty, wonder is oriented to being-itself. After thus attributing wonder *the* capacity central to *Being and Time*, however, Heidegger does not mention the mood again, concentrating instead on the ontological attunement of anxiety.[14] It is not until his Freiburg lecture series in 1937–38 that he addresses the question of wonder at greater length, affirming thaumazein as the "basic disposition" of the first beginning over against the curiosity that obscures it. If Socrates had named curiosity as the origin of philosophy, Heidegger suggests, then thinking might be justified in trying to explain (away) the whole world. However, "the reference to *thaumazein* as the origin of philosophy indicates precisely the inexplicability of philosophy, inexplicability in the sense that here in general to explain and the will to explain are mistakes."[15] At this point the distinction between curiosity and wonder is absolutely crucial for Heidegger, because, again, finding another beginning for thinking depends on thinking through the first one. Curiosity, he insists, can only lodge us more deeply within the calculative confines of metaphysics. Wonder, on the other hand, could be the disposition that "transports [thinking] into the beginning of genuine thinking."[16] Heidegger therefore spends a good deal of time in these lectures trying to get wonder right.

Reserving the term *Erstaunen* to translate thaumazein, Heidegger proceeds to set it apart from four other wondrous moods with which it might be confused: *Verwunderung, Bewunderung, Staunen,* and *Bestaunen.* Similar to the curiosity just described in *Being and Time, Verwunderung* craves, marvels at, and collects novelties, leaping from one fascinating phenomenon to another like children in a natural history museum. It does not ultimately dwell anywhere, but rather is perpetually "carried away by something particular and unusual and hence is an abandonment of what in its own sphere is particular and usual."[17] *Bewunderung* also occupies itself with that which is unusual, but, unlike *Verwunderung,* it always maintains a certain distance from the object of its admiration. It is perhaps helpful here to note that, in the second *Critique,* Kant confesses that the two things that fill him with *Bewunderung* are "the starry sky above me and the moral law within me."[18] In the third *Critique,* Kant commends such *Bewunderung,* "an amazement that does not cease once the novelty is gone," over against *Verwunderung,* which fades as soon as it understands the unusual object before it.[19] Heidegger, however, suggests that even *Bewunderung* falls short of thaumazein because it remains grounded in the known even as it gazes upon the unknown, while wonder makes the known itself unknown. *Bewunderung,* Heidegger says, is ultimately marked by measurement, comprehension, and *self*-affirmation and therefore has very little to do with the constant dispossession of thaumazein. Finally, *Staunen* and *Bestaunen,* while prisoners neither to *Verwunderung*'s flightiness nor to *Bewunderung*'s myth of self-mastery, lose themselves completely in a sort of stupefied amazement (think here of Protagoras's disciples), abandoning the ordinary in favor of one particularly extraordinary thing.

As it turns out, each of these moods amounts to an inadequate interpretation of thaumazein because of its failed relationship to the everyday. Whether forgetting it in favor of the newest craze or standing firmly in it to examine the highest attainments of rocket science, each of these forms of intrigue takes for granted what is most usual of all, holding the great unknown against the drab (and therefore perpetually uninterrogated) background of the known. In *Erstaunen*, on the other hand, the source of wonder is the everyday itself: "precisely the most usual whose usualness goes so far that it is not even known or noticed in its usualness—this *most usual itself* becomes *in* and *for* wonder what is most unusual."[20] And, as readers of Heidegger will doubtless leap ahead to ask, what is more "usual" than being itself? What, therefore, is more deserving of wonder? "*For manifestly you have long been aware of what you mean when you use the expression* 'being.'"

Heidegger does not, however—at least not in any straightforward fashion—call Erstaunen the mood appropriate to a thinking of being. Despite his momentary designation of thaumazein in *Being and Time* as "the contemplation that wonders at being," he is not willing to go this far ten years later. Or, insofar as he *is*, it is only because his understanding of "being" has shifted: in later works, Heidegger will declare that what he had called "being" in *Being and Time* was still lodged within a metaphysical understanding of being as "beingness," or "the being of beings." So, while Erstaunen may be the fundamental mood of the first beginning, it will not ultimately suffice for the second. But we are getting ahead of ourselves.

Almost immediately after naming wonder in the 1937–38 lecture series as the mark of philosophy's fundamental "inexplicability," Heidegger goes on, astonishingly, to explain wonder. In thirteen bullet points, he lists wonder's various attributes, eventually abandoning it as an unregenerately ontic attunement. One might say that Heidegger, packaging and rejecting philosophy's vertiginous origin in this manner, displays a modified—but nonetheless familiar—metaphysical ambivalence toward thaumazein. The first bullet point promisingly declares that wonder reveals the strangeness of the everyday: "In wonder what is most usual itself becomes the most unusual" (*Grundfragen*, 166/144). We might recall here the thaumazein professed by Socrates and Theaetetus when their most commonsensical presuppositions were shown to be philosophically untenable. As the list goes on, however, Heidegger begins to suggest that even the "usual" that wonder uncovers covers over something even more fundamental—something *more* ordinary than the ordinary ordinary. This reservation can already be read in Heidegger's second bullet point, in which he suggests that, as distinct from all other *–staunen*s and *–wunderungs*, the object of *Erstaunen* is nothing in particular. Wonder wonders at an unobjectified "everything," in such a way that the most usual becomes "the most unusual itself in this one respect: that it is *what* it is" (*Grundfragen*,

166–167/144; emphasis added). With this "what," however, Heidegger reigns in the uncanniness he had unleashed in the first point. For in his writings on the "end" of metaphysics, Heidegger locates its beginning in the ancient and artificial rift between that-ness (existence) and what-ness (essence). Along with the ascendancy of adequation over unconcealment, beings over being, and the human will over every other force comes the increasing privilege of essence over existence—of the supposedly measurable "what" of a being over the immeasurable "that" of being's very event. By saying, then, that wonder wonders at the whatness of the most usual, Heidegger swiftly confines wonder to ontic determinations, declaring it ultimately incapable of opening onto the ontological thatness to which genuine thinking must be attuned.

Thaumazein's relegation to the first beginning is both confirmed and undermined throughout Heidegger's remaining eleven theses. In these we learn, for example, that Erstaunen cannot find a sure footing in either the usual or the unusual once it discloses the former as the latter. Rather, "wonder dwells in a between, between the most usual, beings, and their unusualness, their 'is'" (Grundfragen, 168/145). Sustaining this perpetual intermediacy, wonder clears the space-time "in which beings come into play as such"; that is, wonder opens the very open in which beings show themselves in relation to being. The wonderer thus takes shape as a sort of guardian of beings—as the one who "must experience and sustain alêtheia, unconcealedness, as the primordial essence of beings" (Grundfragen, 169/146). The wonderer, in other words, neither abandons nor manipulates beings for the sake of his own security, but rather attends to what appears as such, uncovering and preserving the profoundly disturbing force of the mysterious within the everyday. Heidegger calls this aweful willingness to be unsettled a "thoughtful questioning." Renouncing the "intrusive and rash curiosity" that seeks increasingly detailed "explanations," this sort of inquiry "sustain[s] the unexplainable as such, despite being overwhelmed by the pressure of what reveals itself" (Grundfragen, 172/148–149). Dwelling in wonder, then, is a kind of existential suffering, and it is a suffering that metaphysics cannot ultimately endure.

The "thoughtful questioning" that wonder inspires would ideally remain wondrous, maintaining what Heidegger calls "a creative tolerance for the unconditioned." The problem—at least historically—has been that this questioning is carried out by means of technê (craft, art, skill), which, at least initially, is the concerned, concerted effort "to grasp beings emerging as themselves . . . and, in accord with this, to care for beings themselves and to let them grow" (Grundfragen, 179/155). "Grasping" beings in order to care for them, however, technê begins to make beings into objects of techno-logy, tolerating less and less of that which remains incalculable. With the rise of representation as the only form of truth and the concomitant decline of "the original essence of alêtheia," there therefore comes "the loss of the basic disposition" (that is, wonder) and the rise of curiosity as the dominant mood of science and philosophy (*Grundfragen*, 181/156). Because it is carried out through *technê*, then, wonder essentially gives rise to its own demise: "in carrying out the basic disposition itself there resides the danger of its disturbance and destruction" (*Grundfragen*, 180/155). *Wonder en is gheen wonder.*

It seems, then, that we are no closer to understanding what it would mean for thinking to stay with wonder than we were at the outset. Either that, or we have determined such a remaining-with to be impossible and may as well stop asking. For, at least according to the fall narrative recounted here and encapsulated in Servinus's motto, wonder tumbles inexorably into curiosity because of the very nature of the *technique* that seeks to preserve it. If this is the case, however, why does Heidegger go to such lengths earlier in the lecture series to rupture all presumed ancestral continuity between curiosity, its manifold variants (*Verwunderung, Bewunderung, Staunen, Bestaunen*), and wonder? To be sure, in the raging course of Western thought wonder *has not* persisted as wonder. Is it, however, the case that wonder *cannot* persist as wonder? Must wondering always cause wonder's demise?

After opening up the possibility that thinking might think thaumazein as such, Heidegger presents a sustained effort to do so with two considerable obstacles. The first is his conviction that, now that the whole earth has been made into a stockpile for humanity's techno-calculative will toward global domination, modernity is incapable of wonder. With all beings reduced to mere objects of a self-placed subject's projections, being ceases to amaze us. "For centuries the *being of beings*, which was for the Greeks the most wondrous, has passed as the most obvious of everything obvious and is for us the most common: what everybody knows. For who is supposed not to know what he means when he says the stone *is*, the sky *is* overcast? . . . On account of its obviousness, being is something forgotten" (*Grundfragen*, 184/159; emphasis in the original has been returned to the translation). Because "we" are unable to be shocked by beings in their being, the mood of our thinking can no longer be one of wonder. And, of course, we cannot just muster up such a mood any more than we go out and catch the being that has given us by abandoning us. So, according to the problematic sketched in these lectures, the reason "we are still not thinking" is that we're quite literally not in the mood for it: we cannot think being because we cannot be *surprised* by being. But then again, is it not Heidegger's most pressing task—and his most lasting contribution—to work through scenes of impossibility such as this one? Is he not continually seeking to render shocking and strange that which modernity considers most familiar, and thereby to bring to thought that which seems least to require any thought? *And is this not precisely the work of wonder?* Could it be, then, that wonder is only truly possible where it is most impossible?

Yes and no.

It is certainly Heidegger's suggestion that, even when wonder was "possible" (that is, for "the Greeks"), it was, strictly speaking, impossible, for it was the very effort to sustain wonder *technê*logically that ended up propelling thinking into such manic curiosity in the first place. If, then, wonder is impossible where it seems possible, its only possibility would indeed lie in its impossibility. Wonder would have to break into the time-space in which it is *most* unlikely—the one in which beings are least preserved, least cared for, most objectified, most abandoned. There, where wonder *could not be*, the eruption of wonder would be truly wondrous. What this would mean would be that, insofar as the "first beginning" can only shut down the wonder that opens it, a truly sustained Erstaunen would open thinking onto another beginning in which thaumazein would be possible by virtue of its sheer impossibility.

But the moment we clear away one obstruction in this manner, another presents itself in its place. Even if we read Heidegger's proclamation of impossibility like good Heideggerians, locating all possibility in impossibility, we are still faced with the problem of the ontic confinement to which Heidegger subjects wonder—and therefore with the filial ambivalence that thaumazein always seems to inspire. If wonder, the "basic disposition" that is currently "absent and denied us," were somehow to break into this ruined earth, it would, according to Heidegger, unsettle the most sovereign of subjects and "primordially displace humanity again into beings as a whole" (*Grundfragen*, 183/158; translation modified slightly to retain the gender neutrality of the German *Mensch*). With this declaration, however, Heidegger both grants and revokes Erstaunen's ability to effect a primordial displacement, for he places the destination of wondering humankind not in being or the event of being, but in "beings as a whole." Wonder, along *this* line of thought, would have the power to take thinking back to the *Gestell*-bound beginning, but not *beyond* it. And yet, we recall that a genuine thinking of the beginning—the beginning that metaphysics has never been able to think—could never be simply lodged within metaphysics. So the question of wonder becomes a question of the status of repetition: would a sustained wonder, in all its impossible possibility, remain trapped within the circular mechanisms of metaphysics, or could this repetition open thought nonidentically onto a different horizon?

### Wonder and the "Other Beginning"

The 1937–38 lectures, which announce themselves as a preparation for "futural philosophy," come to an end almost immediately after treating the question of Erstaunen as the fundamental mood of philosophy. Just before he falls silent, however, Heidegger makes an oblique reference to a "still veiled basic disposition," which, now that wonder is impossible, might push thought "into another necessity of another original questioning and beginning" (*Grundfragen*, 186/160). Heidegger had named this "other" basic disposition only once during the lecture series, and he does not do his audience the service of repeating or elaborating upon it at the end. He invoked it at the very beginning of his first lecture, calling upon the "basic disposition of the relation to beyng"—the one that would be "open to the uniquely uncanny fact: that there *are* beings, rather than not" (*Grundfragen*, 2/3); the one that would be attuned to the self-concealing thatness that metaphysics (and presumably Erstaunen) misses. For the few minutes during which it is addressed, this disposition finds a provisional name in *Verhaltenheit*, which is usually translated as "restraint" or "reservedness." Inherent in this disposition are two equiprimordial comportments, which *Verhaltenheit* keeps in perpetual tension: "terror [*Erschrecken*] in the face of what is closest and most obtrusive, namely that beings are, and awe [*Scheu*] in the face of what is remotest, namely that in beings, and before each being, being holds sway" (*Grundfragen*, 2/4). After effectively assigning to this aweful *Verhaltenheit* the status of the Disposition of the Other Beginning, however, Heidegger forbids any further discussion of it. He warns his audience that "only one who throws himself into the all-consuming fire of the questioning of what is most worthy of questioning has the right to say more of the basic disposition than its elusive name." Yet he goes on to say that even the one who seeks thus to immolate himself will not discuss Verhaltenheit at any length; rather, having "wrested for himself this right, he will not employ it, but will keep silent" (*Grundfragen*, 2/4). And as we have seen, this is what Heidegger himself proceeds to do. Unlike Erstaunen, that Great Inexplicable so systematically explained in Heidegger's thirteen bullet points, the ever veiled Verhaltenheit is protected from direct communication—animating, perhaps, but never suffering dissection within, Heidegger's analysis.

Well, not quite "never." At the same time that he was preparing and delivering the 1937–38 lecture series, Heidegger was also composing his *Contributions to Philosophy (from Enowning)*, a quasi-aphoristic outline intended to accomplish the crossing from metaphysics into "beyng-historical thinking." It is in this text, intentionally never published during his lifetime, that Heidegger indulges in a meditation upon the foundational mood of the "other" beginning. Aside from this, the only remaining elaborations upon this disposition can be found in the passages Heidegger deleted from the first draft of the Freiburg lectures he was composing at the same time.[21] Heidegger, then, does not exactly "keep silent" about this veiled disposition. Rather, one might say that he both reveals and conceals Verhaltenheit by performing it; that is, by restraining "restraint" to pages that would only be circulated posthumously.

Before clinging too closely to this rather generous reading, however, one would also do well to consider the historical particularities surrounding the emergence of Heidegger's beyng-historical thinking (a thinking that, of course, rejects as "historiography" such petty concerns as dates and dictators and wars). Heidegger deletes the passages on Verhaltenheit, Erschreken, and Scheu from his public lectures in 1937. The Nuremburg laws had passed two years earlier, *Krystallnacht* was looming on the horizon, and Karl Jaspers had just been barred from the German universities because his wife was Jewish. Heidegger, perhaps not so blissfully unaware of these events as some might like to imagine, had renounced his position as rector of Freiburg in 1934, but had still worn a Nazi badge to his friend Karl Löwith's house in 1936: a troubling wardrobe choice, even if Löwith had been a gentile.[22] While it falls out of the scope of this project to offer psychological conjectures about the extent of Heidegger's loyalty to the Nazi party, it had doubtless become clear to him by 1937 that it was a less-than-perfect alliance. National Socialism had not catapulted Germany into the new and glorious metaphysical beginning Heidegger envisioned, his own work had come under intense scrutiny by party members and opponents alike, and he may have anticipated that any direct appeal to *Erschrecken und Scheu* might look a bit too much like Nazi propaganda[23]—especially in light of unfortunate sound bites like "we must first call for someone capable of instilling terror into our *Dasein* again."[24] Whether compelled by philo-literary or political necessity (or both), then, Heidegger reserves "reservedness" for later.

A signal that his concern to veil this material is not *solely* political, however, the mood of the "other" beginning does not, when it is finally treated explicitly, find systematic explication in thirteen theses. It is, instead, illuminated in periodic flashes scattered throughout the deleted and unpublished material. Heidegger even hesitates to assign it any one name, lest a conceptual stranglehold render it powerless to deliver thinking from conceptuality: "the grounding-attunement of another beginning can hardly ever be known merely by one name—and especially in crossing to that beginning. And yet, the manifold names do not deny the onefoldness of this grounding-attunement; they only point to the ungraspable of all that is simple in the onefold."[25] Among these manifold names are "intimating" and "deep foreboding," which echo wonder's portentous resonances. Yet Heidegger spends most time on the triumvirate, nameable only "in a distant way," of *Verhaltenheit, Erschrecken*, and *Scheu*.[26]

As we have seen, Heidegger limits the wonder he calls Erstaunen to the first beginning when he limits its "object" to the "being of beings." Focused as it is on beings as they appear, Erstaunen overlooks the event of appearance itself; that is, the event of being. This seems a strange failure to attribute to wonder, inasmuch as Heidegger holds thaumazein to be the disposition attuned to the unconcealment that adequation obscures. If wonder wonders at unconcealment itself, then how can wonder possibly miss the truth of being? The missing link here is provided in a deleted passage from the 1937–38 lectures in which Heidegger explicitly declares even *unconceal-ment* to be an insufficiently primordial name for "truth." What unconceal-ment presupposes, and for this reason cannot see, is the *concealment* to which it is perpetually bound: "truth is not simply the unconcealedness of beings—*alêtheia*—but, more originally understood, is the clearing for the vacillating self-concealment. The name 'vacillating self-concealment' is a name for being itself" (*Grundfragen*, 211/179). In the *Contributions to Philosophy*, this self-donating double movement of being is rebaptized *Ereignis*, or "the event [of being's appropriation to beings]."

It is Heidegger's abandonment of truth as alêtheia, then, that necessitates his abandonment of wonder as Erstaunen. As he pushes on to Ereignis, he announces that now he must find a new foundational mood. It is crucial to remember, however, that Ereignis is no radical departure from alêtheia. It is, rather, both unconcealment *and* concealment, so that truth cannot open onto Ereignis without going back to truth as alêtheia. So it is with wonder. Verhaltenheit, as it turns out, is nothing more—and nothing less—than a more primordially thought Erstaunen, a new incarnation of thaumazein that holds itself between wonder and *its* opposite—a wonderstruck, horrified, amazed kind of fright that becomes the dispositional possibility of futural thinking itself.

We will recall that the work of this futural philosophy will be to think the being (at this point rendered "beyng") that has *withdrawn* from beings, and through this abandonment, has given beings over to the objectifying forces of *Gestell*. Brought into being abandoned, beings can only appear as calcu-lable objects, and so, severed from being, beings are not themselves. And yet, beings are. This, for Heidegger, is absolutely terrifying. The disposition that might unsettle thought out of its comfortable representative manipula-tions, then, is not a simple wonder at the thatness of beings—for who could possibly be surprised that beings are?—but rather, depending on the source, shock (*Schrecken*) and/or terror (*Erschrecken*) that, strictly speaking, beings cannot be. What instills this terrifying shock is the sudden realization "that beings can *be* while the truth of being remains forgotten"—that, like wind-up dolls with lost keys, "beings strut as beings and yet are abandoned by beyng" (*Grundfragen*, 197/169). Such unfamiliarity of the familiar is reminiscent of the sudden impossibility of the pseudês doxa, which produces in Socrates a kind of harrowed astonishment. And, in fact, Heidegger acknowledges that "just as wonder bears in itself its own sort of terror, so does terror involve its own mode of self-composure, calm steadfastness, and new wonder" (*Grund-fragen*, 197/169).

The "calm" with which such wondrous terror is endured calls to mind the anxiety that withstands a similar scene of uncanniness in Heidegger's earlier work. As it poses the foundational question, "why are there beings at all, rather than nothing,"[27] the Dasein of Heidegger's early work exposes itself to the frightful "nothing" that both transcends and constitutes beings themselves. Shocked by the no-thingness of what it had always held to be being, Dasein is plunged into anxiety, a state in which "everyday familiarity collapses."[28] Anxiety thus ruptures all of Dasein's usual relations to itself and other beings (namely, subjectivity and objectivity) and confronts Dasein with bare thatness in the face of "the nothing." From this place of terrifying openness, however, anxiety opens the possibility of Dasein's relating genuinely to inner-worldly beings and to itself. This will be addressed more carefully in chapter 3, but the significance of anxiety to the discussion at hand is its double movement: insofar as Dasein does not busily cover over anxiety but rather *persists* in it with "a peculiar calm,"[29] it is lifted out of beings and then back into beings. Its horror at the nothing gives onto a wonder that, by virtue of this very "nothing," beings are. Thus "the lucid courage for existential anxiety assures us the enigmatic possibility of experiencing being. For close by essential anxiety as the horror [*Schrecken*] of the abyss dwells awe [*Scheu*]."[30]

*Scheu*, it turns out, is Heidegger's name for the aforementioned "new wonder," a mood Heidegger describes as "awe in the face of what is remotest, namely that in beings, and before each being, beyng holds sway" (*Grundfragen*, 2/4). Awe is the second, more enduring movement of this new wonder, a response to the shock of *Er/schrecken*. If Erschrecken registers that that which is cannot possibly be, then Scheu sees that it nonetheless *is*. While Erschrecken recoils at the abandonment of being, Scheu marvels that being nonetheless gives itself through this withdrawal. In short, this "new wonder" marvels that beings cannot be, and yet beings are, that is to say, being *happens*. Where being cannot possibly happen.

This particular double movement recalls the passage in Blaise Pascal's *Pensées* (1670) wherein the reader is invited to contemplate the vast infinity of the entire cosmos, in comparison with which "man" is "lost" in insignificance. Pascal then suggests we turn to think upon the "equally astonishing" and vastly *minute* infinity revealed in the tiniest cells of a mite under a microscope, in comparison to which "man" seems a veritable "colossus."[31] Existing between these two ontological "abysses," the person attuned by wonder will "marvel" to the point of being "terrified" at himself. For he knows that his very existence is nothing, and yet, at the same time, this nothingness constitutes his very existence. Contemplating the infinitely vast and the infinitely minute, he will "tremble at these marvels."[32] Giving proto-Heideggerian voice to the shock of being's abandonment and the simultaneous awe at its thereness, Pascal writes,

When I see the blind and wretched state of man, when I survey the whole universe in its dumbness and man left to himself with no light, as though lost in this corner of the universe, without knowing who put him there, what he has come to do, what will become of him when he dies, incapable of knowing anything, I am moved to terror, like a man transported in his sleep to some terrifying desert island, who wakes up quite lost and with no means of escape. Then I marvel that so wretched a state does not drive people to despair.[33]

The ambivalence of terror and wonder to which Pascal attests gains an almost prophetic valence in Heidegger's work. Whereas Pascal's wonder, like Heidegger's, marvels at that which (impossibly) is, Heideggerian Scheu is also attuned to that which (impossibly) might *yet be*. Maintaining itself in the wake of being's withdrawing self-donation, Scheu not only attends to whatever arrives but also awaits the appearance or nonappearance of Hölderlin's "saving power," whom Heidegger comes enigmatically to call "the last god." Precisely because the being to which it is attuned is not present, Scheu becomes "the way of getting nearer and remaining near to what is most remote as such (cf. The Last God), that in its hinting—when held in awe—still becomes the nearest and gathers in itself all relations of beyng."[34] While terror withstands the sudden departure of everything that is, awe watches in the midst of the impossible for the arrival of the unexpected.

Thus caught between Erschrecken and Scheu, Heidegger's futural thinking is called to a perpetual openness—one that constantly suffers the impossibility of the possible and the possibility of the impossible. "Unsupported and unprotected," such thinking continually exposes itself to the "storm" of ceaseless withdrawal and arrival, as terror witnesses the unfamiliarity of the familiar and awe holds near what is most strange.[35] It is the constancy of thinking in the midst of this storm that Heidegger calls Verhaltenheit: the calm dedication to "withstanding the fury" of the relentless oscillation of terror and awe.[36] Heidegger locates the sole possibility of another beginning in this mood, for only restraint can endure the simultaneous shock of being's revelation as concealed and the awe of its concealed revelation. Holding itself in irresolution and uncertainty, Verhaltenheit prepares the way for the possible arrival of the gods and the event of being itself.

At this point, one might be tempted to reconfirm Arendt's diagnosis of Heidegger's "stupidity" as an excess of thaumazein. "Of course he made bad political decisions," one might say: "who could see clearly with his head so firmly in the clouds? With his eyes trained on the cosmic departures and arrivals of last gods and "events of being," how could Heidegger have possibly noticed the arrivals and departures of everyday people on everyday train cars?" Yet neglecting beings for the sake of being—or the actual for the sake of the possible, or the usual for the sake of the unusual—is *not* a function of thaumazein as Heidegger understands it, either in wonder's first incarnation as Erstaunen or its "other" incarnation as Verhaltenheit. For Erstaunen, we will recall, is distinguished from every other type of raptness by its constant attention to the strangeness of that which is most usual of all, whether its strangeness be a function of its beauty, its insubstantiality, or its offensiveness. Similarly, the moment he mentions the reservedness of shock and awe, Heidegger tells us that by opening itself to the event of unconcealment Verhaltenheit "does not justify evading of beings, but the opposite."[37] In order to underline this engagement, Heidegger even shifts his emphasis in the *Contributions to Philosophy* from the *ek-stasis* of Dasein to its *in-stasis*. If *Angst* delivers Dasein out of beings into the "nothing" that *then* "directs us precisely toward beings,"[38] Verhaltenheit delivers Dasein directly into and as being-in. As constituted in the fire of this veiled attunement, Dasein exists as *ecstatic* standing-in. Somehow, Heidegger suggests, genuine attention to beings is only possible in and through a genuine attunement to the being that gives them to be; and, conversely, only a relation to being can restore beings to themselves (that is, out of "subjectivity" and "objectivity"). But how? This is the seeming aporia with which Heidegger consistently leaves us—both philosophically and autobiographically. How is thinking to stay attuned to being *and* the beings it abandons, the clouds *and* the trains, the stars *and* the well, *at the same time*? What would "the opposite of the evading of beings" look like? To echo Heidegger (who ultimately could not stand it), what kind of being might be "capable" of Verhaltenheit?[39] "What *steadfastness* does this inabiding have? Or put in another way: Who is capable—and when and how—of *being Dasein*?"[40]

At this point, we are a bit closer to being able to begin to think through the possibility of a philosophically sustained thaumazein, that is, a wonder that neither neglects particular beings nor collapses into frenzied curiosity about them. The best name Heidegger can find for this disposition is *Verhaltenheit*, a mood whose steady liminality is maintained through the equiprimordial countermovements of Erschrecken and Scheu. Heidegger's suggestion is that Dasein attuned through reservedness indulges in "neither a romantic flight nor a bourgeois repose,"[41] but rather holds itself perpetually between the transcendent and the everyday. This tension, somehow, holds out the possibility of finally letting both beings and being be. It is this persistent "somehow" that now becomes of foremost concern. What does it mean to inhabit the stormy "between" that, for Heidegger, makes Dasein itself by letting what is be? Seeking a clearer view of the open terrain between being and the beings it leaves behind, we are led back, of all places, to the *Theaetetus*.

### *Theaetetus* Redux: The Ghost of the Pseudês Doxa

Heidegger's lecture course of 1931–32 at Freiburg comprises detailed interpretations of both Plato's *Republic* and his *Theaetetus*. Together, these two studies ultimately service Heidegger's refinement of truth's downward trajectory—from the unalloyed unconcealment of Parmenides and Heraclitus through the Enlightenment's certitude and adquation through to modern technology's unrestrained "will to will." Heidegger's readings of both these dialogues operate under two crucial convictions concerning Plato's relationship to truth. First, insofar as the superbeings of the Forms are "most true" in the Platonic universe, "being" is for Plato (says Heidegger) already limited to the being of beings. Second, while Plato still uses the word *alêtheia* to mean truth, unconcealment begins its steady decline toward adequation with Plato's own elaboration of truth as the correspondence between the act of knowing and the Forms themselves. What is significant for our purposes here is that as he sifts through the *Theaetetus* in order to distinguish Plato's understanding of truth from his own, Heidegger is looking primarily for a *mood*. Throughout his exegetical tour of the *"wonderful* structure"[42] of this dialogue, Heidegger grounds his search for the truth of being in a search for a double-edged comportment: one that would relate both to beings and to being itself.

In order to find this comportment, Heidegger elucidates in turn Theaetetus's numerous efforts to define knowledge, rejecting each of them as each fails to meet Heidegger's own "twofold requirement" that it attend to beings and being (*Vom Wesen der Wahrheit*, 257/183). Theaetetus's first venture, we will recall, is that knowledge is perception. Perception, Heidegger explains, always refers both to what it perceives (or what it "has present") and to the perceiving itself (or what it "makes present"). Perhaps, he muses, perception might condition a relation to beings and their unconcealment at the same time? (*Vom Wesen der Wahrheit*, 166/121). Yet Socrates reveals that perception alone cannot produce knowledge of beings, because all perception relies upon a prior knowledge. Specifically, perception relies upon the knowledge of shared properties (*koina*) like sameness, difference, being, and nonbeing.

Characteristically, Heidegger assimilates all these properties within the excessive expanse of being. The reason "the soul" can have a perceptual relationship to "objects" and properties at all is that it is constitutively related to being. And so as Socrates and Theaetetus abandon perception in search of the knowledge that relates the soul to the *koina*, Heidegger narrates their journey as a quest for a comportment that relates to being itself. He again emphasizes that the comportment that relates itself primordially to being would also have to relate authentically to beings: "the question is which human comportment exhibits [the] character of *pragmatenesthai* [engagement] concerning beings, of engaging directly with beings in relationship to them, and in such a way that precisely this comportment makes possible what we call possession of truth, i.e. unhiddenness of beings" (*Vom Wesen der Wahrheit*, 251/179).

Trying now to name the knowledge that perception presupposes, Theaetetus suggests doxa (usually "opinion" or "knowledge," as we saw with Arendt, but Heidegger often prefers "view"). Heidegger points out that, like perception, opinion has "two objects": it must both see something *and* see that something *as* something else (*Vom Wesen der Wahrheit*, 270/192). Recalling the doubleness of the unnamed comportment he seeks, Heidegger says that "at first sight this twofold requirement seems to be met by the *doxa*" (*Vom Wesen der Wahrheit*, 257/183). The problem with a point of view, however, is the internal possibility of its distortion. Taking something *as* something means that one can take it for something it is *not*. The inauguration of judgment, in other words, is the inauguration of bad judgment. And so once again we meet up with the problem of false opinion (pseudês doxa), which is always attended in the *Theaetetus* by thaumazein. Heidegger carefully marks Socrates' discomfort with the appearance of the pseudês doxa, noting in particular the infectious quality of Socrates' uncertainty: "we too are pressed by Plato into the role of Theaetetus; for like Theaetetus we too are *initially* wonder-struck only by Socrates' wonder and unease" (*Vom Wesen der Wahrheit*, 260/185; translation modified, emphasis added).[43] Yet what does Heidegger mean by "initially"? Does he mean that "our" astonishment will increase during the course of the dialogue, so that we wonder not just at Socrates' wonder, but at the very elusive figure that confounds him and ultimately, perhaps, at the whole "astonishing" dialogue itself? Or does this "initially" signal that the wonder we initially experience will eventually wear off?

At first, it seems as though Heidegger is suggesting the former: that "our" initial, Theaetetus-identified wonder will open onto the full-fledged groundlessness I have been referring to as Socratic thaumazein. As Heidegger follows the ancient pair through their various attempts to secure the possibility of the pseudês doxa, he affirms that "all three discussions come to the conclusion that the distorted view is in essence utterly null, therefore cannot exist at all." And yet, of course, the "distorted view" *does* exist: "on the one hand, the existence of distorted views is an indubitable *fact*, grounded in the nature of man; on the other hand the conclusion is reached that such a thing as a distorted view *cannot exist*" (*Vom Wesen der Wahrheit*, 264/188). The discovery of this simultaneous "factuality and impossibility" brings the conversation into "the full force of [its] astonishment and wonder" (*Vom Wesen der Wahrheit*, 264/188)[44]—a wonder, one imagines, that persists throughout the equally "wonderful [*wondervoll*] composition of the dialogue" (*Vom Wesen der*

*Wahrheit*, 290/206). In naming this "full" wonder, however, one might note that Heidegger does not use the word *erstaunlich*. He uses, rather, two forms of *Wunder*, which as we recall will be associated throughout the 1937–38 lectures with the feverish drive toward amassing knowledge of marvelous things.[45] Somehow, then, Heidegger's analysis of the *Theaetetus* has begun to slip out of thaumazein and into the realm of curiosity.

In these Plato lectures Heidegger calls upon *Wunder* to translate the Greek word *teras*, which connotes that which is wondrous, prodigious, or even monstrous and which Theaetetus utters in reference to the possibility that a person might mistake something he knows for something he does not know.[46] In keeping with the typology of wonder he will offer six years later, Heidegger goes on to explain that a *Wunder* is only temporarily wonderful:

> Especially in the later dialogues, Plato always employs the expression *teras*, miracle [*Wunder*], when something initially appears as absolutely impossible and miraculous [*verwunderlich*] to the common understanding, but is later shown by philosophical reflection to be *demonstrated* in its own inner possibility. For the moment, however, we have not yet come so far, but we remain with Theaetetus, more and more amazed as the distorted view becomes more and more puzzling. (*Vom Wesen der Wahrheit*, 269/191; translation modified)

In this manner, Heidegger tells us that the puzzle of the distorted view will at some point cease to confound us. As soon as the pseudês doxa is *demonstrated* in its "inner possibility," our identification with Theaetetus will be broken and our "initial wonder" will simply have been a particularly stubborn variant of curiosity. A mere *Wunder*, the impossible possibility of the pseudês doxa is, in other words, a mystery whose intrigue will fade as soon as it is philosophically resolved.

But the pseudês doxa cannot *be* philosophically resolved! Is this not the whole astonishing and pointless "point" of the pseudês doxa . . . and of the dialogue as a "whole"? We will recall that, far from deploying Philosophy to put an end to the disturbance of the pseudês doxa, Socrates allows this unruly guest to disturb philosophy itself, to the point at which he is forced by the persistent impossibility of this phenomenon to retract even his most fundamental guiding principle; that is, the mutual exclusivity of knowledge and nonknowledge of being and nonbeing. Heidegger recognizes this, even going so far as to say that, when this Socratic presupposition is revoked, "the entire foundation of previous philosophy becomes unstable . . . we can have an intimation of what power the phenomenon of the *pseudos* possesses to disturb and amaze, i.e. such that it forces this fundamental principle of all previous philosophy to be questioned" (*Vom Wesen der Wahrheit*, 287/204). As Heidegger also knows, there *is* no "demonstration" of the pos-

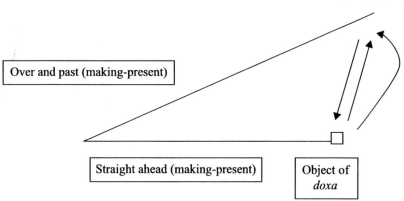

Fig. 1.1. Platonic doxazein according to Heidegger

sibility of false judgment in the *Theaetetus*. On the contrary, Socrates leaves us, with Theaetetus, surrounded by the persistent uncertainty and impossibility that provoke and sustain thaumazein. Perhaps the greatest mystery of all, then, is that after marking the profoundly disturbing character of the pseudês doxa, even to the point of admitting that it never finds "final determination or definition" in the *Theaetetus* (*Vom Wesen der Wahrheit*, 291/207), Heidegger himself goes on to demonstrate its "inner possibility," closing precisely that which Socrates keeps dangerously open and putting Philosophy back on solid ground. He even draws a diagram (*Vom Wesen der Wahrheit*, 313/221).[47]

As a means of dragging himself and his audience out of the philosophical quagmire of the pseudês doxa, Heidegger reminds us that we fell into it while we were seeking a twofold comportment that relates authentically to beings and to being as concealment. Puzzlingly, even though he had already said that it would not ultimately suffice, Heidegger proceeds to equate *doxazein* with the very phantom comportment he seeks—at least as far as Plato's thought takes him. Heidegger illustrates Platonic opinion by drawing an acute angle, designating its base the "having-present" that sees something and its upward-reaching ray the "making-present" that sees this something *as* something. The former looks straight ahead to the object of opinion and the latter runs "over and past" it, representing it "in advance." Both of these movements together constitute doxazein, whose essence is "neither one prong nor the other, but rather to see something approaching in the distance *as*" (*Vom Wesen der Wahrheit*, 313/222). Because of the constant duplicity of doxazein, Heidegger concludes, an object of this "view" can be said to be simultaneously known and not-known; distortion in this case is merely a matter of "looking past" the object to its previously formed representation. In terms of the diagram, the false view emerges when the making-present vector overshoots the having-present vector, so that the object of doxa ends up somewhere in right field. And here ends the problem of the pseudês doxa.

Plato's mistake, Heidegger insists, is to split opinion into true and false opinion. In so doing, Plato locates distortion's possibility in the failure of doxazein's two prongs to coincide properly, or in "incorrectness"—a move that ultimately results in the simple equation of truth with the correctness of representation. What Plato fails to realize, Heidegger argues, is that untruth shows itself in the pseudês doxa to be constitutive of truth itself. The object of the distorted view is simultaneously revealed and concealed and therefore demonstrates (for those who have eyes to see) the "self-hiding *in* and *through* self-showing" of alêtheia (*Vom Wesen der Wahrheit*, 320–321/227). Properly thought, then, Platonic doxazein becomes the twofold foundation of truth as the comportment to beings in their being. Of course, Heidegger is looking to find a comportment that relates to individual beings, the being of beings, *and* "being itself." So he draws another diagram—adding two more tines to his original forking. The lower of these added vectors is pointed toward "being." The higher, arching above all of them to return to the object of doxa, encapsulates "striving for being," which becomes Heidegger's provisional name for the combined comportment to the occurrence of truth as the event of being (*Vom Wesen der Wahrheit*, 321/228).[48]

Marked by its "striving for being," this comportment to truth-as-unconcealment is tantamount to a sort of doxazein plus. or super-doxazein. It grounds itself in the originary division of Platonic judgment, but then also thinks through to the coimplication therein of truth and untruth *and for this reason* strives toward the "being" that remains hopelessly hidden from Plato and his descendants (apart from Heidegger). The resultant fourfold forking, Heidegger maintains, demonstrates the essence of truth as both concealment and unconcealment, that is, it diagrams the originary meaning of alêtheia:

> This *primordial* forking (as distinct from the secondary forking of comportment to beings) belongs to the essential constitution of our Dasein, i.e. our comportment to beings is always already oriented to being. However, with this forking there is given . . . the possibility of mis-taking not only in regard to *beings* (as in the *doxa*) but in regard to *being*. Anything which can *be* existent to us can, in so far as it shows itself as unhidden, also *seem*. So much being, so much seeming. Untruth belongs to the most primordial essence of truth as the hiddenness of being; i.e. to the inner possibility of truth. The question of being is thus thoroughly *ambiguous*—it is a question of the deepest truth and at the same time it is on the edge of, and in the zone of, the deepest untruth. (*Vom Wesen der Wahrheit*, 322/228)

We see in this passage that Heidegger's super-doxazein gives rise to a super-pseudês doxa. False judgments and distorted views do not just appear as

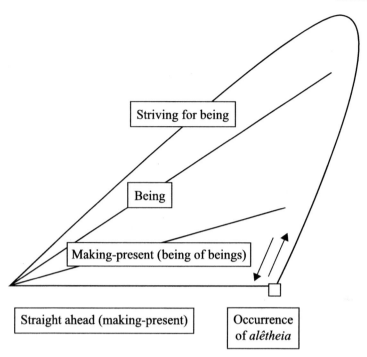

Fig. 1.2. Heidegger's combined comportment to alêtheia

occasional misfirings but rather congeal into the condition of possibility of truth itself.

The aim of this brief excursion into Heidegger's reading of the *Theaetetus* is not to contest the equiprimordiality of concealment and unconcealment, or of truth and untruth, insofar as the former is understood as alêtheia. It is also not to ask—at least not directly—whether or not Heidegger capitulates to the temptation of representational thought when he grounds his "primordial forking" in the primordial in advanceness of making-present. The aim, rather, is to note the *means* by which Heidegger in these particular lectures secures the fourfold "essential constitution of our Dasein." He is able to draw and label the truth of being only by resolving the riddle of the pseudês doxa, which he accomplishes by positing an originary split between having- and making-present and elevating it into a full-blown ontological doctrine. Building upon this "foundation," however, Heidegger not only rests the "essential constitution" of Dasein upon notoriously unstable ground; he also misses the mark of the dialogue, which ultimately aims simply to teach a young philosopher "the good sense not to fancy you know what you do not know."[49] The point is that there is no point: no end to the uncertainty and no solid ground on which to construct a doctrine of knowledge or, for that matter, of being or its truth.

In the *Theaetetus*, of course, the response that such stubborn indeterminacy provokes, whether endured or fled, is wonder, awe, or astonishment. What is perhaps most astonishing of all, then, is that as he combs this very dialogue for an appropriate comportment to the ancestor that metaphysics obscures, Heidegger does not once consider thaumazein.

Its shadowy form certainly haunts these lectures, showing itself briefly in Heidegger's recognition of the dialogue's "astonishing structure" or "wonderful composition" and most tantalizingly in his discussion of the "miracle [*Wunder*]" of the pseudês doxa (*Vom Wesen der Wahrheit*, 269/191, 289/206, 269/191). Yet we have seen the lengths to which Heidegger goes *not* to unleash thaumazein in its fully unsettling force—confining Erstaunen to Wunder and repeatedly qualifying it as an "initial" reaction to that which will later be "demonstrated in its inner possibility"—for example, the pseudês doxa. To those of us who might object that the pseudês doxa cannot be resolved and who might suggest that the wonder it provokes does not go away, Heidegger implicitly responds that while *Plato* has not been able to demonstrate the inner possibility of the pseudês doxa, *he* (Heidegger) has. Even continuing to bracket the question of this solution's reliance upon representation, however, one might remember here that Plato was not incapable of demonstrating the possibility of false opinion—or even of providing a diagram of it. Socrates himself offers one such illustration in the image of the two misaligned wax imprints, representing perception and knowledge respectively. Structurally, these two elements bear a striking resemblance both to the having-present and making-present that compose Heidegger's rendition of doxazein and to the extrapronged version of it that eventually composes his *Über-doxazein*. With his fourfold reduction to bare, fork'd being, then, Heidegger recapitulates Socrates' "greatest stupidity," attempting to secure Dasein against that which *cannot* reach a "final determination or definition."

Soon after drawing his waxen image of the pseudês doxa, Socrates retracts it, horrified at his dumb mistake. And for his part, Heidegger will discretely poke fun at his own angle-with-the-fringe-on-top twenty-five years after the Plato lectures, when he designates reason (*ratio*) in Descartes and Leibniz as a "bifurcated" structure (thereby confirming our heretofore bracketed suspicion about such a structure's inherently representational nature). *Ratio*, for this "later" Heidegger, operates by means of a kind of refashioned having- and making-present, or a "bringing-before-oneself that deals with some particular thing that lies present, and in such a dealing-with perceives the condition it is in vis-à-vis that in terms of which and by which it is reckoned."[50] But, unlike the Heidegger of the Plato lectures who tried to get to the truth of being by standing on doxazein, this Heidegger ridicules the notion that thinking might rediscover being by climbing onto the top rung of *ratio*. It would be very stupid indeed to think that "being" might constitute some "third thing, like a roof, a vault that stands ready, as it were, to accommodate [thinking]. To think this would be cockeyed. Rather, the belonging-together must already light up from what has its abode in it." What prevents any simple bifurcation of Heidegger himself, however, is that even in these "later" lectures, he is still looking to leap into that which "has its abode" in being: he is still seeking the comportment heralded in his "earlier" lectures—the one that might relate authentically to both being and beings.

As is probably already clear, it is my hope here to think Heidegger's nameless comportment, which would engage beings from its abode in being, together with the many-named disposition that holds terror or shock in continual tension with wonder or awe. The 1937–38 lectures, along with the *Contributions to Philosophy*, introduce the latter dispositional complex, tracing the contours of Erstaunen, Verhaltenheit, (Er)schrecken, and Scheu, which I have tried to illuminate as varying interpretations of Socratic thaumazein— both at and beyond the origin of what Heidegger considers to be metaphysics. In these writings, what Heidegger claims, but leaves unelaborated, is that the twofold nature of Verhaltenheit holds out the possibility of letting being and beings *be* in and through their encounter within the twofold openness of Dasein. Hoping to learn more about this ontico-ontological relation, we looked back to Heidegger's lectures on the *Theaetetus*, which are driven by the search for such a comportment. What we have discovered in both sets of texts, however, is that the closer Heidegger comes to thaumazein, the farther he runs from it. In the Plato lectures he goes so far as to foreclose not only the question of thaumazein but also the openness of Dasein, protecting Dasein by means of a four-pronged bulwark against the persistent uncertainty of the pseudês doxa. In order to attempt to connect the aweful duplicity of thaumazein with ontico-ontological betweenness, then, it will be necessary to step a bit farther away from this specter of false opinion, whose appearance prompts both Socrates and Heidegger to abandon their dwelling place in wonder. Attempting to discern what it would mean both philosophically and politically to take up "this wondering as one's abode,"[51] it is helpful to look instead to Heidegger's interpretation of the philo-political ur-abode: Plato's cave.

### Once Again to the Cave

Heidegger considers the cave allegory in book 7 of Plato's *Republic* to be so provocative that he reads it *twice*: once in the 1931 lectures that immediately precede the *Theaetetus* series and again in an essay written in 1947, after Freiburg University's denazification committee had prohibited him from lecturing in public.[52] Each reading is accompanied by Heidegger's own translation of the tale—the 1931 version a Heidegger-inflected revision of the then-standard Schleiermacher rendition[53] and the 1947 version a substantial revision of the first.

In his 1931 effort, Heidegger divides his translation and commentary into four parts, which, he will argue, correspond to the four stages of the occurrence of truth as alêtheia. The first part of the story introduces us to the hypothetical inhabitants of a hypothetical cave underground. Held in chains from the time of their birth, the people who live there can only see a wall in front of them, onto which shadows of various objects behind their backs are projected by means of a hidden fire and screen.[54] From the viewpoint of the prisoners, as Plato tells us, these shadows are not shadows but things-in-themselves. In a more Heideggerian register, these images are what is unconcealed and therefore constitute "the true" (alêthes) at this stage. For the cave dwellers, in other words, the shadows are beings. In the second stage (515c–15e) one man somehow loses his chains and turns to face the objects and the fire behind him. In comparison to the shadows to which he was accustomed, the things he now sees are truer, "more unconcealed" [alêthetera], and therefore "more beingful beings," although he cannot yet recognize them as such (Vom Wesen der Wahrheit, 33/26).[55] The third stage (515e–16e) follows this man as he is dragged from the cave into the blinding light of day, learning how to gaze upon objects under the sun and ultimately the sun itself, which is an allegory for the Good. To refer to this "truest" truth, as well as the other forms, Heidegger borrows a term from book 6 of the Republic (484c): ta alêthestata, the "most unconcealed, the essentially unconcealed, the primordially unconcealed, because the unconcealment of beings originates in them" (Vom Wesen der Wahrheit, 66/49; translation modified). Finally, the fourth part of the translation and commentary (516e–517a) tracks the liberated man's return to the cave, where he is ridiculed and quite possibly killed by those who believe the shadows on the wall of the cave to be the only truth.

One great insight that emerges during the course of Heidegger's analysis is that truth—here narrated as a process of liberation—does not reside statically in any one of these stages. Rather, it takes place in the transitions between them. Accustomed as the prisoner is to two-dimensional projections, he will initially not understand what he sees when he turns around to face the objects and the fire behind him. In fact, simply because they are more familiar, he will probably be inclined to think the shadows to be "more unconcealed, more clear, more present . . . more beingful" than what is now revealed to him (Vom Wesen der Wahrheit, 33/26; translation modified). Similarly, when this man is hauled out of the cave, the sunlight will seem so bright by comparison to the darkness in which he usually sees that, at first, he will be unable to see anything. Once his eyes adjust a bit, he will be able to see the things that most resemble the projections inside the cave; that is, shadows. Gradually, he will be able to look at reflections, then objects in a dim light, objects in the sunlight, and finally the sunlight itself. Only at that point will he finally understand the shadows in the cave *to be shadows*. Liberation—that is, the *occurrence* of truth itself, and not simply its recognition—therefore depends upon the gradual adjustment of one's vision: "to become free now means to see in the light, or more precisely, to gradually adapt from darkness to brightness, from what is visible *in* the brightness to brightness and light itself" (*Vom Wesen der Wahrheit*, 59/44).

Heidegger argues that Plato misses the import of these transitions by locating truth in the Forms rather than in the unconcealing work of truth itself. Had he been attuned to the decisiveness of the transitions between stages rather than the stages themselves, Plato would have seen that hiddenness belongs to revelation: the essence of truth as unconcealment relies upon an equiprimordial concealment. After all, what is ontologically most unconcealed (i.e., the realm of the Forms) is most *concealed* from the perspective of the cave dwellers and vice versa. Perhaps most radical of all, then, is Heidegger's recognition that the prisoner is not fully freed for the truth in the "third" stage, when he looks upon the forms, but rather in the "fourth" stage, when he returns to the cave: "the ascent does not proceed upwards, to something higher, but *backwards*" (*Vom Wesen der Wahrheit*, 79/58). Of course, Plato crowns as philosopher-king the one who chooses to endure the pain of this homeward journey, but for Heidegger the redescent is not just a matter of compassion or duty; it is a matter of the happening of truth itself. The coimplication of concealment and unconcealment inherent to truth as alêtheia means that truth is not lodged within the forms: that the one who simply takes up residence outside the cave *is not actually free*. For "whoever comes out of the cave only to lose himself in the 'appearing' of the ideas would not truly understand these, i.e., he would not perceive the ideas . . . as wrenching beings from hiddenness and overcoming their concealment. He would regard the ideas themselves as just beings of a higher order. Deconcealment would not *occur* at all" (*Vom Wesen der Wahrheit*, 90–91/66).Since truth only takes place as the transition from hiddenness to unhiddenness, there *is* no truth without hiddenness. Truth's very occurrence therefore depends upon "*a return* from the sunlight" (*Vom Wesen der Wahrheit*, 87/63).

It is at this point, however, that matters begin to get complicated. As we have seen, Heidegger sets forth his understanding of the occurrence of truth through his narration of the one man's progression from the cave to "the open" and back again. As it turns out, this simultaneity is not only allegorical, but *actual* for Heidegger: the truth itself depends on the liberated person it forms. "The essence of truth *qua alêtheia* is deconcealment, therefore located in man himself," Heidegger argues, adding to this "daring" reduction of Truth to "something human" the qualification that, of course, "everything depends on what 'human' means here" (*Vom Wesen der Wahrheit*, 73–74/54, 55). The truth does not come into being through everyday, cavely people (cf. "the they" of *Being and Time*), but only through the one who makes it out of and back into the cave. Attuned to truth as alêtheia, "man comes to himself" and "in that event of deconcealment which constitutes the unconcealment of beings" he comes to himself *as* the essence of truth. In the 1931 lectures, in particular, the equiprimordiality of this "man" with truth as unconcealment makes him the unconceal*er* of beings: man is finally liberated when he becomes libera*tor*. Ultimately, then, the fourth stage in the gradual emergence of truth is decisive for Heidegger because it marks the reappearance of this reformed man:

> Liberation does not achieve its final goal merely by ascent to the sun. Freedom is not *just* a matter of being *un*shackled, nor just a matter of being free *for* the light. Rather, genuine freedom means *to be a liberator* from the dark. The descent back into the cave is not some subsequent diversion on the part of those who have become free, perhaps undertaken from curiosity about how the cave looks from above, but is the only manner through which freedom is genuinely *realized*. (*Vom Wesen der Wahrheit*, 91/66)

As we know both from Plato's account and Heidegger's gloss, though, this liberator's homecoming is not exactly celebrated with a ticker tape parade. Just as his eyes were blinded by the sun in the transition to the third stage, they are again blinded by the darkness in the transition to the fourth. Far from greeting him as their leader and following him to freedom, his compatriots begin say of him "that he [has] returned from his upward journey with his eyesight ruined and that it isn't worthwhile even to try to travel upward. . . . And, as for anyone who tried to free them and lead them upward, if they could somehow get their hands on him, wouldn't they kill him?" (517a). With this difficulty in mind, the Platonic narrative goes on to discuss the gradual readjustment from light to darkness that the philosopher-king would first have to undergo before helping the other cave dwellers to adjust their eyes from darkness to light: "Therefore each of you in turn must go down to live in the common dwelling place of the others and grow accustomed to seeing in the dark. *When you are used to it*, you'll see vastly better than the people down there" (520c; emphasis mine). Concretely, this acclamation takes shape for Plato as fifteen years of practical political training in the cave (539e–40a). The Heideggerian account, on the other hand—both in 1931 and in 1947—ends at 517a with the likely martyrdom of the newborn liberator.

Literally (and literarily) bound by this execution, Heidegger's account of the occurrence of truth—particularly in its 1931 incarnation—is inextricably tied up with violence. The liberator's tendency to be murdered is merely the final phase of what has been an ethically questionable process from the beginning: "liberation, in the sense of turning around towards the light of the sun, is *violent*. Attaining what is . . . unhidden involves violence, thus . . . resistance, such that the one to be freed is forced up along a rugged path. The ascent demands work and exertion, causing strain and suffering . . . a sudden ripping loose, followed by, outside the cave, a *slow adaptation*" (*Vom Wesen der Wahrheit*, 42/32). What is offensive to Heidegger about the murder of the philosopher, it seems, is not the introduction of force into the history of truth, but rather the use of force by the *wrong party*. As attuned to truth, it is only the liberator who may exert force over others. Through his vision of beings' unconcealment, this man is transformed into beings' unconcealer, and "only then does he gain power to the violence he *must* employ in liberation" (*Vom Wesen der Wahrheit*, 81/60; emphasis added). This necessary violence takes two different forms in Heidegger's 1931 lectures. The first is the process we have just encountered of the philosopher's "dragging . . . the others out into the light which already fills and binds his own view" (*Vom Wesen der Wahrheit*, 81/60). It should be noted here that, inasmuch as his vision is still exclusively "bound" to the light, the liberator has not taken any time at all—let alone fifteen years—to learn how to see in the dark before dragging others out of it. The "slow adaptation" to which Heidegger refers is for some reason limited to the space outside the cave. Inside the cave, Heidegger does not seem to hold out much hope at all for any equal and opposite readjustment period. He maintains instead that, since the liberator's "assertions fail to correspond to what everyone down there agrees upon is correct," the liberator will not even try to see from their perspective in order to turn their views around (in the manner, one might say, of Socrates): "The philosopher will not himself challenge this all too obligatory cave-chatter," Heidegger announces, "but will leave it to itself, instead immediately seizing hold of *one* person (or a few) and pulling him out, attempting to lead him on the long journey out of the cave" (*Vom Wesen der Wahrheit*, 86/63).

We see from what follows this passage, however, that while the philosopher will not stoop to the level of engaging such mindless "cave-chatter," he nevertheless does not always just "leave it to itself." Rather, he openly contradicts all cavely utterances by means of "assertions" the people will never understand—that is, whenever he is not leading forced marches out of the cave. These assertions, I would argue, constitute the second form of violence. "The liberated one returns to the cave with an eye for *being*," Heidegger explains,

This means that he who has been filled with the illuminating view for the being of beings will make known to the cave-dwellers his thoughts on what *they*, down there, take for beings. He can only do this if he remains true to himself in his liberated stance. He will report what he sees in the cave from the standpoint of his view of essence. . . . On the basis of his view of essence, *he knows in advance, before he returns to the cave*, what "shadows" mean, and upon what their possibility is grounded. Only because he *already knows* this is he able, returning to the cave, to demonstrate that the unhidden now showing itself upon the wall is caused by the fire in the cave, that this unhidden is shadow. (*Vom Wesen der Wahrheit*, 88–89/64–65; emphasis added)

Again, there is no mention here of the slow and painful recalibration that the being-dazzled philosopher must undergo in order once again to see the mere "beings" of the cave. He knows everything he needs to know before he heads back down and so never takes the time to learn to see what the cave folk see. This is the reason that his view will remain utterly incompatible with theirs. His relationship with the people in the cave is thus irremediably agonistic, for all this "liberator" can do is lecture at an audience that will never understand him or to force a few of them to understand him by tearing them away from the cave, at which point the others will want to kill him. And, in the midst of all this violence and counterviolence, Heidegger mentions incidentally that these philosophers "are to become *phulakês*, guardians. Control and organization of the state is to be undertaken by philosophers" (*Vom Wesen der Wahrheit*, 100/73). Somehow, even though they have "a view only for essence" (91/66), fail to communicate with others, provoke homicidal tendencies in their subjects, and spend most of their time wresting one or two promising young boys into the "open," the philosophers will rule the world of the cave.

What has happened here?

Heidegger, it seems, has lost sight of his most profound insight: that truth takes place in the *transitions*, or encounters, between darkness (the cave, beings, hiddenness) and light (the "open," being, unhiddenness) *and vice versa*. By ignoring the considerable problem of the neophyte philosopher's inability to see in the dark, by insisting that his focus is solely on being and light and essence, Heidegger not only makes a violent and ultimately impotent polemicist out of the philosopher-king but also reinscribes precisely what he sets forth in these lectures as "Plato's doctrine of truth." For, if the liberator returns to the cave with his eyes trained only on what is *not* in the cave, then the implication is that, *before* he returns, he already has—and already *is*—the truth. If nothing in the thoughtless chatter of the cave people can teach him anything about the being and truth and essence that he knows "in advance," then *truth does not occur in the cave at all*. Truth is simply located, just as it is for Heidegger's Plato, outside the cave: in a being without beings, transcendence without worldliness, and unconcealment without concealment.

Heidegger, I would argue, is partly justified and partly unjustified in reading *Plato* in this manner, although Heidegger's *own* lapse into the vision he attributes to Plato remains puzzling indeed. On the one hand, Plato seems to authorize the notion that the return to the cave cannot teach the philosopher anything. In the illustration of the divided line, for example, Plato describes the highest form of *nous* as reaching conclusions "without making use of anything visible at all, but only of forms themselves, moving on from forms to forms, and ending in forms" (511b–c). On the other hand, Plato has Socrates ridicule those otherworldly philosophers who live out their days on the "Isles of the Blessed," and who stubbornly refuse "to go down again to the prisoners in the cave and share their labors and honors" (519c–d). In this notion of "sharing," Socrates preemptively repudiates Heidegger's insistence that the returned philosopher will refuse to listen to "cave chatter." Even more radical, however, is Socrates's account of the end of the cavely readjustment period that Heidegger does not discuss. After fifteen years of political training in the cave, Socrates says, "at the age of fifty, those who've survived the tests and been successful both in practical matters and in the sciences must be led to the goal and compelled to lift up the radiant light of their souls to what itself provides light for everything. And *once they've seen the Good itself*, they must each in turn put the city, its citizens, and themselves in order, using it as their model" (540a–b; emphasis added). This is nothing if not astonishing: what Socrates says quite explicitly here is that it is only *after* the philosophers have readjusted their vision to the blinding darkness that they finally see the Good itself. *In the midst of the cave.* Had Heidegger attended more closely to this strand, he would have had ample ancient support for the insight he is ultimately unable to sustain: truth always and only opens in and through the untruth that conceals and reveals it.

Instead, Heidegger insists, for the sake of attributing the adequation problem to Plato, that Plato does not understand "concealment is always and necessarily present at the occurrence of unconcealment" (*Vom Wesen der Wahrheit*, 145/104; translation modified). This would be a relatively harmless selective reading of Plato, if Heidegger himself had stayed with the insight that concealment is part of the unfolding of truth, so that the ascent and descent could have been seen as equally integral to the occurrence of unconcealment. But why is this not reflected in Heidegger's meditations upon the philosopher-king? Why does Heidegger resort to such a facile bifurcation between untruth and truth, concealment and revelation, shadows and things-in-themselves? And what would it mean to retell the story in such a way that the truth of being, in "genuine" Heideggerian fashion, might refuse this simple dichotomy, taking place instead in the interstices of all that is embodied in the "cave" and all that is promised in the "open"?

Heidegger's second translation and interpretation of this allegory gets us a bit closer than the first to opening this betweenness, if by ultimately shutting it down in the opposite direction. In his 1947 essay on the cave, Heidegger stresses even more strongly the priority of the transitions over the stages themselves and, promisingly, almost always counters his references to the upward adjustment with equal and opposite rhetorical nods to the downward adjustment. So, in the first few pages of the 1947 essay, he argues that "the 'allegory' recounts a series of movements rather than just reporting on the dwelling places and conditions of people inside and outside the cave. In fact, the movements that it recounts are movements of passage out of the cave into the daylight and then back out of the daylight into the cave."[56] In this second version of the allegory, even more explicitly than in the first, the one who makes his way out of the cave is meant to make his way back *down* to free those who are still imprisoned within it. The most striking difference between the two narratives, however, is that the second presents its reader with a liberator who has very little confidence in his ability to liberate.

In 1947, what concerns Heidegger far more than it had sixteen years earlier—before the war, before the rectorship, before the humiliating appearances in front of the denazification committee—is the problem of the philosopher's night blindness. In marked contrast to the picture of poorly received triumphalism he paints in his earlier account, Heidegger now steeps his philosopher in political impotence:

> the one who has been freed is *supposed to* lead these people too away from what is unhidden for them and to bring them face to face with the most unhidden. But the *would-be* liberator no longer knows his or her way around the cave and risks the danger of succumbing to the overwhelming power of the kind of truth that is normative down there, the danger of being *overcome* by the claim of the common "reality" to be the only reality. ("Platons Lehre von der Wahrheit," 129/171; emphasis added)

In this version, as in the earlier one, the philosopher is "threatened with the possibility of being put to death" and the downward descent is portrayed agonistically as a "battle waged within the cave between the liberator and the prisoners who resist all liberation." Unlike the pontificator/body-snatcher of the first scenario, however, the philosopher in this second one is a profoundly *vulnerable* character whose grasp on his "vision for essence," once he returns to the cave, is tenuous at best ("Platons Lehre von der Wahrheit," 129/171). In marked contrast to the Liberator who descends with a full knowledge of the truth and remains blind to his blindness, this more circumspect would-be liberator of 1947 recognizes not only that it is difficult to hold fast to the truth of the "open" but also that he "no longer knows his way around the cave" ("Platons Lehre von der Wahrheit," 129/171).

Frustratingly, however, the new awareness that troubles this text does not give onto a meditation upon the philosopher's necessary visual readjustment. The philosopher can only learn to see in the dark again, at least according to Heidegger, insofar as he ceases to be what he has become, giving up his vision of the truth in order to recall "the kind of truth that is normative down there." Just as in the 1931 reading, then, the viewpoints of the cave and the open are thoroughly exclusive of one another. And only the latter is the locus of philosophy. Even though there is no talk of violent draggings or impassioned speeches in the 1947 text, there are still two utterly separate abodes: "the one inside and the one outside the cave. . . . The kind of astuteness that is normative down there in the cave . . . is surpassed by another *sophia*. This latter strives solely and above all to glimpse the being of beings in the 'ideas.' . . . Outside the cave *sophia* is *philosophia*" ("Platons Lehre von der Wahrheit," 140/180). Like the first, then, the second retelling self-deconstructs, reconsolidating truth into its "Platonic" abode in the third stage. In fact, this second collapse is even more explicit than the first, because while Heidegger had at least initially tried in 1931 to maintain the decisiveness of the passage to the fourth stage, here he argues that "real freedom is only attained in stage three. Here someone who has been unshackled is at the same time conveyed outside the cave 'into the open'" ("Platons Lehre von der Wahrheit," 127/169). And, again, "authentic liberation is the steadiness of being oriented toward that which appears in its visible form and which is the most unconcealed in this appearing" ("Platons Lehre von der Wahrheit," 128/170; translation modified slightly). So, while it is the philosopher's destiny to become a misunderstood politician in the first interpretation, his best option in the second would probably be to remain out in the open where his vision of "the most unconcealed" is the most unobstructed. Equally problematic positions, the liberator of '31 reenters the world to wage war with it, while the philosopher of '47 would be wise, in the words of David Hume, to "make [his] escape into the calm, though obscure, regions of philosophy."[57]

Perhaps this is an unfair ascription. Then, again, perhaps not. There is no way of knowing for certain, because Heidegger provides an even shorter exposition of the "fourth stage" in 1947 than he did in 1931, breaking off the narrative to attack Plato's "doctrine" of truth, more forcefully this time around. Again, Heidegger accuses Plato of failing to pay attention to the hidden implied in every act of unhiding. Again, he faults the ancient philosopher for reifying truth into an attribute of beings rather than recognizing it as an occurrence. And, in this reading, he blames all these errors, which set philosophy on its disastrous course toward modern technology, on Plato's gradual subordination of unconcealment itself to the Forms; in particular, the idea of the Good. From this point forward, Heidegger's illustration of this epic blunder becomes the sole focus of his analysis: "the 'allegory' is grounded in the unspoken event whereby *idea* gains dominance over *alêtheia*" ("Platons Lehre von der Wahrheit," 135/176)—and the story of the liberated one is again, and this time forever, deferred.

At the very end of this second commentary on the cave allegory, however, Heidegger begins to point toward a path for future thinking. He writes that while thought must return to its origins in order to begin again, this repetition must be nonidentical to move thinking forward. Any "recollection" of Platonic truth cannot "take over unconcealment merely in Plato's sense"; it must also attune itself to "the 'positive' in the 'privative' essence of *alêtheia*" ("Platons Lehre von der Wahrheit," 238/182)—that is, to forgetting, hiddenness, and untruth. Presumably, then, insofar as genuine attention to truth as unconcealment would always reveal an equiprimordial concealment, such thinking would have to maintain itself within their relentless, mutually dependent oscillation. It would have to take its placeless place *between* hiddenness and revelation, darkness and light, beings and being, and earth and sky. While Heidegger's analysis never returns to the story of the cave, the last moments of this essay can nevertheless be heard as a call for *another* rereading of it—one that might *stay with* the liminality and caveliness from which both Heidegger's own accounts ultimately ran. One clue Heidegger gives to those who might take on such a task is that, for such thinking/reading to take place, something will have to "break in on us": "that exigency whereby we are compelled to question not just beings in their being but first of all being itself (that is, the difference)" ("Platons Lehre von der Wahrheit," 144/182). Something will have to awaken us out of our cave-bound *or* sky-dwelling stupors—something that places and sustains us in the unrelenting difference of the between.

### Rethinking Thaumazein

In his unpublished writings from 1937–38, Heidegger argues that Erstaunen will not suffice as the disposition that carries thinking into its "other beginning" because its object, being, has become utterly commonplace. No one wonders anymore that being is—or that beings are. Again, this failure is the sign—rather than the cause—of being's withdrawal, by virtue of which thinking has lost the capacity for that which initially calls forth and calls for thinking. Thinking cannot think being *or* the beings being has abandoned. Yet it remains blind to this incapacity. Because of the in-advance certainty of calculation, modern natural and social sciences are oblivious to their own oblivion of being. They *think* they think being, they *know* they know what beings are, and so they remain completely unaware that there is any need to think thinking, being, and knowing themselves. Again, Heidegger maintains that the Erstaunen that might awaken this need is inaccessible to us now. But Verhaltenheit—with its constituent attunements of Erschrecken and Scheu—just might displace thinking into the exigency of thinking. And in so doing it might awaken thaumazein from its slumber in impossibility.

Ten years later, in Heidegger's second reading of the cave, the possibility of thinking is once again a matter of somehow shocking thinking into its own exigency. Something must break into "the kind of thinking that is normative down [here]," orient our vision toward being, and thereby reveal the objects we call "beings" to be just shadows of beings. This sudden displacement, whereby even the most familiar shadows on the wall would be revealed in their insubstantiality, would provoke a kind of shock or terror (Er/schrecken). It might therefore be possible to think this first movement of Verhaltenheit together with the ascent from the cave. Allowing this to be the case, Heidegger's reluctance to dwell upon (or in) the countermovement, by which the eyes would gradually be able to see in the dark *without losing sight of the light*, can be seen as a reluctance to dwell upon awe (Scheu). In the flight from any comportment that would engage the cave chatter, we thus see yet another flight from wonder. Yet, even as we mark his repeated attempts to close it, we can now begin to piece together a way of thinking (in) the space of thaumazein that Heidegger reopens.

Dwelling in the wonder of the "other beginning" would mean learning, like the philosopher-king, to understand the truths of the cave and the "open" *simultaneously*. It would mean turning away from beings in their terrifying strangeness *and back toward them* in the midst of being's withdrawal without ever losing the capacity for shock (by falling into the comforting arms of unthinking everydayness) or the capacity for awe (by maintaining too comfortable a distance from this everydayness). Turning and returning in this manner, Dasein-in-thaumazein would be continually interrupted and displaced by the shock of what arrives or fails to arrive, so that "everything that has been heretofore manifest to human beings, as well as the way in which it has been manifest, gets transformed" ("Platons Lehre von der Wahrheit," 124/168). Unable to know anything "in advance," thaumazein would resist the objectifying mediations of calculation *and* the officious certainty animating the self-appointed liberator.

"Perhaps . . . " interrupts the ghost of Hannah Arendt. "But, even so, it would make for a miserable political strategy." Living responsibly in the public sphere, Arendt would argue, requires that individuals make decisions based on their own convictions, the discernment of which depends upon the very opinion-solidification that wonder persistently unsettles. For Arendt, the trouble with attuning oneself to the "withdrawal of being" is that the "annul-ment of this 'withdrawal' on the other side, is always paid for by a with-drawal from the world of human affairs."[58] Yet the aim of such thinking, as John Caputo has phrased it, is not to "annul" the withdrawal at all, but rather to "awake[n] *to* the withdrawal of [b]eing *as* a withdrawal . . . entering into that withdrawal all the more primordially."[59] Arendt is right to say that trying to cancel the distance between oneself and "being-itself" would most likely amount to abandoning the world completely. She is right, moreover, to suggest that the one who speaks from within "total terror" speaks in ideo-logical clichés that tolerate no relation to particularity. The possibility that Arendt does not raise, however, is that *withstanding* the distance of being's terrifying withdrawal might block the machinations of "total terror" that seek to collapse all critical distance. A constantly sustained double move-ment between something like Erschrecken and something like Scheu might condition a more attentive, awed relationship to the very beings being leaves in its horrifying wake.

For, as it is now possible to see, Heidegger's "stupidity" was hardly the result of a wonder-struck inability to form an opinion. Rather, it seems to have emerged from his resorting to the kind of packaged opinion that depends upon *closure* of thaumazein. Had Heidgegger's response to the "terror" the Führer "instilled in our Dasein" been to maintain an aweful attunement to the beings and Daseins around him, one wonders whether he would have been able to walk the totalitarian party line, which required, as they all do, that a person insulate himself from every particularity that might unsettle the knowledge it instills "in advance." Performing his own understanding of the formation of false opinion, Heidegger failed to see the treatment of, say, Hus-serl, Jaspers, or Blochmann; gazing *past them* toward canned slogans such as "The Führer alone *is* the present and future of German reality and its law."[60] To be sure, Heidegger was operating in his political speeches under some sort of spell—Jaspers said he was under the sway of the same "mass intoxica-tion" as the majority of the nation[61]—but this degree of uncritical acceptance resembles the stupor of the chained cave dwellers or the reverence of the Sophists' pupils; not the tireless questioning and steadily endured uncertainty of Socratic thaumazein. The 1933 commitment roughly follows the trajectory of the cave interpretation of 1931: the philosopher who returns to the cave with the truth preaches it to mostly unconvinced audiences and dismisses any divergent viewpoints as cave chatter. Conversely, one might say that Hei-degger's withdrawal in the last months of the war from all public affairs—his escape to Wildenstein castle to read Heraclitus, Parmenides, and Hölderlin in "pastoral idyll" with a few devoted followers—was merely a reversal of this same failure to attend to the world.[62] This withdrawal followed the path of the philosopher, sketched in 1947, for whom "genuine liberation" takes place when he has made his way outside the cave entirely, perhaps dragging one or two others along behind him.

In the years leading up to his separation from the polis, Heidegger began to reverse his initial conviction that philosophers ought to be the guardians of the state, insisting, with increasing vehemence, that genuine philosophy is politically useless.[63] During this period he also forgot the philosopher's awed attention to the everyday, citing Nietzsche to argue (perhaps as nothing more than a proleptic defense of his time spent in an unheated cabin in the woods of Todtnauberg and his flight to Wildenstein Castle) that "'philosophy . . . means living voluntarily amid ice and mountain ranges.' Philosophizing, we can now say, is extra-ordinary questioning about the extra-ordinary."[64] Most shockingly, however, all of this immanence renouncing led him to forget his finitude, writing in 1943 that "being presumably prevails in its essence without beings." (He came back to his senses—at least partially—in 1949, when he revised the manuscript and changed the "presumably" to "never.")[65]

Heidegger's "own" decisions, then, whether in the form of his attempts to command or to abandon the polis, represent particularly extreme failures to negotiate both the cave and the "open," both the world and the sky. Nevertheless, this is precisely what his thought calls us to do: neither to abandon the usual for the unusual nor to force the usual to become something else, but rather to see the ordinary and the extraordinary in and through one another, thereby letting what *is* finally *be*. This, he tells us, is the work of thaumazein: "wonder—understood transitively—brings forth the showing of what is most usual in its unusualness. . . . Wonder does not divert itself from the usual but on the contrary adverts to it, precisely as what is the most usual of everything and in everything."[66] "Bringing forth" the ordinary *as* extraordinary, wonder neither escapes the cave to gaze upon the open nor ignores the open to see in the cave, but rather dismantles this binary altogether, opening the open *in and through the cave*. And how could it be otherwise? What is so strange about Heidegger's insistence upon the "two abodes" of the cave and the open is that in the work both preceding and following the 1947 Plato piece, there is no such separation. In *Sein und Zeit*, for example, Heidegger repeatedly insists that authenticity is not a matter of somehow removing oneself from everydayness but of living in a different relationship to it instead. "Authentic being-a-self," he maintains, is not a liberation from "the they," but rather an "existentiel modification" of it; it is "nothing which hovers over entangled everydayness, but is existentially only a modified grasp of everydayness."[67] Had he read this insight into the cave allegory, Heidegger would have had to concede that the everydayness of the cave *cannot* be escaped; it can only be taken on in the open resoluteness he calls *Ent-schlossenheit*. This unclosedness, in the language of the "early" work, is openness to anxiety—to being shocked by the groundlessness of things and to enduring this uncanniness until it places Dasein back into the world as care. Modulated according to the dynamic of Verhaltenheit, Dasein is the being that stands ex-statically in the *there* of the world, holding open the shock of being's withdrawal so that it might give way to a "new wonder" at the impossible thatness of being. Always renewed by the surprise conditioning it, this awe keeps open the uncertain questioning that allows thinking neither to abandon nor to instrumentalize beings, but to preserve them in being. In these technophilic times, would amount to "re-creating a being unto the ownmost of its destiny and unto freeing it from the misuse of machinations, which, turning everything upside down, exhaust a being in exploitation."[68] The double movement of wonder takes us out of the world *only to put us back into the world*, dismantling old possibilities to uncover new ones, exposing as "wind-eggs" all we think we know in order to reveal everything as different—as more itself—than it had been before. Genuine relation and decision, then, do not depend upon closing off wonder into a momentary "spark," but upon keeping it open.

All things have come out of nothingness and are carried onwards to infinity.
Who can follow these astonishing processes?

　　　—Blaise Pascal, *Pensées*

## 2. OPENNESS: Emmanuel Levinas

### Passivity and Responsibility

What does thinking open when it (re-)opens wonder? Insofar as wonder opens thinking to begin with, might one venture that opening wonder would open openness itself? Or that wonder keeps the open open? And if so, what are the implications of keeping thinking so profoundly exposed?

Because of the irreducibly ambivalent nature of thaumazein, we have seen that remaining with wonder opens onto a kind of horror: horror at the sudden uncanniness of the everyday; at the groundlessness of the thinking self and the objects it clearly and distinctly perceives; at the monstrous slippage between friend and foe, Harpies and rainbows, known and unknown. The problem under consideration in this chapter, then, is this: how is thinking to sustain the twofold attunement to Erschrecken (shock, terror) and Scheu (wonder, awe), considering the prevalent tendency to cover it over in opening it up? In its tireless oscillation between withdrawal and arrival, strangeness and familiarity, and monstrousness and godliness, how might Verhaltenheit keep openness open? And how might this double exposure help us to understand what Heidegger meant when he mentioned in passing that Verhaltenheit "does not justify evading of beings, but the opposite"?[1] Does "the opposite" of evading beings mean attending to the concrete needs of others? And, if so, how might the twofold wound of wonder open and sustain this attentiveness?

To be sure, the ethical dangers of wonder are clear: Socrates warns The-aetetus that the same thaumazein that makes him a philosopher might leave him enslaved to the "inexorable logic" of mercenary sophists. Socrates also tells the story of Thales, whose wide-eyed admiration of the stars above him led him to tumble into an open well below him. Two thousand years later, Descartes will warn that wonder occupies a space anterior to the distinction between good and evil, leaving the wonderer unable to distinguish between his savior and his destroyer. And, of course, there is Aristophanes' caricature in the *Clouds* of Socrates himself, who first appears in a basket in midair, as if unable to land anywhere.[2] Common sense would seem to dictate that living responsibly in the world requires a closure—or, at the very least, a strong sublimation—of wonder's primordial openness. And yet the thought experiment at hand will seek to reopen this wound in the name of "attentiveness to beings," to consider the possibility that responsibility relies upon vulnerability rather than mastery or certainty.

The counterintuitive notion that ethics depends upon philosophical, emotional, and physical *exposure* is perhaps most compellingly set forth in the work of Emmanuel Levinas. Pitting much of his thought directly against Heidegger's (and, for that reason, often remaining squarely within the very "climate" he continually attempts to "leave"),[3] Levinas counters what he perceives to be a residual will toward comprehension in Heidegger with a thoroughgoing submission to the will of the other: a "passivity beyond passivity." Levinas most frequently distinguishes this passivity from Heideggerian *Gelassenheit*, a mood to which it nevertheless remains closer than Levinas might prefer. *Gelassenheit*, or "letting be" (also *Seinlassen*) could be called a disempowered modification of *Being and Time's Ent-schlossenheit* and a close (anti-) conceptual cousin to Verhaltenheit. It emerges in the middle of Heidegger's authorship as a mood of releasement, a total receptivity to that which exceeds and constitutes Dasein; a resistance to the metaphysical impulses to calculate, represent, and assimilate the unknown. In and as Gelassenheit, Dasein places itself within the terrifying withdrawal of the "being" that metaphysics takes for granted, allowing beings finally to be *as beings* rather than as objects (which can only be stably constituted against the uninterrogated façade of being-as-presence). Stripping Dasein of the raw material for its techno-ontological adventure, Gelassenheit, moreover, signals an abandonment of the will-toward-fixity that seeks to consolidate the transcendental subject, its objects, and its God into mutually stabilizing monads.

The main reason Levinas rejects Gelassenheit as a model for his "passivity more passive still than any receptivity"[4] is that he believes it supports Heidegger's alleged "priority" of being over beings, ultimately subsuming the beings it "lets be" under the comprehensive rubric of being-itself.[5] Along Levinas's reading of Heidegger, then, openness to being *precludes* openness to individual beings. By only "allowing" beings to appear in the light and on the horizon of being, Gelassenheit assembles them all under "a totality that gives them meaning." As it consumes more and more objects of knowledge, the knowing subject becomes subject over it all: "everything . . . that comes to me in terms of being in general certainly offers itself to my understanding and my possession."[6] In short, Gelassenheit remains lodged within the register of comprehension, neglecting beings for the sake of being and shoring up the supremacy of the representing self. This critique is similar to Arendt's insistence that attuning oneself to being "is always paid for by a withdrawal from the world of human affairs."[7] Or, as Levinas puts it, "the understanding of a being consists in going beyond that being—precisely into openness— and perceiving it upon the *horizon of being*. . . . To understand the particular being is already to place oneself beyond the particular."[8] To place oneself beyond the particular is for Levinas to place oneself beyond (or above) ethics, so that "Heideggerian ontology, which subordinates the relationship with the Other to the relationship with Being in general, remains under obedience to the anonymous, and leads inevitably to another power, to imperialist domination, to tyranny."[9]

Looking to obstruct this seemingly relentless march from fundamental ontology to dictatorship, Levinas insists that "the terms must be reversed" and, against Heidegger's alleged privilege of being over beings, proceeds to hold up "the philosophical priority of the existent over Being."[10] In Levinasian shorthand, this amounts to an absolute priority of ethics over ontology. It should be noted that this privilege of individual beings over being itself recapitulates the mutual exclusivity Levinas critiques in Heidegger. Moreover, Levinas's separation of being and beings is founded upon a reading of Heidegger that Jacques Derrida has described as "embedded" with "misunderstandings," since being for Heidegger is *only* ever articulated in and through beings—apart, we should interject, from a brief stint between 1943 and 1949.[11] As Derrida explains it, "Being, since *it is nothing* outside the existent . . . could in no way *precede* the existent, whether in time, or in dignity, etc. Nothing is more clear, as concerns this, in Heidegger's thought. Henceforth one cannot legitimately speak of the 'subordination of the existent to Being,' or, for example, of the ethical relation to the ontological relation."[12]

Logically speaking at least, Derrida's defense of Heidegger all but invalidates Levinas's critique of him. Insofar as being "never prevails in its essence without beings,"[13] insofar as beings only *are* as *beings*, and insofar as the failure to interrogate being as such is the source of ontic instrumentalization in the first place, any "ethical" attention to particular beings as such requires "ontological" attention to the beings they are—to the unthought being they instantiate. In fact, especially in Heidegger's later work, Dasein enters into the vortex of being for the explicit purpose of releasing beings from "objectivity" back to their integrity as beings: "to *let be* is to engage oneself with beings . . . such engagement withdraws in the face of beings in order that they might reveal themselves with respect to what and how they are."[14] Any well-executed "priority" of being would thus necessarily entail an equiprimordial "priority" of beings in their particularity.

All of that said, it is not the case that "nothing is more clear" than the consistent interarticulation of being and beings throughout Heidegger's work. In addition to Heidegger's brief insistence between 1943 and 1947 that being "presumably" holds sway without beings,[15] we also might cite Heidegger's comparative inattention to the Scheu that marvels at beings as distinct from the Erschrecken that wakes to being's withdrawal. Most significantly, we should remember Heidegger's two equally cave-ophobic treatments of Plato's *Republic*, both of which end up reinscribing truth as otherworldly. All these betray a certain self-betrayal within Heidegger's work with respect to the integrity of beings. And so, while Levinas's direct attacks on Heidegger do remain lodged in a reactionary and self-defeating strategy of inversion, his sense that Heidegger shortchanges the concrete, particular, and ethical is hardly without justification. As will become clear, the moments in Levinas's thought that are *not* explicitly framed as critiques of Heidegger will be most helpful to us as we consider the ethical implications of the bilateral wonder Heidegger opens and closes.

### The Ethics of the Cave

Far more nuanced than his attempts simply to reverse Heidegger's alleged "priority" of being over beings, of existence over existents, or of the "universal" over the particular is Levinas's ethical interdetermination of all of these terms in his notion of infinity. Much the way that Heidegger at his most careful insists that being only takes place through its appropriation to beings, Levinas maintains that any talk of the infinite-itself (or God, or the Good, all of which he uses more or less interchangeably) is an absurdity as well as an act of violence. Both phenomenologically and ethically speaking, the "metaphysical" event of infinity only takes place insofar as it "comes to mind"—to a finite, human, embodied mind—in the face of another.[16] The infinite, in other words, only becomes itself by means of its revelation *to and through* that which it exceeds. This revelation, then, always issues in a profound responsibility to the particular one through whom the infinite comes to mind: "The coming to mind of God is always linked, in my analyses, to the responsibility for the other person and all religious affectivity signifies in its concreteness a relation to others; the fear of God would be concretely a fear for my neighbor."[17] In his musings on infinity, Levinas therefore stays with the insight that Heidegger posits and then retracts: since truth takes place in and through the cave it transforms, the so-called two abodes are inextricably bound up with one another. In fact, it may be unhelpful even to count two of them. Exposure to the Good is neither a matter of preaching the truth of the sky to deluded cave dwellers nor of abandoning them for Philosophy, nor of dragging a few promising pupils into the blinding sun of the "open," but rather of recognizing the opening of the open in the faces of the enslaved ones as such. Far from transporting the thinker into the glimmering realm of the Forms, infinity keeps her focused on the naked, hungry, and suffering people through which it calls her. Exposure to Levinasian infinity, in other words, *would prevent our escape into some rarefied "infinity-itself"*: "The goodness of the Good—of the Good that neither sleeps nor slumbers—inclines the movement it calls forth to turn away from the Good and orient it toward the other, and only thus toward the Good."[18] Here then we find the sort of perpetual displacement we anticipated through Heidegger's Erschrecken and Scheu. Along Levinas's understanding of infinity the wonder of being "itself" redirects the wondering gaze immediately back to the everyday, from the "open" right back into the cave.

The ethical relationship that Levinas designates as the occurrence of the Good entails a reciprocal openness: the abject vulnerability of the other is mirrored by my vulnerability to that vulnerability.[19] This exposure that responds *as* exposure *to* exposure, and without deliberation or reservation, goes by the names of *discourse, speaking*, or, in Levinas's later work, *saying*. Unlike denomination, which conquers the unknown by assimilating it to the known (or the "said"), saying responds to the unknown *as unknown*, that is, before all determination of its intensity or intentions. Saying is therefore ex-pression; saying "expos[es] one's very exposedness." As such, "the act of speaking is the passivity in passivity"; it is the assent to the command of the other without any understanding. In sum, saying is a "response without a question," which calls out, like the most obedient of servants, "here I am."[20] Because saying-without-understanding interrupts the phenomenological return from known object to knowing self, the subject-as-saying is not, strictly speaking, itself. At its most extreme, the self is nothing more than a solicitous reference to the other, and, in fact, this hyperbolic ethic could be the unattainable telos of Levinas's whole oeuvre: "to make oneself completely into a sign, perhaps that is it."[21]

Beginning with *Otherwise Than Being* (1974), Levinas calls the subject's constant departure from itself in responsibility a process of "de-nucleation": insofar as the self responds to the other without stopping to gather itself onto-epistemologically, the "nucleus of the ego is cored out/cores itself out."[22] And yet this ceaseless turning inside out does not dissolve me into nothingness, for a complete annihilation of self would relieve me of my responsibility. On the contrary, the self's self-divestment *enacts* its responsibility as vulnerability without annulling it: "as a responsible I, I never finish emptying myself of myself."[23] Thus there is in Levinas's thought a profound tension, which will be examined in further detail toward the end of this chapter, between the self's utter diremption and its ethical singularity, which are equiprimordial and irreconcilable effects of responsibility. Opening myself without reserve to the suffering and demands of others, I am constituted (in the accusative) as *me*—as the irreplaceably responsible one. Yet, at the same time, the very command that singularizes me continually divests me of myself, so that I *am* as eroding, aging, passing passively and inexorably beyond my own reach: I am as wounded.

It is this infinite passivity as infinite responsibility that Levinas takes pains to distinguish from Gelassenheit, which in his view ends up objectifying beings and returning the self to itself because it remains within the register of comprehension. Like the temporary "passivity" of Kantian rationality, Heideggerian receptivity for Levinas always re-acts with "a grasping, as transcendental apperception—the passivity of the wound received turning back into assumption, synthesis."[24] "Passivity beyond passivity," by contrast, keeps responsibility open, leaving the eroding ego increasingly susceptible to further "woundedness and outrage," to the point of being responsible for the very suffering it undergoes as responsible.[25] The revelation of the infinite through the ethical relation can thus perhaps be best described as a *trauma*—a wound in the everyday that no act of memory, anticipation, will, or cognition can heal.

### Infinity and Astonishment

As trauma, infinity takes place as the discomfiting nonadequation of knowledge and the known; infinity is the thought the thinking self cannot think. Surprisingly, Levinas finds the prototype for this cognitive insufficiency in Descartes' *Meditations*, at the moment when the "I think" comes upon the idea of God. Rather than confirming the integrity of the thinking self, Descartes' God ruptures it, according to Levinas, since infinity is the only idea too great to have come from finitude. Objects, other people, angels: Descartes tells us that all these could be his own cognitive projections. "The *cogito* can give itself the sun and the sky," Levinas reminds us; "the only thing it cannot give itself is the idea of the Infinite,"[26] because finitude cannot possibly give rise to infinity. This is what leads Descartes to infer that God must have placed the idea of himself within him, "like the mark of the craftsman impressed upon his work."[27] Thinking God, Levinas explains, the cogito thinks more than it can think and therefore ceases to be able to tout itself as self-determined. Tracing the cogito's progression from radical doubt to God, "Descartes has sketched, with unequaled rigor, the extraordinary course of a thought proceeding to the breakup of the I think."[28] Undone by the "monstrous" indwelling of infinity, the self becomes not-itself, inscrutable; with the clearest and most distinct suddenly obscure.

Descartes himself recognizes that the idea of infinity exceeds his own capacity, going on to parley this excess into a proof of God's existence. Levinas, however, goes further, locating in this philosophic interruption the inauguration of ethics. What is important, Levinas tells us, is not whether or not Descartes manages to prove the existence of God, but rather the "astonishment" one feels at the very idea of God in me or infinity in finitude, insofar as it testifies to "the very paradox—so anti-Greek—of an idea 'put' into me."[29] This astonishment interrupts the project of thinking, cores out the self, and redirects it to the other. Before moving on to investigate this relationship, however, it is important to tease out the particularities of the "anti-Greek paradox." First, Levinas's suggestion here that the infinite is "'put' into me" works against his own insight that infinity does not exist on its own before breaking into finitude. Rather infinity *is* nothing apart from its trace in (and as) the wounded finite; conversely, the finite cannot be itself apart from the infinite. It is misleading to say that one could be "put" in another, because, strictly speaking, the two emerge in and through one another. The reason this is important is that it signals the total priority of the ethical relation: for Levinas, there is no way to the Otherness of God/Infinity except through my denucleation by and for the otherness of my neighbor and vice versa.

Second, Levinas makes oblique reference here to the "Greek" doctrine of recollection as a foil for the idea of infinity. If the soul contains everything it needs to know from eternity, the theory goes, then it merely needs to be prompted to remember what is already within it. The reason infinity ruptures such recollection for Levinas is that it cannot be contained properly in the soul's vision or memory; rather, it must come from *outside* the thinking self.[30] While the rhetorical value of this distinction is clear, however, Levinas seems strategically to ignore here the moments in the Platonic corpus that unsettle any simple myth of self-constitution. In addition to Socrates's daimon, his possession by Diotima, and Plato's dispossessing "fourth delirium," with which Levinas is well acquainted,[31] one might also mention the thaumazein of the *Theaetetus*. The recognition of the groundlessness of knowledge in this dialogue comes neither from Socrates nor from Theaetetus, but rather from the conversation between them. Far from attesting to some memory from eternity, and equally far from thanking Socrates for "putting" an idea into him, Theaetetus tells his teacher, "for my part I have already, thanks to you, given utterance to more than I had in me."[32] This testimony, coming as it does as the consummation of the effort to know the nature of knowledge, already attests to a progressive "breakup of the I think" similar to the "anti-Greek" one Levinas reads through Descartes.

Third, the connection to the *Theaetetus* is particularly compelling given Levinas's suggestion that Descartes provokes *astonishment*. How are we to read this, given Descartes' own proclamation in the *Passions of the Soul* that "astonishment . . . can never be anything but bad"?[33] Furthermore, looking back to the *Meditations*, one finds that Descartes actually goes out of his way to say that the idea of God is not astonishing at all: "To be sure, *it is not astonishing* that in creating me, God should have endowed me with this idea."[34] The Latin text actually has an imperative, even prohibitive, valence that the English translation is missing here: "Et sane *non mirum est* Deum, me creandum, ideam illam mihi indidisse." That God should have placed the infinite in me is not only not wondrous for Descartes; it is *not to be* wondered at. The French translation of the Latin can also be read as retaining this sense of a duty not to wonder: "Et certes on *ne doit pas* trouver étrange, que Dieu en me créant ait mis en moi cette idée." Is it possible that Levinas senses some sort of repression at work here? Does Descartes' mild prohibition of astonishment or surprise or wonder (depending on how one translates *mirare*) actually show something of a slip on his part—perhaps a dangerous tendency in the face of the idea of God toward that dreaded "excess of wonder"? Most importantly, why does Levinas bring up the passion of astonishment in relation to infinity?

Throughout his authorship, Levinas calls the idea of infinity a "miracle," a "wonder" or source of wonder, a "marvel," a "monstrosity," a "shock," an "astonishment" or source of astonishment, a surprise, and a "trauma."[35] He also locates in this aweful monstrosity the original possibility of thinking itself, thereby explicitly tying it to thaumazein: "the figure of the Infinite-placed-in-me, which if we believe Descartes is contemporary with my creation, would signify that the not-able-to-comprehend-the-Infinite-by-thought is, in some way, a positive relation with this thought. . . . The not-able-to-comprehend-the-Infinite-by-thought would signify precisely this condition—or non-condition— of thought."[36] Binding and rebinding his thought to philosophy's origin in this manner, Levinas claims an epistemological anteriority for "infinity"; that is, for the nonadequation of the thinker and the thought, for the surprise of the unexpected and immemorial, and for the un-re-cognizability of the most familiar (in the enigmatic traces of the face, neighbor, self). It is at this point that the interruption of ontology and epistemology gives way to ethics. Prompted by the shock of originary, unassimilable alterity, thinking is nothing other than a response to the infinity in the finite; a constant turning away from oneself and toward the other. Levinas thus reopens the wound of wonder in the strange figures of infinity, God, the Good, or the other. Most important, Levinas isolates this "traumatism of astonishment"[37] not in the service of some otherworldly and egoistic escapism, but rather for the sake of a concrete responsibility that interrupts all subjectivity: "the wonder of the *I* claimed by God in the face of my neighbor—the marvel of the *I* rid of self and fearing God—is thus tantamount to the suspension of the eternal and irreversible return from the identical in itself to itself and of the inviolability of its logical and ontological privilege."[38] Because it prevents me from getting myself together, the wonder that makes me vulnerable to my neighbor makes me responsive to her in her vulnerability.

To recapitulate, the infinite exceeds every conceptual boundary. It therefore shatters all myths of interiority, all aspirations toward mastery, and, through its revelation in the particular face or gaze of the other, disables my ability to kill or assert power over the other. The infinite as beyond-the-determinate is, for this reason, the Good: the paradigm of every ethic. It seems, then, as though we have solved the problem of thaumazein by unraveling this particular knot through our reading of Levinas: if, in the figure of infinity, all indeterminacy opens onto the Good, then the wonder that constantly opens onto the in- and overdeterminate must necessarily open onto ethics as concrete responsibility to and for the suffering of others. And Arendt's concern about the wonderer's selfishness, otherworldliness, and obscured judgment need trouble us no more. Indeed, the matter would be closed (at which point it would look suspicious anyway) were it not for what Derrida calls a "strange symmetry" between the vulnerability of the responsible ego and the vulnerability of the *aliter*-ego to whom he responds.[39]

The infinite passivity of Levinasian ethics responds, without prior comprehension, to the command issued by the suffering of the other. This non-comprehension, it is important to emphasize, is not a *failure* to comprehend; rather, it is a renunciation of comprehension. Any effort to comprehend the other's plight is unacceptable to Levinas, since explaining suffering always entails a degree of explaining it *away*.[40] Ultimately, the evil that the other undergoes must be the figure of incomprehensibility itself: "Is not the evil of suffering—extreme passivity, helplessness, abandonment and solitude—also the unassimilable . . . the half-opening that a moan, a cry, a groan or a sigh slips through—the original call for aid . . . original opening toward merciful care."[41] I must respond to this opening precisely because I cannot understand it, because evil exceeds every effort to understand it. "It is . . . a counter-nature, a monstrosity, the disturbing and foreign in itself. *And in this sense transcendence*."[42] Evil is therefore the monstrous and unassimilable original opening of ethics as transcendence. But, then again, we have just seen that the Good is the monstrous and unassimilable original opening of ethics as transcendence. So wonder's indeterminacy has opened us onto the goodness of the good *and* the essence of evil, and we return once more to our dilemma.

Richard Bernstein offers us one possibility for thinking through this "strange symmetry," between good and evil in Levinas. Bernstein suggests they are structurally similar in Levinas because "the only adequate response to the malignancy of evil is a response that is 'commensurate' with this transcendence of evil."[43] But this seems to install good and evil as two equal and opposite sides of a tug-of-war, and ethics as a call to get on the right side and pull. Levinas's thought is more nuanced than this: he suggests that the Good pulls not so much *against* evil as *through* it, awakening the complacent self to the suffering of others and to its own responsibility to suffer *for* others. "Evil strikes me in my horror of evil," Levinas writes, "and thus reveals—or is already—my association with the Good. The excess of evil by which it is in surplus to the world is also the impossibility of our accepting it."[44] Suddenly exposed to meaningless suffering, the Levinasian *moi* embarks on its continual, constitutive departure from itself, an absolute passivity which, because it suffers for others, is *not* meaningless for Levinas. In fact, while the suffering of others is always unacceptable, mine is so important that it singularizes me: "meaning begins . . . in the relation of the soul to God, starting from its being awakened by evil. God hurts me to tear me from the world as unique and exceptional: as a soul."[45]

It is of little consequence to this study to determine whether or not Levinas sneaks in a back-door theodicy here, despite his protests to the contrary. What is more pressing for investigation is, rather, the distinction of the other's unacceptable suffering (evil) from my necessary suffering (good). Asked in an interview how on earth I can be responsible for the other if his very gaze lodges me in extreme and powerless passivity, Levinas is ultimately pushed to answer that passivity only goes so far. I must be utterly nonreactive to the violence done *against me*, he says, but highly reactive to the violence done against the other. "My resistance begins when the harm he does me is done to a third party who is also my neighbor," he writes, "it is the violence suffered by the third party that justifies stopping the violence of the other with violence."[46] What this means is that no matter how cored out and dispersed "I" become, I must retain the ability: 1. to know myself-as-suffering apart from the other-as-suffering, and 2. to tell the difference between what appears to be a "bad" indeterminacy (evil) and what appears to be a "good" indeterminacy (infinity). Yet if these two figures are similar by virtue of their fundamental unknowability, then how is one to know the difference between them? Does ethical openness to the "good" other insulate the self from evil, or leave the denucleated self exposed to the possibility of goods and evils alike? To explore these questions, the rest of this chapter will work through two figures of indeterminacy in Levinas's corpus: the *il y a* and the *Ille*. This exploration will track the shifting relationship between these "bad" and "good" infinities as they evolve from Levinas's earliest works,

*Existence and Existents, Time and the Other*, through *Totality and Infinity*, and finally through Levinas's most mature and perhaps most compelling major study, *Otherwise Than Being*. Ultimately, I will suggest both with and against Levinas that an ethic of vulnerability must remain open to an indeterminacy *beyond* good and evil.

### Opening Out: From Existent to Existence

Written while Levinas was a prisoner of war and published in 1947, *Existence and Existents* sets itself within a "world in pieces," a "world turned upside down."[47] And although this early text of Levinas's seems at times to construct an utterly decontextualized philosophy of the subject, still the all too real, unworlded world lurking in its background serves as the model for "the central concept of this study": the anonymous, impersonal field of naked existence that Levinas calls the *il y a* (there is).[48] Both in this work and in his 1946–47 lecture series at the Collège Philosophique (published in 1948 as *Time and the Other*),[49] Levinas takes his audience through a strikingly Cartesian meditation, encouraging us to "imagine" with him a scene in which all worldly beings, orders, and relations as we know them were to disappear completely. The postapocalyptic remnant would be the *il y a*: existence without existents, sheer thatness. Another way Levinas isolates phenomenologically the *there is* that exceeds all phenomenology is through an analysis of insomnia. Exposed to an endless night, the self-in-insomnia, along with the objects it knows, undergoes continual "extinction," so that "in insomnia one can and one cannot say there is an 'I' which cannot manage to fall asleep. . . . I do not stay awake: 'it' stays awake."[50] And elsewhere: "it is not that there is *my* vigilance in the night; in insomnia it is the night itself that watches. It watches."[51] When "they" and "I" and all the elements of the insomniac world dissolve into oblivion, there is nothing left but the elemental itself—neither being nor nothing but, like the *tehom* over which *Elohim* breathes in Genesis 1:2, the impersonal flux that gives rise to their difference.[52]

Levinas admits that Heidegger would find the notion of existence without existents "absurd." At the same time, however, Levinas claims to find a philosophical precedent for the "there is" in Heidegger's work. He finds it not in Heidegger's own "there is" (*es gibt*), but rather in the theme of thrownness (*Geworfenheit*), which undermines all human pretension to possession and mastery.[53] Thrown into a set of commitments and relations we did not choose, Levinas argues, we are always in a certain manner preceded by our own existence. This is not to say that Levinas's "existence without existents" is ultimately convertible with Heideggerian being. In fact, it is not clear that Levinas's isolation of the il y a is exhaustively—or even primarily—an ontological effort. The point seems rather that no matter how hard the imagination tries, it cannot think away existence "itself." Insofar as thinking thinks, it necessarily relies not on the solitary integrity of the thinking self (contra Descartes), but rather on *some notion of existence*—no matter how diminished or dispersed. In this manner, sheer thatness always returns to haunt even the starkest absence: even as the very insistence, or "presence," of that absence.

Levinas also goes to great length in this work to distinguish the terrifying experience of the il y a from Heideggerian anxiety and Sartrean nausea, claiming that neither of these sufficiently divests the anxious or nauseous subject of itself or its "experience."[54] Yet while it is debatable whether such disavowals signal a successful elusion of Sartre,[55] it is far less certain that they free him of Heidegger. At some moments, Levinas characterizes the "experience" of the il y a as terror *at* being itself; whereas Heideggerian anxiety, he maintains, is anxious *for* being-in-the-face-of-nothingness. At other moments, Levinas places the "experience" of the il y a in the nonplace *beyond* being and nothingness, an opposition to which Heidegger's early work ostensibly remains confined. Yet, even here, Levinas remains within the Heideggerian climate by unwittingly launching his analysis into the orbit of Verhaltenheit. Of course, even if Levinas had paid much attention to Heidegger's work after *Being and Time*—even if he had not decided in 1933 to abandon his full-length study of the rector's thought—Levinas would not have known much during the war about this transvaluation of thaumazein into Verhaltenheit, since, we will recall, this mood only finds explicit (and still gap-ridden) elaboration in the deleted passages from the Freiburg lectures and the posthumous *Contributions to Philosophy*. Levinas does, however, link the "astonishing" revelation of the il y a to "the wonder [*l'étonnement*] which Plato put at the origin of philosophy," because, like thaumazein, the il y a reveals the unfamiliarity of the most familiar. "Its strangeness is, we might say, due to its very reality, to the very fact that there is existence."[56] And, sounding strikingly close to Heidegger in his description of Erschrecken, Levinas calls this astonishment, which responds to the strange appearance of sheer thatness through the sudden disappearance of the self and its objects, horror (*l'horreur*).

Faced with the extinction of the world and all its inhabitants, the subject that faces the bare il y a is turned inside out, rendered utterly passive: "horror is somehow a movement which will strip consciousness of its very 'subjectivity.' Not in lulling it into unconsciousness, but in throwing it into an *impersonal vigilance, a participation*."[57] Thus emptied of itself, however, the self cannot be said to be obliterated by, or absorbed into, the elemental flux of the il y a in which it "participates." Exposure to sheer existence "prevents the subject from gathering itself up, reacting, being someone," but it does not thereby relieve it of the burden of existing. Unlike the fear of death, which at the very least promises an end to suffering, "horror carries out the condemnation to perpetual reality, to existence with 'no exits.'" Divesting the self of itself, the il y a reveals the "impossibility of death," the "unbreakable commitment" to existence, the "eternal responsibility of being."[58] Could it be, then, that we have found our double movement? Facing the il y a, the self is exposed and undone in horror at the disappearance of the world, but at the same time is bound, *precisely as un-selfed*, to the unassimilable strangeness of thatness. *Horreur* at the "there is" would therefore map onto a terror at the withdrawal of being, while the *vigilance* of insomnia would marvel at the self-donation of this very withdrawal. It moreover seems as if, in the "astonishing" figure of the il y a, Levinas sketches an ethical forerunner of the "astonish-ing" idea of infinity that in his later work will order and ordain, unravel and bind, "denucleate" and singularize me as such. *Existence and Existents*, then, would set us on our way to thinking wonder as the twofold opening of worldly ethics *through* the unworldly opening to existence. It *would*, that is, if, in trying to travel such a road, we did not skid to a stop before the resurrected body of the cogito.

### Closing Down: From Existence to Existent

Having begun this work with the horrifying march from the existent out to bare existence, Levinas now undertakes the opposite journey, which becomes his title, *De l'existence à l'existant*. (The English translation, *Existence and Existents*, completely obscures this directionality as well as the singularity of the existent.) After uncovering the faceless, "mute, absolutely indeterminate menace" that unsettles every self-constituted self,[59] Levinas proceeds to work not through the *il y a* but rather *against it*, ultimately reconstituting the decon-stituted self. Opposing his figure of the "existent" to Heidegger's Dasein, who is always already bound to being and related to others as *Mit-dasein*, Levinas argues that a relationship to existence and others is not simply given, but rather accomplished, achieved. "It is banal to say we never exist in the singular," Levi-nas declares, going on to establish the ontological priority of solitude over togetherness.[60] Far from giving itself over to its primordial dispersion in the *il y a*, then, the existent must gather itself together by taking up a position—an ontic solidification that Levinas names *l'hypostase*. The Greek ancestor of the Latin concept of substance, *hypo-stasis* literally names that which stands under or causes to stand under. Along Levinas's reading of the metaphysical tradition, this term refers to a certain becoming noun: "the event by which the act expressed by a verb became a being designated by a substantive."[61] In the self-positing moment of *hypostasis*, the existent becomes itself by gathering itself together against the *il y a* that tends to dispossess it. "Contracting" exis-tence in this manner, the hypostatic self puts a kind of ontological restraining order against the de-creative, pre-creative flux of the *il y a*—a "thus far shall you come, but no further."[62]

In the language of *Existence and Existents*, the action of *hypostasis* establishes the existent itself as spatiotemporally *present*. It thus puts an end to the insomniac night of the *il y a*, and the subject becomes capable of sleep. And with the possibility of sleep's *un*consciousness, Levinas explains, comes the possibility of consciousness, which accomplishes the establishment of the self: "To be conscious is to be torn away from the *there is*, since the existence of consciousness constitutes a subjectivity." With consciousness and subjectivity, then, resurge immanence, presence, intentionality, distance, will, knowledge—in short, everything the *il y a* would unsettle, were it not now "contracted" by the existent, who has hypostatically made himself "a master of being": "In positioning itself on a base the subject encumbered with being gathers itself together, stands up and masters all that encumbers it; its *here* gives to it a point of departure."[63] This "contraction" of existence on the part of the existent calls to mind Hobbes's *Leviathan*, in which the primordial chaos is kept at bay by means of a contract whose efficacy can only be guaranteed by an absolute sovereign.[64] It is a similarly sovereign subject that must arise in order to close off the indeterminate *il y a*. Furthermore, this sovereign subject becomes for Levinas the condition of genuine transcendence: "good" infinity can only break in through a subject firmly grounded against the ravages of sheer existence. Before the subject can be opened to the needs of the other, in other words, he must make himself master of the astonishing horror of being. Once more undermining his argument by "opposing" Heidegger, Levinas thus puts substance before *ecstasis*, insisting that "transcendence is not the fundamental movement of the ontological adventure; it is founded on the non-transcendence of position."[65] This position, however, is always and only "founded" on the repressed chaos of the raging *il y a*. Any account of the progression of this hypostatic master will therefore do well to look out for ghostly resurgences of the "indeterminate menace" against which this determinate subject asserts itself.

It will not have to wait long. Soon after establishing the subject's dominion over "all that encumbers it," Levinas admits that the hypostatic stage is not yet freedom from the raging *il y a*, but rather a necessary step toward this freedom. Like any good master, consciousness predicates its integrity upon the enslavement of all that might threaten it, in this case pulling indeterminacy along behind it on an existential leash. Levinas presents an image of the hypostatic self as "chained" to itself, in bondage to itself, dragging its own existence behind it like a late afternoon shadow: "the I is already riveted to itself, its freedom is not as light as grace but already a heaviness."[66] This unbearable burden of being is described in Levinas's lectures as the weight of embodiment itself. It is *matter* that is the matter with the subject, matter that keeps lagging behind the master to whom it is tied: "matter is the misfortune of hypostasis. . . . Everyday existence [is] haunted by matter."[67] As with all slave/master pairs, then, it is hard to know whether the "existent dominates existence," or whether "existence," in all its indeterminacy and messy materiality, actually troubles the existent's dominance.[68] Either way, with this statement of the materiality of existence comes the first explicit suggestion of its *femininity*. And as the binary rigidifies between the "bad" and "good" infinities in Levinas's work, it becomes increasingly sexed and increasingly mapped onto the psychoanalytic drama of male becoming. The existent must do everything he can to free himself from the chaotic multiplicity of material-maternal existence in order to become a single substance, worthy of the psychic bonds of "paternity" in Levinas's early work, or the (very male) Other/Go(o)d in his later work. And so the "there is" turns out to be not so much an *il y a* as an *elle y a*.

In *Existence and Existents,* Levinas focuses more on the self's position against bad infinity than he does on its liberation at the hands of good infinity. The text does briefly suggest that such liberation is necessary, for insofar as the sovereign subject posits itself as simple presence, it is coiled up within its own position and unable to open its own future. But Levinas does not go much further into an analysis of "good" alterity here than to say that "salvation . . . can only come from elsewhere, while everything in the subject is here."[69] It is not until his next publication, *Time and the Other*, that one finds a sustained attempt to describe this "elsewhere," which Levinas designates as the opening of futural time through the encounter with the other. In an interview, he will tell Philippe Nemo that these lectures represent "an attempt to escape from this isolation of existing, as the preceding book signified an attempt to escape from the *il y a*."[70] *Time and the Other*, in other words, focuses on the "second" stage of liberation; that is, freedom from the very self that has "freed" itself hypostatically from the *il y a*.

In this text, Levinas reiterates his conviction that the subject establishes itself in and as presence by positioning itself against the material flux of the *il y a*, which he now compares to Heraclitus's river as reimagined by Cratylus: one cannot even step into it once.[71] Having established its own presence over against the unassimilable (and now *watery*) "there is," the self can only be opened to the *future* by an other, which, strangely enough, also confronts the self as unassimilable: "the future is what is in no way grasped . . . the future is absolutely surprising."[72] To reinforce its difference from the *il y a*, this other will be named with the masculine demonstrative pronoun *Ille*, "that one," in *Totality and Infinity*. For now, the good other remains an other other, a second other that opens futurity by remaining refractory to all knowledge. Face-to-face with alterity, the self undergoes "the situation where something absolutely unknowable appears. Absolutely unknowable means foreign to all light, rendering every assumption of possibility impossible, but where we ourselves are seized."[73] The self is thus unchained from its stubbornly present self in its encounter with that which it cannot foresee or comprehend. In the manner of some cavely liberator, the "other" "seizes" and "takes hold" of the hypostatic self, freeing it for the future by loosening its own grasp on itself and others. Levinas describes this "second" liberation as a kind of suffering for and at the hands of the other: the opening to the future is "that whereby the subject finds itself in relationship with the event that it does not assume, which is absolutely other, and in regard to which it is a pure passivity and no longer able to be able."[74] In other words, only that which dispossesses the subject can save it. Taken from itself, the self is restored to itself as a reference to otherness—a *sign*.

Yet the question remains: if Levinas is going to locate the possibility of ethics in the rupture of this intentional subject—in passivity, powerlessness, cognitive failure, etc.—why would he first reconstitute the subject over against the *il y a*, which already performs such a rupture? Why does he hinge the opening of the ethical future upon the presentist frame of a hypostatic monadology? Why must an *other* other interrupt the ego's mastery; why could this mastery not be unsettled through the *primordial*, presubjective indeterminacy of the *il y a* that interrupts it at the outset?

During the first half of an essay on aesthetics published in 1948, Levinas seems to suggest that it could. Again in declared opposition to Heidegger, Levinas argues in "Reality and Its Shadow" that the work of art neither unconceals the clearing of being nor "worlds" the world, but rather "darkens" being and *empties out* the world.[75] Just as the hypostatic subject of *Existence and Existents* comprises two elements—the materiality of existence and the masterful existent that drags it around—a being for Levinas is both itself and its image. Like the matter that haunts the sovereign subject, the material qualities of an object (its color, texture, weight, etc.) lag behind it, keeping it riveted to itself as a being in the world and giving it a particular place and shape. In the work of art, Levinas argues, the image is divorced from the object and the ghosts of materiality are set loose to *unworld* the world. Art thus reduces objects to their primal "thickness, coarseness, massiveness, wretchedness," the unchained image converting the object "into a non-object," ultimately effecting a complete "disincarnation of reality."[76] Art, one might say, reveals the il y a as "reality's" uncanny doppelganger: its shadow.

Plunged into the shadow box that art makes of the world, the self loses all self-position and possession. Because it cannot recognize the image as an object—that is, as something it can own, master, or know—the self cannot get a hold of itself as owner, master, or knower and becomes "a fundamental passivity." Art thus carries the self beyond itself, performing a dreamlike "reversal of power into participation."[77] One scholar, looking to connect this early essay with Levinas's later work, has noted that "art turns the sovereign ego out of its house in a deposition that anticipates the trauma or obsession of the ethical relation."[78] And indeed, recalling that the idea of infinity dispossesses the thinking self it establishes, we might expect Levinas to conclude that art effects the opening (or at least *an* opening) onto infinite responsibility; that the "dream" into which poetry or music throws us might open as the traum-a of alterity that renders the self unable to gather itself together.

Expectations, however, seem destined to fail when thinking concerns itself with indeterminacy and its various attunements. Levinas, perhaps already intuiting a troubling resemblance between the *il y a* that art uncovers and the *Ille* that will occupy him from *Totality and Infinity* onward, ends the essay by constructing various roadblocks between art and alterity. First, he argues that art (unlike the other as sketched in his lectures) cannot open the future or even the present, presenting us with nothing but petrified instants and immobilized shadows of things. Even the "temporal" arts remain static and lifeless, condemning their characters to "infinite repetitions of the same acts and the same thoughts."[79] As far as Levinas is concerned, then, literature and film as much as the plastic arts are forever "immobilized . . . never finished, still enduring—something inhuman and monstrous."[80] And, lest we be tempted to connect this particular monstrosity with, say, the "monstrous" idea-of-the-infinite-in-me, Levinas ends the essay by condemning art as refractory to all ethics, religion, philosophy, politics, and science. "There is something wicked and egoist and cowardly in artistic enjoyment," he cautions, "there are times when one can be ashamed of it, as of feasting during a plague."[81] Somehow forgetting the *horreur* induced by the exposure of/to the *il y a*, Levinas argues that art "charms as lightness and grace," lulling its creators as well as its participants into thoughtlessness, complacency, and a kind of bourgeois *jouissance*. To dwell in the *il y a* that art reveals is not to open oneself to and as responsibility, but rather to *evade* it: "To make or appreciate a novel and a picture is to no longer have to conceive, is to renounce the effort of science, philosophy, and action. Do not speak, do not reflect, admire in silence and in peace—such are the counsels of wisdom satisfied before the beautiful."[82] Becoming responsible, Levinas advises his readers, requires self-control, hypostasis, activity, "the refusal of art's bewitching rhythms"[83]; in other words, the refusal of the il y a.

## Locking Up: *Totality and Infinity*

Traveling through Levinas's early work, we have pieced together what seems to take shape as a mutual exclusivity between the two "astonishing" figures of the *il y a* and the Other: the opening of the latter is said to rely upon the closure of the former. Turning now to *Totality and Infinity: An Essay on Exteriority* (1961), we see this separation between "bad" indeterminacy and "good," or ethical, indeterminacy grow clearer and more aggressively patrolled. Yet, as one might anticipate, this safeguarding is so anxious that it signals the distinction's impending collapse. It is therefore upon this particular textual strain that we now focus.

Perhaps his best-known book, *Totality and Infinity* represents Levinas's own post-Hegelian effort to shatter all "comprehensive" systems by rehabilitating the inappropriable core of all philosophy, history, memory, and teleology. Levinas finds the totality-demolishing antistructure he seeks in the ethical, or "metaphysical" relation, by virtue of which the singular self escapes the slaughter bench of history and the other is neither anticipated nor understood, but rather preserved in discourse as the infinite. The unfamiliar thus troubles the heart of the familiar, turning the self inside out and holding it open as unconditional hospitality—as the "welcoming of the other by the same, of the Other by me."[84] By virtue of this radical welcome, Levinas seeks to provoke the disruption of all ontology and phenomenology by stirring up everything that eludes their assimilation of the other to the same, the unknown to the known, and the saying to the said. It is almost as if this work is set to the rhythms of Hamlet ("Oh day and night, but this is wondrous strange. / And therefore as a stranger give it welcome. / There are more things in / heaven and earth . . . "). Yet how many "more things" is Levinas willing to acknowledge in his philosophy? How hospitable is this unconditional hospitality? Are there limits to ethics' openness to the strangeness of infinity? Restrictions upon the kind of stranger it will welcome? And if infinity does suffer any sort of delimitation in this work, does it remain infinity?

As *Totality and Infinity* unfolds, it stages the perplexing emergence of what could perhaps be described as an ethical teleology—in a work committed to the ethical destruction of all teleologies. Levinas paves an existential path from what he calls the "elemental" through egoity to illeity, which is also characterized as a voyage from "primitive" "paganism" (or the "sacred") through robust atheism to ethical monotheism (or the "Holy"). This "path," explicitly avowed as such in an essay of the same period called "Signature,"[85] is certainly not inexorable, but is nonetheless *prescriptive* in its tracking of the journey of the properly ethical subject from a "wicked" indeterminacy through self-interested determinacy to the "Good" indeterminacy of the face-to-face relation. The analysis at hand will take the time to follow this particular yellow brick road, but in the service neither of an uncritical adoption nor a triumphalist rejection of it. Rather, this gradual reading seeks to trace *Totality's* contours in order to clarify the distinctions Levinas attempts to draw between these two bewitching figures of infinity. Perhaps more importantly, it will look to glimpse the fleeting conflations that motivate their frenzied separation and begin to envision an alternate route.

Levinas begins the ethical analytic of *Totality* not in the horror of the il y a, but rather in the sheltered, sensible enjoyment of what he calls "the elemental," which comprises all the generous and generative forces that create and sustain the cosmos. Phylogenically, Levinas calls this stage "pagan," since humanity-in-enjoyment attributes all it has, and all that stands in its way, to the gods of the wind, fire, earth, and sea. Ontogenically, "the elemental" recalls each person's infancy, in which the self is maintained as contented, unseparated, and immediately nourished. And so the feminine resonances of the initial stage multiply themselves. Similar to Freud's primary narcissism, this maternal, material, stage of the elemental is one in which "the simultaneity of hunger and food constitutes the paradisal initial condition of enjoyment."[86] In enjoyment, the proto-self's needs are all instantaneously met; it *desires nothing*. Levinas is careful, however, to distinguish this immediate, elemental existence from any sort of totality. Unlike a comprehensive system that would dissolve all particularity within it, primordial nourishment takes place within, and by virtue of, that which remains essentially untotalizable, "essentially non-possessable, 'nobody's': earth, sea, light, city. Every relation or possession is situated within the non-possessable which envelops or contains without being able to be contained or enveloped. We shall call it the elemental."[87] The womblike envelope of the elemental, then, cannot herself be contained, which is to say she is unpredictable; she can be neither controlled nor guaranteed. Much like the moment when the Freudian infant's mother does not come, Levinasian enjoyment is fatefully interrupted by the profound *uncertainty* that it will continue to be nourished by the unruly elemental. Thus Levinas's text begins to tremble, and one begins to hear the rumbling annunciation of something wicked in increasingly paradoxical utterances: the elemental *is* sensibility/the elemental *disturbs* sensibility; the element nourishes/the element "menaces"; the element constitutes me/the element "overflows" me; the element saves me from absorption into a totality/the element is a "wave that engulfs and submerges and drowns."[88]

Hidden within enjoyment, both as its condition and its impossibility, "lurks" what Levinas calls "the fathomless depth of the element . . . opaque density without origin, the bad infinite or the indefinite, the *a-peiron*."[89] Variously translated throughout the course of Greek-inflected philosophy as "indeterminate," "infinite," or "indefinite," *a-peiron* literally means "unbounded" or "without limit." Simplicius and Aristotle tell us it is Anaximander's term for the absolute origin, which, Anaximander insists contra Thales, is not water quite but rather an ur-elemental material, out of which all things arise (if Thales's contemplation of the watery indefinite led him to fall into a well, one would be hard-pressed to imagine a sufficiently primordial receptacle for Anaximander to tumble into).[90] For Levinas, the utterly form-less, proto-creative stuff of the *apeiron*, insofar as it remains refractory to all calculation and comprehension, "opens up an abyss within enjoyment," unsettling the self's blissful existence with an "unforeseeable future."[91] The more he endures this uncertainty, however, the more our unstable narcissist experiences the elemental not just as unreliable, or even threatening, but as *terrifying*—as "the anonymous *there is*, horror, trembling, and vertigo."[92] Suddenly uncertain of its future, the fragile ego encounters indeterminacy itself, to the point that "the absolute void, the 'nowhere' in which the element loses itself and from which it arises, on all sides beats against the islet of the I who lives interiorly."[93] Two options present themselves here. The first, which Levinas condemns as mythology, unregenerate "paganism," irresponsibility, and wickedness, is that this "islet of the I" might undergo a complete unselfing at the hands of this sacred, wicked infinite. The second, which the rest of the book explores as the only properly *ethical* possibility, requires that the self gird up its proverbial loins and declare egoistic war against the *apeiron*, the primal giver that now threatens to destroy him.[94]

Faced with the faceless element that both generates and destroys, the proto-subject becomes a laborer, making himself a dwelling that is strong enough to withstand the elements. Rather than succumb passively to the *apeiretic* excess revealed in uncertainty, the good Levinasian self *acts* against the indeterminate with all his might to carve out an inviolable interiority—a "home" that will allow him not so much to escape the element as to possess and control it. Breaking the ground, erecting walls, installing occasional windows and doors, the laborer puts the element at his disposal—securing for himself all the air, water, fire, and earth he needs, when and as he needs (or wants) it.[95] The mastery of domestic interiority is so comprehensive, it seems, that the individual who toils against the elements is likely to forget that *there is* anything at all outside his carefully patrolled inside. Even Levinas capitulates to this forgetting, eventually reducing everything apart from the laboring self to insignificance: "The laborer will subjugate the fallacious resistance of *nameless* matter in the infinity of its *nothingness*. Thus in the last analysis labor cannot be called violence; it is applied to what is *faceless*, to the resistance of *nothing-ness*. . . . It attacks only the facelessness of the pagan gods whose *nothingness* is henceforth exposed."[96] By divesting the bad infinite, along with its "pagan gods," of all names—even names like *il y a*, *apeiron*, and *tehom*—Levinas effectively takes it out of existence, insisting (three times) it is "nothing." This is perhaps the most perplexing move Levinas has made so far, since the *il y a* has always named for Levinas the figure of "bare existence." Inasmuch as *Totality and Infinity* establishes the "there is" as the wind and earth and sea and fire that provide the matter for all that is, it would seem more appropriate to invoke it as "everythingness" than as "nothingness."

Most strikingly for the thinker of the *visage-à-visage*, Levinas declares the elemental to be "faceless" in order to exempt the ethical subject from any responsibility toward this bad infinite. He marks it, in other words, as undeniably distinct from the "good infinite" that calls through and as the face of the other. Earlier in this work, Levinas had not been quite this clear about the matter; in fact, the question of whether or not the apeiron has a face undergoes a number of significant mutations throughout *Totality and Infinity*. At first, Levinas distinguishes the two infinites by assigning a "side" (*face*) to the elemental and a "face" (*visage*) to the properly infinite, but this separation is tenuous at best, especially considering Levinas's occasional designation of the ethical relation as *le face-à-face* rather than *le visage-à-visage* (*Totalité et infini*, 39/68). He later abandons this attribution, suggesting that the elemental "only has one side [*côté*]: the surface of the sea and of the field, the edge of the wind"—but insisting that this side is not a *face*: "to tell the truth, the element has no face [*face*] at all" (*Totalité et infini*, 104/131; translation modified). In each case Levinas is concerned to establish that the ego-exceeding apeiron "does not have a face," in order to insist that it "be distinguished from the presence of the infinite in the finite" (*Totalité et infini*, 115/141). Again we see Levinas open and reopen the connection between the il y a and the Ille, only to shut it down each time.

Insofar as the element against which our recovering pagan fights has now been refigured as "nothingness," the war he wages against its nonface is "nonviolent." Moreover, since the elemental gods he kills never existed in the first place, the laborer becomes a full-blooded atheist: "One can call atheism this separation so complete that the separated being maintains itself in existence all by itself, without participating in the Being from which it has separated" (*Totalité et infini*, 29/58). With this characterization of atheism, we witness what is perhaps a *further* degradation of the il y a it annihilates: having already been demoted from sacred element to abject facelessness, the apeiron is now identified with Being and therefore saddled with all of Levinas's anti-ontological rage. The "separated being" effectively frees himself from Heidegger in freeing himself from the apeiron. But is it not the case that Levinas just said (three times) that the apeiron was "nothingness"? Furthermore, we will recall that, in *Existence and Existents*, the il y a was also characterized as "neither being nor nothingness," but rather the generator of the distinction between them.[97] This peculiar triad (the apeiron as being, as nothing, *and* as the origin of their differentiation) is perhaps less inscrutable than it seems if one considers Heidegger's insight that from the standpoint of metaphysics, which can only think in terms of beings as objects, "being itself" *is* the same thing as "nothing."[98] From the standpoint of Heidegger's "other" beginning, however, "being" designates the event of appropriation and disappropriation itself: the *es gibt*. In a manner of speaking, then, the il y a actually does find articulation in Levinas's work as everything, characterized variously as everything that is, everything that is not, and everything that gives rise to is-ness and not-ness. Setting himself against the il y a, then, the "atheist" unwittingly sets himself against the whole world—including all of its beings, gods, and creative/destructive forces.

It is remarkable that such an "individual"—perhaps we might call him a secondary narcissist, or an evolved narcissist—can even *survive* in his solipsism; Levinas himself remarks that "it is certainly a great glory for the creator to have set up a being capable of atheism" (*Totalité et infini*, 30/58). What is even more astonishing than this individual's bare survival, however, is his ethical commendation in *Totality and Infinity*. In the same way that otherness relies upon hypostasis in his early work, Levinas affirms that "the atheist separation is *required* by the idea of Infinity" (*Totalité et infini*, 31/60). Infinity cannot come on the scene until the master of the elements overcomes every exteriority and becomes Himself by himself. As we saw with the hypostatic subject, however, possessing the unpossessable is hard work. The atheist laborer's mastery is ultimately just a "suspension" of the "unforeseeable future of the element"—a "postponement" of the indeterminate (*Totalité et infini*, 132/159). Sooner or later, even the most stalwart of houses will be flooded, infested, or burned to the ground. Yet for Levinas, once the house is built, the indeterminacy that "breaks the ceiling of the totality" is never the wind and the rain, but rather "the relation with the Other" (*Totalité et infini*, 146/171).

When this other Other finally comes on the scene in *Totality and Infinity*, He bears a striking resemblance to the elemental "It" against which "I" have been maintaining my solipsistic closure all along. Just like the "coarse, massive, wretched" materiality uncovered in the work of art, the Ille appears on my doorstep as bare, poor, and miserable: "a nudity disengaged from every form" (*Totalité et infini*, 51/79). This formlessness effectively *disincarnates* the Other, rendering him fundamentally *strange*—unassimilable and as unpossessable as the sea. Exposed to this other, I am exposed to the incomprehensible itself. Faced with the face of the other, which divests me of all cognitive capacity to reduce the unknown to the known, I am unable to gather myself together: a stranger to myself. Again, what is curious about this event is that it is practically indistinguishable from my prior exposure to the indeterminacy of the apeiron. Just as the nocturnal revelation of the il y a divests the insomniac self of itself, the interruption of the Other bursts open the interiority I have so laboriously constituted. "The Stranger . . . disturbs the being at home with oneself" (*Totalité et infini*, 9/39),[99] uprooting the very home into which I welcome him and yet demanding my response, like a voice from the whirlwind.

Lest we get too carried away with such elemental resonances and, say, read the Other's illeity as some tidal recurrence of *il y a-ity*, however, Levinas interjects throughout *Totality and Infinity* to prohibit such readings—usually when they are most tempting. In addition to the facelessness and name-lessness addressed above, a dramatic example of these efforts comes at the end of the first section on "The Same and the Other," when Levinas tries to separate the disincarnating work of the elemental from the disincarnating function of the infinite:

> The element presents us as it were the reverse of reality . . . as though we were in the bowels of being. Hence we can say the element comes to us from nowhere; the side [la face] it presents does not determine an object, remains entirely anonymous. It is wind, earth, sea, sky, air. Indetermination here is not equivalent to the infinite surpassing limits; *it precedes the distinction between the finite and the infinite.* (*Totalité et infini,* 105/132; emphasis added)

So the element comes from nowhere, resists objectification, and has no name, but *not* because it is the same thing as the infinite. In fact, the element precedes the difference between finitude and infinity themselves. To be sure, this is a deeply problematic way to distinguish the elemental from the infinite, particularly if Levinas is looking to prioritize the relation to the infinite as "first philosophy." For Levinas, we remember, the difference between the finite and the infinite *is* the occurrence of the infinite. If a kind of elemental indetermination "precedes" this distinction, however, then the elemental either 1. precedes the infinite or 2. *is* the infinite.

Perhaps recognizing this difficulty, Levinas tries again, saying a moment later that the element does not so much precede, as it "lies *outside* the distinction between the finite and the infinite" (*Totalité et infini,* 105/132). This is not much of an improvement, insofar as "the distinction between the finite and the infinite," again the very occurrence of infinity, is *itself* supposed to be the figure of outsideness. To locate the elemental as outside what is already the outside would again be to exalt it above infinity and thus above everything within (and without) the universe of this *Essay on Exteriority.* So Levinas tries once more: "the element as it were *stops up* the infinite by relation to which it should have had to have been thought. . . . The element separates us from the infinite" (*Totalité et infini,* 105/132; emphasis added). So the relation upon which Levinas finally settles is an antirelation—neither one of priority nor exteriority but rather of *obstruction.* The element *blocks* our way to the infinite; moreover, it is the element that prevents us from thinking the element in relation to the infinite. A relation that, Levinas says, "should have had to have been thought." But by whom? And why the passive, modal pluperfect? Why and when and by what sort of thinking *should* this relation between the element and the infinite *have had to have been* thought?

To sum up an admittedly complicated line of argument, there are three primary presentational differences between the elemental and the infinite, all of which keep a reading of Levinas from thinking what it perhaps "should have had to have been" thinking. First, unlike the face of the Other, which is refractory to all form, the formless elemental, as we have seen, *has no face at all*. Because the elemental lacks a face, it remains anonymous and indistinct, calling for no response on my part. The one to whom I *must* respond is rather the Ille, whose face renders him personal, unique, and (unlike the nameless pagan gods) radically *unsubstitutable*. Substitution, which will ironically become the cornerstone of Levinas's late ethics, is dismissed in *Totality and Infinity* as unethical. Substitution is even called "the primal disrespect, [which] makes possible exploitation itself" (*Totalité et infini*, 274/298). As unsubstitutable, then, the other is afforded respect and response, while the interchangeable gods of the elements are not.

Second, Levinas denies all violence in relation to the infinite. Not only does my war against the faceless element not count as violence, but when infinity finally does come, it comes in a gentlemanly fashion. Unlike the raging elements that shock the fragile ego-system, "the other precisely *reveals* himself in his alterity not in a shock negating the I, but as the primordial phenomenon of gentleness" (*Totalité et infini*, 124/150). While I would not know how to go about judging whether or not this "primordial" phenomenon is gentle or not, it nevertheless seems clear that not *everything* can be primordial. Either, as Levinas maintains throughout his ethical analytic, the Other makes his entrance once the self has already separated itself from the elemental, in which case the *elemental* is primordial; or the Other's alleged gentleness really is primordial, in which case He would become indistinguishable from the manifold "primitive," faceless, nurturing/devastating elements that precede the formation of the Levinasian ego. The distinction Levinas tries to maintain between the shocking element and the Gentle Other becomes even more problematic when he argues that the suffering Other eventually *masters* the self it interrupts. The Other, Levinas explains, becomes my *maître*, a master/teacher who breaks my interiority not by drawing otherness Socratically out of me, but rather by *placing* otherness inside me, planting "into me what was not in me" and shattering my finitude by "placing in me . . . the idea of infinity" (*Totalité et infini*, 178/203, 155/180).[100] This teaching method might strike one as forceful; even reminiscent of Heidegger's Liberator of 1931. Yet Levinas insists throughout *Totalitiy* that the entrance of the infinite is always nonviolent, because regardless of what it forcefully gives to or takes from the subject, it does not rob him of his "own" existence.

This leads us to the third and last distinction that Levinas tries to draw between the elemental and the infinite, which is that whereas the former prevents all interiority, the latter *relies upon* and even, in a sense, preserves it: "the whole dimension of interiority—the articulations of separation—are necessary for the idea of Infinity, the relation with the Other which opens forth from the separated and finite being" (*Totalité et infini*, 122/148). Or: "truth presupposes a being autonomous in separation" (*Totalité et infini*, 32/61). Or again: "*The individual and the personal are necessary for Infinity to be able to be produced as infinite*" (*Totalité et infini*, 193/218). Thanks to this dependency, the Infinite as Good Other does not *ultimately* threaten this autonomous being, but rather reconfirms its integrity after shaking it up a bit: "the other absolutely other—the Other—does not limit the freedom of the same; calling it to responsibility, it founds and justifies it" (*Totalité et infini*, 171/197). Freedom for Levinas "denotes the mode of remaining the same in the midst of the other" (*Totalité et infini*, 15/45). To say, then, that the other maintains me in my freedom is to say that while I may be interrupted by the other, I eventually *return* from the ethical encounter to myself as myself. Approaching, interrupting, and reconfirming the same in the full force of its self-enclosed sameness, the Other in *Totality and Infinity* maintains Himself and myself as two existentially distinct terms, so that even the violence that he might inflict upon me "maintains" me in my "subjectivity" (and consequently, is said always to be a "gentle" violence). The ethical relation with the master thus performs the dialectical reversal we have been anticipating, for I-as-slave am reconfirmed as *me-and-me-alone* through that which I undergo at the hands of the other: as Levinas himself writes at one point, "extreme passivity becomes extreme mastery" (*Totalité et infini*, 216/239).

Just as the hypostatic self of *Existence and Existents* remains encumbered with its own materiality until another human being comes along and opens its future, the domestic self of *Totality* remains at war with the elements until his roof is knocked in by *Illeity*. If only I let infinity break and rebuild it, my little mortal house will "fear no more the heat o' the sun / nor the furious winter's rages."[101] For once the Other breaks in, the elements are not just suspended, but silenced: "Society with the Other . . . marks the end of the absurd rumbling of the *there is*" (*Totalité et infini*, 239/261). Yet one begins to wonder just what sort of existence, ethical or otherwise, would persist by virtue of a complete annihilation of the elemental, of "existence itself." In response to the arrival of the "wondrous strange" vision of his father's ghost, a haunted Hamlet tells Horatio, "therefore as a stranger give it welcome." In *Totality and Infinity* we find the welcome qualified, learning that there are some strangers to whom I must offer hospitality and other strangers that this hospitality literally excludes—whose "end" my welcome actually brings about. Levinas tells us, "I welcome the Other who presents himself in my home by opening my home to him" (*Totalité et infini*, 146/171). That is to say, "I" welcome the Other as long as he *presents* himself, as long as he is *presentable*— in a Levinasian register, as long as he has a "face," as long as he does not take me by surprise, and as long as he is not *so* other that he threatens my hard-earned same-ness. And, in extending this particular welcome to the more presentable of the two infinities (the Ille rather than the il/elle y a), I terminate the inchoate murmur of the un(re)presentable itself. But what exactly does the infinite annihilate when it silences the voice of the element? Differently put, *can* the element be silenced? Or does this exclusion amount to yet another deferral of her inevitable return?

### The Phantom of the *Autrement*

In the major works investigated so far, we have traced the uneasy relationship between the twin indeterminacies of the il y a/apeiron/elemental/bad infinite, and the Other/Ille/ethical/good infinite. We have explored Levinas's various attempts to purify the latter of its primordial counterpart—attempts that, in one way or another, end up erecting or resurrecting the monadic self between the shock of the il y a and the marvel of the Infinite. Yet it is still not clear that a closure of the primordial-soupy bad infinite is desirable, or even possible, and one might suspect it will return like any good ghost to disturb any structure that excludes it. We thus turn to Levinas's last monograph, *Otherwise Than Being: Or Beyond Essence* (1974), which complicates this astonishing terrain even further by abandoning—or attempting to abandon—the very structures Levinas developed in his previous work in order to protect the ethical against the chaotic flux of existence.

In the previous section Levinas's primary defenses were grouped into three primary distinctions. Over against the anonymous, shocking, subject-obstructing It, which is often feminized, the Other is figured as a personal, unsubstitutable He who announces himself gently and relies upon the very monadic subject He interrupts and then reconfirms. Turning now to *Otherwise Than Being,* we find that each of these distinctions has collapsed during the turbulent years between 1961 and 1974. And as we track Levinas's final efforts to reign back in the raging il y a he has once again unleashed, we will begin to think genuine "openness" as that which neither closes the subject into itself nor closes off the apeiron, but rather that which opens the ethical *through* the primordial open of the il y a, turning and returning through the shocking to the marvelous, through the infinite to the material, through evil to responsibility, and through the bright exteriority of the open back into the worldly darkness of the cave.

Perhaps the most radical philo-ethical move that *Otherwise* makes is its interiorization of alterity. In Levinas's early, Buber- and Marcel-inflected work, the other opened the hypostatic subject through discourse. In *Totality and Infinity* otherness came from outside to shatter the self's laboriously constituted interiority. In *Otherwise Than Being,* far from relying upon a previously consolidated subject into which it might make its entrance, the other prevents all such interiority from the very beginning: the other is *already within* the "subject" itself.[102] Looking to unseat its traditional philosophical position as substance, Levinas emphasizes that the subject only is as *subjected*— as thrown under a will and command that are not his own. Because it is radically heteronomous, the subject is in a sense the one who can never be a subject, a paradox Levinas marks in his case-bending use of the word *moi*. The subject as subjected is never an "I," but always and only a "me," a "subject" ungrammatically relegated to the accusative. As that which accuses me, this "alterity in identity"[103] aboriginally thwarts the formation of any stable identity on my part, prevents all being-at-home, and renders me a perpetual departure from myself. In fact, alterity's original interiority issues in a complete transvaluation of the solitary subject. Whereas the self-made self had been the condition of responsibility for action in the world, the same hypostatic master is now figured as the very paradigm of irresponsibility. Thus in an essay published in 1968 called "Humanism and An-archy," Levinas writes that the denucleation of the ethical self is difficult to maintain, and that "there is, in the midst of the submission to the Good, the seduction of irresponsibility, the probability of egoism in the subject responsible for his responsibility, that is, the very birth of the ego in the obeying will."[104] This "birth of the ego," once the condition sine qua non for Levinasian ethics, now signals "the refusal of responsibilities," since the subject-as-substance only responds to the other after he has gathered himself together. Such insularity, in fact, becomes the figure of evil itself, the self's self-position, "the very egoism of the ego that posits itself as its own origin, an uncreated, sovereign principle, a prince."[105] Preceding and forbidding the subject's emergence as consciousness, cogito, sovereign, hypostasis, monad, etc., this other-in-me is very strange indeed and actually bears a closer resemblance to the mater(n)(i)al il y a than to the spiritual He-Other of *Totality and Infinity* who approaches and then maintains me in my so-called freedom.

The anteriority of exteriority's interiority thus leads Levinas to rethink "sensibility" as his starting point. In *Otherwise Than Being* we find no edenic simultaneity of need and fulfillment, no carefree enjoyment that one day gives onto uncertainty. From the outset in this work, the self is "sensible," but sensible here means sensitive, vulnerable, susceptible, *exposed*. The subject's sensibility is its "subjection to everything"[106]—to the pain of others, to the violence of others, to every force that assaults the inside-out subject as selfless, as persistently inessential and sensible, as "having-the-other-in-one's-skin."[107] The other, then, does not appear as some mild-mannered stranger at my threshold. Always already inside my house, emptying it of everything I might purport to own, unhinging all the windows and doors to expose me to the outside, this other behaves in just as violently and elemental a fashion as the rumbling apeiron. We will recall that, although the Other of *Totality* certainly opened the self to suffering, Levinas maintained that this violence was in fact "nonviolent" because the terms *self* and *other* always remained essentially separated. The "other" always allowed "me" to have the most *essential* bit of myself left over, for in the ethical relationship, "each contributes everything, except the private fact of one's existence."[108] Because the ego remains the same, or "free," in the midst of the other, its diremption is only temporary; moreover, its "extreme passivity" eventually becomes "extreme mastery." To the contrary, in *Otherwise Than Being* there is no such "gentle" redemption. Insofar as I am always already exposed to the other, my passivity only deepens into "passivity beyond passivity," making me nothing but an erosion, a wearing away, an open wound. The stranger, always already inside the self, dispossesses the self itself. The most familiar of all, I become a stranger to myself.

To be sure, there is a certain singularization that takes place even through this subjection; as was mentioned at the beginning of this journey with Levinas, the subject's infinite responsibility requires that no one else take her place. She is irreplaceable, however, only insofar as she dis-places herself; in other words, singularity for Levinas only functions through its unreleasable tension with substitution. We are thus led to consider what was designated earlier as the first mark of the infinite as distinct from the elemental, which is that it is *not anonymous*: that in establishing the self and the other as primarily individual and only secondarily relational, infinity preserves them as fundamentally unique and unsubstitutable. Once *Otherwise* posits an interior alterity that obstructs all identity-formation, however, the other to whom I respond is *not* actually unique. This is because, as continual dis-placement, *I* can and must take his place: "subjectivity undoes/defeats *essence* by substituting itself for another."[109]

We have thus witnessed the breach of the three conceptual levees that dammed the il y a to keep infinity high and dry; for responsibility in *Otherwise*, much like the "bad infinite" of the earlier works, entails substitution, violent shock, and the disruption of all interiority. In addition to this, we find that the temporal "locus" of otherness in *Otherwise* has shifted onto the colloidal turf of the apeiron. Rather than opening the self-present ego to the unforeseeable future, the otherness of *Otherwise* installs itself in and as an "immemorial" *past*. As infinitely responsible, the *moi* is always subject to a command it has not freely adopted, burdened with transgressions it has not committed, hostage to a past that is not its own. As Levinas explains it, "In my responsibility for the other, the past of the other, which has never been my present, 'concerns me': it is not a re-presentation for me. The past of the other and, in a sense, the history of humanity in which I have never participated, in which I have never been present, is my past."[110] "My past" is recalcitrant to all recuperation, for all the healing workings of memory cannot close the aboriginal wound it installs in (and as) "me." In this never-present past, we thus hear the rattling chains of yet another apeiretic phantom. For, as Anaximander tells us, as Levinas's early work demonstrates, and as even the most advanced physics must admit, there is nothing more resistant to the synchronizing efforts of the understanding than the diachronous no-thing that stands under everything: the time "before" time, the primordial stuff productive of all matter and form, the horrifying sludge through and against which the world takes shape. Implicitly confirming this connection, Levinas begins as early as *Totality and Infinity* to compare Cratylus's river to the immemoriality of the Other, when, in his previous work, he had installed this water feature to highlight the impersonal, primordial flux of the il y a.[111]

This retemporalization of alterity finally provokes Levinas to admit outright in "God and Philosophy" (1975) what we saw him try to avoid in *Totality*. To claim the temporal anteriority of infinity/Otherness/God, he confesses, is to place it/Him dangerously close to the mythic realm of the il/elle y a: "God is not simply the 'first other,' or the 'other *par excellence*,' or the 'absolutely other,' but other than the other, other otherwise, and other with an alterity prior to the alterity of the other, prior to the ethical obligation to the other and different from every neighbor, transcendent to the point of absence, to the point of his possible confusion with the agitation of the *there is*."[112] How, then, is one to receive this admission? How is thinking to treat this "possible confusion," and does this amount to asking how such confusion "should have had to have been thought""—in some unrecuperable past? This exploration has already witnessed (and perhaps even assisted) the failure of every effort to separate God/ethics/other from element/existence/il y a, but does this consistent self-destruction necessarily mean that the two indeterminacies cannot be distinguished by any means whatsoever? If, in fact, they do prove inseparable and equiprimordial, does this mean they are identical, or might some other sort of relation bind them together? And how on earth is human, stubbornly determinate thinking to gain any ground at all in trying to discern the relationship of one indeterminacy to another?

In the introduction, we noted that Descartes characterizes wonder as the "first of the passions" because it strikes before all judgments of good and evil. Descartes' striking declaration that astonishment, as an "excess" of wonder, "can never be anything but bad" signals an anxiety over wonder's prenoetic, premoral functioning and leads him to suggest that the will should drag itself out of all wonder by gaining concrete knowledge of everything "wondrous."[113] When Levinas marks the Cartesian interruption of the infinite as "astonishing," he therefore displaces the infinite, despite his best intentions, to the immemorial no-place beyond good and evil. And once again, "good" infinity ends up in the middle of the desert of the il y a. It is no wonder that Levinas's numerous attempts to separate the Good from the bad infinite all self-destruct. Yet what is one to make of this astonishing indeterminacy between good and bad indeterminacy?

Responding not to Levinas in particular but to the general problem of wonder's openness, Jerome Miller argues that since wonder's exposure is existentially originary, it must be utterly indiscriminate: "all one can do is surrender to the throe of the unknown and to let it transport one wherever it will. . . . One takes the unknown so seriously that, instead of setting out to master it, one gives up all one thinks one knows and becomes its servant. . . . [One must be] open to it and even willing to be devastated by it."[114] As Levinas's own work demonstrates, however, absolute servitude displays a structural tendency to become precisely the absolute mastery it is trying to avoid. Moreover, even if wonder managed to "accomplish" such a state of unmitigated subservience, is this the most helpful expression of the openness of wonder as the beginning of thinking? If so, would it not become impossible to make any kind of distinction between wonder and ideological manipulation? Problematic as it is, however, this position is a helpful one to keep in play: according to Miller, diverse figures of the unknowable cannot and should not be distinguished by the wondering selves they open, master, and even devastate.

Over against this position, one might set a scholar like Adriaan Peperzak, who condemns such reveling in indeterminacy as "a product of unmoved and passionless thought." He insists that it is sheer laziness to collapse everything that seems to exceed conceptual thinking into an undifferentiated "undecidability." The proper path of all philosophical thought from the pre-Socratics onward, Peperzak argues, moves "from the initial indeterminacy through experience, phenomenology, and ontological determinations to the overdeterminacy of the One."[115] The only acceptable way to read Levinas, for Peperzak, is to follow his lead in the "Signature" essay and to separate the Levinasian universe into three linear, vertical stages. At the bottom is the material: the "unorderly, chaotic, 'elementary,' indeterminate, and ununderstandably dark non-being." In the center lies the "noetic realm," between matter and spirit. Finally, in a realm of light and form above the knowing self, hovers "the One that is 'beyond' the essence of determinable being."[116] Peperzak gives little more than a dismissive nod to a "possible confusion" between the infinity below and the infinity above, asking rhetorically, "But are we able to keep the beneath (the *hypo*) and the above (the *hyper*) apart? Is it thinkable that they coincide, thus producing a confusion of the 'highest' and the 'lowest'?" Peperzak's tautological answer is that, insofar as it is *desire* that propels the soul from the indeterminate material to the overdeterminate spiritual, a conflation of the two is "thinkable" only by a "thought without desire." Without providing any illustrations, Peperzak simply insists that properly desirous thought *will* be able to discern the "*infinity* that separates the *hyper* from the *hypo.*"[117] And yet the infinity Peperzak adds in between the hyper and the hypo only complicates matters for those of us uncertain types who, perhaps deficient in the ways of desire, cannot see a clear way to separate infinity from infinity—especially by means of infinity. And particularly when doing so seems to undermine the infinite by reinscribing a series of totalizing binaries: below/above, evil/good, dark/light, elle/il, chaos/order, etc.

If Miller asserts that discerning infinities is impossible and unnecessary, and if Peperzak maintains it is possible and necessary, a scholar like Richard Kearney can be invoked to counter that such work might well be impossible, but it is nevertheless necessary. Finding an ethical model in literary narrative, which speaks even and especially in the face of the unspeakable, Kearney recognizes the impossibility of telling good indeterminacies from bad ones, especially as seen through the work of Levinas and Derrida. That said, he accuses these two thinkers of a certain "romanticizing" of unassimilable otherness as such. Kearney acknowledges the ethical "indispensability" of radical openness, but also emphasizes the need for some sort of separation—however "provisional," "between different kinds of otherness."[118] Kearney's problem with the Levinasian ethic, particularly as filtered through Derrida, is that

> in such non-discriminate openness to alterity we find ourselves unable to differentiate between good and evil. A fine lesson in tolerance, to be sure, but not necessarily in moral judgement. If there is a difference between Jesus and Jim Jones, between Saint Francis and Stalin, between Melena and Mengele, between Siddharta and de Sade—and I think most of us would want to say there is—then some further philosophical reflections are needed to supplement the deconstructive scruple of absolute hospitality. . . . For if we need a logic of undecidability to keep us tolerant—preventing us from setting ourselves up as Chief High Executioners—we need an ethics of judgement to commit us, as much as possible, to right action.[119]

As we try to think the relation of two figures of indeterminacy in Emmanuel Levinas, the primary obstacle to adopting Kearney's position is that it would map the il y a and the Ille, both of which *precede* the distinction between good and evil, onto evil and good respectively. Reestablishing them from the beginning as binary opposites, this move would prevent a more complicated coimplication from rearing its monstrous head within this analysis. The most deleterious effect of such a stark separation would be its inability to think the shock of the il y a and the awe of the infinite as unfolding *through* one another. For, all Levinas's protestations to the contrary aside, one insight that has emerged repeatedly throughout the foregoing sections is this mutual unfolding: even when Levinas tries to prevent it, his own work continually reveals these horrifying-astonishing-revolting-compelling figures *in one another's wake*, as one another's shadows.

In conversation with all of these accounts, I therefore propose to explore the possibility that distinguishing between horizons of openness in this situation might most productively be read as possible but unnecessary. "Possible" because, as we have witnessed again and again, even the most radical openness tends toward limitation and exclusion, whether in the stubborn reconsolidation of the thinking subject, the possession of the unpossessable, the reinscription of ancient names for the unnameable, or the persistence of two-column schemes to separate good from evil. All these stabilizing moments remain, to be sure, "possible" for a thought that makes itself too dizzy with indeterminacy. Yet they are not *necessary*, and, in fact, their indefinite suspension in a kind of wondrous openness might deliver thinking *through* the possible, the subject, the good, and the evil to "reach a more open terrain."[120]

## Awakening

Looking now to think the horrifying il y a and the wondrous Ille as folded in on one another, it is helpful to consider a certain "shadow" of the text that most fervently separates them. Levinas's essays *On Maurice Blanchot* (1956) build on *and* depart from the aesthetic theory that "Reality and Its Shadow" had set forth a decade earlier. In *On Maurice Blanchot*, Levinas complicates somewhat the simple opposition he had drawn in "Reality" between illumination and darkening, calling art's disincarnating, decreating, and nonetheless disclosive function its "black light" and locating the paradigm of this paradox in Blanchot. "Art is light," Levinas affirms, "Light from on high in Heidegger, making the world, founding place. In Blanchot it is a black light, a night coming from below—a light that undoes the world, leading it back to its origin, to the over and over again, the murmur, ceaseless lapping of waves, a 'deep past, never long enough ago.'"[121] This dark, nocturnal, precreative, murmuring, watery immemorial onto which Blanchot's art opens for Levinas has hopefully by now become a familiar unfamiliarity; as in the earlier essay, art still uncovers the shadow of reality: the elemental materiality of the *there is*. In this later piece, we find the effects of art not so much altered as intensified: as art, Blanchot's writing exposes the horrifying materiality of things. Unmaking everything by which the "subject" might get its bearings, this writing dispossesses the writer/reader to such an extent that s/he becomes an "it," exiled into the impersonal desert of the shadow of the real. Under the spell of Blanchot's dark art, Levinas writes that, "as before death, the 'I,' mainstay of our powers, dissolves into an anonymous 'one' in a land of peregrination."[122]

In Blanchot, writing condemns the deposed subject to the endless vigilance or insomnia refractory to all consciousness, all hypostasis, all house building, mastery, activity. What is strange in the Blanchot essays, however, is that the endless insomnia writing provokes is not condemned as evil, wicked, or inimical to responsibility, as it was in "Reality." In fact, as he sets Blanchot's black light against Heidegger's purported whiteness, Levinas seems to be suggesting that the work of art that obscures might preserve the very possibility of the ethical that Heidegger forecloses by means of his presentist, immanentist, totalizing structures of being, truth, light, etc. Art's darkness, Levinas suggests, could allow the other to "appear" and remain utterly other. Again, it must be said that the distinction between Blanchot's darkening and Heidegger's unveiling, Blanchot's "uprooting" and Heidegger's self-possessed position, Blanchot's "non-truth" and Heidegger's truth is a feeble one at best, if only because Heidegger's thought attempts to dwell in the clearing before and between all these pairs. What remains significant, however, is that in pitting Blanchot against Heidegger, Levinas intimates that the nocturnal primordiality onto which Blanchot's work opens might lead philosophy somewhere other than the egotistical "priority of Being over beings" to which we have seen Heidegger capitulate in a number of crucial places in his authorship. Art's revelation of the il y a might, in other words, open onto something like the "opposite of the abandonment of beings" toward which Heidegger gestured without elaborating upon it. It might be that in art one can see the face of the Other, not in spite of, but precisely *in* the wretched materiality of the il y a. "In the accursed cities where dwelling is stripped of all its architectural wonders," Levinas writes—and here one might envision a split-screen between Levinas's depiction of Blanchot's disaster and St. Augustine's account of Sodom's transformation into a "wondrous, blackened horror"[123]—"not only are the gods absent, but the sky itself. But in monosyllabic hunger, in the wretched poverty in which houses and objects revert to their material function, and enjoyment is closed in on both sides, the face of the man shines forth."[124]

In this essay, then, there shines a glimmer of an "otherwise" to the vertical teleology that insists itself throughout Levinas's major works, and that an interlocutor like Peperzak solidifies, from the lower, material, cavely indeterminate, through the self-made-self, unchained but still not free, to the highest, disembodied, utopian inessentiality of the good infinite. Here it seems rather that the "highest" just might open in and through the lowest—that art, by illuminating/obscuring the primal (de-) constitution of things, might allow "me" finally to see, *without gathering myself up beforehand*, the "face of the man" who suffers. It should be noted that at the same time that he writes this meditation on Blanchot, Levinas is also writing *Totality and Infinity*, which will argue, in no uncertain terms, that the element dominated by Laboring Man is *faceless* and thus cannot suffer violence. Through Levinas's reconsideration of art, however, this certainty begins to tremble: "Violence is applied to the thing, it seizes and disposes of the thing. Things *give*, they do not offer a face. They are beings without a face. *Perhaps art seeks to give a face to things*, and in this its greatness and its deceit simultaneously reside."[125] Perhaps art seeks to give a face to things; perhaps through art the infinite might be unable to exert violence against the il y a and open in the face of it instead. Here we have finally stumbled upon a possibility that faces (transitively and intransitively) the monstrosity of the logic of the *Infini* that Levinas himself gives us to think: the possibility that the highest might be itself only insofar as it speaks through the lowest, that God might only be God as revealed in the gutteral plea of the most unpresentable, that the Good might only be *realized* as such through the terrifying face of evil.

Wherein lies the possibility of this possibility? It is the conviction of this study that thinking can only short-circuit the age-old, unidirectional passage from "bad indeterminacy" through determinacy to "good indeterminacy"—figured in the *Republic* as the movement from the cave to the fire to the light—by (once again) interrogating the integrity of the "subject" upon which such a teleology ultimately rests. For his part, Levinas from *Otherwise* onward tries to keep the conscious self divested of itself through the logic of substitution: the *moi* is continually prevented from establishing itself hypostatically because, as infinitely responsible, it takes the place of all the others without ever establishing its "own" place. Levinas is insistent, however, that this process be nonreciprocal: "I substitute myself for him, whereas no one can replace me."[126] This, for Levinas, is the "paradox" of substitution and singularity: "no one can take my place when I am the one responsible: I cannot shrink before the other man, I am *I* by way of that uniqueness, I am *I* as if I had been chosen."[127]

Here, however, arises another difficulty. In putting "myself" in the place of every other other, do I not destroy the uniqueness, the irreplaceability, the particularity, the *alterity* of these others? If each other is an other for whom I can and must stand in, then how can I still maintain the "exclusive alterity" and "exclusive singularity" of each of them?[128] How is the ceaseless place taking that constitutes my "inalienable identity"[129] any different from a reasserted assimilation of all the others to the inalienable identity of the same? How does it differ from the domineering stance of taking-another's-care-away, against which Heidegger warns in *Being and Time*?[130] Ultimately, I would submit that the "paradox" between substitution and singularity does not hold; it is not a paradox. I am not singularized through my *own* substitutability, for I am unsubstitutable. Rather, since the responsible "I" must put myself in everyone else's place, I am singularized through the infinite substitutability of all the others. I am singularized, in other words, *because "they" are de-singularized*, which is to say that I am singularized because I am Singular, and unique, and they are not.

Once again, despite Levinas's best intentions, the most extreme passivity inverts itself to become the most masterful mastery. Another illustration of this surprising reversal is can be found in Levinas's description of the responsible subject's abject heteronomy as *être-ordonné*: "the self is 'ordered,' and the word 'to order' is very good in French: when you become a priest, you are ordained, you take orders; but in reality, you receive powers. The word '*ordonné*' in French means both having received orders and having been consecrated."[131] This mastery-through-submission is even more disturbingly enacted in Levinas's explanation that "the commandment I receive must also be the commandment to command the one who commands me. It consists in commanding a being to command me."[132] It does not take a sophisticated theorist to discern the true commandant here; nonetheless, we could invite the scandal of calling upon Gilles Deleuze's study of Sacher-Masoch to support our sense that the one who commands the commander to command—*even if he himself suffers under the commandment he thus commands*—is the Master behind the "master" who masters him. Distinguishing between the sadist who controls his victim and the masochist who actually controls his torturer, Deleuze writes that

> the torturer of masochism cannot be sadistic precisely because she is *in the masochistic situation*, she is an integral part of it, a realization of the masochistic fantasy. . . . The masochist appears to be held by real chains, but in fact he is bound by his word alone. The masochistic contract implies not only the necessity of the victim's consent, but his ability to persuade, and his pedagogical and judicial efforts to *train his torturer*.[133]

"Receiving powers" by virtue of his "ordination," the only orders that the self-substituting self obeys are the ones he issues himself, for who else remains to order the one who takes everyone else's place?

Thus the extreme logic of Levinas's displacement is an omniplacement: at the very moment one expects to witness the utter diremption of the cogito, one witnesses instead its awesome resurrection as the very "God" who provoked the diremption in the first place. This upside-down deification (at my most passive, I become master of all) can also be detected, for example, in Levinas's comparison of the vulnerable, responsible self to the One of Plato's *Parmenides*,[134] or to the One in Plotinus,[135] or, indeed, to Atlas: "The self is a *sub-jectum*; it is under the weight of the universe, responsible for everything."[136] The theotic workings of substitution are perhaps most shockingly elaborated, however, in Levinas's shift of responsibility's watch cry. With the notion that the self is always already subject to a command it does not understand, Levinas replaces the "here I am" he had commended earlier in *Otherwise* with Isaiah 65:25: "Before they will call, I will answer."[137] While this may at first seem a fair replacement for the Abrahamic "here I am," there are two significant differences. First, while Abraham responds before he knows what he is going to be asked to do, he does not respond *before he is called*. His response precedes understanding, but it remains (unless of course he misheard) a *response*.[138] Second and relatedly, the "I" of the "here I am"—whether it be Abraham, Samuel, or Ezekiel—is a *human* I. The "I" of the passage in Isaiah, on the other hand, is *God*, who proclaims, according to the JPS translation, "Before they *pray*, I will answer / While they are still speaking, I will respond."[139] Who, then, *is* this ostensibly "displaced" Levinasian self, that he proclaims himself the one to whom our needs are known before we ask?

Despite Levinas's repeated assertions that the human other is neither God nor an avatar of God nor even a mediator of God, interlocutors such as Jacques Derrida and Edith Wyschogrod have famously argued that the distinction between other and Other does not hold up in Levinas's work—that there is ultimately no way to tell the face of the widowed and orphaned from the face of God.[140] This may in fact be the case, and it presents its own set of problems and possibilities, some of which I will address in chapter 4. What concerns me here, however, is the strangely neglected conflation in Levinas's work, not of the other and God, but of the *self* and God. Responsible for the cosmos itself, this He who's got the whole world in his hands signals that, once again, Levinasian openness has been closed down by means of a sovereign subject—in this case, a *very* sovereign subject, but nonetheless the princely inheritor of the crown that in the course of his work has passed, across swampy terrain and through back doors and windows, from the hypostatic subject, to the self-made homeowner, to the One Who Out-Passive-fies the Rest. Each of these characters, including a certain kind of "God," represents the reinstallation of the "pure and impassive identity of the transcendental ego" in the face of an increasingly threatening il y a.[141] Levinas cannot keep the subject out of the way long enough to allow thinking to pass from the horrifying opening of the elemental to the astonishing openness of ethics as responsibility—much less to permit the unfolding of these indeterminacies in and through one another—*even though it is his thought* that suggests such openings "should have had to have been thought."

The result of this repeated leveling down into sovereign subjectivity is not only that the apeiron is once again relegated to the "bowels of being," but that the "ethical relation" itself—which Levinas continually sought to establish as more fundamental than the fundament—is not only displaced, but precluded. Perhaps because it takes everybody's place and answers without listening, the "infinitely vulnerable" self does not admit of anything like genuine responsibility, for "through substitution for others, the Self-itself escapes *relation*" and is left in the most egoistic solitude.[142] It is thus possible to ask:

is there a relation that resists the hyperresponsible eclipse of relation *and* the solipsistic closure to the il y a? If there were a way truly to maintain the absolute originality of relation—that is, the impossibility of any form of "inalienable identity"—would it perhaps open a "face" upon the protoplasmic stuff that the subject-as-substance can only see as "faceless"? Is it possible that openness as *relation*, and not just as self-immolation, might open the existent as "an incessant awakening"? And might something like a relational insomnia set thinking on its way to a ceaseless awakening, prevented at all turns from reconsolidating the transcendental subject in the face of the horrifying? Looking now to Jean-Luc Nancy to sharpen this progressive sketch of wonder's double movement, my working hypothesis is that, by remaining between suffering and responsibility, existents and existence, the holy and the sacred, destruction and creation, relation might sustain the openness that subjectivity always shuts.

Each one is one. There are many of them. Each one is one. Each one is any one, any one is each one. Each one is one. Each one is one and each one is the one each one is being in being that one. Each one in being one is one being that one, is one being one especially being that one. Each one is one. There are many of them.

—Gertrude Stein, "Galleries Lafayettes"

It would be wondrous—that aporetic principle that declares, "the one is many and indefinite; the multiple, the indefinite: one."

—Sarah Kofman, *Comment s'en sortir?*


## 3. RELATION: Jean-Luc Nancy


### The Problem of *Mitsein*

During the course of our journey with Levinas, we saw a steady correspondence between the closure of indeterminacy and the erection of a self-determined subject. Remaining with indeterminacy, then, will be a matter of preventing this solidification at all turns. We return, therefore, to the Heideggerian insight the early Levinas charged with "banality": that, from the outset, Dasein is *Mit-sein*. Insofar as being [*sein*] *is*, being is *there*, insofar as it is there, it is in a *world*, and insofar as it is in-the-world, being there is always already engaged in various relations of concern with other innerworldly beings.[1] At this point two readings emerge. There is, on the one hand, the still dominant interpretation of Heidegger's early work. If one were to summarize eighty years of such reactions to and against *Being and Time*, such an interpretation would sound something like the following:

Initially and for the most part, Dasein exists in the midst of things and people from which it does not distinguish itself. Lost in or entangled with "everyday" concerns, Dasein initially and for the most part remains in a state of "inauthenticity," living out cultural norms without any critical reflection, comporting itself according to the mediocre standards of "what 'they' say."[2] Thus assimilated under the "dictatorship of the they," Dasein's only hope is to hear and follow its innermost conscience, whose call summons Dasein out of its absorption in the they-self by means of a dose of anxiety so strong it makes the whole world strange. At this point, Dasein can either flee this sudden unhomeliness and level back down into worldly inauthenticity or maintain itself in relation to that which is revealed when the rest of the world drops away: death. Because no one can die in Dasein's place, Heidegger tells us, death "belongs" to Dasein alone; death is Dasein's "nonrelational ownmost possibility."[3] As being-toward-its-own-death, then, Dasein finally lives "authentically," resolutely tuned toward its "own" possibilities rather than blindly following the leveled-down pursuits of the masses. As "authentic," in other words, being-there is "an isolated I,"[4] for while Dasein is always *in* the world, it is no longer *of* it, remaining a "stranger" to the mindless chatter and average cares of the "they."[5] As authentic, *Dasein is itself*; that is, no longer *Mit-sein*.

This sort of reading, which invariably supports an elitist and escapist Dasein, reminiscent of one or the other of Heidegger's Platonic liberators, seems to undergird Levinas's rejection of *Mitsein* as "banal" at the beginning of his lectures at the Collège Philosophique. Linking Heidegger's ethicopolitical failure to his ontology, Levinas initially reverses what he reads as the Heideggerian progression from being-with to being-alone, tracing instead an ontological path from being-alone to being-with, that is, from an initial hypostatic unity out to ethical relation. Even in this early work, however, the "solitary existent" is not Levinas's real starting point, for, as we will recall, the individual subject only emerges by working to posit itself in one way or another *against* the elemental flux that both precedes and exceeds it. The proper Levinasian subject first becomes itself by hauling itself out of the primordial anonymity of the il y a. As is well known, Levinas abandons ontology in his later work, insisting upon the absolute anteriority of the asymmetrical ethical *relation*, but, as we saw repeatedly in the last chapter, the self-identical transcendental subject returns to disrupt even the most other-oriented Levinasian schematic, provoking him to declare that, at the height of self-abnegating responsibility, "through substitution for others, the oneself escapes relations."[6] Ontologies, it seems, die hard. One could, in fact, argue that every ethic operates according to an ontology, if because every mode of comportment toward the "world" or the "other" demands that I recognize the world and other as such and either account or fail to account for their relation to me.[7] In effect, Levinas's attempt to divorce ethics from ontology ends up inscribing a new, other-directed ethic on top of an old, monadic ontology. The latter, precisely as disavowed, cannot help but resurge at the limits of the former. And the limits of Levinas's radical vulnerability—the borders that ultimately close his ethical openness—give again and again onto the unfixable terrain of the il y a. There is, in other words, a kind of hydraulic in operation here: the closure of the subject demands and effects a closure of the elemental materiality of 'bare' is-ness, and vice versa. If, then, an irreducible relationality can prevent the "subject" from consolidating as such, it will offer no security against the il y a. Conversely, opening the inessentiality of existence will require a relational demolition of the subject. Either way, ethics can only be sustained as relational ontology, which can only take shape *through* the shape-shifting il y a.

A fruitful place to begin an exploration of such an (anti-)ontology might be a less standard interpretation of *Being and Time*: one that would track the persistence of Dasein as *Mitsein* throughout the existential analytic, rather than presuming its disappearance at the moment of Dasein's self-decision.[8] To be sure, the individualistic, otherworldly Dasein of the received reading can find ample textual support in *Being and Time*, and some of the classic prooftexts have been cited in the footnotes to my admittedly parodic gloss of this perspective. Yet something in Heidegger's thought continually unravels even the most snobbish and agoraphobic strands of his own thought, namely, his philosophically revolutionary conviction that the possibility of authenticity is opened *through*, rather than against, inauthenticity; that "*authentic* existence is nothing which hovers over entangled everydayness, but is existentially only a modified grasp of everydayness."[9] This notion finds repeated iteration throughout *Being and Time* and is deepened in many of the texts after the self-proclaimed turn [*Kehre*] in his thought.[10] Hence the frustration vented in chapter 1 concerning Heidegger's refusal or inability to read the "open" as an existentially modified grasp of the cave. Separating the (authentic) open and the (inauthentic) cave into "two abodes," Heidegger consigns Dasein to an agonistic and solitary unhomeliness: the liberator may have returned to the cave, but he *belongs* to the open and cannot even *communicate* with the cave folk, much less coexist with them in relations of care. Again, the figure of the Lone Liberator could easily be derived from any number of readings of Dasein's unregenerate selfishness, from Theodore Adorno's *Jargon of Authenticity* through Richard Farías's philo-historical "exposé" of Heidegger's Nazism as well as the anti-Heideggerian responses it has generated.[11] To rest too quickly with such an understanding of Dasein, however, would require focusing on the passages in which Heidegger announces the disappearance of "the world," "the others," and relations of care, without wrestling with the ones in which he announces their persistence—or, as the case may be, their return. Both these conflicting strands in Heidegger's thought can be found in mind-boggling succession in a single paragraph toward the end of the section on "being-toward-death," which I quote here in full:

> The ownmost possibility is *nonrelational*. Anticipation lets Dasein understand that it has to take over solely from itself the potentiality-of-being in which it is concerned absolutely about its ownmost being. Death does not just "belong" in an undifferentiated way to one's own Dasein, but it *lays claim* on it as something *individual*. The nonrelational character of death understood in anticipation individualizes Dasein down to itself. This individualizing is a way in which the "there" is disclosed for

existence. It reveals the fact that any being-together-with what is taken care of and any being-with the others fails when one's ownmost potentiality-of-being is at stake. Dasein can *authentically* be *itself* only when it makes that possible of its own accord. But if taking care of things and being concerned fail us, this does not, however, mean at all that these modes of Dasein have been cut off from its authentic being a self. As essential structures of the constitution of Dasein they also belong to the condition of the possibility of existence in general. Dasein is authentically itself only if it projects itself, *as* being-together with things taken care of and concernful being-with . . . primarily upon its ownmost potentiality-of-being, rather than upon the possibility of the they-self. Anticipation of its nonrelational possibility forces the being that anticipates into the possibility of taking over its ownmost being of its own accord.[12]

The first half of this passage announces what we readers of Heidegger think we already know: that, when it comes down to it, Dasein is all alone. Not only *does* Dasein neglect "the others," but it *must* neglect them simply in order to make itself itself. But the passage then goes on to say that the *failure* of all relations does not signal relation's extinction and, in fact, that Dasein can only relate to its nonrelational possibility as a relational being; that is, "as being-together with things taken care of and concernful being-with." In relation to death as nonrelationality, relation itself both fails and asserts itself. How is one to read this profound violation of the principle of noncontradiction?

If it is indeed the case that, as Giorgio Agamben puts it, "Dasein is co-originarily in truth and non-truth, in the proper and the improper," then authenticity can only be attained *through* inauthenticity: "In *Sein und Zeit*, every time it is a matter of seizing the experience of authenticity (thus for example in being-toward-one's-own-death), the way is always and only cleared by way of an analysis of inauthenticity (for example, being-toward-factical-death). The factical link between these two dimensions of *Dasein* is . . . intimate and original."[13] Is it possible that the "relation" that falls away in authenticity is not relation *tout court*, but rather a particular *kind* of relation? If so, then being-toward-death would not dissolve the world, the others, and relations of care, but would rather *transform* Dasein into a more authentic being-in-the-world-with-what-is-taken-care-of. Something along these lines could be at work in Heidegger's suggestion that, from Dasein's lostness in taking care of things,

> *authentic* disclosedness then modifies equiprimordially the discoveredness of "world" grounded in it and the disclosedness of being-with the others. The "world" at hand does not become different as far as "content," the circle of the others is not exchanged for a new one, and yet the being toward things at hand which understands and takes care of things, and the concerned being-with with the others is now defined in terms of their ownmost potentiality-of-being-a-self. As *authentic being a self*, resoluteness does not detach Dasein from its world, nor does it isolate it as a free floating ego.

How could it, if resoluteness as authentic disclosedness is, after all, nothing other than *authentically being-in-the-world*? Resoluteness brings the self right into its being together with things at hand, actually taking care of them, and pushes it toward concerned being-with with the others.[14]

The implication here is that relations of concern, far from dropping away in being-toward-death, are transformed through it into *genuine* relations of care. Not all relation, as it turns out, is good relation and not all care is helpful care. In fact, the relations of care for things and people in which Dasein-as-Mitsein is initially and for the most part engaged include "being-for, against-, and without-one-another, passing-one-another-by, not-mattering-to-one-another. . . . And precisely the last named modes of deficiency and indifference characterize the everyday and average being-with-one-another."[15] By comparison to the entangled, chattering, everyday Mitsein he so colorfully depicts, Heidegger seems reluctant to elucidate what "authentic" Mitsein might look like, especially in *Being and Time*. He does, however, hint at what will find further clarification (and sink into further obscurity) in his later work: that the authentic comportment toward the beings with which Dasein irreducibly *is* would be a matter of letting them be: "The resoluteness toward itself first brings Dasein to the possibility of letting the others who are with it 'be' in their ownmost potentiality-of-being. . . . It is from the authentic being a self of resoluteness that authentic being-with-one-another first arises, not from ambiguous and jealous stipulations and talkative fraternizing in the they and what they wants to undertake."[16] Once again, we see Heidegger sneak in what seems to be an ontological separation between the they and authenticity toward the end of this passage: authentic communication seems to depend upon the silencing of the commoners' confabulation. If, however, the possibility of authenticity is only opened in and through the everyday, then it could only be through the idle talk of "the they" that other possibilities of communication and concern could open. I will return to this problem, but Heidegger's reinscription of the pesky "two abodes" aside, it is important to note this early articulation of authentic relation as concernful being-with-others involves letting them be "in their ownmost potentiality of being."

This theme deepens throughout Heidegger's work as Entschlossenheit gives way to Gelassenheit and Gelassenheit morphs for a brief, unannounced period into Verhaltenheit. For Heidegger, "relating authentically" to inner-worldly beings and other people always has to do with "freeing" the other for his or her or its own care; that is, preserving the clearing in which mere objects might become beings and humans Dasein. Later in the Heideggerian corpus, Dasein will take on even more of a salvific role, becoming the clearing-concealment through which the era of "enframing" (*Ge-stell*) might open onto a new relation to being that Heidegger calls the "fourfold" (*Ge-viert*).

The *Geviert* would relate earth, sky, gods, and humans to one another in such a manner that thinking might leap into "another beginning" and the coming or staying-away of the gods might be decided—or at least prepared. Still, it is arguable that Heidegger never paints a detailed enough picture of Dasein's living into these roles; that is, of Dasein in its authentic mode of caring for others—especially not one that manages to resist portraying this caretaker as either a demigod or a storm trooper. As Jean-Luc Nancy phrases it, Mitsein "remains a moment, which is not returned to thematically, in a general analytic where Dasein appears initially and for the most part as in some way isolated, even though Heidegger himself emphasizes that there is solitude 'only *in* and *for* a being-with.'"[17] The problem, Nancy argues, is that "Dasein's 'being-toward-death' was never radically implicated in its being-with—in *Mitsein*— and . . . it is this implication that remains to be thought."[18] These two existentials (being-toward-death and being-with-the-others, which is always also being-in-the-world) eventually find stunning interarticulation through Nancy's onto-ethic of "being-toward-the-world," which will be elaborated shortly. Before turning to Nancy's (un)work, however, the question of relation in Heidegger will be examined from a perspective that Nancy (doubtless intentionally)[19] leaves unconsidered, but which arguably goes farther than any of Heidegger's other works toward sketching "authentic" relations of care: the (un)grounding-attunement of the "other beginning," or Verhaltenheit.

Immediately after introducing reservedness as a doubled and transvalued thaumazein, Heidegger writes:

> Reservedness, the tuning of the midpoint of *Erschrecken* and *Scheu*—and the basic *thrust* of the grounding-attunement—in this reservedness Dasein attunes itself to the *stillness* of the passing of the last god. Situated creatively in this grounding-attunement of Dasein, man becomes the *guardian and caretaker* of this stillness. . . . Seeker, preserver, guardian, and caretaker: this is what *care* means as the basic trait of Dasein.[20]

In the *Contributions to Philosophy*, then, Heidegger offers further clues as to what genuine care might entail, and it has everything to do with Dasein's maintaining itself at the midpoint between shock and awe. We will recall from chapter 1 that Verhaltenheit, or reservedness, faces the abandonment of being, with Erschrecken disclosing being's donation as a withdrawal and Scheu disclosing being's withdrawal as a donation. Put another way, Dasein-in-Verhaltenheit is shocked, stunned, terrified at "beyng's abandonment," and *simultaneously* awestruck "before the resonating enowning [*Ereignis*]."[21] Beings as we know them—and "we" ourselves—have been abandoned by being, and yet this abandonment constitutes all that is, precisely as deconstituted. Furthermore, it is by maintaining this twofold attunement, through which the unusual continually opens in and through the everyday, that Dasein might finally let beings be *as beings*, rather than as elements in the standing-reserve into which *Gestell* has transformed the world. To be sure, the existential analytic already laid most of the groundwork for this: anxiety is as a forerunner of sorts for Erschrecken, because in both experiences, the world and all innerworldly beings are revealed as utterly unfamiliar. Conversely, enduring the uncanniness that anxiety discloses, rather than fleeing it, presages the "renewed awe" proclaimed in the *Contributions* and the deleted passages from the *Basic Questions of Philosophy*. What has changed is that it has become much more difficult to read the Dasein of Heidegger's later period as other-worldly or escapist, for the ecstatic *Verhaltenheit* that lifts Dasein out of its ordinary relationships delivers it *at the same time* into a more profound *instasis*. In the introductory chapter, we saw Hannah Arendt argue that because *thaumazein* lifts the philosopher out of the world, it destroys the possibility of inter-human relationships.[22] By means of Heidegger's later work, however, it can be demonstrated that far from obliterating relationships, reservedness holds out the most promising possibility of *turning them around*, transforming and deepening the existential structure of *Mitsein* by lifting Dasein not out of the world, but back into it as ecstatic "inabiding" (*Inständigkeit*).

As early as the essay "On the Essence of Truth" (1930), Heidegger argued that "*as ek-sistent, Dasein is insistent*," and that this out-standing-inabiding is maintained by "the resolutely open bearing" that resists all conceptual closure in order to let beings be.[23] In his 1949 introduction to the fifth edition of *What Is Metaphysics?*, Heidegger explicitly links this *ek-stasis* to the structure of care by characterizing it as "the being of those beings who stand open for the openness of being in which they stand, by standing it. This 'standing it,' this enduring, is experienced under the name of 'care.' The ecstatic essence of being-there is approached by way of care, and conversely, care is experienced adequately only in its ecstatic essence."[24] What becomes clearer when one turns to the writings from the period of the *Contributions* (1936–38) is that through the traumatic double movement of Verhaltenheit, being-in (like being-with, being-there, and care) undergoes what might be called a repetition. "Dasein always already stands within the openness of being,"[25] Heidegger reaffirms, yet it is not until Dasein is attuned as reservedness that it can become the relation that truly cares for beings: "Reservedness of Dasein first of all grounds care as the inabiding that sustains the 't/here.'"[26] Because the standing-in into which Erschrecken and Scheu project Dasein *is* care, Heidegger thus speaks of awe as preparing and effecting a leap that leaps (contra Arendt) not beyond the world but rather deeper *into* it. Through this aweful leap, standing-in becomes inabiding, neglectful or manipulative "concern" becomes care, objects become beings, the "others" become *Mitdasein*, and the "world" becomes world. Most centrally for Heidegger, being becomes genuinely there—Dasein now stands as a kind of ontological airport for the departures and arrivals of beings, other Daseins, gods, and monsters. This, then, is the point at which Heidegger's "other beginning" opens onto a concrete ethic, especially insofar as ethos means "dwelling place."[27] In and through the movements of Erschrecken and Scheu, Dasein leaps into its inessential existence. Maintaining itself like Socrates in the vertiginous draft of being's withdrawal, it becomes the clearing in which beings come to be as such. Dasein as reservedness (Verhaltenheit) lets the world be world precisely by dwelling *in* it, that is, in relation (*Verhältnis*) with beings as beings. Ultimately, then, it can be said that wonder, doubled into Erschrecken and Scheu, conditions the possibility of withness, of relations of care.[28]

While such a reading finds ample support within the *Contributions*, however, there is still something unsettling about the Dasein that emerges in this text—a kind of heroic elitism that announces itself most vociferously in the section on "The Ones to Come." In this part of the sixfold fragmentary "fugue" composing the *Contributions*, the person who is able (that is, strong, single-minded, and "steadfast" enough) to become genuine Dasein is figured as the "seeker of beyng," "preserver of the truth of beyng," "guardian of the stillness of the passing of the last god," etc.[29] Echoing and rendering extreme the pastoral metaphor announced in a work like "The Letter on Humanism," where Heidegger calls "man" "the shepherd of being,"[30] Heidegger announces in the *Contributions* the autosacrifice of the Dasein-shepherds who undergo the ordeal of the furious storm of beyng: *"Our hour is the epoch of going-under. . . .* Those who *are going-under* in the essential sense are those who are suffused with what is coming (what is futural) and sacrifice themselves to it as its future invisible ground."[31] In other words, the many are able to *be* thanks to the self-abnegation of the few. The opening onto thinking's other beginning thus relies upon the immolation of those who are best at "withstanding the fury"[32]—those who, precisely through their self-denial, become lionized, deified, sacri-ficed. And, insofar as there is one or there are a few solitary, "futural" Daseins who will ground, shelter, and preserve the clearing in which beings can come to be, the condition of possibility of relations of care—however persistent or "authenticated" these relations may be—is still the existence of one, *individual* Dasein in relation to his ownmost nonrelational possibility.

The problem, it seems, which Nancy will affirm, is that even at Heidegger's most relational, Dasein remains self-identical in the midst of the ties it binds.[33] Like the troubling image of the airline passenger who secures her own oxygen mask before helping her child with his, Dasein secures its own lifeline to being (or rope ladder out of the cave) before sharing it with others, learning/becoming the "truth" in the unrelational "open" and then bringing it with/as him back to the others. Between unreflected and "authentic" relation, there is a complete rupture in which Dasein becomes itself all by itself. So while it might remain the case that authenticity does *not* dissolve relation, even that it *restores* it as such, Heidegger sustains the line set forth in a 1928 essay in which he writes that it is "insofar—and only insofar—as Dasein exists as a self [that] it can comport 'itself' *toward* beings, which prior to this must have been surpassed," and that "only because Dasein as such is determined by selfhood can an I-self comport itself toward a you-self."[34] This egoism haunts the *Contributions*, asserting itself so strongly as to unravel (once again) Heidegger's careful weaving of all otherworldliness through this-worldliness: "Beyng itself must set us out from beings and set us—who are *in the midst of* beings, and besieged by beings—free from this being besieged."[35] Yet to what "free" land could beyng possibly take us? Where could we be but "in the midst of beings"? In particular, how might existential relations of care become "authentic" except through relation to other beings?

I would argue that Dasein is held between twin temptations toward narcissistic closure within Heidegger's work. The first, which Heidegger thematizes in various ways, is Dasein's desire to secure itself against the "nothing" anxiety unveils, an ultimately violent self-defense strategy, later echoed in the will-toward-representation that rages as *Gestell* or the curious not-staying that cannot sustain the uncertainty of Erschrecken and Scheu. The other, which Heidegger inscribes in spite of himself, is Dasein's effort to "save" itself by lifting itself out of the they, inauthenticity, or its situatedness "in the midst of beings." As if the authenticating structures of anxiety, resoluteness, letting-be, and reservedness did not all function *through* these inauthentic antistructures in the first (and only) place. In effect, then, Dasein's everyday flight into some myth of self-constitution is structurally repeated in its flight from everydayness into some myth of self-sacrifice. Dasein flees both its dispersion in the anxiety or awe *and* its dispersion in the everyday in order to secure itself against the anonymous, ego-exploding forces that both bear an uncanny resemblance to the il y a. Jean-Luc Nancy's bold rethinking of Mitsein as "essential to the constitution of Dasein itself"[36] therefore threatens, and promises, to prevent this incessant return to solipsism, opening a kind of ethico-ontological Pandora's box from which the most unworldly and the most ordinary, the most charming and the most frightening, the most routine and the most transformative forces might be unleashed.

### *Mitsein* as Essential Inessentiality

In a book called *Being Singular Plural*, Jean-Luc Nancy sets forth, both with and against Heidegger, what he calls a "coexistential analytic."[37] This text offers a careful elaboration of the (anti-)ontology that runs through Nancy's corpus to date, beginning from the "originary coexistence" of existence itself.[38] Crucial to this project are numerous interarticulated themes that Heidegger introduces, but, for one reason or another, does not sustain, and that I will assemble for the sake of this brief exposition under three makeshift headings: 1. the *singular plurality* of existence, 2. the *inessentiality* of existence, and 3. the *finitude* of this singular plural inessentiality.

Short-circuiting classical ontology's thorniest problem, Nancy insists from the beginning that the One and the Many are absolutely equiprimordial. That which exists only exists insofar as it coexists; Dasein, one might say, is always already and always *always* Mitsein. This is not to say that the existent is in any way dissolved into some massive plurality; on the contrary, it is because beings coexist that they are singular. Conversely, it is because beings are singular that they are irreducibly *with* one another. Hence the title "Being Singular Plural": "Because none of these three terms precedes or grounds the other," Nancy explains, "each designates the coessence with the others."[39] Or, one might say, because none of these three terms grounds the other, each of them grounds—and precisely thereby *ungrounds*—the others as such. Being is only being insofar as it is singular, which is only singular insofar as it is plural, which is only plural insofar as it is singular, which is only singular insofar as it *is*. There is, in other words, no such thing as being-itself, singularity-itself, or even multiplicity-itself. They are all, as Nancy writes, "coessential." And that which is coessential is essentially *shared*, essentially shared out (*partagé*).[40]

Beings, then, do not simply appear indifferently next to one another as nodes in some anonymous methexis. Rather, they appear in and through one another by means of that which they have in common, that which they share: being "itself." *Esse* always only presents itself as *inter-esse*, blocking from the outset all dis-interest, all self-enclosed existence alongside, in spite of, or without "the others." Nancy articulates this irreducibly inter-ested singular plurality in *The Inoperative Community* as an onto-ethico-phenomenology of *comparution*, usually translated "compearance" to preserve the word's derivation as well as its strangeness. He explains: "Being *in* common means that singular beings are, present themselves, and appear only to the extent that they compear, to the extent that they are exposed, presented, or offered to one another. This compearance is not something added on to their being; rather being comes to be in it."[41] The sharing that originally constitutes beings as shared therefore sets them from the outset in concerned, inter-ested relation with one another. This withness thus constitutes the essence of existence itself: "existence is with: otherwise nothing exists."[42]

Yet what kind of essence is "with"? How is one to make any sort of substance out of a preposition? The second Nancean theme thus asserts itself as a countermelody to the first: insofar as existence is essentially shared, it is *essentially inessential.* These two themes echo the Madhyamika doctrines of *pratitya-samutpada* (dependent coarising) and *sunyata* (emptiness); insofar as all things arise in and through one another, the substance of any of them is insubstantial. Nagarjuna writes, "The real is suchness where there is an identification of emptiness and co-arising whereby empty non-being hollows out every trace of inner selfhood."[43] Similarly, in Nancy's terms, since existence is only ever singular plural, no thing can ever solidify into any individual or collective "essence." Essence, in other words, is nothing other than the inessentiality of existence. Although Heidegger was arguably the first modern Western philosopher to reunite the long-estranged essence and existence in this explicit a manner (at least without reserving their identity for the being of God),[44] Nancy and Philippe Lacoue-Labarthe mention in their *Literary Absolute* that it is Kant who first desubstantiates the existent by relating the "subject" *essentially* to its own representations and moral judgments. Although Kant does everything he can to avoid recognizing as much, the "subject" that emerges out of the three critiques is ultimately nothing more than a synthetic function"—*itself*, one might say, only as that which makes sense of *objects*. In this manner, there is in Kant, in spite of Kant, a "hiatus introduced at the heart of the subject," for "as a moral subject, in sum, the subject recovers none of its substance."[45] And, for Nancy, it is this space, irrecoverably hollowed out within the core of the "subject," that opens being as relation: "the 'with' at the heart of being."[46]

Insofar as being is, being is *with*, which means that the moment being comes on the scene it prevents all reifications of essence, identity, or substance. Nancy characterizes the ceaseless opening effected by and as existence with the verb *transir*, which marks the simultaneously transitive and intransitive function of being: being *transit*—that is to say, both is and is-es—the existent. Also, in ordinary usage, *transir* means to chill or be chilled, or to paralyze or be paralyzed, as in the phrase *ce vent me transit* ("this wind is going right through me"). *L'être transit l'essence,* therefore, means that being is essence, being constitutes essence, and being freezes the formation of essence at its core or *coeur*:

> Being . . . is transitively . . . the essence before the latter even has a chance to be or to constitute the essence it is. Being, therefore, does not deprive the essence of essence; essence simply does not take place. *Being entrances* [transit] *the essence. This is what we call* existing. . . . The singular as essence is the essence existed, eksisted, expelled from essence itself, disencysted of its essentiality, and this, once again, before the cyst has even formed.[47]

A radicalization of Levinas's denucleation, Nancean "entrancement" names the essential inessentiality of existence, by which existence is (in)essentially shared among existents. Each of Nancy's projects endeavors from different perspectives to expose this essential exposure, so that existence in Nancy is figured variously as singular plurality, being-in-common, compearance, inter-esse, sharing, being-with, being-toward, being-offered, "whatever," freedom, sense, community, exposure, touching, communication, and transcendence.[48] To say, then, that existence is inessential is *not* to say it is "nothing"; on the contrary, existence is that which "we" all share and that which shares us among one another. This inessentiality is, in fact, all there is.

There is, in other words, no reserve of is-ness—no infinite well of essence—independent of being's singular interarticulations. Simply put, being is *finite*. This is the third of the opened-and-closed insights that Nancy takes on from Heidegger,[49] and, strangely enough, finitude in Nancy looks more or less like infinity in Levinas. We will recall that Levinas names infinity as the opening of all egoistic closure and the transcendence of all immanence. Most importantly, infinity only *is* for Levinas insofar as it constitutes and exceeds the finite "mind" to which it "comes." This is perhaps Levinas's most lasting insight: that there *is* no "infinity" without "finitude," no Go(o)d except insofar as it calls from the face of "the other" and leads the self not out to "infinity" but inexorably back to concrete responsibility for its neighbor. Infinity, in this sense, is *finite*, and, for that reason, it calls people into ethical relation with one another. Like Heidegger, however, Levinas often forgets infinity's finitude, inscribing the ethical as some immaterial, extraworldly realm in which the subject is infinitely substantialized against all *there is* by putting itself in every place. If Nancy focuses on being's *finitude*, then, it is not in the service of a sheer, undifferentiated immanence[50] or of a renucleation of the essence that Levinasian "infinity" is meant to denucleate. To the contrary, being's finitude *is* precisely the inessentiality that neither Heidegger nor Levinas could ultimately sustain, that is to say, its *transcendence* of every essential reification. As finite, existence transcends because it always exceeds its own grasp, whereas the infinite subject of, say, speculative idealism, ultimately remains immanent by grasping itself infinitely. "We are *infinitely* finite," Nancy writes, "infinitely exposed to our own existence as a nonessence, infinitely exposed to the otherness of our own 'being.'"[51] If the infinitely infinite (Hegel), the finitely finite (Heidegger), and even the finitely infinite (Levinas) all ultimately congeal into self-identical essence, then what Nancy seems to suggest is that existence as inessential can only remain infinitely inessential as *infinitely finite*.

Again, because the three themes introduced here only become themselves in resonance with one another, one would have to read this infinite finitude not only as inessentiality but also as singular plurality. If being only *is* in finite instances of being, then existence-with must be radically singular: existence happens each time as "just once, this time."[52] Absolute singularity, occurring only by virtue of its equiprimordiality with multiplicity, can thus be seen as an interweaving of *Mitsein*, the "each-time-mineness" (*Jemeinigkeit*) of *Being and Time*, and Heidegger's later insight that all appropriation takes place as depropriation.[53] When being takes place as "just once, this time," it is both irreducibly "mine" and utterly inappropriable; its position *is* its disposition and dispossession by the sharing, freedom, towardness, etc., that delivers it over to itself, in excess of itself: "'Singularity' isn't simply understood as the singularity of an individual (not simply as Heidegger's 'in each case mine'), but as the singularity of punctuations, of encounters and events that are as much individual as they are preindividual or common, at every level of community."[54] Moreover, the differences between singularities take place *within* what ordinary parlance designates as the "individual" itself, for "It is never the case that I have met Pierre or Marie per se, but I have met him or her in such and such a 'form,' in such and such a 'state,' in such and such a 'mood,' and so on."[55] And so we are back to the equiprimordiality of the One and the Many: for Nancy, that which is "individual" *is* that which is "common": finitude, inessentiality, sharing: the incoherence of any self-identical essence, immanence, "individual," or "community."

## The Myth of Essentialism

Much like Socrates' vaporization of the pseudês doxa, however, this ontology of inessentiality opens onto a dilemma. Concepts such as essence, the individual, and the community inevitably reveal themselves to be windeggs when held up to Nancy's neomaieutic scrutiny, and yet, much like false opinions, essential identities are posited all the time. While it might certainly be the case that they cannot *be*-in-the-world, identities and essences certainly *work* in the world. In fact, every major source of politicosocioeconomic power—from the nation-state to the consumer to the majority to the minority to the corporation to the private sector to the Establishment to the Anti-Establishment to the "secular left" to the "religious right"—does the work it does by positing itself as a stable, nonrelational entity, however "impossible" such entities might, (anti-)ontologically speaking, *be*.[56] Figures such as substance, the subject, the individual, and the community thus assume for Nancy the structure of *myth*. Often revolving around a metonymic individual hero, myth grounds the identity of an individual race or nation. Insofar as myth is a myth, however, this grounding negates itself as soon as it affirms itself: "The phrase 'myth is a myth' means in effect that myth, as inauguration or foundation, is a myth, in other words, a fiction, a simple invention."[57]

To call "pure identity" a myth, a "simple invention," an "absurdity," or even an impossibility,[58] is therefore not to deny that it *functions* as if it were necessary, substantial, and complete. In fact, simple identities of all sorts *work* precisely by constituting themselves *as works*. Any thing that masquerades as absolute (that is, constituted in relation only to itself) is in a Nancean register a work: "Man," this race, that nation, this idea, that teleology—all these mythic substances effectively wage war against *existence itself* in order to posit themselves as infinitely self- (that is, un-) relational. Thus, as Nancy and Lacoue-Labarthe have also illustrated in their analysis of the neomythological constitution of German identity, the will-toward-essence becomes the source of all violence: in any movement that attempts to establish its own necessity, "essence is set to work . . . it becomes its own work. This is what we have called 'totalitarianism,' but it might be better named 'immanentism.'"[59] The evil of totalitarianism is in this manner transgressively linked to numerous configurations from which political philosophies and religious orthodoxies, to name a few, would doubtless want to keep it separated. Far from representing anomalous occurrences within the otherwise peaceful history of the West, regimes of "total terror" show themselves by virtue of Nancy's critique of immanentism to be grossly metastasized products of the everyday metaphysical will toward certainty, identity, and simple location.

In *The Experience of Freedom*, Nancy calls this mythic essentialism "wickedness" itself. If freedom is the "essence" of existence, Nancy ventures, then existence has no "essence"; if freedom is the ground of being, then being itself is groundless. The denial of this groundlessness is what Nancy calls evil, or wickedness [*la méchanceté*], insofar as denying groundlessness means denying existence itself. A reconfigured death drive, evil functions as a desire to pin down Being, the Origin, God, or the Other by projecting them into some sphere of necessity outside the world, where they turn into superessences that guarantee the integrity of the self, its community, its race, and its ideology. It is evil, then, that replaces the inessentiality of existence with the myth of essence, leveling singular plurality down into "this people," "that nation," or "this idea." Evil does everything it can to deny existence-as-relational-inessentiality, to the point of positing itself in a rage—or fury. It cannot *stand* being unable to stand on its own ground or being so thoroughly bound up with others; it "hates singularity as such and the singular relation of singularities"[60] because singularity and relation can only divest essence of its essentiality. So evil posits *itself* as its own origin, obliterating the inessentiality that makes relation possible. (Shockingly, then, the current president of the United States is right to say that evil "hates freedom." What is ironic, however, is his failure to attribute such evil and hatred to his own sacred duty to impose "freedom," as the Hero of This Nation, the unwavering supporter of That Idea, and the self-appointed avatar of This God.)[61]

As the denial of inessentiality, evil amounts to a renunciation of freedom. Since only freedom could renounce freedom, the possibility of evil is opened in the opening of freedom itself, as the possibility of its own foreclosure. Freedom, in a sense, *destroys itself* in the furious self-grounding of evil, which works as a sort of autoimmune pathology: asserting itself by consuming itself.[62] Freedom's anteriority to the determinations of good and evil is discomfiting, yet Nancy refuses to offer any sort of theodicy to account for the entrance of evil into existence. To the contrary, freedom's capacity to be freely refused resists all efforts to understand it: "In the final analysis nothing else is incomprehensible about freedom except the possibility of wickedness—and this to the extent that this 'possibility' is a reality effectively present in freedom's factuality."[63] Persistently incomprehensible, the self-positing of evil as the free obliteration of freedom remains at the absolute limits of thought. Yet it is at the limits of thought, Nancy tells us, that thought must dwell (Derrida says the same, as did Kierkegaard).[64] The unthinkable is the ethos of thinking.

If thinking is genuinely to open itself to the unthinkability of evil, however, it cannot take the triumphalist form of a philosophy of "the problem of evil." To assimilate evil under some "free will defense" or any other dialecticizing scheme would be to deny the unthinkability of wickedness as such. Here, the word *unthinkable* must be heard in both its logical and its ethical resonances: thinking evil as unthinkable means staying with its resistance to all conceptual or teleological frameworks *and* maintaining its utter unacceptability. That which is evil is neither philosophically nor ethically comprehensible; it is *indefensible*. Thinking must think evil without defending it; that is, without theodicy and without positing an ethereal realm in which justice will finally be done. Only in this way can thinking truly become an ethic:

> "Neither *dike* [destiny as justice] nor *dicy* [justificatory redemption]": this is a call neither for despair nor for hope, neither for a judgment of this world nor for a "just world"—but for justice *in* this world, for justice rendered *unto* the world: that is, for resistance, intervention, compassion, and struggle that would be tireless and oriented toward the incommensurability of the world, the incommensurability of the totality of the singular outline, without religious and tragic remuneration, without sublation, and thus without discourse. Without discourse: for discourse, all discourse, sublates everything.[65]

Thinking, then, is a matter of freeing thinking for that which precedes it and exceeds it—that which opens, and for that reason constantly slips away from, philosophical discourse itself. In *Being Singular Plural*, Nancy briefly refers to such an ur-condition—we will even dare to call it a mood—as "the most primitive layer of curiosity, the level on which we are primarily *interested* by what is interesting par excellence (the origin)."[66]

In contrast to the curiosity against which Heidegger rails in *Being and Time*,[67] what Nancy calls "primitive curiosity" is interested not in appropriating strange new things but rather in the inappropriable "origin" of things *tout court*. And of course, the origin in which a primitive curiosity would be interested would be inter-esse itself: the absolute originality of existence as inessential relationality; its thoroughly interdependent just-this-onceness. So Nancy tells us that thinking the freedom of existence—which would also mean thinking the monstrous possibility of the free renunciation of freedom— is not a matter of finding a proof, launching a defense, providing a calculation, or securing a determination, but rather of holding thinking within a certain original openness. The task of thinking is to dwell as openness within an ethos that is inter-ested in the relational constitution and deconstitution of singular plurality—and in the furiousness with which such groundlessness is denied.

To say that this "primitive curiosity" is interested in the origin of beings is not to say, along with Heidegger at one of his moments of escapist indulgence, that such ethical openness loses interest in beings themselves. For, when being is nothing but "just once, this time," each instance of existence is, in effect, "the origin." The origin does not stand as a *punctum aeternum* outside the world or outside time, rather, as the withness, interest, or singular multiplicity of beings themselves/being itself, "the origin of the world occurs at each moment of the world." If it is the case that "the world springs forth everywhere and in each instant, simultaneously,"[68] then the origin is what is most familiar, most ordinary, most *common* and in-common of all. Yet, precisely because it presences itself differently at each moment, this origin is unobjectifiable, unanticipatable, always coming as a complete surprise. For Nancy, as for Heidegger and Socrates, thinking the unthinkable is a matter of finding the strange in the familiar—in this case, the origin in everyday things:

> As English [and French] allows us to say, other beings are *curious* (or *bizarre*) to me because they give me access to the origin; they allow me to touch it; they leave me before it, leave me before its turning, which is concealed each time. Whether an other is another person, animal, plant, or star, it is above all the glaring presence of a place and moment of absolute origin, irrefutable, offered as such and vanishing in its passing. This occurs in the face of a newborn child, a face encountered by chance on the street, an insect, a shark, a pebble . . . but if one really wants to understand it, it is not a matter of making all these curious presences equal.[69]

As the previous chapters have shown, however, an attentiveness to the strange within the familiar leaves itself open to strangenesses both helpful and harmful. The "primitive curiosity" of thaumazein can become unthinking dogmatic assent merely by closing itself down. Similarly, for Nancy, freedom's potential opening onto wickedness remains of considerable concern: "If we do not have access to the other in the mode just described, but seek to appropriate the origin—which is something we always do—then this same curiosity transforms itself into appropriative, destructive rage."[70] Contrary to the more outlandish aspirations of some contemporary philosophical projects, then, thinking amounts to the humble effort not to appropriate. It is not an activity carried out by the best and bravest forces of good (the anti-essentialists, anticolonialists, antifoundationalists, antimisogynists, etc.) against the forces of evil (the corresponding contingents, minus the anti-). Thinking is, far more perilously, the continually renewed and, for the most part, continually failed attempt to expose itself to exposure itself, when exposure is only itself as relation. The task of thinking is therefore to undo the "work" it will always be tempted to do: the origin-fixing, sense-restricting, community-consolidating, identity-assigning, self-positing, other-demonizing, and Other-deifying that erect some edificial essence to guard against the vertiginous inessentiality, the ceaseless relationality, of existence itself. The work of thinking is, in other words, unworking.

### Unworking

Nancy treats this curious movement most thoroughly in *La communauté désoeuvrée*, which has been translated into English as *The Inoperative Community*, but literally says that community is as unworked.[71] Ultimately, this adjective functions both descriptively and prescriptively for Nancy: insofar as a work designates an essence, community is not a work, and furthermore, it must resist being made into one. Although these descriptive and prescriptive senses of *désoeuvrement* are inextricable, they will be treated in turn for the sake of clarity (and so, here, I am already failing to attend to the relational as such).

When Nancy says that community is *désoeuvrée*, he means it both historically and philosophically. Historically speaking, communities are unworked in the sense that they have at this point broken down along traditional fault lines of race, ideology, geography, ethnicity, and religion. If, in the nebulous temporality of the "old days,"[72] This or That Nation of This or That People was founded by a primal myth, a heroic sacrifice, and a nationalist god or gods, modernity has witnessed the dissolution of all these foundations: myth has revealed itself as *myth*, the value of sacrifice has been horrifyingly closed in the genocides of the last century (particularly, for Nancy, the Shoah),[73] and God's death has asserted itself with perverse and unparalleled fervor in the recent resurgence of religious fundamentalisms and proliferation of consumerist spiritualities across the globe. So there is no longer any *communion*,

which is Nancy's term for a mythic community bound by a solid racial, eth-
nic, or national identity. Nancy's marking of this historic disappearance opens,
furthermore, onto a broader, philosophical insight: there has never been any
properly substantial race, ethnicity, or nationality at all. As Nancy puts it, the
myth that grounds identity has always been a myth. And yet, in everyday parlance, politics, legislation, and cultural products, such identities continue to
rage in full force. One might think here of the tension within critical race
theory between the biological groundlessness of race, on the one hand, and its
embodied categorical insistence, on the other. Just because race turns out to
be scientifically and theoretically insubstantial, this does not mean it ceases
to function, and to function violently, in the world. If there is any way through
this double bind, Nancy locates it within community itself. Community as
Nancy understands it cannot possibly consolidate into a work, because it
takes place *in common*; like the singular plural *essence* of existence itself, community only *is* insofar as it is *shared*. Unlike a communion, then, *community*
always exceeds the frames that *working* attempts to place around it. Because
the withness of community undermines all essence and identity, "community
is, in a sense, resistance itself, namely, the resistance to immanence."[74]

Within the Nancean corpus, the inessentiality of community is an instance
of a broader, haunting theme: the sense in which, along with myth, sacrifice,
God, and communion, *sense itself* has abandoned "us." ("We" who have, for
some time now, been coming after the "modernists" and yet still have nothing
sensible to call ourselves.) This abandonment by sense, or meaning (*sens*),
is what Nancy understands by the closure of metaphysics, whose task has
always been to determine meaning by fixing essences. In response to sneers
on both sides of the analytic/continental divide at the purportedly baseless
abstraction of "the end of philosophy" (which also finds articulation as "the
death of God"), Nancy testifies continually to the relentless and concrete
*embodiment* of Nietzsche's and Heidegger's seemingly hyperbolic declarations of senselessness: "[the end of philosophy] is what we have at present,
very concretely, right before our eyes. Think a moment about the sense of
words like 'nation,' 'people,' 'sovereignty,' 'right,' 'beauty,' 'community,' 'humanity,' 'life,' 'death,' and so many others. It is not just a matter of the traditional
complexity and difficulty of notions such as these; rather, it is a question of
their exhaustion."[75] Turning again and again *toward* the senselessness of the
world, Nancy begins a number of his essays with one or another "litany that's
both unbearable and entirely necessary"[76] of names and places of absolute
unthinkability—from Vietnam to Kosovo to the Armenian genocide to the
"end" of apartheid to Hiroshima and Nagasaki. To this unbearable litany, any
reflection of the shock of being in *this* world would be remiss not to detail its
own terrifying mise-en-scène: at this moment, I would name Iraq, Afghanistan, Haiti, Sudan, Guantánamo Bay, East Timor, the Gaza Strip, the Patriot

Act, the slow erosion of academic freedom in the United States and the rapid erosion of beaches and glaciers across the globe, the so-called clash of civilizations, New Orleans, "family values," Abu Ghraib. To be sure,

> We'll not come to the end of the list of places and marks of uncertainty, of helplessness, of anguish. There is something like a general loss of sense. Sense, that's the word that matters to me today. A general flight of sense, whether it occurs in a political or esthetic or religious or whatever other form. Sense matters to me since, finally, "philosophy" deals with nothing else but sense. Absolutely nothing else. If sense is screwed to hell everywhere (forgive me for being vulgar, but it's deliberate, that's what's going on right now, and vulgarity is not necessarily what one thinks it is), this is obviously a philosophical concern, and also because philosophy is screwed to hell everywhere.[77]

The "end of philosophy" says nothing more, and nothing less, than the senselessness of existing with an exhausted set of concepts.

In the same way that existence's inessentiality does not signify "nothing," however, the abject failure of the old methods of making sense does not mean "there is no sense," especially inasmuch as such a declaration would only encourage ethical and philosophical complacency. Philosophy's being screwed to hell everywhere is no license to stop thinking; on the contrary, since the unthinkable is precisely what calls for thinking, the senselessness of "our" existence *is our sense.* "Today," Nancy writes, "all sense has been abandoned. This makes us feel a little faint, but still we sense (we have the *sense*) that it is precisely this exposition to the abandonment of sense that makes up our lives."[78] Lest Nancy be accused of an unreconstructed historical narcissism, it should be pointed out that he realizes ours is hardly the first age to be characterized by a "general loss of sense." The collapses of ancient Greece, classical Greece, the Roman Empire, and the Christian Empire were cataclysms no less complete than the collapse of the modern world. In a sense, then, this senselessness is nothing new: "The twenty-eight or so centuries of the Occident seem punctuated by the periodic repetition of crises during which a configuration of sense comes undone, a philosophical, political, or spiritual order decays, and, in the general vacillation of certainties and reference points, one is alarmed at the lost sense—one seeks to retrieve it, or even to invent a new sense."[79]

This invention, however, is the point at which the senselessness that currently assails us can and *must* be endured differently from the others, and so we now turn to the prescriptive sense of Nancy's invocation of working. The reaction to the loss of sense has traditionally been one of regression or creative denial. Faced with the groundlessness of identity, of "man," of "God," etc., the usual theopolitical reaction is either a fervent effort to return to the great men and gods of a mythic past or to consolidate new, stronger men and gods in their place. The responsible response to unworking, to the contrary, is unworking itself. "Alarmed" at its loss of all solid foundations, thinking must try to resist all temptations to ground itself—perhaps, one might say, by keeping itself alarmed, "eyes wide open to the absence of sense, to sense as absence of sense."[80] This is the manner in which Nancy understands Marx's injunction to change the world or Nietzsche's Zarathustran call "to introduce a new sense, it being understood that this task itself has no sense."[81] Remaining with the senselessness of sense would, in a sense, give rise to a "new sense," but, far from emerging triumphant from its jaunt through the labor of the negative, such new sense would be nothing more and nothing less than a kind of alarmed-remaining-with-the-impossibility-of-sense. Wide-eyed at the insubstantiality of things. "This is all my art can achieve." (*Theaetetus*, 210c).

As it is with sense, so it is with community: unworking is not merely what *has* happened to being-with, but, more importantly, what *must* happen *as* being-with in the absence, or the interruption, of community. Being-in-common is only itself as constantly unworking—as shared, communicated, and resistant to all attempts to solidify community under some essentialist myth. Community, Nancy insists, does and must constantly *interrupt* all mythic reification in such a way that this resistance (unlike most of what comes to call itself the Resistance) does not form a new foundation for a communion, but rather remains open to and as inessentiality, nonidentical circulation, relation. Community *is* the very exposure that unworks it, so that "in a certain sense community acknowledges and inscribes—this is a peculiar gesture— the impossibility of community."[82] Ultimately, this sustained inessentiality might condition the emergence of a new kind of community, much like the new sense of sense's absence. For, if community emerges in the interruption of community, it emerges in the interruption of the myth that founds it, and "there is no myth of the interruption of myth. But the interruption of myth defines the possibility of a 'passion' equal to mythic passion—and yet unleashed by the suspension of mythic passion: a 'conscious,' 'lucid' passion, as Bataille calls it, a passion opened up by compearance and for it. It is not the passion for dissolution, but the passion to be exposed."[83] Ceaselessly exposing the fault lines of essential calcifications, shattering all self-identical closure, the task of unleashing this "lucid passion" is not unlike that of freeing the "primitive curiosity" that interests itself in inter-esse. In both cases, it is a matter of unworking.

In the phenomenon of unworking, we thus see ontology give immediately onto ethics and vice versa; unworking is both "our" existential (de)situation and our responsibility. Again, however, it must be emphasized that, like the much maligned, little understood "unworking" of deconstruction, the task of exposing the failures and interruptions of sense *is first and foremost a way of making sense*, precisely by refusing to assimilate the unthinkable under ready-made categories of thought. Adapting Marx's theses on Feuerbach, Nancy argues that "we can no longer refer to available senses; we have to take absolute responsibility for making-sense of the world."[84] Yet, unlike Marx and Engels, for whom "man" is always a producing, laboring animal, Nancy insists we must make sense by *unmaking* it—by constantly exposing the exhaustion of every work and stable signification in order to get to the sense that exceeds all signification, the community that interrupts all communion, the freedom that frees existence from the totalitarian reign of essence. What is exposed in this ceaseless *frayage* (which has been translated "marking" but which also means path clearing, opening, and generation all at once) is ontological exposure itself. And exposure is always already existence's aboriginal relation. As a politics of unworking, then, "all of our politics are politics of the undoing within self-sufficiency."[85]

The undoing of all violently established and jealously guarded "autonomy" reveals, and in this manner frees, a network of absolute interdependence. Just as Nagarjuna's emptiness reveals the dependent coarising of all things, Nancy's act of unworking is always also the act of relating: linking, enchaining, connecting, tying. Of his unworked politics of radical heteronomy, Nancy can thus say that "such a politics consists, first of all, in testifying that there is singularity only where a singularity ties itself up with other singularities, but that there is no tie except where the tie is taken up again, recast, and retied without end, nowhere purely tied or untied."[86] And again, this ethicopolitical praxis can only take shape through and as ontology, however improperly ontological: "This politics requires an entire ontology of being as tying, that is, precisely perhaps where all ontology, as such, gets tied up with something other than itself."[87] The tie (*lien*), which can also be translated as the knot, is Nancy's disfiguring figure for this politics of unworking and enchaining.[88] Strictly speaking, the knot is no thing at all, but rather the sort of twisted "not" that never returns to itself from its tarrying with the negative, or that returns, but as still tarrying, that is, as perpetually differing from itself. The tie, the knot, *le lien*: the very unworking linking by virtue of which things become themselves as not-themselves, as *more than themselves*.

## Interruption

In an uncharacteristic moment of foreclosure, hidden away in a footnote to his discussion of *lier* and *le lien*, Nancy writes, "to avoid all ambiguity, one must emphasize that religion has nothing to do with the tie, contrary to what a false etymology might pretend. *Religio* is scrupulous observance, and consequently, it implies that the tie is tied, given."[89] A number of questions would need to be asked here. First, since when has Nancy looked to "avoid all ambiguity"? Or, for that matter, to refrain from the use of anything but watertight etymologies? In light of this particular intervention, how is one to read, for example, his linking of the words *penser* and *pèser*, his playing with the revealing and concealing inherent in the word *dérobement*, his reading of exposure as ex-position, interest as *inter-esse,* and sharing as division—not to mention his work on the overdetermination of the sense of the word *sens*—if not as productive musings on the ambiguity generated by what he himself (in an essay, we might add, that reads the word *Europe* as potentially meaning both "wide-eyed" and "far-sounding") calls a "questionable etymology"?[90]

Moreover, as Nancy must know, the "scrupulous observance" to which he confines "religion" is precisely a signal that the ties tied in ritual practice are not at all stable or simply given, but are rather continually untying themselves. This is the reason, we might say, that they need to be retied, *reliés.* The always already tied and untied ties of "religion" (as if these could be simply divorced from economic circulation, the communication of information, or the alliances and networks that make and unmake the political) are therefore no more—and no less—*given* than the relations of Nancy's inoperative community. What seems an allergic reaction to the "religious" on Nancy's part, especially in the face of the sorts of practices and ideologies that have recently resurged to combat so-called secularism, is certainly understandable. That said, forbidding the linkage between a politics of enchainment and the problem of religion is not only self-defeating but also irresponsible. The contemporary global landscape is veritably knotted with sites of theopolitical struggle between and among shifting communities, where the religious is always already political and the political always already religious.

Nancy himself could be said to explore the dangerous linkages he forbids here in a number of recent essays. By virtue of the inextricability of the history of the Occident and the "Abrahamic traditions," he argues, a rethinking of philosophy's most basic terms (community, man, duty, etc.) will require a complete phenomenologico-deconstruction of monotheism in general and of Christianity in particular.[91] Nancy does not, however, explicitly link these recent projects on "religion" to the politics of enchaining. All this is merely to say that it remains to those of us who, despite everything, cannot manage to leave such questions alone to think through a possible—even a necessary— *religion désoeuvrée,* whose very self-exposure might reconfigure "the religious" precisely *as deconfigured.* But already I feel inclined to reserve such absurd and impossible possibilities for another time.

Il n'y a qu'il y a

As we have seen, the ceaseless relation that unworking-as-(re)tying exposes is literally the undoing of all bounded interiority, whether it be communal, institutional, or "subjective." Unworking is the obstruction, in other words, of all *hypostasis*, and for this reason, the sense it makes performs the constant uncovering of what Levinas calls the il y a. Through the action of unworking, one might say that Nancy flattens out Levinas's stratified universe, pulling everything down Jacob's ladder—angels and stars and all—into the unground of everyday existence. In this very gesture, however, he folds the finite in on itself and out of itself, staging an infinite resistance to all immanentist recuperation. Thinking alongside Nancy, we are moreover able to touch upon what can only be intuited from close readings of Heidegger and Levinas: that the self-positing of the hypostatic ego is nothing short of suicide (which, by virtue of the stubborn singular plurality of existence, is also autricide—not to mention deicide).[92] The self that denies its own displacement, relation, and materiality destroys itself because displacement *is* its position, relation *is* its singularity, and the "there is," in all its materiality and multiplicity, *is all there is*. "'Matter,'" Nancy writes, "is first the very difference through which *something* is possible, as *thing* and as *some*. . . . If there is something, there are several things; otherwise, there is nothing, no 'there is.'"[93] The Levinasian effort to "put an end to the absurd rumbling of the *il y a*,"[94] insofar as such work rages against relation, materiality, plurality, sharing, contamination, and elementality, announces precisely the nihilistic task it seems upon first hearing to announce: the effort to put an end not only to what there is, but to *that there is*—to existence itself.

Of course, the attempt to obliterate isness itself is as doomed to failure as the attempt to render inviolable the borders of a house, nation, race, or subject. All these "wicked" operations of self-grounding, however furious the devastation they wreak upon the world, cannot annihilate it: "We can't destroy the world any more than we can destroy what has to be called *being*: the *fact* that 'there is' something, without this being either for us or because of us." In keeping with the principle of conservation of mass energy, nothing that truly is can be destroyed. Everything is indestructible: appearing, disappearing, existence, world, exchange, exposure, matter, il y a. "Granted," Nancy continues, "it's little comfort knowing that being is indestructible if this knowledge is only granted on the verge of our destruction, if there is no one to know it. In truth, though, we already know this, here and now. 'Being' or the 'there is' or 'existence' is, in us, what happens before us and ahead of us, arising from the very step beyond us."[95] To "be there," then, is to think thereness as such, which means to practice a thinking that faces up to the inessential withness of existence itself. For it might very well be the case that freedom and relation and everything that *is* cannot be annihilated. But "none of this . . . is accessible to the ego. Indeed, it is always *from out of this* that the ego emerges in order to contemplate blindly the desert of what it has destroyed. Whoever would contemplate the world would, in truth, contemplate the effacement of the ego."[96] And of the nation, and the people, and the solution, and this god, and that book, and this gender, and that class, and this history, and that idea, and this hero, and that enemy. This effacement, which would constantly expose the face of the il y a, would be the (un)work of a perpetually incomplete ethics as ontology.

Throughout his corpus, Nancy thematizes a number of different concrete practices through which thinking the senseless *makes* sense, knowing that it's senseless, by exposing and retying the relational network of the there is. All of these can be read as one or another strategy of touching—of quite literally sense-ing the radical heteronomy of all beings by getting in touch with them. As distinct from the idealist specularity that sees things from a safe, ultimately appropriative distance, a thinking of touch exposes the physical and philosophical structure of being-toward-the-world as such: "the world is nothing other than the touch of all things and wherever nothing is touching, wherever contact is severed, there is nothing; this is the absolute exposure of the world."[97] In a sense, Nancy's recognition is the most mundane of all: things in the world exist on one another's edges as well as their own, bumping into, brushing up against, leaning on, colliding into, just missing, circumventing, heading toward, fusing with, bleeding onto themselves and other things. Thinking's (un)work is to get in touch with this chaotic touch of the world—and not, it cannot be emphasized enough, to hold itself above the fray. For unlike vision, which always collapses a perceived otherness back into the gazing self, touch exposes the infinitely inappropriable alterity between and within all beings, preventing the self's self-position. Such position can only be established *against* the "there," against the material, the indeterminate; against the world. And thinking must think *with* and *toward* the world, touching all the elements the ego tries so hard to keep out of its little house.

The touching-thinking that exposes the infinite inter-esse of finite things is, for Nancy, carried out through writing. By bringing the world to language, literature writes the singular plurality of being (which is its inessentiality, its touch, its communication—these themes all build fugally upon one another). In other words, literature unworks precisely that which myth works into essence by working it out of being: "literature's revelation, unlike myth's, does not reveal a completed reality, nor the reality of a completion. . . . It interrupts myth by giving voice to being-in-common, which has no myth and cannot have one."[98] However, since myth—like the self-identical subject, community, and history it validates—always returns and will always return to assert itself, there can be no end to writing or to the disruption it performs.

Literature has always been and will always be haunted by the myth of myth, and, "forasmuch as it is haunted by this myth, the stroke of writing, bravely confronting this haunting memory, must never stop interrupting it again."[99]

Constantly unworking essence, writing becomes nothing short of a political ontology of radical hospitality. Exposing at each turn the *myth* of pure identity, whether it be individual or collective, writing literalizes the literary, letting being come to presence as such: "bringing to language . . . means literally . . . *bringing* being itself, as ek-sisting, to the advent or the event that it is: to the action of making-sense. Language doesn't signify being but makes it be."[100] Of course, "being" and "presence" in Nancy are at once less and more than they seem to be. On the one hand, that which "is" is not in any stable sense, since that which copresents itself does not present itself to be comprehended, appropriated, or simply located. That which comes into being always slips away from optic and aptic *grasping*, and, in this sense, that which presents itself is never present. On the other hand, this ceaseless elision and elusion *is* the essence of being itself: spacing, disposition, relation. By exposing the inessentiality of essential structures *and* refusing to inscribe new ones, writing touches on existence itself. Thus we can sense the proximity of Nancy to Heidegger in his very distance from Heidegger. Hollowing out the space within all solidified "presence," writing clears the clearing in which "being-itself" (as the relational inessentiality of beings) can finally come to pass. Writing, then, is nothing if not a practice of care.

Precisely by referring the praxis of thinking (as writing, touch, exposure, unworking, tying, letting-come-to-presence) to a relational, inessential ontology, Nancy thus maintains the very priority of the ethical that Heidegger's "two abodes" keep him from maintaining and that Levinas's undead transcendental ego keeps *him* from maintaining. The opening of the ethical, far from relying upon a closure of the frightful il y a, depends upon an ever-renewed exposure to it, which Nancy calls "being-toward-the-world." In the very construction of this particular phrase is announced something like a double movement—"being-toward" draws existence outward, beyond itself, and "the world" draws it back, simultaneously, as more than itself. Nancy refers to this self-exceeding finitude of being as "the 'transcendence' of its 'immanence'—its *transimmanence*"[101] or, in the language with which we are becoming increasingly familiar, the hollowed-out space of the "toward" or the "with" that conditions relation both between *and within* beings. Insofar as it is transimmanent, being-there is being-here; ecstasis is instasis; Dasein is *Mit-sein*, precisely because there is no "other world" into which the existent might be transported. In the Nancean universe, we might say, "Il n'y a qu'il y a": or, in his words, "the *there* of the 'there is' is nothing but spacing as such. . . . As such, then, the *there* is nothing other than the Wittgensteinian 'That' of the world, while at the same time being the world's original 'how.'"[102]

We would be remiss not to swerve momentarily off course to note here that, for Ludwig Wittgenstein, the "that" and the "how" of the world is the source of a most profound wonder. At a lecture at Cambridge University in 1929–30, Wittgenstein told his audience of a certain existential overwhelmedness he frequently experienced: "I believe the best way of describing it is to say that when I have it *I wonder at the existence of the world.* And I am inclined to use such phrases as 'how extraordinary that anything should exist' or 'how extraordinary that the world should exist.'"[103] Likewise, toward the beginning of Nancy's "Forgetting of Philosophy," he writes that "philosophy is not, perhaps is never, *that* which happens; but the wonder [*l'étonnement*] before the fact that it happens bears the name and form of the philosophical for the Occident."[104] We should not be too quick to tie Nancy to Wittgenstein on this point, because Wittgenstein goes on to describe the "world" this wonder reveals as simultaneously too immanent and too transcendent to resound with Nancean transimmanence or "infinite finitude." Wonder, Wittgenstein tells us, gives us the ability to see the world as a "limited whole," in other words, *sub specie aeternitatis.*[105] Wittgenstein writes in his notebooks that such a globalized wonder is usually the provenance of the artist: "The aesthetic miracle [*Wunder*] is *that* the world exists."[106] In *Culture and Value,* he suggests that since philosophy opens with wonder, it can also "capture the world" from a heavenly perspective: "Thought has such a way—so I believe—it is as though it flies above the world and leaves it as it is, observing it from above, in flight."[107] Were we to read this through Nancy's understanding of the *that* of the world, however, we would be prevented from any such self-extrication; Nancy warns explicitly that "themes of 'wonder' and the 'marvel of Being' are suspect if they refer to an ecstatic mysticism that pretends to escape the world."[108] If it is the case that il n'y a qu'il y a, then there is no place—whether it be *punctum* or flight pattern—of dispassionate observation from which we might indulge in the quiet passion of *Wunder*. We would instead need to begin to think through the entangled, everyday way in which wonder opens us within—and *toward*—the infinitely finite "there" from which thinking can never take flight. To reverse the metaphor, we might say that in order to expose the wonder of the *that*, thinking would have to sink down into it. In fact, although it is unlikely that he is explicitly referring to Wittgenstein here, Nancy writes, contra any sort of flighty, artistic *Wunder,* that "we need an art—if it is an 'art'—of thickness, of gravity. We need figures that weigh upon the bottom rather than extracting themselves from it."[109]

Having stumbled into another spectral emanation of thaumazein, this exploration once again finds itself on dangerous (un)ground. As seen in Nancy's reading of the whole world as the il y a, the very nature of the *that* at which wonder wonders dismantles such calcifications as Wittgenstein's outerworldly perspective. The places that wonder finds to sink down are infi-

nitely entangled, infinitely finite. And yet, the aboriginal openness of thaumazein does seem to provoke the very escapism it ought to prevent (Thales,
Plato, Protagoras's disciples, Heidegger, Wittgenstein). If the "there is" is
all there is, why on earth would the *Wunder* that wonders at it attempt so
completely to leave it? Toward the beginning of this study, I set forth the
hypothesis that there is no such thing as "good wonder" or "bad wonder";
rather, there is wonder and there is the denial of wonder.[110] If this is indeed
the case, then a great deal of what announces itself as wonder is more like
wonder's foreclosure than its opening. And insofar as we are faced with an
opening that permits its own closure, we are thrown back upon the problem
of freedom.

What Nancy's analysis of freedom reveals is that most of what goes by the
name of freedom ("autonomy," the breaking of relations, "free" choice among
a number of given options, diet soda, unlimited cell phone minutes) really
asserts itself as the autofoundational wickedness that *destroys freedom at its
core* by filling in the hollowness of freedom's "with." Similarly, I would argue
that the cloud hovering, the stargazing, the slavish devotion, or the uncavely
dwelling that masquerades as wonder is not only *not* wonder, but goes so far
as to destroy wonder by closing off the inessentiality of that which is. Just
as the opening of freedom gives freedom either to be freed or renounced,
however, it must also be said that, insofar as wonder attunes thinking to the
"there is" of the world, it also opens the possibility of its own refusal, even in
the form of the hero worship, metaphysical elitism, or otherworldiness that
in turn brands itself "wonder."

Although he does not explicitly thematize wonder's parallelism with freedom, Nancy does seem interested in distinguishing a primordial philosophical wonder ("Ever since its foundation, wonder has been philosophy's virtue")[111] from the various essentializing closures with which it might be falsely
conflated. In a brief chapter called "On Wonder," he writes of this aboriginal
mood that "in no way is this a blissful contemplation, but, rather, a difficult,
complex, and delicate set of decisions acts, positions, and gestures of thought
and writing."[112] Wonder as the origin of all philosophy is therefore inimical
to the various sorts of "wonder" Nancy denigrates from time to time in his
writing—such as perverse fascination, progressive causal reasoning, or, one
would imagine, Wittgenstein's world-abandoning rapture.[113] Wonder as "philosophy's virtue" has something, rather, to do with keeping things difficult—
with thinking at the limits of thinkability and making sense at the fault lines
of sensibility. "In the final analysis," Nancy suggests, "wonder is nothing other
than that which happens or arrives at the limit. Wonder itself is a kind of sign
without signification, and the sign—the index or the signal—that signification
is verging upon its limit, and that sense is laid bare."[114] In this manner, Nancy
aligns wonder with his aforementioned "primitive curiosity" that wonders at

the origin of things, linking this "lucid" passion with the action of unworking, exposing, enchaining, letting-come-to-presence, and being-toward-the-world that makes sense in and as the absence of sense. Amidst the senselessness to which the inoperative community remains stubbornly exposed, "to wonder today is nothing other than to wonder before this resistance and insistence of our strange community in sense, in the exposure toward sense."[115]


### Repetition

As Nancy tirelessly demonstrates, the community that unworks is the event of being itself: the originary singular plurality that resists the formation of self-enclosed communities, whether they be individual or collective. A wonder that wonders at this strange inessentiality thus wonders, much like the *Wunder* of Wittgenstein's lectures or Heidegger's *What Is Metaphysics?*[116] at isness or thatness itself. What differentiates Nancy's from these two formulations, however, is a certain double movement by virtue of which astonished thought cannot dissociate from the mundanity at which it wonders—a repetition announced in the out-and-back motion of being-toward-the-world that renders all flight a kind of diving down. It is likely that Nancy would hesitate to characterize his ontology in terms of a dynamic of repetition, especially considering the latter's thematic proximity to—and frequent conflation with—one or another version of dialectical return. Nevertheless this proximity, which might turn out to be the greatest distance, must be risked in order to flesh out the sort of *étonnement* that haunts and propels Nancy's thought.

For Nancy, wonder wonders at "the resistance and insistence of our strange community in sense." Yet this sort of "sense," we will recall, is only ever exposed insofar as thinking thinks through the *loss* of sense. And since, for example, the so-called substances of self and other ordinarily seem most familiar, most reliable, and most understandable of all, the sudden loss of these must *each time* be experienced as a surprise or shock. In *The Gravity of Thought*, Nancy describes the thinking self's experience of its own inessentiality thus: "Thinking is presumably nothing other than the sensation of a 'self' that falls outside of itself *even before* having been a self. And what is then felt is neither a dizziness nor an intoxication but, indeed, a violent shock (no grandiloquence or melodrama here: a good shot that hits hard, that is all, yet that is quite enough). It is a calm and opaque *hardness*."[117] The "hardness" up against which thinking runs is both a weightiness that keeps drawing us back down into isness and a *difficulty*. Exposed to the abandonment of sense, thinking runs up against a hardness at the limits of thinking—an unthinkability—a *resistance* to thought. Yet this is precisely the way in which thinking makes sense; the self or community's infinite exceeding of immanence *is* its ontological insistence. Such resistance, then, comes as a shock *and* gives rise to a kind of "new awe."

Throughout both *The Experience of Freedom* and *Being Singular Plural*, being's event as advent is characterized as essentially surprising. If every moment is the origin of existence as "just once, this time," then coming-to-presence cannot be calculated in advance or precomprehended.[118] Existence surprises us *every time*, so that, ultimately, there is no being at all without surprise: "What makes the event an event is not only that it happens, but that it surprises."[119] In order to let beings come, thinking must therefore learn how to be astonished: "Again, it is necessary to stay precisely within the element of wonder—that is, within what could never properly be made into an 'element,' but is instead an event. How is one to stay in the event? How is one to hold onto it (if that is even an appropriate expression) without turning it into an 'element' or a 'moment'? Under what conditions can one keep thinking within the surprise, which is its task to think?"[120]

We begin here to witness a dedramatized Verhaltenheit beginning to take shape in Nancy's thought. What we might call the moment of (Er)schrecken finds exposition in Nancy as the disappearance of the structures—like selves, others, gods, ideas, and nations—that habitually assert themselves as substances to keep senselessness at bay. So shock registers the revelation of the "insignificance" of being, the senselessness of sense. This means it can take the form of surprise, distress, terror, and even rage. It is shock that keeps our "eyes wide open to the absence of sense," shock that attunes us to senseless suffering and cruelty, shock that prevents a so-called thinking from working evil into a triumphalist soteriological scheme. Alphonso Lingis thus understands the most important sort of surprise in Nancy to be the shock of *anger*. For Lingis, the "chthonic, oceanic, celestial rage" that overwhelms us in the face of "starved, deported, massacred, tortured bodies" is what finally brings us out of our mythic self-enclosure into genuine relation with one another.[121] He thus adds his voice to Nancy's declaration that anger is "the political sentiment *par excellence*. Anger concerns the inadmissible, the intolerable, and a refusal, a resistance that casts itself from the first beyond all it can reasonably accomplish—to mark forth the possible ways of a new negotiation with what is reasonable, but also the ways for an untractable vigilance."[122]

Shock, in all of its forms, preserves the unacceptability of the unacceptable, the unthinkability of the unthinkable, the meaninglessness of the meaningless. It is almost excruciatingly difficult to say at this point that such shock gives way to anything else, because it seems any "anything else" would work in service of a theodicy (e.g., "the evil that provokes outrage serves to bring us closer together," "watching my neighbor suffer makes me into a better person," "the surprise I feel at my own heteronomy provokes me to become more autonomous," etc.) Yet one can detect in Lingis a conviction that runs throughout Nancy's work as well, and which tries always to remain on this side of any redemption narrative: the senseless as senseless has become "our" sense. The ways we used to make meaning no longer *mean*, but "the exhaustion and the opening indicate only one thing: that there is sense to our existence, sense in withdrawal from, or in excess of, all signification."[123] Hence the repetition. The interruption of every thing—signification, the autonomous subject, communion, myth, politics, identity, essence, continuity, history, "mythic passion," and the cosmos itself—somehow conditions the emergence of sense, singularity, community, literature, the political, sharing, existence, contiguity, happening, "primitive curiosity," and *world*. So while it is obviously not right to say that the shock of the inessentiality of things gives rise to a new essence, it is not exactly wrong, either. For the inessentiality that remains relationally inessential *is* essence "itself." In the shock of unworking, "we are exposed to the risk of no longer being able to understand or interpret ourselves—but also . . . we are thereby exposed once again to ourselves, and once again to one another, to our language and to our world."[124] And this exposure (de)constitutes the strange community that "dwells in" wonder.

*Etonnement* in Nancy is thus reminiscent of Heideggerian *Scheu*. The mood that marvels at the donation of abandonment, for Heidegger, attunes itself to the sense of senselessness, in Nancy. If the movement by which the familiar becomes strange can be called shock (or surprise, anger, horror, or terror, depending on one's situation), then the reciprocal, nonidentical movement by which this strangeness presents itself as *all there is* is indeed awe (or astonishment, marveling, etc.—but these terms can almost all be used in both of the senses we are attempting to distinguish here). Shock reveals the inessentiality of things; awe reveals the thingliness of inessentiality. Shock brings us out of "subject-object" relations; awe brings us into being-toward. Shock demolishes autonomy; awe frees us for freedom. Shock unworks; awe makes sense. Shock punctuates; awe enchains.[125] In shock, thinking loses everything, and in awe, everything returns, at once more and less than thinking had thought it to be.

Again, we are in dangerous waters here. First, we risk reinscribing any number of self-identical categories of thought as conditions of possibility, however negative, for ethical opening. One such disastrous reading could assert that, much like the house that the early Levinasian ego must construct against the elements before the Other can break into it properly, the Nancean existent must be a "self" before it is *toward*; an identity must form and harden before it is shattered. And, once again, we would find that an attempted ethics of relation would depend for its integrity upon an ontology of the Subject-as-Substance. If we are going to try to think through the repetition that seems to take place here, we must each time resist pinning necessity onto these monstrous concretions, for as Nancy shows us in numerous ways, a lone individual is a logical absurdity as well as an ethical nightmare. Figures such as the self, the other, this nation, that god must be thought not as substances to be torn down, but rather as *myths* to be interrupted. The logic of myth accounts for the seeming priority of the substantial, in spite of its ontological impossibility: the solid identities that unworking unworks have always only been myths. On the other hand, it also announces the endlessness of the unwork of writing, for the mythic, however "simply mythic," is that which refuses to stay dead. The shock of inessentiality and the awe at its insistence as such are therefore constantly renewed—each time different, each time a surprise.

If the Scylla threatening this aweful navigation here is a monadic ontology, the Charybdis, which reared its head a moment ago, is theodicy. One risks asserting too easily that awe restores what shock takes away—that, once the dust settles, senselessness comes to signify something truer and more certain than the old significations. And indeed, something does *come* here—or come back to—or come *toward*—a surprised thinking. But this "something" is hardly certainty and can only in the most qualified sense be called truth. In "Euryopa," for example, Nancy argues that the uncanny dissipation of all "other worlds," whether they be "new, ancient, celestial or infernal," opens this world as the only world there is, that is, as finite—which is to say free and singular plural and each time entirely new. Here, then, thinking touches upon the sort of repetition around which it tends inexorably to circle: "This world is finite because it is entirely returned to itself. It no longer opens onto any other worlds, neither new, nor ancient, nor celestial, nor infernal worlds. . . . It is the world, which is nothing but the world."[126] And if shock witnesses the terrifying withdrawal of the mythic elsewhere; awe senses the infinite complexity of all *there is*.

Yet what *is* the "there is" at which this wonder wonders? It is uncertainty, heteronomy, freedom, inessentiality—*vanity* [*hebel*], in the language of Ecclesiastes: breath, wind, nothingness, air. To echo Derrida's sizing up of the strange community of philosophers whose task it is to question the possibility of philosophy, existence itself is "very little—almost nothing."[127] Thus Nancy warns, "Let's not speak too hastily of the 'wonder [*merveille*] of being.' This 'wonder' is a mere trifle: only the thing, almost nothing. But," he continues, "almost nothing suffices to make a world—which means also that a world is no big thing, that this world *here* is no big thing (and, of course, *there isn't* any other)."[128] The "almost nothing" of the il y a—what Nancy will later call "scant being"[129]—is far closer to everything than it is to nothing, and yet it is no thing, nothing with strong walls that might protect thinking from the senselessness it exposes. It does not "make things better." In fact, far from presenting thought with stable significations or assuring teleologies, the shared (in)essence to which awe attunes thinking only leaves it open to new and further outrage at and by the self-positing pretensions of evil. Even more dangerously, the surprised thinking one encounters in Nancy risks working in their service.

For, as Nancy reveals, freedom can either be freed or renounced; it both precedes and opens the possibilities of good and evil. Again we recall that for Descartes wonder as the first of all the passions also precedes all determinations of good and evil. It can therefore now be said that, to the extent that wonder wonders at thatness, wonder wonders at the "almost nothing" of freedom, the inessential essence of being-with. This towardness, however—this shared freedom—is only exposed in the shock of unworking, a worldly entanglement with senselessness that, when followed to its limits, provokes horror, terror, and even what Lingis calls "oceanic rage." But what is to prevent this entanglement from becoming the very identity-positing it exposes? What stands between this particular oceanic feeling and the demonic fury of wickedness? What is it that separates rage from rage?

It is very little, but enough to make a world, and Nancy, in an unusual proximity to Christian theology, calls it "grace" or "decided existence. As distinct from self-grounding wickedness, grace is a being-toward-the-world that "withdraws from the essential 'self' and properly holds back its possibility for devastating fury."[130] Nancy seems for a moment here to want draw an excessively neat distinction between the two possibilities that freedom presents, calling evil the renunciation of freedom, and grace its endurance. Unlike evil, he explains, grace as decided existence makes "a free decision that frees freedom for itself, for its finitude, for its sharing, for equality, for community, for fraternity, and for their justice—singularly, singularly shared/divided, singularly withdrawn from the hatred of existence."[131] However, as Nancy himself teaches us never to forget, all of this graceful being-toward takes place right in the midst of the hatred of existence. Moreover, a certain kind of outrage is the basis of all Nancean politics insofar as it *exposes* the very "with" against which wickedness rages. It seems from this short analysis, then, that the existent would do well not so much to repudiate fury in favor of grace as she would to hold out in the one for the passing of the other. Grace would come, were it to come, in the midst of a furious world *as* an ever-renewed exposure to worldly fury. This is precisely what ties "decided existence" into the Heideggerian mood it most powerfully evokes: the reservedness that "withstands the fury" of the withdrawal of being. In Nancy, the fury that rages in the wake of being's abandonment is the violent denial of the relation, inessentiality, and freedom that constitute existence itself. "Withstanding the fury" thus means standing with it, rather than against or in spite of it—standing with and among the infuriating beings, communities, nations, and histories that continually assert their own necessity. This with-standing *is* the opening of responsibility in Nancy. And as we are sensing more and more strongly, its possibility is exposed right along with the possibility for the most thorough destruction.

The question then becomes, how does "decided existence" remain decided? How does withstanding remain *with*? Is decision a matter of choosing a course and holding to it, or would such a teleology reinscribe the violent, autonomous subject? Could it be something closer to indecision that holds existence in genuine decision, preventing its furious closure by keeping it open, shared, shattered, exposed? And how might such (in)decision (un)work? How would it make sense in and of the senseless as such, that is, without asserting it as some "new mythology"? What kind of decision would it be that "frees freedom for itself," putting an ocean of interdependence, strategic alliances, and wide-awake outrage between grace and fury?

We do not decide on impossible things—anyone claiming to decide on them would be a fool.

> —Aristotle, *Nicomachean Ethics*, trans. Terence Irwin

I am trying, precisely, to put myself at a point so that I do not know any longer where I am going.

> —Jacques Derrida, response following "Structure, Sign, and Play in the Discourse of the Human Sciences"

# 4. DECISION: Jacques Derrida

## *Thaumazein*, the Irresponsible, and the Undecidable

In the introductory chapter, the problematic of thaumazein was preliminarily articulated through Hannah Arendt's fourfold suspicion of it. For Arendt, we recall, dwelling in wonder is inimical to responsible participation in civil society because it delivers the wonderer out of the world of everyday affairs, exposes him to all manner of good and evil forces, singularizes him at the expense of all earthly relations, and prevents him from forming any stable opinion, which means he has no base upon which to make concrete decisions. Through analyses of Heidegger, Levinas, and Nancy, I have gradually sketched thaumazein as a double movement through which the familiar is rendered strange and the strange is endured and awaited as such. In this manner, I have hoped to show that, far from disabling ethical being-in-the-world, a truly sustained thaumazein would expose existents neither as escapist nor as egocentric, but rather as always and only (in)essentially bound up with one another. At their most consonant, Heidegger, Levinas, and Nancy all demonstrate that such wondrous openness to alterity can be sustained only by an onto-ethical "unworking"—a tireless refusal to ground once and for all the identity of the self, the other, our god, this nation, or that people. Nancy calls this relationally sustained vulnerability "decided existence," but the question of what it means to decide remains to be explored. This chapter will therefore approach Arendt's final and most strenuously maintained conviction: that inasmuch as thaumazein blocks the sure functioning of dox-azein, it is inimical to opinion, decision, and the political responsibility that relies upon them.

For Arendt, decision relies upon the autonomous political subject, who clearly discerns and then strongly adheres to her *own* opinions. Arendt believes this process of determinate (self-)formation to be encouraged most powerfully through Socratic midwifery, which allegedly calls upon wonder as a momentary "leaping spark"—just enough to get thinking going. As I have argued by means of the *Theaetetus*, however, the maieutic process stabilizes neither the self nor its opinions: under Socratic scrutiny, each of Theaetetus's baby *doxai* turns out to be a mere image, wind-egg, or phantom. It is in this dialogue, moreover, that the so-called eternal Platonic self is ruptured at its anamnesic core: as Theaete-tus confesses at the end of his fruitless labor, the unworks "he" has produced were never his "own" in the first place: "For my part I have already, thanks to you, given utterance to more than I had in me."[1] Arendt is therefore correct to attribute to wonder a pesky tendency to expose both the autonomous self and its uninterrogated convictions as radically inessential. What she does not con-cede is that, in this dialogue at the very least, the maieutics she always places on the side of political decision and responsibility operates *through*, rather than against, thaumazein. Far from functioning as a temporary goad, the wonder that strikes Theaetetus is never resolved into a determinate knowledge that would have the last, decisive word. Yet simply repositioning Socrates into the "camp" of thaumazein hardly constitutes an adequate demonstration of wonder's rela-tion to ethicopolitical responsibility. Regardless of the way we align the ancient teacher "himself" with respect to thaumazein, the question remains: how can a mood that precedes and undermines the integrity of the knowing self and its opinions be said to condition the possibility of everyday decisions? For, having followed the traces and echoes of Socratic wonder through Heidegger, Levinas, and Nancy, this is the paradox upon which we have stumbled: things can only be decided insofar as they remain open; inessential; un-, inter-, and overdeter-mined; in short, undecidable.

To be sure, this is a counterintuitive position to take. It is not Hannah Arendt alone whose work weighs against decision's fundamental undecid-ability, but more or less the entirety of modern ethics, such that one need not cite any particular thinker to make the self-evident claim that a deci-sion can only be made by a self-determined, responsible subject who can approach any particular situation knowing, at the very least, good from evil and right from wrong. Against this more or less uncontested "commonsense" conviction, however, each of the thinkers we have engaged so far argues, in different ways and with varying levels of consistency, that a certain indeci-sion and heteronomy actually condition decision. In his "Origin of the Work of Art," for example, Heidegger ventures that "every decision . . . bases itself on something not mastered, something concealed, confusing; else it would never be a decision," and the *Contributions to Philosophy* tell us that insofar as it is "decided," Dasein is not "resolved," but rather resolutely "un-closed."[2] For Levinas, responsibility to and for the other precedes all freely chosen commitments I might make or fail to make to him, so that I am bound by a "responsibility for him without deliberation, and without the compulsion of truths in which commitments arise, without certainty."[3] Because this responsibility precedes all knowledge, I am radically heteronomous: given, temporalized, and decided not by myself, but by the other-in-and-as-me. Complicating and expanding upon Levinas's work, Nancy argues that the "freedom" upon which neo-Kantian ethics insists as the condition of decision actually *prevents* the self-gathering that neo-Kantian "autonomy" presupposes. According to an understanding of freedom as that which ungrounds existence relationally, decision takes shape as standing-with this inessential withness; decision decides again and again for the essential sharing that freezes all essentiality. Decision therefore relies upon precisely the uncertainty and indecision that a proper ethical system would judge inimical to all ethics: "Every decision surprises itself. Every decision is made, by definition, in the undecidable. . . . This is also why my decision is identically, each time, a decision for relation and for sharing—to the point that the *subject* of *my* decision can appear to itself as not being simply 'me' (but also a 'you' or an 'us') without its being any less singularly mine."[4] The most thorough thinker of the undecidability at the heart of every decision, however, has been Jacques Derrida, who remains in close critical conversation with each of the interlocutors we have called upon so far and whom we now invoke to help us navigate the unpredictable waters upon which thinking sets sail when it attempts to dwell in the realm of Thaumas the sea god.

In *The Gift of Death*, one of his most widely read recent works, Derrida begins what might be called a genealogical deconstruction of the autonomous subject and its "free" decision. This particular reading both relies upon and destabilizes a particular genealogy set forth in Czech phenomenologist Jan Patočka's *Heretical Essays*. According to Patočka, human (that is, Western) history is divided into the progressive stages of the "prehistoric" (which is also designated as the sacred, orgiastic, and demonic), the "Platonic," and the "Christian." This narrative, at least according to Derrida's reading of Patočka, testifies above all to a particular European testimony: Patočka retells the story that the West tells about its own progress from "paganism" through a kind of Christian secularism. And of all the concepts upon which its ethics, philosophy, and religion rely, the West is particularly proud of the emergence of its responsible subject.

Patočka's first stage, "prehistorical humanity" designates preresponsible humanity, in which people exist in uninterrupted continuity with gods and mortals. One should therefore start to think here of the elemental, the apeiron, the maternal—everything Levinas ties together as "paganism." At this "sacred" stage, Patočka tells us, people view all occurrences as necessary components of the divinely ordered cosmos and do not therefore endeavor to shape their lives or souls in accordance with any external (or internal) "Good."[5] As Derrida explains it, "the demonic is originally defined as irresponsibility or, if one wishes, as nonresponsibility. It belongs to a space in which there has not yet resounded the injunction to *respond*; a space in which one does not yet hear the call to explain oneself, one's actions or one's thoughts, to respond to the other and answer for oneself before the other."[6]

This prehistoric nonresponsibility is initially ruptured for Patočka by the Platonic doctrine of individual immortality: the soul for the first time is now charged with the task of making itself itself in accordance with a force with which it is not in immediate relation: the Good. In the fifth essay, Patočka announces his reading as an echo of Eugen Fink's interpretation of Plato's cave, which traces the allegory as a passage from sacred irresponsibility to Platonic responsibility. Along Fink's and Patočka's reading, the cave of the *Republic* can be seen as "a remnant of the subterranean gathering place of the mysteries; it is the womb of Earth Mother. Plato's novel idea is the will to leave the womb of Earth Mother and to follow the pure 'path of light,' that is, to subordinate the orgiastic entirely to responsibility. Hence the path of the Platonic soul leads directly to eternity and to the source of all eternity, the sun of 'The Good.'"[7] It is interesting to note where this path does not lead, that is, back into the cave. If Heidegger and Levinas each shortchange this return, consolidating the true dwelling place in the immaterial "open," neither Fink nor Patočka nor Derrida treats this countermovement at all. Instead, they track the soul's gradual procession from the maternal, material site of nonresponsibility out to the vision of the ethereal light of the Good, never accounting for its return. Responsibility, for Patočka, is a unidirectional journey, and Derrida explains that undertaking. It demands the soul's refinement of two "disciplines": the continual suppression of the demonic and *meletê thanatou*, "the 'practicing (for) death' that Socrates speaks of in the *Phaedo*."[8]

The stakes of both "parts" of the philosophic discipline sketched here are incalculably raised with the emergence of Christianity (Judaism falls somewhere, it seems, into the chasm between the pre-Socratics and Paul, and Islam into the chasm between Paul and Hegel). Unlike the Platonic soul, Patočka tells us, the Christian soul exists not in external relation to an ultimately comprehensible Good, but rather "in an inscrutable relation to the absolute highest being in whose hands we are not externally, but internally."[9] It is the terrifying unapproachability of this absolute highest being that gives rise to the Pauline injunction to work out one's salvation in fear and trembling. The Christian lives in unseeing response to the *mysterium tremendum*, which both represses the Platonism that suppresses the orgiastic and issues in a new relationship to death. Insofar as—in this Heidegger-inflected Christianity—no one can die in my place, the secret God that calls me from within-me-beyond-me calls me to absolute responsibility. The gift of Christian death is my radical singularity, in absolute relation to an inscrutable God. The disciplines of repression and being-toward-death are thus doubled and intensified. Responsibility must work increasingly hard to incorporate and repress its primordial *irresponsibility*, and the singular subject of responsibility must constitute itself through an increasingly mysterious relationship to death. The second half of this particular pairing—and the pairing itself—will be more directly addressed toward the end of this chapter, but for the moment let us begin by focusing on the first: responsibility's irresponsible core.

In the first section of *The Gift of Death*, entitled "Secrets of European Responsibility," Derrida's concern is simply to establish that responsibility has a *history*: that, far from being eternal, necessary, or self-evident, the very notion of the responsible self upon which "ethics" and "religion" rely is the product of a series of incorporations and repressions of irresponsibility. What this means, however, is that responsibility's history can never fully present itself to itself. Insofar as the mysterium tremendum that explicitly issues in responsibility remains absolutely inaccessible *and* insofar as the "demonic" or "orgiastic" irresponsibility that remains at responsibility's foundation must be continually denied, the history of responsibility is, fundamentally, a secret—a multilayered history of the secret.[10] Responsibility, in other words, is never fully responsible, but always relies on irresponsibility as its condition of possibility. But because this foundational irresponsibility effectively prevents responsibility from ever becoming itself (that is, thoroughly responsible), irresponsibility is *also* responsibility's condition of *im*possibility.

Derrida locates a similarly aporetic configuration in the decision upon which responsibility rests: undecidability is at once decision's condition of possibility and its condition of impossibility. Unlike his unearthing of responsibility's "nucleus of irresponsibility,"[11] however, Derrida's exposure of the aporetic (un-)structure of undecidability tends to proceed more logically than genealogically. For a decision to be worthy of the name, Derrida insists, it cannot be a matter of applying a predetermined "ethical" theorem to a particular range of determinate options and then of emerging from the scene assured of having chosen the Right One. Something about decision must remain utterly refractory to all such calculation, otherwise, "we could simply unfold knowledge into a program or course of action. Nothing could make us more irresponsible; nothing could be more totalitarian."[12] Unless decision undergoes what Derrida variously calls "the test of the antinomy" or "the aporia" or "the undecidable," decision is not decision at all, but rather the unthinking execution of a program.[13]

The notion that decision might rely on undecidability has always stirred up a great deal of scholarly concern. In a response to charges from a number of British and American critics that taking undecidability seriously amounts to advocating indifference at best and anarchy at worst, Derrida distinguishes three possible meanings of undecidability. First, this undecidability can refer to that which "resists," but still remains within, the onto-logic of binary opposition. Second, it can refer to that which delimits, but therefore also remains within, the boundaries of calculation. Finally, the undecidable can name that which "remains heterogeneous both to the dialectic and to the calculable." It is Derrida's insistence that undecidability understood in this last sense, far from abandoning us to some apolitical and anethical zone of complacency, indifference, or "complete freeplay," actually opens the space of ethics, politics, and responsibility itself:

> In accordance with what is only ostensibly a paradox, *this particular* undecidable opens the field of decision or of decidability. It calls for decision in the order of ethical-political responsibility. It is even its necessary condition. A decision can only come into being in a space that exceeds the calculable program that would destroy all responsibility by transforming it into a programmable effect of determinate causes. There can be no moral or political responsibility without this trial and this passage by way of the undecidable. Even if a decision seems to take a second and not to be preceded by any deliberation, it is structured by this *experience and experiment of the undecidable*. If I insist on this point from now on, it is, I repeat, because this discussion is, will be, and ought to be at bottom an ethical-political one.[14]

If it is the case that decision can only decide the undecidable and that responsibility can only respond by virtue of irresponsibility, then the very work of pushing these concepts out to their logical extremes is itself an ethicopolitical task. If decision and responsibility are only possible as impossible, then it is perhaps banal but nevertheless necessary to point out that they cannot be possible where they are simply "possible." It can thus be seen that Derrida's tireless uncovering of impossibility is performed for the sake of possibility itself. To reveal the impossibility of decision *as the very possibility of decision* is, in other words, to condition the possibility (but never the necessity) of the emergence of genuine (that is, impossible) decision.

Of course, decision and responsibility are not the only concepts whose aporetic configurations Derrida has thematized. In his earlier writings, Derrida ascribed the provisional name *différance* to the ur-condition of spatial differentiation and temporal delay. Neither a word nor a concept, *différance* (or writing, trace, *pharmakon*, etc.) both produces and disrupts—renders possible and impossible—the structural distinctions that undergird the metaphysical edifice, such as presence/absence, light/darkness, speech/writing, and inside/outside. In the later writings upon which we will explicitly focus here, Derrida treats problems that are more identifiably political: decision, responsibility, the gift, forgiveness, the messianic, mourning, justice, hospitality, and democracy, to name a few. It has thus become commonplace to say that sometime around the collapse of the Berlin Wall, amidst declarations of the concomitant "end of history,"[15] Derrida's thought took an ethicopolitical "turn."[16] Nevertheless, these more recent themes bear a striking (anti-)structural resemblance not only to one another but also to the "quasi-concepts" of *écriture, différance,* etc. All of them destabilize precisely that which they "produce."

Examining terms that most of us use daily and (we imagine) quite unproblematically, Derrida shows each of them to be possible only as impossible: forgiveness can only forgive the unforgivable, hospitality violates all laws of hospitality, the truest friend is an enemy, and a gift can only be a gift if it is not recognized as such.[17] As I have just done with the aporia of decision, the claim could be made in conversation with Derrida's readings of each of these utterly commonplace, utterly aporetic concepts that he marches thinking out to impossibility in order to clear room for more possibility—to expand the boundaries of the ordinary, the acceptable, the *imaginable.* Insofar as the possible only becomes truly possible when it opens out to impossibility, opening out to impossibility opens out new possibilities for ethical and political engagement. Granted, such a claim remains to be demonstrated, but assuming for the moment that it is the case, then thinking cannot know in advance what such reenvisioned possibilities will look like. Nor can it see in advance the impossibility that alone conditions these possibilities. It must therefore prepare itself not to know what it is looking for: thinking must find a way not to know its way, to put itself in a position where it cannot know where it is going, what is coming toward it, or what floodgates it might open when it opens onto aporia. In other words, the course of thinking must itself become undecidable, learning to *welcome* what it cannot determine or decide ahead of time. Which means it must learn to welcome what it will not know *how* to welcome—to prepare for the arrival of that whose arrival it cannot prepare. And so, in order to continue to think through the (im)possibility of decision, this exploration will take a detour through the (im)possibility of welcoming, of hospitality.

## Hospitality

In a lecture on the quasi-concept of forgiveness, Derrida reflects on the family resemblance between forgiveness and the gift, saying that these two are not by any means identical or equivalent, but are "analogous" and "linked."[18] In an essay on the concept of aporia itself, he ventures that perhaps all the various quasi-concepts he has welcomed into thought might *haunt* one another.[19] Among all these phantoms, however, hospitality seems to be the most frequent *arrivant*, constantly supplementing the elaboration of each of the others' impossible possibility. I would suggest that this is because the very gesture of opening thinking out to impossibility is *already* a gesture of radical hospitality toward the unexpected and indeterminable, and, in fact, Derrida seems to be considering something like this when he muses, "It is a little as if 'hospitality,' the name *hospitality*, came to name, but also to give a kind of proper name to this opening of the possible onto the impossible, and reciprocally: when hospitality take place, the impossible becomes possible but *as* impossible."[20] As we explore the contours of this particular (im)possibility in search of a fuller understanding of ethicopolitical decision, we should therefore at the very least mark the abyss into which thinking is thrown when it approaches hospitality: insofar as there can be no genuine openness to impossibility without a certain hospitality, hospitality is the condition of (im)possibility of the very analysis that reveals hospitality's own possibility as impossible.

Each of Derrida's aporetic analyses proceeds out to impossibility in different ways and in conversation with a vast range of works of literature and philosophy. In his writings on hospitality, Derrida offers careful readings of *Hamlet*, Emile Benveniste, Pierre Klossowski, Immanuel Kant, and Emmanuel Levinas to reveal two distinct, yet interdependent, imperatives at work throughout the Western tradition. On the one hand, there is the idea of a "conditional" hospitality: a warm welcome extended to the stranger or foreigner who appears at the threshold of my home, community, or nation. Of course, for a stranger even to be recognized as a "foreigner" in the first place, she must fulfill certain obligations. She must, for instance, state her intentions, pledge her goodwill, tell me where her home is and when she intends to return there, and, most important, she must disclose her identity. According to the conditional hospitality that governs—to cite one modest example— international law, entrance would never be offered to "an anonymous new arrival . . . someone who has neither name, nor patronym, nor family, nor social status."[21] All these conditions, which constitute the "juridico-political" laws of hospitality, ultimately serve the same purpose: to ensure the sovereignty of the people or institutions that welcome the foreigner into their territory. The laws of hospitality attempt to guarantee that the guest I welcome is not the type who will stay too long, wreck my house, or take my place and put me out on the (literal or metaphorical) street. Much like the mediocre "ethic" of tolerance, conditional hospitality says to the one it welcomes, "I am leaving you a place in my home, but do not forget that this is my home." By means of this conditional economy, I remain master of my own house and "retain power" over the other,[22] whom I only welcome after a series of careful pre-screenings . . . perhaps I even take her fingerprints. Yet this power play hardly seems to square with what we understand as hospitality. Gradually, then, we begin to see that the very "laws" meant to guarantee the possibility of hospitality also disable it. Or, in tune with Derrida's now familiar refrain, hospitality's very conditions of possibility become its conditions of impossibility.

What exactly is it, though, that prompts one to look at a set of regulations of hospitality and respond, "that doesn't seem like hospitality"? Something else must govern our common understanding of this concept—something that remains distinct from hospitality's concrete juridico-political instantiations. This "something else" is the "other hand" heralded by the "one hand" we have just described: the "other" injunction toward hospitality, the one that would remain "unconditional." As distinct from the particular laws of hospitality, then, the unconditional welcome that Derrida aligns with the medieval "Great Law of Hospitality"[23] would open itself completely, indiscriminately: leaving itself vulnerable to the nameless, to the unexpected, to the one whose intentions cannot be discerned ahead of time. Unlike the conditions of hospitality that preserve the autonomy of the sovereign self, this unconditional Law would ultimately allow the guest to interrupt and displace the very host that welcomes her (and in fact, the French word *hôte* means both "host" *and* "guest"). Along the lines of Levinas's ethics and Nancy's ex-istence, unconditional hospitality would install absolute alterity at the very heart of the welcoming "self," freezing it before any egological consolidation, in such a manner that "hospitality precedes property."[24] Unsettling all stability, calculability, and identity, this Law that transcends all laws would "say yes *to who or what turns up*, before any determination, before any anticipation, before any *identification*, whether or not it has to do with a foreigner, an immigrant, an invited guest, or an unexpected visitor, whether or not the new arrival is the citizen of another country, a human, animal, or divine creature, a living or dead thing, male or female."[25] This Great Law thus announces a "pure" hospitality—hospitality "itself" (if there is such a thing)—uncontaminated by conditions, limitations, or econo-dialectical reappropriation.

It is important to emphasize at this point that Derrida does not insist upon this rigorous conceptual "purity" for its own sake but rather as a means of thinking beyond what is ordinarily considered to be possible. Derrida recognizes that, even "if there is such a thing,"[26] the "unconditional hospitality" imagined in these thought experiments could never become, for example, state policy. He admits that an ethic of welcoming anything and everything that arrives is a "hyperbolic" one, exceeding even the most liberal of "juridico-political" configurations. It is precisely this hyperbolic excess, however, that makes it necessary to keep a state's conditional regulations and laws in constant tension with the "unconditional principles"[27] upon which they are ostensibly based:

> An unconditional hospitality is, to be sure, practically impossible to live: one cannot in any case, and by definition, organize it. Whatever happens, happens, whatever comes, comes, and that, in the end, is the only event worthy of this name. And I well recognize that this concept of pure hospitality can have no legal or political status. No state can write it into its laws. But without at least the thought of this pure and unconditional hospitality, of hospitality *itself*, we would have no concept of hospitality in general and would not even be able to determine any rules for conditional hospitality (with its rituals, its legal status, its norms, its national or international conventions).[28]

Without a rigorously defined concept of hospitality itself, we citizens, friends, in-laws, and strangers would be incapable even of setting forth our everyday, all-too-human hospitalities, much less of evaluating them, much less of reevaluating, reimagining, and expanding their limits in accordance with the ideal they both embody and fail to embody.

But is this not a familiar line of thought, found in chapter after chapter of the all-too-ontotheological book of metaphysics? What distinguishes Derrida here from the Kant of the second Critique? Or, for that matter, from Plato's philosopher-king who regulates the city-state by virtue of his uncorrupted vision of the Ideas? It is perhaps very little, but enough to signal at least an attempted departure from classical political theory and metaphysics. What sets Derrida apart from both neo-Kantianism and Neoplatonism is his insistence that the dependency of the conditional upon the unconditional is really a codependency. Just as the conditional pole of hospitality is both logically and practically reliant upon its unconditional referent, the unconditional pole literally cannot exist unless it *exists*; there *is* no "hospitality" independent of the limiting conditions that both instantiate and occlude it. There are no Forms outside the cave, no regulative ideals that might be approached asymptotically through the course of human history.[29] To the contrary, the very idea of the Ideas only emerges *within* that which attempts, with varying success, to reflect the Ideas. For this reason, Derrida maintains, "even while keeping itself above the laws of hospitality, *the* unconditional law of hospitality needs the laws, it *requires* them."[30]

In one of his essays on forgiveness, Derrida describes a similar, mutual reliance between the "pure" concept of forgiveness and the conditions that render forgiveness impure: "if our idea of forgiveness falls into ruin as soon as it is deprived of its pole of absolute reference, namely, its unconditional purity, it remains nonetheless inseparable from what is heterogeneous to it, namely the order of conditions . . . as many things as allow it to inscribe itself in history, law, politics, existence itself."[31] Likewise, the only true hospitality would be an absolutely unconditional hospitality, which in turn would have no hope of existing at all unless it were embodied in a particular, and necessarily impure, ethicopolitical setting. Hospitality itself, in other words, would only truly be itself by not being itself. This bears witness to the "non-dialectizable antinomy" Derrida locates between the conditional and unconditional injunctions to offer hospitality to the other. Insofar as "they both imply and exclude one another, simultaneously," these "irreconcilable but indissociable" concepts of hospitality tell us once again that hospitality is only possible as impossible: "It is . . . as though hospitality were the impossible: as though the law of hospitality defined this very impossibility, as though it were only possible to transgress it."[32]

Unconditional conditions of the impossible possibility of a hospitality that is only itself as not-itself . . . it would perhaps not be out of order to confess to Derrida that along with Theaetetus, our heads are beginning to swim. Once again, we find ourselves surrounded by aporia, and once again it is crucial to emphasize that unlike the sophists about whom Socrates warns his wide-eyed interlocutor, Derrida (which is certainly not to speak for all Derrideans) is not interested in leaving logic stranded in impossibility for its own sake or even in the name of some god of postmodern "play" (whatever postmodernity means, and as if play were ever simply play). We saw earlier that the effort to delimit "pure" concepts in all their impossibility is an effort to reimagine the "possibility" in which thinking tends to get stuck. Similarly, the with-standing of aporia holds in constant, productive tension both terms of a "non-dialectizable antinomy" in the hopes of making things—real, live, everyday things: policies, laws, social practices—*better*. And it is Derrida's unshakable conviction that things cannot get better if they remain easy or self-evident. "All these questions remain obscure and difficult," he admits, but

> we must neither conceal them from ourselves nor, for a moment, imagine ourselves to have mastered them. It is a question of knowing how to transform and improve the law, and of knowing if this improvement is possible within an historical space which takes place *between* the Law of an unconditional hospitality, offered *a priori* to every other, to all newcomers, *whoever they may be*, and *the* conditional laws of a right to hospitality without which *The* unconditional Law of hospitality would be in danger of remaining a pious and irresponsible desire without form and without potency, and even of being perverted at any moment.[33]

From this we can begin to see that the (at times excruciating) practice of dwelling in aporia would allow thinking neither to capitulate to the unreflective living out of uncontested sociopolitical norms, nor to take refuge from the conditional mire in the unconditional ether. For, as we have seen, each of these spaces exceeds and intrudes upon the other, endlessly, allowing us to count neither "two abodes" nor simply one, but the one *as*, *in*, and *through* the other to which it remains nevertheless irreducible and with which it remains in constant, mutually corrective tension.

Remaining in this particularly fraught "between," thinking remains neither in Aristophanes' clouds nor down Thales' well, but rather in the opening of the political as such, a space that Derrida, more pragmatically than usual, calls one of "negotiation." Simply put, "if we want to embody an unconditional forgiveness in history and society, we have to go through conditions. We have to negotiate between the unconditional and conditional."[34] Or, as Derrida says of democracy, we must negotiate in order to "reduce the gap *as much as possible*" between the ideal of democracy and the miserably corrupt democracies around us. This process must be "infinite," lest the space of the political be closed: the conditional and the unconditional "must be implicated with each other in the course of a complex and constantly re-evaluated strategy. There will be no re-politication, there will be no politics otherwise."[35] Or, as Derrida explains in relation to hospitality, the negotiable "must enjoin a negotiation with the non-negotiable so as to find the "better" or the least bad."[36] And here another distinction from Kant arises: for Derrida, this "process" of negotiation, if it can even be called a process, is not at all guaranteed. For it belongs to the very nature of unconditional hospitality that one *cannot know* in advance whether what is coming will be better or worse than what one has already got. I cannot know, for example, whether the other I welcome into my house will renovate or destroy it. Derrida concedes that this is an extremely dangerous, even "terrible" situation in which to put oneself, one's family, one's nation, "because the newcomer may be a good person, or may be the devil; but if you exclude the possibility that the newcomer is coming to destroy your house—if you want to control and exclude in advance this possibility—there is no hospitality."[37]

It is at this point that the aporia of hospitality intersects again with the aporia of decision. In fact, this is the same vertiginous crossroads we glimpsed during our journey with Levinas, when an aporia-sick Richard Kearney finally placed ethicopolitical limits around Levinasian ethics and its Derridean derivatives, insofar as "such non-discriminate openness to alterity," renders us "unable to differentiate between good and evil."[38] This statement represents an explicit break from Derrida, who had insisted in a discussion with Richard Kearney and others a few years earlier that "we should not know, in terms of knowledge, what is the distinction between good and evil."[39] It is certainly tempting, for this reader at least, to take refuge in the distinction Kearney eventually draws between "a logic of undecidability to keep us tolerant" and "an ethics of judgement to commit us as much as possible to right action,"[40] but I am attempting here to stay with aporia as long as I can stomach it, particularly now that decision has explicitly become a matter of knowing the difference between good and evil. For, according to Descartes, the only passion that precedes the distinction between good and evil is wonder. So, insofar as wonder's relation to genuine decision is under examination here, the question that arose at the beginning of this chapter reasserts itself. How is it possible for decision to emerge from sheer undecidability?

### Undecidability Revisited

First, and at the risk of diminishing its dramatic impact, the "sheerness" of undecidability should be qualified somewhat. Undecidability as Derrida thematizes it does not designate some force field of indifference, or even of "indeterminacy" as it is frequently understood (usually by those who accuse "deconstructionists" and "postmodernists" of "advocating" it). Undecidability is *not* indecision; far more simply and far more inscrutably, undecidability refers to the situation that gives rise to any decision that can be called a decision. For example, when my (determinate) obligations to my family and my nation oppose one another; or when two, five, or eight (determinate) people I love make mutually exclusive demands of me; or when I cannot know what the outcome of one or another (determinate) course of action will be, I find myself thrown into a position in which I *do not know* how to decide. This is the sense in which undecidability is "indeterminate." And yet it is from this undecidability that I must decide; it is from this impossibility that decision becomes possible. For, to return for a moment to ground we have already covered, a decidable decision is not a decision, but just a formula or a program. Hence decision's impossible possibility: for a decision to be itself, it must be undecidable, otherwise it is mere calculation.

To deromanticize this scene even further, saying that decision cannot be reduced to calculation is not the same as declaring decision to be Utterly Incalculable. As Derrida has said repeatedly, every decision must begin by accumulating as much knowledge as possible—by "learning, reading, understanding, interpreting the rule, and even calculating."[41] A certain calculation must prepare for decision with the utmost rigor—not only because responsibility demands that I educate myself as thoroughly as possible about the situation at hand but also because it is only through this process of preparation that the impending decision announces itself as impossible. It is at the *end* of this process that calculation fails us: "the decision remains heterogeneous to the calculations, knowledge, science, and consciousness that nonetheless condition it."[42] There is, in other words, a point of absolute rupture between preparing for a decision and actually making it, which nonetheless does not invalidate the preparation as such.

For yet again, one *must* certainly *know, one must know it,* knowledge is necessary if one is to assume responsibility, but the decisive or deciding moment of responsibility supposes a leap by which an act takes off, ceasing in that instant to follow the consequence of what is—that is, of that which can be determined by science or consciousness—and thereby *frees itself* (this is what is called freedom), by the act of its act, of what is therefore heterogeneous to it, that is, knowledge.[43]

It is this "leap" between calculation and the incalculable that is ultimately decisive for decision, and, perhaps not surprisingly, this leap is the point at which even sympathetic readers of Derrida tend to grow uncomfortable with his notion of undecidability.

It is this very leap into unknowability that prompts Richard Kearney to supplement undecidability with a more decidable "ethics of judgment," and this same moment that provokes countless interlocutors to ask Derrida how decision can possibly be made there where a decision cannot be made. As Graham Ward ventured after one of Derrida's lectures on the (im)possibility of forgiveness, "is there not the danger that you make aporia itself a transcendental, so that we are just paralyzed in front of an absolute abyss and therefore unable to do anything, let alone forgive?"[44] Derrida has tended to respond to these questions by reiterating in one way or another the first premise of his argument: namely, that undecidability is the condition of possibility of decision. It is only undecidability that allows decisions to be made (or forgiveness to take place or the gift to be given, etc.) in the first place. For this reason alone, "the aporia is not a paralyzing structure."[45] Furthermore, Derrida maintains in a number of essays that if in a given situation a decision is necessary, then it is *urgent*. There is no time for paralysis, simply because the negotiation between the conditional and the unconditional "cannot wait . . . [it] calls for an urgent response, a just response, more just in any case than the existing law."[46] Or, as Derrida insists elsewhere, "justice, however unpresentable it remains, does not wait. It is that which must not wait . . . a just decision is always required *immediately*, right away, as quickly as possible. It cannot provide itself with the infinite information and the unlimited knowledge of conditions, rules, or hypothetical imperatives that could justify it."[47] And yet, we might wonder, how is thinking to process out to undecidability, much less *recognize* it, if decision admits of no delay? How would calculation be prevented from running its ordinarily programmed course if there were no delay, no hesitation at all between the calculable and the incalculable? Is there not something that works against urgency and immediacy in the very "rupture" just marked out between preparation and the decision?

It seems we have stumbled upon yet another aporetic scene: if decision is undecidable, then there must be some interruption or suspension of everyday knowledge in order for decision to emerge. Some hesitation. And yet if the decision as undecidable is the condition of responsibility, then it must respond to the countless others, whose appeals for more justice, more freedom, and better laws *cannot wait*. Urgency and hesitation, right now and not yet, seem to be as strangely intertwined as the conditional and the unconditional, and, in fact, looking a bit farther back in the Derridean corpus, we can find this simultaneity of delay and responsibility foreshadowed in the quasi-concept of *différance*. As Derrida emphasizes at one point in response to yet another criticism of what we might call the "paralysis problem,"

> it is because there is this possibility of postponing that we can and we must make decisions. If there was [sic] no possibility of delay, there would be no urgency, either. *Différance*, therefore, is not opposed to ethics and politics, but is their condition: on the one hand, it is the condition of history, of process, strategy, delay, postponement, mediation, and on the other hand, because there is an absolute difference or an irreducible heterogeneity, there is the urge to act and respond immediately and to face political and ethical responsibilities.[48]

It is because the decision is undecidable and instantaneous, paralyzing and urgent, possible as impossible that Derrida places a "leap"—in which all knowledge is suspended—between preparation and decision. It is for this same reason that he appeals in *The Gift of Death* to Johannes Climacus's conviction that "the instant of decision is madness."[49] Yes, we must take pains to gather as much knowledge as humanly possible, but, in the absence of "universal" moral rules that might make our decisions for us, "a certain 'madness' *must* keep a lookout over every step, and finally watch over thinking, as reason does, too."[50] So a decision must be as reason-able as possible in order to be as "mad" as (im)possible. And once again our heads are swimming. We have already discussed the first, arguably less aporetic, part of this aporia: a decision must be carefully prepared before the undecidability that eventually (un)conditions decision can emerge. But how is one to go about discussing the second part—the leap into the unknown? Is it enough to say, "decision is madness" and end one's hypothetical chapter on decision? Or is there a way to begin to think *through* this madness? What is it that *takes place* in the instant of decision?

## Much Madness Is Divinest Sense
## (or, Who Comes After the Decision?)[51]

Perhaps the most profound impediment to pinning down the moment of decision conceptually is the problem of knowing just who or what it is that makes this mad leap. To be sure, it cannot be the transcendental subject of classical philosophy, for decision requires the suspension of everything that might secure subjectivity as such: substance, continuity, identity, essence, certainty, knowledge, autonomy, etc. In other words, the progression out to impossibility and undecidability exposes as fallacious any "subject" or "object" that might stabilize or guarantee the decision's outcome. In fact, the very persistence of a "subject of decision" would ruin the possibility of decision entirely, standing as a roadblock between possibility and impossibility, calculability and the incalculable. Or, as Derrida has argued, "at the risk of shocking, one could even say that a subject can never decide anything: a subject is even that to *which* a decision cannot come or happen."[52] So if there is no subject who makes a decision, who bears the responsibility for it? How is it that undecidability gives way to decision at all? Who or what would ensure and then claim this passage?

The question of what happens "between" undecidability and decision has been perhaps most systematically treated by Ernesto Laclau. Together with Chantal Mouffe, Laclau has been one of the few political theorists to think through the impact "deconstruction" might make, and, indeed, has already made, on political philosophy.[53] Interestingly enough, Laclau and Mouffe locate deconstruction's most significant contribution to the political arena in its emphasis on undecidability. Democracy, they maintain, is only itself as the tension, contestation, and negotiation between divergent viewpoints. To the extent that a democracy is democratic, then, it relies on something like deconstruction to keep its constitutive differences as different (and, with any luck, as transformative) as possible. Laclau thus argues that deconstruction has been, and will continue to be, indispensable for democratic political theory because it "widen[s] the field of undecidability."[54]

This, however, is where Laclau veers from the Derridean course, as it were, asserting that once deconstruction makes this crucial movement outward to undecidability, it ceases to be helpful to the democratic process. Much like Kearney and Ward, Laclau welcomes the destructive or destructuring operation of deconstruction (what in a Nancean register we might call unworking), but judges insufficient the simultaneous *con*structive operation that deconstruction presumes also to entail: "Deconstruction, in its first movement, has immensely enlarged the areas of structural undecidability, but what the second movement—the logic of the decision taken in an undecidable terrain—would consist of, is far from clear."[55] Laclau thus suggests a necessary (and, I would argue, "dangerous") supplement to deconstructive expansiveness: a certain contraction that would move from the destructured "field of undecidability" back to a single, concrete decision: from unworking back to the work. This supplement is what Laclau understands by "hegemony," that is, the consolidation and self-grounding of that which lacks any necessary identity to begin with. For Laclau, deconstruction unworks all essentiality, and then hegemony reposits it *as* (re-)*constructed*, so that "deconstruction and hegemony are the two essential dimensions of a single theoretico-practical operation."[56] So what, for Laclau, does hegemony hegemonize?

In an essay entitled "New Reflections on the Revolution of Our Time," Laclau sets forth the thesis that the space between undecidability and decision is filled by the self-positing *subject*.[57] Basing his ontology upon a particularly Lacanian strand of psychoanalysis, Laclau argues that, insofar as subjectivity is "founded" upon a constitutive lack, a subject must *make* itself itself in order to become anything at all. This self-fashioning, he states even more explicitly during a 1993 conference on "Deconstruction and Pragmatism," *is* the instant of the decision. If undecidability prevents the consolidation of everything that might secure subjectivity, then decision finally enables it, making the decision and the subject utterly coextensive: "This moment of decision as something left to itself and unable to provide its grounds through any system of rules transcending itself, is the moment of the subject."[58] Now if, at this point, we were to decide to go along with Laclau, there would be no more aporia of undecidability. We would be able to describe—or even diagram—the linear progression from undecidability to decision by way of hegemonic formation. We would thus remain true(ish) to what we have learned in different ways from Heidegger, Levinas, Derrida, and Nancy about the archaic inessentiality of things, but would also have a way to resolve this inessentiality into the autonomous (but contingent, imperfect, and made-not-begotten, so presumably acceptable from a post-Heideggerian perspective) subjects we need in order to assign responsibility somewhere. But would this do justice to the problem of decision?

For Laclau, the hegemonic subject does not just appear out of nowhere, or even out of undecidability itself. Rather, it forms itself in the *transition* "*between*" undecidability and the decision, making itself a subject (and thus hauling itself out of its own impossibility) by first *pretending to be a subject*: "the impossibility of a free, substantial subject, of a consciousness identical to itself which is the *causa sui*, does not eliminate its need, but just relocates the chooser in the aporetical situation of having to act as if he were a subject, without being endowed with any of the means of a fully fledged subjectivity."[59] Upon hearing this, one's Nancean ears might sharpen and one might recall that "acting as if" one were a subject is tantamount to "being" a subject, insofar as the myth of subjectivity has *always* been a myth. Moreover, it is precisely insofar as such attempted self-grounding denies freedom, inessentiality, and relationality that it becomes "wickedness," ultimately exalting itself above everything else in the world. And indeed, as one might suspect, Laclau's account of the subject's playing make-believe in the absence of the *causa sui* ultimately amounts to the subject's playing the role of the Almighty himself: "To take a decision is like impersonating God. It is like asserting that one does not have the means of being God, and one has, however, to proceed as if one were Him [*sic*]."[60] According to this logic, much madness quite flat-footedly renders sense divine. In Laclau's "aporetical situation," a subject acts as though he were secure, which means he effectively acts as though he were God. But, one might interject, there is nothing aporetical about the "situation" of feigning existential security. It just takes an average, everyday denial of groundlessness and uncertainty—perhaps the most commonplace comportment in the world—for a contingent, heteronomous existent to pretend it is a subject. And there is certainly nothing new about an insecure person playing God. In short, if the structure of decision still relies upon the human subject, if the subject's impossibility "does not eliminate its need," then there is no significant difference between Laclau's "deconstructive" hegemony and good old hegemonic hegemony: according to both accounts, a self-constituted subject decides.

It is therefore surprising that, in a response to Laclau's and a number of other scholars' papers on the question of deconstruction's relation to pragmatism, Derrida testifies (perhaps as a counterbalance to his nearly complete *dis*agreement with Richard Rorty), "I am completely in agreement with everything that Ernesto Laclau has said on the question of hegemony and power."[61] Without wanting to make too much out of an impromptu reflection at an academic conference, it does seem important to pause here before this seemingly un-Derridean profession of "complete agreement" and, at the very least, to refrain from considering Laclau's thesis simply "refuted" by the foregoing analysis. Derrida expresses his agreement with Laclau's opening of an aboriginal groundlessness and then draws it from a Lacanian to a Levinasian register by saying that "it becomes necessary to stabilize because stability is not natural . . . it is because *there is* chaos that *there is* a need for stability."[62] So *il y a du chaos*; most primordially, there is the undecidable *there is*. This Levinasian invocation can be heard again a moment later, when Derrida refers to "this chaos and instability, which is fundamental."[63] It seems particularly unlikely, then, that Derrida would endorse Laclau's lack-denying hegemonic subject, so subtly substituted here for Levinas's il y a–denying hypostatic subject. And, indeed, Derrida goes on to compromise his "complete agreement" with Laclau when the question of the subject arises, maintaining that "the question here is whether it is through the decision that one becomes a subject who decides something." Sounding far more like "himself," Derrida reminds his audience that, "with regard to the subject and the object, there will never be a decision."[64] And yet, something about Laclau's theory of hegemony did provoke Derrida's momentary assent—and this something also conjured Levinas. Could it be that the sort of "stabilization" to which Derrida would grant his signature might resemble, as opposed to Laclau's hegemonic subject or the "early" Levinasian hypostasis it echoes, something like the "late" Levinasian sub-ject of radical passivity? Could it be the perpetually accused *moi* that takes place in the madness of the instant of decision?

Such a position would find support in the work of Simon Critchley, who, like Laclau, believes that deconstruction on its own ultimately falls short of the decision it thematizes. In a paper delivered at the same conference on pragmatism, Critchley writes, "Derrida insists that judgements have to be made and decisions have to be taken, provided it is understood that to be responsible they must pass through an experience of the undecidable. But my *critical* question to Derrida would be: *what* decisions are taken, *which* judgements are made?"[65] We are back, then, to the problem we have been considering for some time now: exactly *how* does undecidability give way to decision? For Laclau, this mad passage relies on the subjective pretensions of one who is not, technically speaking, a subject. And, to a certain extent, as he will argue in an essay on *Specters of Marx*, Critchley agrees with Laclau's supplementation of deconstruction with a theory of hegemony.[66] But the "subject" that emerges at the moment of decision for Critchley differs from Laclau's paper tiger god by virtue of its infinite responsibility to and for the other who always already interrupts its autonomy—whether genuine or pretended. Along this line of thought, my boundless responsibility for the inappropriable and singular other holds "me" hostage to the other who interrupts me *essentially*; that is, who holds me in undecidability. This condition will complicate itself exponentially in *The Gift of Death*, where Derrida reflects upon the irreconcilable conflict between any one obligation and my boundless responsibility for every *other* inappropriable and singular other. But in any event, from this condition of being bound to those who make me me as not-me, "I" obviously cannot be the one who makes a decision, for I am infinitely not-"I." The decider can therefore only be the other to whom I am infinitely sub-jected: as Derrida says in an essay on Levinas, the one who decides is "the other in me."[67]

According to this view, one might say that something is hegemonized over against the il y a at the moment of decision, but that it is "the other" rather than the "self." If undecidability divests the "self" of itself, then the decision goes on not to reinscribe the self-as-fictional-construct (*pace* Laclau), but rather to install the *other* at the very core of anything that might be called a self, making "me" utterly responsible for the decision the other makes—in me. Something like Levinas's "passivity more passive still than any receptivity"[68] would thus characterize the instant of decision. Its "madness" would refer to the position into which "I" am thrown at the moment of decision: responsible for that which "I" could not have decided. This is the way, at the very least, that this "madness" takes shape in *The Politics of Friendship* (1994), particularly when Derrida wonders rhetorically whether a "passive" decision might not invalidate ethics and politics entirely, precisely by divesting

philosophy of the "free," autonomous self who believes he has made a decision on his own:

> But should one imagine, for all that, a "passive" decision, as it were, without free-
> dom, without that freedom? Without that activity, and without the passivity that is
> mated to it? But not, for all that, without responsibility? Would one have to show
> hospitality to be the impossible itself—that is, to what the *good sense of all phi-
> losophy* can only exclude as madness or nonsense: *a passive decision,* an originarily
> affected decision? Such an undesirable guest . . . signifies in me the other who
> decides and rends. The passive decision, condition of the event, is always in me,
> structurally, another event, a rending decision as the decision of the other. Of the
> absolutely other in me, the other as the absolute that decides in me. Absolutely
> singular in principle, according to its most traditional concept, the decision is not
> always exceptional, *it makes an exception for/of me.* In me, I decide, I make up my
> mind in all sovereignty—this would mean: the other than myself, the me as other
> and other than myself, *he makes or I make* an exception of the same. This normal
> exception, the supposed norm of all decision, exonerates from no responsibility.
> Responsible for myself before the other, I am first of all and also *responsible for the
> other before the other.* This heteronomy, which is undoubtedly rebellious against the
> decisionist conception of sovereignty or the exception (Schmitt), does not contra-
> dict; it opens autonomy on to itself, it is a figure of its heartbeat.[69]

Tracking the Levinasian self from hypostatic ontology to *Otherwise Than
Being* in chapter 2, it was established that even the supposedly unselfed self
of "extreme passivity" eventually and inexorably slides into "extreme mastery."
Just as it puts an end to the "absurd rumbling of the *il y a*," the Levinasian
*moi* places itself into every other's place, infinitely reconsolidating itself as
the very subject whose consolidation the "other" had, supposedly, infinitely
obstructed. This argument accounts for a good deal of the sympathy between,
for example, Critchley's appeal to the Levinasian sub-ject of infinite substitution and Laclau's appeal to a "subject" of infinite sovereignty. They are equal
and opposite guarantors of the inscrutable passage between undecidability
and decision: they are both silencers of the il y a. In the passage just cited,
Derrida seems to be siding with Critchley's half of this equation, insofar as
he insists that, if there is a decision, it is the *other* who makes it. If this were
the case, of course, Derrida would be siding with Laclau as well, inasmuch
as both the "self" and the "other" take shape in Laclau and Levinas-Critchley
respectively as twinned, self-identical guardrails against excessive undecidability. And, were this the case, one would be able to proclaim that because
(as he has said elsewhere) Derrida "agrees completely" with Emmanuel Levinas,[70] he does indeed, by virtue of the transitive property, agree completely
with Ernesto Laclau. But could it be that this passage in *Politics* signals a

subtle refusal of both of these solutions? And could this refusal have something to do with these solutions' being *solutions* in the first place?

Even in his most "other"-oriented accounts of the instant of decision, Derrida almost never names an identifiable, self-identical other whose first letter
ought to be capitalized. He speaks, rather, of an other "in me"; that is, an
"other" who would be *just as divested and interrupted as the "self" it divests and
interrupts.* This strange "other" would not be other in his own right, but rather
only *in,* through, and in spite of its inherence in a self (that is, an other) that
is not itself in its own right, precisely by virtue of said inherence. As Sylviane
Agacinski has phrased it, "the other is neither [a] wholly-other nor [a] similar
self who would hold himself over there, far from me, elsewhere. It is already
that which distances me from myself and forbids all self-sufficiency."[71] The
moment of decision would perform this disruption of self-sufficiency: "self"
and "other" would be prevented in decision's madness from all reification,
held between and through one another by an unconditional hospitality—that
is, hospitality toward the kind of "other" who neither stays in his own place
nor lets me stay in mine. If this is a justifiable reading of Derrida's "me as
other and other than myself" then, contra Laclau and Critchley-Levinas, I
would insist that there is neither a self *nor* an other who might smooth the
transition from undecidability to decision. On the contrary, both of these
terms are as entangled and unstable at the moment of decision as they are
in the agony of undecidability. The only difference between them is that
the decision issues in *responsibility:* the decision makes the utterly singular,
utterly mixed-up exception that "I" am, *responsible* for the decision I both
made and did not make; that is, the decision that made me the one in whose
name a decision was made in the name of the other in me-as-not-me. And
yet, could one not also say that there is a certain responsibility adhering to
undecidability as well? "Before" the decision? In the throes of the undecidable, am I-as-not-I not responsible for making a decision—indeed, in as swift
and informed a manner as humanly possible? Moreover, is there not a certain
responsibility that provokes me to face up to and "freeze" before the undecidable, in the first place, rather than simply to march in time to the sure
rhythms of calculation? Responsibility's inherence in each of the "stages" of
the decision means that, once again, it is impossible to map the decision on
to stages at all. In fact, every sure distinction examined so far between the
undecidable and decision has flown from us: first the self-creation of the
Subject, then the interruption of the Other, and now the moment of responsibility's inauguration. If, then, there is anything more to be said about the
"madness" of the instant of decision (if, that is, one is not simply exhausted
and derailed by so much impossibility), then this thought experiment will
have to abandon the effort to erect a sturdy ontological bridge "between"
undecidability and the decision. That said, it should not simply abandon the

conviction that something or some*one takes place* at the moment of decision; indeed, Critchley and Laclau are both right to suggest that the crucial question with respect to the decision is "Qu'est ce qui se passe?" It just might be that we are going to have to complicate our understanding of this *qui* and of this *passage*.

### How to Avoid the Subject (or, "That's Not My Hedgehog!")

As is well known, Derrida's work resists setting forth theories of any sort, looking instead to unearth the conditions of possibility and impossibility of propositional logic itself.[72] Perhaps the most striking avoidance of all has been Derrida's stubborn refusal to set forth any sort of theory of "the subject" or even of the "who" who "comes after the subject." There seem to be two main reasons for this. First, as Derrida insists as justification for his (non-)response to Jean-Luc Nancy, even the question of "who comes after the subject? . . . implies that for a certain philosophical opinion today, in its most visible configuration, something named 'subject' can be identified, as its alleged passing might also be identified in certain identifiable thoughts or discourses. This 'opinion' is confused."[73] The term *subject,* Derrida finally goes on to say, means vastly different things for different thinkers, and in different contexts, and has not even persisted uninterrupted through the course of modern Western philosophy.[74] Second and more problematically, Derrida has been attuned to the tirelessly reappropriative power of anthropocentrism ever since his earliest work on Hegel, Husserl, and Heidegger, in whose oeuvres, their best intention(alitie)s aside, something like "the human subject" inevitably returns: "phenomenology is the *relève* of anthropology. It is *no longer,* but it is *still* a science of man."[75] Or, as Derrida says in his discussion of Heidegger on the question of the postsubjective *qui*, "in spite of everything it opens up and encourages us to think, to question, and to redistribute, *Dasein* still occupies a place analogous to that of the transcendental subject."[76] So if Derrida avoids setting forth his "own" theory of Dasein, or of the *moi*, or even of the singular, heteronomous existent, it is most likely because he has witnessed and, in many cases, provoked the collapse of most such figures back into the very subject-objective frameworks they aim to unsettle.

That said, it is not the case that Derrida never says *anything* about the "who" that might elude the consolidating grasp of the transcendental subject. He does seem to be alluding to some unelaborated understanding of this "who" in the passage on decision and alterity from *Politics of Friendship* quoted at length above: "I" am only "sovereign" as radically heteronomous. In fact, a difference-in-identity-in-difference similar to this "me as other and other than myself" had already turned up in the opening pages of *The Other*

*Heading* (1991), in which Derrida offers an utterly uncharacteristic account of "all identity or all identification." Here he argues that identity always recapitulates the logic of culture itself, and that, contrary to what one might ordinarily think, "What is proper to a culture is not to be identical to itself. Not to not have an identity, but not to be able to identify itself, to be able to say 'me' or 'we'; to be able to take the form of a subject only in the non-identity to itself or, if you prefer, only in the difference *with itself*."[77] Referring to this text three years later at a discussion at Villanova University, Derrida makes explicit the ethical significance of this identity as nonself-identity: "it is a duty, an ethical and political duty, to take into account this impossibility of being one with oneself. It is because I am not one with myself that I can speak with the other and address the other. That is not a way of avoiding responsibility. On the contrary, it is the only way for me to take responsibility and to make decisions."[78] This responsibility of and for not-being-one-with-oneself is perhaps most compellingly articulated in *Specters of Marx* (1993), whose ethic of learning to welcome and to "live *with* ghosts" depends upon an understanding of difference-in-identity articulated as being-as-haunted: "Ego = ghost. Therefore 'I am' would mean 'I am haunted': I am haunted by myself who am (haunted by myself who am haunted by myself who am . . . and so forth)."[79] This ghostly ego is not only haunted by itself, but also by its ancestors, its dead friends and enemies, its living friends and enemies, and by the literally countless specters of "the heritage" that make it what it "is": both more and less than "itself." There are, then, brief moments during which something like a "who," resistant to all simple or self-identical "selfhood" and "otherness," is briefly sketched in Derrida's work as something like a self-in-other-in-self. What we continue to seek, to refocus what has admittedly been a rather tortuous journey so far, is a sustained treatment of such a *qui* as the one *qui passe* at the instant of decision, in order to understand a bit more about this passage itself and, ultimately, its relation to concrete ethicopolitical engagement.

The first place one might look for a (perhaps inadvertent) figure of decision's "who" is in a short piece entitled "Che cos'è la poesia?" that Derrida wrote for the Italian journal *Poesia* in 1988. In this strange little response, Derrida offers—dare we say "proposes"?—as an emblem of the poem the figure of a hedgehog (*hérisson* in French, *istrice* in Italian) thrown into the middle of a highway. The poem, frozen and blinded like a hedgehog in the headlights, "hears but does not see death coming."[80] All alone in the middle of the road, facing oncoming cars and trucks, the poem *is* as sheer response to whatever comes its way. What is interesting about Derrida's description of this endangered hedgehog, though, is that it is not simply receptive, rather, it is active in its very passivity, wounding in its very vulnerability, for it only exposes itself by means of the act of violence by which it seeks to defend itself: "Rolled up in a ball, prickly with spines, vulnerable and dangerous, calculating and ill-adapted (because it makes itself into a ball, sensing the danger on the autoroute, it exposes itself to an accident). No poem without accident, no poem that does not open itself like a wound, but no poem that is not also just a wounding."[81] Insofar as the poem is merely an open, wounding wound, Derrida emphasizes that it is not a *work*: even rolled up into itself, the hedgehog is not an entity that would be the object of any *poeisis*, for it never coincides with itself. With this poematic (as distinct from poetic) hedgehog, there is simply "nothing to be done (*poiesis*), neither 'pure poetry,' nor pure rhetoric, nor *reine Sprache*, nor 'setting-forth-of-the-truth-in-the-work.' Just this contamination, at this crossroads, this accident here."[82] In this occasional text, at least, this accidental contamination is figured as an active-passive-wounding-wounded *response* to whatever it is that comes toward it on the highway. What account can be derived from this accident scene of the one who decides to respond?

In an article on the problem of responsibility in Derrida and Kierkegaard, David Goicoechea describes Derrida's notion of undecidability almost exclusively by means of the poematic hedgehog. Goicoechea narrates the journey of the hedgehog as a kind of trek up Mount Moriah, saying that the hedgehog is *called* to cross the road (in fact, Derrida's hedgehog is *thrown* . . . ), steps out into the middle of it, stops, rolls up into a ball, and either does or does not get flattened by oncoming traffic. For Goicoechea, the decision takes place the moment the hedgehog freezes and the truck either hits it or does not hit it. This is where he begins to read Kierkegaard's knight through Derrida's hedgehog: the hesitation is the "leap of the decision" itself.[83] We thus have in this little hedgehog a model for all human ethicopolitical becoming: "the hedgehog in her rolled-up interiority is an image of the responsible person."[84] A few things should be pointed out here, and I will proceed through them quickly by moving backward through this brief summary of Goicoechea's summary of Derrida. First, Derrida never goes so far as to personify the poematic hedgehog. It could, and will, be argued that a certain anthropocentrism, subjectivism, or indeed even an un- , pre- , or postsubjective "who" can be said to be hiding under the quills of this tropelet, but such a claim is in no way self-evident. Second, the reason this hedgehog should be at least temporarily resistant to any anthropic appropriation is precisely her resistance to, or at the very least her complication of, the "rolled up interiority" to which Goicoechea refers. According to Derrida's analysis, the sort of "rolling up" that this hedgehog does advertises its extreme vulnerability *at the same time* that it makes the whole exposed hedgehog into a weapon. Therefore, any "interiority" to which it might lay claim would be a kind of inside-outness that both makes it violent and leaves it open to violence. From Goicoechea's account, however, we get an exceedingly one-sided, hyper-Levinasian hedgehog, who is called by the other, is stopped by the other, and is either killed or spared by the other. Through every "stage" of the decision (and it is still not clear what such stages might look like), Goicoechea's hedgehog as the "image of the responsible person" remains completely passive and self-identical, mirroring the Other's own active self-identity. So if the instant of decision can in fact be encapsulated in the hedgehog's freezing in the middle of the road in front of an oncoming car—and nothing is less certain—then the act of "freezing" itself would be, somehow, an *act*. The response would take shape as a figure of exposure and danger, activity and passivity, and interiority as exteriority.

For all that, however, could it not be said that the situation of this figure—either it is killed or it isn't—looks more like a kind of fatalism than undecidability? As though the response to the question Che cos'è la responsibilità? might at any moment break out into a rousing chorus of "Que Será Será"? Moreover, how close does this hedgehog come to resembling the self-in-other-in-self Derrida has sporadically sketched in connection to the instant of decision? Does the exposure and vulnerability of the one who stops in the middle of the road, and who lets what is coming come, amount to that self's inherent otherness? In other words, can this particular respondent be taken as an index of a haunted, nonself-identical otherness that inhabits the very selfhood of the nonself-identical-self? Or might this little spiky one, who responds to the death she hears but cannot see, incarnate something more akin to the resurrected subject of phenomenology: to Dasein without Mitsein? And, above all, is it really fair to ask a *hedgehog* to bear the metonymic burden of all this responsibility?

Derrida himself expresses this last concern in an interview given two years later, saying it is not quite fair to "stuff polysemic vitamins down the throat of a humble little mammal" (right before going on to do so anyway).[85] In a rare act of backpedaling, Derrida is primarily concerned in this particular conversation to distinguish "his" poematic hedgehog from two German *poetic* hedgehogs (*Igel*). The first of these, which hovered over the reading of unworking offered in chapter 3, has to do with the Romantic fragment as interpreted by Philippe Lacoue-Labarthe and Jean-Luc Nancy in *The Literary Absolute*.[86] I refer the reader to this remarkable text for a lengthier exposition of this figure, but, briefly, early German Romanticism can be said to have been launched with Friedrich Schlegel's characterization in *Fragment 206* of the fragment itself, "the romantic genre *par excellence*."[87] Schlegel writes, "A fragment, like a small work of art, has to be entirely isolated from the surrounding world and be complete in itself [clos sur lui-même] like a hedgehog."[88] Lacoue-Labarthe and Nancy proceed throughout the rest of their exposition to account for romanticism's annunciation of idealism by virtue of the Fragment's and the System's shared pretensions at self-generation and self-enclosure, both of which are exemplified in the very "fragmentary totality" of "the logic of the hedgehog."[89] According to a certain hologrammatology that takes shape through the course of their analysis, this little tyrant, the totalizing fragment, comes to recapitulate the logic not only of the work of art but also of the "putting-into-work of the work,"[90] which is to say the romantic artist himself. For Schlegel, the artist was the paradigmatic Subject; the absolute image of the divine who, like the hedgehog closed in on himself, "has his center in himself."[91] Ultimately, then, "the romantic Fragment conclusively confirms and installs the figure of the artist as Author and Creator."[92]

Unsurprisingly, Derrida becomes very anxious indeed upon realizing he has unintentionally conjured such a hedgehog. While he does not elaborate the full significance of Schlegel's totalizing fragment in the "*Istrice* 2" interview, he says from the outset that he had most certainly not written "Che cos'è la poesia?" with this particular hedgehog in mind. Nor had he recalled at the time the Grimms' *Igel* who appears toward the end of Heidegger's *Identity and Difference*—the omnipresent one who springs forth from each bend in the road to tell the Hare who can't win, "I'm already here [Ich bünn all hier]!" These two inadvertently invoked hedgehogs, Derrida says, "now come back like ghosts."[93] And while it seems, in accordance with the haunto-ethic he sketches in *Specters of Marx*, that Derrida might try to be as hospitable as possible to these ghostly creatures, his engagement with them takes the form of nothing short of vehement disavowal: "these two hedgehogs don't have much relation to 'mine'; they don't belong to the same family, the same species, or the same genre, even though this non-relation says something about a deep genealogical affinity, but in antagonism, in counter-genealogy." And even this reluctantly conceded "deep genealogical affinity" is denied a moment later, when Derrida maintains that *his* hedgehog "doesn't have the same genealogy [as Schlegel's and Heidegger's]. It doesn't belong to the species or the genre, to the generality of the *gens* 'hedgehog.'"[94]

The genealogical differences upon which Derrida insists can be listed as follows: first, Derrida's hedgehog has nothing to do with the work, the work of art, or the putting-into-work of the work of art. Poematic rather than poetic, "Derrida's" hedgehog is "profoundly estranged" from everything that might be called a *work* at all ("*Istrice* 2," 312/303). Second, "his" hedgehog can never be said to be complete or closed in on itself because, once again, it exposes itself in the act of rolling into a ball. It cannot be classed with romanticism's "fragmentary totality" because "it has no relation to itself—that is, no totalizing individuality—that does not expose it even more to death and to being-torn-apart" (312/303). Third, precisely because it falls infinitely short of the immediate, complete, or closed relation to itself that would make it a work, this particular hedgehog is not a subject, much less an artist, much less a god (who, like Grimm's *Igel*, would always already be "(t)here"): "The *istrice* that came to me can barely say '*Ich*,' and certainly not '*bünn*,' still less '*hier*' and '*da*'" (314/304). And, to divorce his poematic pet as fully as possible from Schlegel's self-centered and infinitely exalted sovereign, Derrida emphasizes as frequently as he can that his hedgehog is nothing but an *accident*—that it is "barely a hedgehog" at all (314/304). He recognizes that this point of distinction does not quite deliver him from the clutches of Heidegger, who infamously *aufhebung*ed even the most accidental occurrence—even, toward the end of his life, his "greatest stupidity"—into a Sending of Being. Thus, Derrida doggedly insists that *his* accident is different from that of Heidegger, whose "propensity to magnify the disastrous accident is foreign to what I called the humility of the poematic hedgehog: low, very low, close to the earth, humble (*humilis*)" (319/309). But even this distinction won't last him very long; Derrida knows better than anyone how easily the lowest, precisely by being the *most low*, can be exalted as highest—how "extreme passivity" tends to assert itself as "extreme mastery."

At this point, there is an interruption in the interview—the first of two. Could it be that running after this hedgehog has exhausted even the infamously inexhaustible Jacques Derrida? Or could it be that some sort of leap takes place in this break? Either way, when the conversation resumes and Derrida is asked to return to the question of Heidegger's hedgehog in relation to his "own," he pulls a momentary Bartleby: "I would rather not re-semanticize this letter" (321/311). Then, immediately upon expressing his reluctance to force-feed his little hedgehog, Derrida goes on to do what he would prefer not to, and sets forth—very briefly, with no fanfare and no lengthy explanation— what a reader unaware of Derrida's persistent resistance to such things might go so far as to call a theory of the subject. At the very least—and Derrida clearly wants to establish "his" hedgehog as the least of all—we seem to be able to glimpse in sporadic instants here the outline of a kind of ghostly Derridean "who."

The most striking difference between the conversations before and after the interruption is that, after the break, Derrida finally admits that his hedgehog *does* have *something* to do with the one who is called to responsibility. He goes on to distinguish this particular respondent quite rigorously from the Dasein that lives in response to the call as being-toward-death, but without recourse to the vehement denials that compose the first half of the interview. As was mentioned earlier, one of Derrida's greatest frustrations with Heidegger is that, for all the work the existential analysis does to unravel the fabric of the self-identical, *human* self, Dasein ultimately capitulates to a more or less unreconstructed anthropocentric subjectivism. In spite of itself, being-toward-death installs the self as exclusively human and self-identical: complete as Schlegel's fragment. And of course, that which is complete is not *toward*-death at all; it is just *dead*. Thus Heidegger's foreclosure of the animal is at the same time a foreclosure of living itself: "In Heidegger, the being-toward-death, as strange as this may seem, is not the being of a living creature. Death does not happen to a living creature. . . . The *Dasein* is not an animal, not even, essentially, an *animal rationale* or a *zoon logon ekhon*." It is at this point that Derrida—very subtly, in the negligible middle of a long answer to a long question about a stupid *hedgehog*—offers his "own" alternative to the cult of the (dead, strictly human) subject: "The catachresis of the *hérisson*, in the very aleatoriness of the letter and of its name for me, is the figure of a being-toward-death *as living creature*, which is, it seems to me, wholly unacceptable to Heidegger's dominant discourse" (321–22/311).[95] So there we have it: "Derrida's" hedgehog, however metaphorically overburdened, is a transvalued Dasein. And a transvalued Dasein in its "authentic" mode at that, insofar as the Dasein that comports itself toward death *is* as *response*. The hedgehog therefore is indeed some sort of figure of responsibility. The difficulty with which Derrida leaves us, however, is this hedgehog's (utterly constitutive) propensity toward "being run over by a great discourse that it cannot/does not resist" (322/312). As Derrida himself has demonstrated through the course of this interview, it is excruciatingly difficult to set forth any sort of "who" who would not be immediately flattened (that is, redeemed, sublated) by the philosophical MACK trucks of Heidegger, Hegel, Schlegel, humanism, or anthropology, to name a few: "it's true, it is truth itself, that one can always bring this hedgehog back into the Heideggerian logic. As we have already seen, this can always happen to it as one of its accidents. As its loss. Its salvation is its loss" (335/325).

One last point before letting go of the poor little hedgehog I too have been pursuing in the manner of some hybrid SUV (well-intentioned but hardly harmless). The most important trait of Derrida's admittedly "catachrestic" hedgehog—the trait upon which he insists right until the end—is its "lowliness," that is to say, its vulnerability; its exposure; its inability to gather itself into some prickly bundle of sovereignty. But just as the hedgehog's vulnerability is also an aggression, just as its exposure is also a defense, Derrida realizes that its "lowliness" could be said to entail some sort of masterful height, setting in motion the dialectical work through which the hedgehog would once more be he(d)gemonized into something like Schlegel's self-effecting work of art or, we might add, something like Laclau's make-believe God. Derrida thus wonders whether it might be possible to speak of "a low without opposition to height. Is that possible? Is it still a 'here-below,' but this time a here-below without beyond? No, it must be something else. A low that would rise up—in order to fall, then fall again—against the background of the All-High or the Beyond, such a low would never be very low, an all-low, absolutely low" (335/325). The "something else" that is required in order to think through the situation of the decision's *qui* will thus be another spatiotemporal configuration from the one to which we are accustomed. It will have to refrain from positing a "high" that stands over the hedgehog's "low" or an "elsewhere, then" that stands against its "here, now" or, as we will continue to argue, even an "other" that stands against its "self," for (if deconstruction has taught us anything, it is this) all these onto-temporo-spatial overs and againsts can only ultimately provoke the exalted term to subsume the humble one. Just as sovereignty and closure-in-itself have managed to inscribe themselves even on the unsuspecting body of a lowly hedgehog.

For if there is no such thing as a "who" who does not immediately roll up into a subject, then there is no undecidability, and the decision is lost.

### Undecidability, Take Three: "Think Here of Kierkegaard"[96]

Of course, the decision is not lost just because the hedgehog is lost—if in fact the hedgehog is lost. It may very well be that the poematic hedgehog is simply not the most appropriate representative of the "who" who decides— if such a who can even be represented—and that the manner in which the hedgehog freezes in front of a car, which either hits it or does not, is simply not the most helpful way to think about the "how" of decision's *passage*. Having traveled apiece with the Derridean *hérisson*, however, we have reached a far better vantage point from which to examine these questions. For we have seen that even Derrida's most elaborate, hyperdetermined strategies of reading, of disavowing, of unsaying, and of re-casting "his" hedgehog all fall short of the decision because of a lingering fatalism, subjectivism, and otherworldiness. These three markers of distance will provide the orientation for the rest of our exploration.

First, as I have suggested, the hedgehog's position, however resolutely attuned she may remain toward the death she can hear but not see, seems to be more one of dumb luck than of active undecidability. The cars and trucks either hit her or they do not. There is uncertainty here, to be sure, but there are no conflicting obligations, no irreconcilable ethical demands. To think the "who" of the decision, thinking must meet him or her not just in any crisis, not just in powerlessness, but in a crisis of *undecidability*. Second, whether it be made at the moment of the hedgehog's hesitation or at the moment of the truck's hitting or missing it, the decision in this scenario seems to be made by a self-sufficient self or other, constituted as such before the moment of decision. What we are seeking, once again, is the *qui* that emerges in and through the instant itself—neither self nor other, but self-as-not-self or self-as/in-other-as/in-self or self-as-haunted-by-itself-as-not-itself, in short, being-toward-death as radically coimplicated with being-with. (I suppose we might spend some time considering the "withness" of self and other at the moment of violent impact on the road between mammal and machine, but although this might do some work to unsettle the "integrity" of the self-in-response, such a reflection would doubtless produce a far too literally "shattered self" for these purposes. . . . But I really must leave this poor little hedgehog alone . . . ). Finally, the positioning of the responsible one whose shadow we are chasing must be refractory to any mythically posited "beyond." The "who" must take place in a *here that is not opposed to a there*—a now not opposed to a then, whether past or futural. Let us begin with the first of these three conditions and hope the others might unfold from it. Let us try to find a scene of genuine undecidability and see whether it might produce a "who" and a "where" that would not immediately cancel the decision.

In "Dialanguages," yet another interview that finds its way to the question of undecidability, one of Derrida's interlocutors explicitly connects the first two of the three concerns elaborated above, asking Derrida whether it is the case that "indecision" entails a necessary division "within oneself, or between the self and the other in the self, or between self and the other outside the self,"[97] and whether this division compromises responsibility. Derrida responds by reiterating once more that "indecision," which he prefers to call undecidability, would not obstruct the decision, but would make decision possible (by making it impossible) in the first place. And, yes, he confesses, such undecidability entails a profound divisibility, but

> it is from the moment one surrenders to the necessity of divisibility and the undecidable that the question of decision can be posed; and the question of knowing what deciding, affirming—which is to say, also deciding—mean. A decision that would be taken otherwise than on the border of this undecidable would not be a decision. Thus the gravest decision—the Wager, the Sacrifice of Isaac—the great decisions that must be taken and must be affirmed are taken and affirmed in this relation to the undecidable itself; at the very moment in which they are no longer possible, they become possible. These are the only decisions possible: impossible ones. Think here of Kierkegaard. The only decision possible is the impossible decision.[98]

Derrida then goes on to illustrate with a number of brief examples the sort of existential division that takes place in the moment of decision, framing them with a suggestion neither he nor any of his various commentators has yet set forth concerning the decision. The decision, Derrida ventures here, "is decided . . . at the moment the great symptom appears." What is this great symptom? Undecidability. "Someone says, 'I don't know if I am going to do this or that, I will never manage to decide if it is better to do this or that.' *This scene betrays decision.*"[99] Let us pause for a moment here.

In this chapter's initial explorations of the aporia of decision, a number of scholars (Kearney, Laclau, Critchley) were shown to supplement a "strictly" Derridean undecidability with something else ("an ethics of judgement," hegemony, substitution) in order to account for the transition or *passage* between undecidability and the decision. Each of them, in other words, decides to provide a second, con-structive movement as a counterbalance to deconstruction's first, de-structive movement. I have argued that, in one way or another, each of these proposed guarantors of the decision relies on an ultimately self-identical subject of responsibility (whether it be the s/Self or the o/Other)—precisely the kind that Derrida insists is inimical to decision: "the decision is barred when there is something like a transcendental subject."[100] Could it be that there is a necessary connection between the desire to pin down the transition from indecision to decision and the impulse to reinscribe some version of the transcendental subject? If so, then the only hope one would have of avoiding the subject would be to refrain from trying to certify this transition—or, perhaps, even from separating undecidability from the decision at all. For, in saying that the decision "is decided . . . at the moment the great symptom appears," Derrida does seem to recommend that those who attempt to think the decision think it *as indecision itself*. Rather than trying to reign in undecidability, then, perhaps thinking should progress all the way out to it *and without theorizing a way to come back*, for, according to Derrida at least, the arrival of the "great symptom" would mark the arrival of the decision itself: its arrival as its "betrayal." If we were to attempt to think along such lines, then perhaps it would become even clearer that the self, like the other it mirrors, cannot be consolidated, hegemonized, hypostasized, or worked into a work of art. Perhaps the self-in-decision would, to the contrary, be "betrayed," and even in a certain sense frozen, *transit*, perpetually unable to close in on itself dialectically. Let us now return to the transcript of "Dialanguages."

Derrida works with two striking examples in response to the interviewer's question about undecidability: the Abraham of Genesis 22 who is called to kill the son he loves beyond measure and a far less lofty, hypothetical person "who says: don't take my picture; and then one has the picture of someone who puts his hand in front of his face and says: don't take my picture. It is the truest photograph."[101] Confirming his barely noticeable suggestion a moment ago that decision might occur at the moment of deepest undecidability—and it should be noted that undecidability has, up until now, been paired with divisibility—Derrida goes on to explain the coextensiveness of *decision* and division:

> To remain undecided means to turn oneself over to the decision of the other. . . .
> Indecision, from this point of view, is in fact being unable to decide as a free subject,

"me," free consciousness, and thus to be paralyzed, but first of all because one turns the decision over to the other: what has to be decided comes back, belongs to the other. In the case of Abraham, it is effectively God who decides. That doesn't mean that Abraham does nothing; he does everything that has to be done, but he knows in a certain sense that he is obeying the Other; it is the Other who will decide what "come" means; that is where the response is.[102]

The question, then, is, does this account of decision-in-indecision come any closer to thinking the madness of the instant than the hedgehog on the highway? From the outset, it seems it might not, for even if both Abraham and the camera-shy John Doe are both divided and interrupted at the moment of decision, the o/Other who interrupts them seems to remain fairly intact, preserving his own subjective integrity from the other side of the camera or of the Ontological Distinction, as the case may be. In the terms of the question to which these examples respond, they may account for the division "within oneself," but they do not seem to thematize the division of the other within the very self it divides. That said, the ontological status or nonstatus of the selves mentioned in this brief interview is far from clear; it may well be that a snapshot of the decision has been taken here, but it is impossible to tell for certain. Luckily, Derrida meditates on one of these figures in a text this chapter has already explored at some length. And here the reader may breathe a sigh of relief to know I shall not be pursuing the person who says "don't take my picture" down any existential autoroute. Rather, let us climb a mountain with a madman. Following Derrida's suggestion to those of us who would think decision, let us try to think here of Kierkegaard, to think here of Abraham.

As we saw in the beginning of this investigation of decision in Derrida, the first half of *The Gift of Death* is a reflection of the irresponsibility at the heart of responsibility, illuminating the extent to which modern ethics, philosophy, and religion are all haunted by the orgiastic/demonic/thaumaturgic traditions they repress. The second half of this book is a Levinas-inflected meditation on Kierkegaard's *Fear and Trembling*, itself a meditation on Genesis 22:1–18: the *akedah* or *korban* of Isaac,[103] which exemplifies for Derrida the crisis of undecidability. Abraham's "ethical" duty to his son and his "religious" obligation to God conflict so thoroughly that there can be no way of resolving the two. Nor can there be any hope of calculating the relative merits and demerits of defying one's god on the one hand and killing one's son on the other. Kierkegaard's pseudonym Johannes de Silentio names this ordeal of undecidability "the teleological suspension of the ethical." Called by God to sacrifice the son he loves absolutely, Abraham is thrown into the absurd position of being tempted *by the ethical*—tempted to do what (ethically speaking) he is *supposed to do*.[104] For his part, Derrida calls this the "aporia of responsibility": a "paradoxical contradiction between responsibility *in general* and *absolute* responsibility."[105] Abraham thus instantiates the impossibility Derrida has already sketched with Patočka in the first two chapters of the book, for Abraham's responsibility indeed relies structurally upon irresponsibility. "Abraham is thus at the same time the most moral and the most immoral, the most responsible and the most irresponsible of men, absolutely irresponsible because he is absolutely responsible, absolutely irresponsible in the face of men and his family, and in the face of the ethical, because he responds absolutely to absolute duty" (*Donner la mort,* 103/72). Since both *Fear and Trembling* and *The Gift of Death* are at once familiar and infinitely complicated texts, I will not attempt to summarize the arguments of either here; what I would like to focus on more narrowly is the question, thematized most explicitly at the end of *The Gift of Death*, of who decides in this sacrificial scene—who is *responsible*—and how it is that the decision emerges out of Abraham's most terrifying crisis of undecidability.

Abraham "does everything that has to be done," Derrida tells us in "Dialanguages." Let us, then, try to tell the story once more of what it is that he does. Abraham makes the preparations, saddles the donkey, climbs the mountain with Isaac, builds the altar, binds Isaac to the wood, raises the knife . . . and at this moment, Derrida tells us, Abraham is paralyzed by God, who decides *for* Abraham and gives Isaac back. Again, God in this scenario "is the Other who will decide what 'come' means; that is where the response is." If "that is where the response is," however, then that is where the responsibility is. According to the Derrida of this interview, in other words, Abraham is initially but not *ultimately* responsible, for although it is Abraham who works his way up and out to undecidability, it is God alone—that is, *not-Abraham*—who decides. Far from displaying any signs of "divisibility" at all at the moment of decision, the two characters in this scenario could not be more discretely constituted. God calls, Abraham listens, Abraham prepares, Abraham freezes, and God decides.

Despite the deconstruction of the "responsible self" with which *The Gift of Death* begins, its analysis thus deepens and further confirms the indivisibility, or self-identity, of both Abraham and God. Looking to prove that even the seemingly incalculable scene on Mount Moriah capitulates to a "secret" economic reappropriation, Derrida ends up ascribing a *separate* decision to each of the story's two main characters. He writes that at the crucial moment of the story, "God *decides* to *give back* . . . the very thing that [Abraham] had already, in the same instance, *decided* to sacrifice" (131–32/96–97; emphasis added on "decides" and "decided"). According to Derrida's account, then, Abraham decides to give Isaac up, and God decides to give him back. Abraham decides to renounce hope of "recouping the loss," and God decides to restore it. Abraham "expects neither response nor reward," and God goes on to reward and respond, that is, to bear the responsibility for the final decision (131/95, 132/96). These two equal-and-opposite decisions are, in fact, the logic with which Derrida decides to conclude *The Gift of Death* itself: Abraham decides to sacrifice all economy, and God decides "to reinscribe sacrifice within an economy" (132/96). The final decision, then, is God's responsibility and not Abraham's at all. In fact, Abraham's responsibility ends the moment he decides to sacrifice Isaac. At this moment, Derrida tells us, Abraham

> considers himself to be all square. He acts as if he were discharged of his duty towards his fellows, his son, and humankind; but he continues to love them. He must *love* them and also *owe* them everything in order to be able to sacrifice them. Without being so, then, he nevertheless feels absolved of his duty towards his family, towards the human species and the generality of the ethical, absolved by the absolute of a unique duty that binds him to God the one. Absolute duty absolves him of every debt and releases him from every duty. (103–4/73)

In other words, despite his having established responsibility's fundamental irresponsibility as a crisis of undecidability between general responsibility (Kierkegaard's "ethical") and absolute responsibility (Kierkegaard's "religious"), Derrida very strangely describes Abraham as making his decision to sacrifice Isaac *not* in undecidability, but rather in perfectly good conscience, absolved of all duty to humanity.

There are two major problems that need to be unraveled here. First, from what Derrida has taught us about ethics and the decision, it is clear that what matters is not whether someone is *actually* responsible—for, after Levinas, one's infinite responsibility more or less goes without saying—but whether or not someone perceives herself to *be* responsible: whether or not she owns up to her "own," infinite obligation to every other other as well as her failure to meet this unrelentingly excessive obligation. In a Derridean register, responsibility *always* means that "one must avoid good conscience at all costs."[106] I must *never* be able to say "I have decided," much less "I have decided *well*," much less "*I am all square*, and my duty is done."[107] Somewhere along the line, then, the Abraham whom Derrida announces as "all square" has lost his undecidability, and with it he has lost his responsibility. Thus the attempt to follow Derrida's prompt and think the emergence of decision at the moment of the greatest difficulty is short-circuited the moment that Abraham is separated from his undecidability. This leads to the second problem with this particular fissure, which is that by splitting the decision of Genesis 22 into two decisions (which might not even be decisions, given the sudden evaporation of undecidability from the Abrahamic psyche) Derrida reifies both the self (Abraham) and the other (God) as autonomous agents of "decision," and, as he himself has warned, "the decision is barred when there is something like a transcendental subject."[108] Furthermore, not only does this scenario produce a transcendental, "all square" subject to bridge a reinstalled rift between undecidability and the decision; but this gesture is then repeated by the Most Transcendental Subject of All, who whimsically decides to put a sensible economic end to Abraham's aneconomic decision, which itself put an end to undecidability. Faced with a subject and a Subject who thus resolve all uncertainty and all undecidability into an economy of the same, it seems quite certain that the decision is lost. How has this happened?

Each of these destroyers of decision—good conscience, the subject, a safe space between undecidability and decision, economy, and an extraordinarily ontotheological God—can be traced back to Derrida's conviction that Abraham thinks he has been absolved of his ethical duty. Kierkegaard's Abraham, for Derrida, has resigned himself to losing everything for the sake of absolute duty, to such an extreme that, deciding to give up Isaac, Abraham has given up all hope of *anything at all*: "Abraham had consented to suffer death or worse, and that without calculating, without investing, beyond any perspective of recuperating the loss; hence, it seems, beyond recompense or retribution, beyond economy, without any hope of remuneration" (*Donner la mort*, 131/95).

"Yes . . . " a ghostly Johannes de Silentio might reply, were we to conjure him here, "yes, he gives up everything absolutely, but you've missed the most decisive part. The 'Abraham' you've described here gives up everything absolutely, knowing nothing can come back, and expects nothing to come back. But Abraham goes farther. He gives up everything absolutely, knowing nothing can come back, and then expects *everything to come back*, impossibly."

Herein lies the problem: in setting forth a "Kierkegaardian" Abraham who renounces everything infinitely and expects nothing back, Derrida has set forth an Abraham without faith in the absurd. Within the worldview of *Fear and Trembling*, Derrida has collapsed this knight of faith into the knight of infinite resignation: a character whom Derrida never actually mentions in *The Gift of Death*. The knight of infinite resignation gives up everything the knight of faith gives up, but does so "without any hope of remuneration," that is, without faith. The knight of faith, by contrast, "makes the infinite movement of resignation and gives up Isaac, which no one can understand because it is a private venture; but next, at every moment, he makes the movement of faith. This is his consolation. In other words, he is saying: But it will not happen, or if it does, the Lord will give me a new Isaac, that is, by virtue of the absurd."[109] *This*, for de Silentio, is what makes Abraham so incomprehensible—not his "decision" to sacrifice Isaac or his renunciation of all hope in economy, for any properly disciplined person can give up everything. What is baffling—even "amazing"—is rather "the little phrase: But it will not happen anyway."[110] This little phrase is what allows the Abraham of *Fear and Trembling*, in distinction to the Abraham of "Dialanguages," *not to hesitate* for even a moment as he raises the knife over Isaac. This nonhesitation provokes Sylviane Agacinski, for one, to profess astonishment at this scene: "That Abraham was able to answer without delay and without hesitation; this is what reinforces the stupefying character of his act."[111] The stupefying "but it will not happen anyway" therefore distinguishes Abraham from both the tragic hero who gives up what he loves for the greater good *and* from the knight of infinite resignation who gives up what he loves for Beauty or Poetry or even God. This little phrase, which expresses Abraham's absolute faith in the absurd precisely because it is absolutely absurd, makes Abraham *Abraham*.

But, one might ask, does this reminder of Abraham's faith in Isaac's return not support even more strongly Derrida's claim in *The Gift of Death* that Abraham acts in good conscience when he decides to sacrifice Isaac? Does it not merely put Derrida's analysis on a faster track to the economy that wins out in the end? No; nothing could be farther from the case. If there is one conviction that all Kiekegaard's pseudonyms share, which they share with the author of his signed works as well, it is that there is absolutely nothing "all square" about faith. Faith is not trust in what is certain or calculable or comprehensible; again, faith is faith in the *absurd* and, as such, is constantly attended by "anxiety, distress, and paradox"[112]—all of which this reader, at least, would like to associate with Derrida's understanding of undecidability. It is faith, in short, that causes one to *tremble*. This sort of terrifying faith, for which nothing is easy and nothing is certain, allows Abraham *truly* to exceed the limits of calculation and economy. For if, having now recalled the knight of faith, one is again to consider Derrida's Abraham, it will become clear that he never actually surpasses calculation at all. It is not the case that God reinscribes the economy Abraham renounces, for this Abraham does not renounce it in the first place. Derrida's Abraham sacrifices everything absolutely and expects nothing back. This is *not* actually aneconomic at all: there is nothing absurd about sacrificing everything and expecting not to have it. In fact, if I were truly to give up everything *absolutely*, I would do best from a mathematical perspective to assume that I had given up everything absolutely, that is, that everything was gone and that it would not come back. To be sure, it would be a calculating gesture to give up something while taking measures to ensure its safe return—like throwing a boomerang, or putting a return label on a package addressed to no one—but this is not what Abraham does. What makes Abraham Abraham is that he gives up everything, *including* all means of making sure it will come back, and that, still, he expects it back. *This* is the moment at which Abraham surpasses calculation—not in renouncing everything infinitely, but in expecting everything back at the same time. And he does this not in spite of the impossibility of such an event, but *because of its impossibility*. Which, as Mark C. Taylor points out by linking *Fear and Trembling* to *The Sickness Unto Death*, means that "everything is possible," that "the past is not closed and the future remain open."[113] So what, we might ask, could be more Derridean than looking toward the event and advent of the possibility of the impossible?

Having reestablished the significance of the expectation of the impossible, by virtue of which Abraham trembles beyond measure but does not hesitate, one ought to consider one remaining possibility that this "faith in the absurd" might indeed stem from what Derrida calls a "secret calculation." It could be that Kierkegaard's Abraham is of a certain soteriological persuasion that assures him that, while Isaac is gone from "this life," God will make it up to him in the eschaton. It is particularly important to consider such a position because this sort of otherworldly Abraham, whom Derrida calls "re-Christianiz[ed] or pre-Christianiz[ed]," is precisely the one who is able to consider himself all square, his duty done (*Donner la mort*, 130/95). With characteristic attention to seemingly negligible details, Derrida zeroes in on the end of the third problema in *Fear and Trembling*, when de Silentio once again insists that Abraham cannot be understood by mortals, but only by God the Father, who "*sees in secret* and recognizes the distress and counts the tears and forgets nothing" (*Fear and Trembling*, 120; cited in Derrida, *Donner la mort*, 131/95; emphasis added). Derrida reminds us here that the God who "sees in secret" is a reference to Matthew 6 and that the quotation in context is,

> when you fast, anoint your head and wash your face, so that your fasting may be seen not by men but by your Father who sees in secret; and your Father who sees in secret will reward you. Do not lay up for yourselves treasures on earth, where moth and rust consume and where thieves break in and steal; but lay up for yourselves treasures in heaven, where neither moth nor rust consumes and where thieves do not break in and steal. For where your treasure is, there will your heart be also.[114]

This Mattheian onto-theo-logic composes *Fear and Trembling*'s secret bottom line for Derrida, who concludes that while Abraham may renounce ordinary calculation, he is repaid by virtue of a divine calculation. Derrida says it is as if Kierkegaard is saying, "You can count on the economy of heaven if you sacrifice the earthly economy" or "Every earthly discomfort will be compensated *in heaven*" or "The real heavenly treasure is constituted on the basis of the salary or price paid for sacrifice or renunciation on earth." In other words, when all is said and done, "There is an economy, but it is an economy that integrates the renunciation of a calculable remuneration" (*Donner la mort*,

134/98, 136/99, 145/107). So when Abraham decides to sacrifice Isaac, he can consider his earthly duty done, his heavenly reward on the way.

To be sure, this "great is your reward in heaven" line can be understood within a particular eschatological framework as perfectly consistent with Matthew 6, and even with the logic of the Sermon on the Mount in general. But, I would argue, it is not a satisfying resolution to the problem of Kierkegaard's Abraham, for the simple reason that the "heavenly economy" allegedly inscribed in *Fear and Trembling* is neither heavenly nor economic. Had Kierkegaard described for us an Abraham who believed that he would be reunited once again with his son on Judgment Day, who had "faith" their resurrected bodies would someday frolic in the fields of Paradise, then we could accuse him of this particular "Christianization" of Abraham.[115] But that is not the kind of "faith" Abraham has. What makes de Silentio's Abraham Abraham (that is, what makes him incomprehensible, undialectizable, and resistant to all efforts to economize him—in short, in need of a silent speaker) is that his hopes are set not on some other world or afterlife but on *this* one:

> Abraham had faith, and had faith for this life. In fact, if his faith had been only for a life to come, he certainly would have more readily discarded everything in order to rush out of a world to which he did not belong. But Abraham's faith was not of this sort, if there is such a faith at all. . . . Abraham had faith specifically for this life— faith that he would grow old in this country, be honored among the people, blessed by posterity, and unforgettable in Isaac, the most precious thing in his life, whom he embraced with a love that is inadequately described by saying he faithfully fulfilled the father's duty to love the son.[116]

It is only by loving Isaac absolutely, renouncing him absolutely, and expecting him back impossibly *in this life* that Abraham is placed beyond the limits of all reason alone into the madness of decision.

Following Derrida's suggestion that decision only takes place in the midst of undecidability, we have been struggling throughout this chapter to find an instance of a genuine decision. From an initial meditation on undecidability through an analysis of hospitality to the situation of the poematic hedgehog on the highway, we have come to try to "think here of Kierkegaard," bearing in mind three conditions of decision's (im)possibility: the persistence of the most difficult undecidability at the very moment of decision, the nonself-identity of any "self" or "other" in the face of their constant mutual interruption, and, finally, the absence of a reassuring spatiotemporal "there" that might promise to sublate the agonizing tensions of the "here." In the course of his own analysis of Kierkegaard's Abraham, Derrida seems to cancel the possibility of the decision by annulling each of these conditions: "God" and "Abraham" remain self-identical beings, in charge of their "own" decisions,

Abraham sacrifices Isaac not in undecidability but in the certainty that he is "all square," and this squareness is ultimately guaranteed by the heavenly reward promised in Matthew 6. Perhaps, then, it is Derrida's conviction that a decision does not, by his standards at least, take place on Mount Moriah. As we have seen, however, this conviction cannot in any simple way be justified by way of *Fear and Trembling*, for de Silentio sketches the outlines of a very different Abraham, who—to address the third concern first—does not have faith for some "there, then," but rather for a "here, now." Abraham's "faith for this life" indicates, in other words, that the infinite double movement is made not for the sake of infinity but for the sake of finitude itself. Abraham expects everything back *here*—precisely where it is impossible. Could this absolute this-worldliness—this here without the background of a Beyond—be something akin to the "something else" that Derrida's hedgehog would require in order to be-toward-death without being immediately sublated by Heidegger? If so, then how would this interpretation in turn thematize the other two conditions, that is, decision out of undecidability and the ghost-ridden self-in-other-in-self?

First, it is crucial to recall that de Silentio's Abraham is not in any way "all square," but rather is caught throughout the entire ordeal *in trembling*: that is, in the anxiety of the very undecidability Derrida thematizes between the ethical and the religious. De Silentio tells us, "The ethical expression for what Abraham did is that he meant to murder Isaac; the religious expression is that he meant to sacrifice Isaac—but precisely in this contradiction is the anxiety that can make a person sleepless, and yet *without this anxiety Abraham is not who he is*."[117] The unbearable tension between incompatible duties must remain utterly unresolved, or else there is no paradox, and if there is no paradox, there is no Abraham (just as, if there is no undecidability, there is no decision). Therefore, Abraham can never, contra Derrida, take refuge in Matthew 6 and consider his duty to his son and his family to be "done" while awaiting his eternal reward. To the contrary, he must love his son as absolutely as he renounces him:

> The absolute duty can lead one to do what ethics would forbid, but it can never lead the knight of faith to stop loving. Abraham demonstrates this. In the moment he is about to sacrifice Isaac, the ethical expression for what he is doing is this: he hates Isaac. But if he actually hates Isaac, he can rest assured that God does not demand this of him, for Cain and Abraham are not identical. He must love Isaac with his whole soul. . . . Only in the moment when his act is in absolute contradiction to his feelings, only then does he sacrifice Isaac.[118]

This "absolute contradiction," this persistent undecidability with all the "distress and the anxiety" it provokes, this total inability to make a decision, conditions the possibility of Abraham's decision as such. Abraham's this-worldliness and his unresolved crisis of undecidability established, the question of "his" "selfhood" remains to be explored—what kind of notion of identity emerges from this undecidable decision?

For Derrida, the actors in the scene at Mount Moriah remain discrete, self-identical figures—precisely the type Derrida establishes in his analysis of Patočka and throughout his corpus as inimical to responsibility. Abraham-himself, believing his duty to Isaac to be done, makes his own "decision," and then God-himself makes *his* own "decision," annulling the "earthly economy" with the "heavenly economy" proclaimed in the Sermon on the Mount. What happens to "Abraham," however, once the anxiety of undecidability is introduced back into this operation? I have already argued that by omitting Abraham's faith in the impossible *in this life*, Derrida collapses the knight of faith into the knight of infinite resignation who gives up everything and expects that everything is gone forever. Further confirmation of this conflation can be found in de Silentio's description of the knight of infinite resignation as free from the anxiety of faith, drowning in the calm pleasure of despair. Speaking as the knight of infinite resignation, de Silentio explains, "I can resign everything by my own strength and find peace and rest in the pain."[119] The absence of anxiety, the conviction that "all is square," the resolution of undecidability are all traits of the knight of infinite resignation, and, as is evidenced by the quotation above, such "rest" indicates the presence of a self-by-itself—a "me" who can renounce everything "by my own strength." De Silentio reiterates this stubborn self-identity of the knight of infinite resignation in a number of places, saying that "the act of resignation . . . is a purely *philosophical* movement. . . . Through resignation, I renounce everything. I make this movement all by myself" (*Fear and Trembling*, 48; emphasis added). Giving up everything and expecting no return is a human possibility or, as Derrida's (perhaps inadvertent) isolation of the discrete selves of this "decision" allows us to extrapolate, what "Abraham" does when he makes the philosophical gesture of renouncing everything is, simply put, *possible* for the transcendental self of philosophy that it ultimately reinscribes. Impossibility, which Derrida himself names the condition of possibility for any decision, only comes on the scene with the *second* movement that he mysteriously leaves out: faith in the absurd.

Having encountered so many mysterious foreclosures in the face of a particularly insistent ghost, it will perhaps not come as such a surprise that the movement occluded in *The Gift of Death* is the movement that opens de Silentio's own musings onto thaumazein. While resignation keeps thinking within the realm of understanding, faith pushes it into wonder. De Silentio marks the entrance of the marvelous at the impossible moment of repetition: "After having made the movements of infinity, [faith] makes the movements

Oxford Brookes University

Title: Attention and value : keys
to understanding museum visitors

ID: 0096266802

Total items: 1
09/12/2016 12:55

Thank you for using the 3M
SelfCheck™ System

of finitude. Fortunate is the person who can make these movements! *He does the marvelous*, and I shall never weary of admiring him" (38; emphasis added). Precisely because Genesis 22 disables all efforts to comprehend it, a certain *admiration* is the only possible reaction to Abraham. Wonder leaps in as the understanding fails: as our narrator confesses, "Abraham I cannot understand; in a certain sense I can learn nothing from him except to be amazed" (37). In other places, de Silentio expresses the darker side of this amazement, writing, "Although Abraham arouses my admiration, he also appalls me" and "One cannot weep over Abraham. One approaches him with a *horror religious*, as Israel approached Mount Sinai (*Fear and Trembling*, 60, 61). Ultimately, the book's central either/or hangs entirely on this mood. Either Abraham is a murderer or he is a man of faith; either there is a teleological suspension of the ethical or Abraham is lost: "Let us then either cancel out Abraham or *learn to be horrified* by the prodigious paradox that is the meaning of his life" (52–53; emphasis added).

Inasmuch as a kind of fearsome wonder is faith's distinction from infinite resignation, de Silentio runs up against it again and again as he tries and fails to get a grip on Abraham. The knight of infinite resignation, he tells us, "is reconciled in pain. But then the marvel happens; he makes one more movement even more wonderful than all the others, for he says, Nevertheless I have faith that I will get her" (46). It is this wonderful movement that offends the understanding, transgresses the boundaries of the sensible, the intelligible, the human, and the possible: "So I can perceive that it takes strength and energy and spiritual freedom to make the infinite movement of resignation; I can also perceive that it can be done. The next [movement] amazes me, my brain reels, for, after having made the movement of resignation, then by virtue of the absurd to get everything, to get one's desire totally and completely—that is over and beyond human powers, that is a marvel" (47). Again: "not to find rest in the pain of resignation but to find joy by virtue of the absurd—this is wonderful" (50), "One, two, three—I can walk upside down in existence, but I cannot make the next movement, for the marvelous I cannot do—I can only be amazed at it" (36). Anyone can give up everything. Anyone can know that everything is gone. Anyone can think himself all square, having lept out to infinity. "But to be able to come down in such a way that instantaneously one seems to stand and to walk, to change the leap into life into walking, absolutely to express the sublime in the pedestrian—only that knight can do it, *and this is the one and only marvel*" (41; emphasis added).

Again, though, to say that Abraham lands without a hitch back into the finite is not to say the finite doesn't come as a surprise. De Silentio is clear on this: Abraham *expects* Isaac back by virtue of the absurd and therefore receives him back with joy, but this expectation is just that—absurd—and has nothing at all to do with knowledge. What can be known is what is possible. What must be *expected*, without being known, and what (like birth or death) always comes as a shock, even though it is fervently awaited, is the possibility of the impossible. Therefore one might say that God does not give Abraham "the same thing" Abraham had given up, for the Isaac who returns is not simply the Isaac who was sacrificed, but rather the one whose arrival Abraham could never anticipate and yet had to anticipate; in Derrida's language, the absolute *arrivant* who would divest the self of its very "self" *as well as* its grasp on the "other," who interrupts "the self" to its very core. This, then, is the sense in which Abraham is "paralyzed" at the moment of decision: he does not hesitate, but rather is *transit*, "frozen" in the Nancean sense—prevented, in trembling, from resting in himself.[120] At the moment of decision, Abraham *is* as more than himself—as disrupted by the other who is more intimate to him than he is to himself.[121] Therefore, because it rests on the (im)possible anticipation of that which cannot be anticipated *and* because it intalls a nonidentical otherness within the very selfhood of the self, the question of "faith" in Kierkegaard can be loosely translated into Derridese as the question of hospitality. If there is such a thing.

Everything short of faith in impossibility would simply be "possible," and, as Derrida knows, possibility without impossibility always underwrites the mastery and certainty of the transcendental subject. Reflecting upon what he would do were God to demand *his* only son, de Silentio writes, "I would have said to myself: Now all is lost, God demands Isaac, I sacrifice him and along with him all my joy. . . . But this is utterly false, for my immense resignation would be a substitute for faith. I would not be able to do more than make the infinite movement in order to find myself and again rest in myself" (*Fear and Trembling*, 35). What Silentio suggests here is that the one who makes not only the possible movement of resignation but also the impossible movement of faith will *not* "find itself again" or "rest in itself." The trembling "singular individual" *will not*, in other words, *return to or coincide with itself* like the speculative subject. If Abraham has indeed made the impossible movement of faith in the impossible, then Abraham is not simply "Abraham," for such a decision could never have been within "his" power. Some sort of "who" utterly resistant to the logic of self-identity will have taken place here, and, indeed, when de Silentio speaks of Abraham's having been restored to himself with the restoration of Isaac, he always describes this repetition as nonidentical. Abraham as the "single individual" is not "himself," rather, he continually exists by virtue of the impossible decision in "absolute relation to the absolute," which prevents all "rest" or, to recall Schlegel's hedgehog, all closure-in-itself. What emerges from the undecidable decision of Genesis 22 is therefore not "Abraham himself" or even "God Himself," but rather an absurd and absolute relation that interrupts the simple identity or agency of either of them.[122] It is impossible to say "who" made the decision, for the decision was made, if it was made, not by a self or an Other, but through their infinitely complicated, mutually interrupted *relation* at the terrifying height of absolute undecidability.

### Mysterium Tremendum

In this attempt to thematize the mad instant of the decision, I have tried to show that the crucial question with respect to decision and undecidability is "Qu'est-ce qui se passe?" Having established the structural dependence of decision's passage with the *qui* it (dis)establishes, this analysis has gone on to mark a stubborn reinscription of one or another figure of the transcendental subject every time a rift is posited between undecidability and the decision: from Laclau's subject who plays God, to the oft-invoked Levinasian Other who is indistinguishable from Him, to the hedgehog who gets flattened by Schlegel or Hegel or Heidegger, to an Abraham who "rests in himself." What has been gained along this often frustrating way, however, is a clearer understanding of strategies by means of which a consideration of the decision might avoid the subject and open onto "something else." And, although I have argued that in his "own" reading of Genesis 22 Derrida ultimately closes down the possibility of the decision, it is his notion of the decision—his insistence that thinking *stay with* the very "ordeal of the undecidable"—that might allow this reflection to reopen the trauma of the *akedah*, in the hopes of reopening decision. Even if it can be said that a genuine decision *does* take place on Mount Moriah because it 1. remains lodged in total undecidability, 2. produces an "Abraham" who does not and cannot coincide with himself, and 3. eschews all otherworldliness—does this not strengthen the case of those critics who charge that Derrida destroys the possibility of everyday decision? By confining the (im)possibility of decision to a scene as unique, incomprehensible, and ahistorical as the binding of Isaac, does one not in effect declare that decision can never take place in the "real" world for "ordinary people" (that is, for those of us who fall short of Abraham)?

This concern leads us directly to the most radical suggestion of *The Gift of Death*. If responsibility is responsibility, Derrida insists, then it is infinite and indiscriminate; I am just as responsible for your mother as I am for my own, for my neighbor's cat as for my tropical fish. It may be—it probably is—the case that I prefer my own family, language, and nation to everyone else's, but, in expressing and acting upon such a preference, I am neglecting my duty to all the other families, languages, and nations to and for which, strictly speaking, I am just as fully responsible.[123] The place this gets tricky is in the difference between Kierkegaard's ethical and religious stages—or what Derrida calls "general" and "absolute" duty. Certainly, one's duty to someone else's cat and one's duty to God can be clearly prioritized . . . unless, of course, one's duty to God happens to have something to do with caring for someone else's cat. The problem is, it is not clear that one can ever be certain of what one's "duty to God" actually entails. This is especially the case if one is operating within the Levinasian conviction that the relation to "infinity" or "God" immediately redirects one to finitude and one's neighbor, or within the notion we derived from Nancy that "il n'y a qu'il y a," or, in fact, within de Silentio's insistence that Abraham had faith for this finite world. In each case, it becomes progressively difficult to untangle one's obligations to God from one's obligations to the world. This is not to say that distinctions must never be made; to the contrary, responsibility demands nothing if not the distinctions that are made in decision. But this also means that responsibility demands undecidability. This is all simply (and impossibly) to say that there is no dependable division between the ethical and the religious, just as there is no law that would permit me to discern who in the world deserves my response more than all the others. From the perspective of what might transgressively be called Derrida's moral law, there is no law; no pregiven formula that might help me to distinguish the call of the other to whom I am generally responsible from the call of the other other to whom I am equally responsible from the call of the Other to whom I am absolutely responsible. Every other is, *from this perspective*, completely other ("tout autre est tout autre"). So, far from confining the possibility of the decision to one mythical man, Derrida opens decision out to everyone at all times precisely by revealing it as impossible: "what can be said about Abraham's relation to God can be said about my relation without relation to *every other (one) as every (bit) other [tout autre comme tout autre]*, in particular my relation to my neighbor or my loved ones who are as inaccessible to me, as secret and transcendent as Yahweh" (*Donner la mort*, 110/78).[124]

What is crucial here for Derrida is to demonstrate that, because my obligation to anyone can only be carried out at the expense of my obligation to everyone else, the "monstrous" story of Abraham and Isaac is actually "the most common and everyday experience of responsibility" (*Donner la mort*, 97/67). (But we who thought we understood responsibility have now become perplexed . . . ) And yet Derrida recognizes as well as anyone that it is not at all "common" to love one's children as much as Abraham loved Isaac or to love one's god as much as Abraham loved God. Decisions are made, and responsibilities carried out all the time, and it is hardly "common" to be so fully aware of the obligations these particular decisions and responsibilities necessarily neglect. To this, of course, Derrida would object that such decisions are not actually decisions at all, because, as we have heard again and again, a decision can only be made from the agonizing space of undecidability. And, as we have seen, the fullest implication of this claim is that the height of undecidability and the ground of decision inhabit the same spatiotemporal instant. It seems, then, that there is a profound ethical project motivating *The Gift of Death*: to condition the possibility of genuine decisions by revealing the undecidability that alone conditions them. As I suggested at the outset of this chapter, Derrida pushes even the most ordinary experience of responsibility (feeding one's cat, for example) out to monstrous impossibility *for the sake of responsibility's possibility*. The crucial passage with respect to the decision, then, is not the so-called gap between undecidability and decision that has troubled so many scholars, for *there is no such gap*, but rather the passage from good conscience out to impossibility; from decidability out to undecidability. Which is to say out to decision. This is the (un)work of responsibility.

What, then, of the "qui qui passe"? Who *is* in response to "tout autre comme tout autre"? "The question of the self," Derrida mentions in passing, would be "'who am I?' not in the sense of 'who am I' but 'who is this "I"' that can say who? What is the 'I,' and what becomes of responsibility once the identity of the 'I' trembles *in secret*?" (*Donner la mort*, 127/92). Although Derrida never answers this question explicitly, one can read the multivectorial alterity of the *tout autre* back into the Abraham I have tried to scrape off the highway and resuscitate after Derrida for some reason declared him to be "all square." If it is the case that every responsibility worthy of the name puts me in a situation of absolute undecidability, which, however lower the stakes, remains as incalculable as Abraham's ordeal, then every responsibility divests me of all self-identity. For a decision can only emerge at the moment when "I" am surrounded by undecidability, to the point of my ceasing to be an "I" over against the "others" to whom I am responsible. The mad instant of decision thus would bind "me" not just to "God," but to, with, and through *each* other to whom I am responsible, every one of whom interrupts my relation to my self absolutely, for I only *am* as *response*. This would be decision's "who": singular in its very heteronomy, itself only as relational.

The final question one might be inclined to explore, then, is this: why does Derrida not only avoid, but *preclude* the emergence of such heteronomous singularity in *The Gift of Death*? Particularly when such a "who" seems to hold in tension the very elements that condition the (im)possibility of decision, that is, the interruption of all sovereignty and the nontransferrability of responsibility? We will recall that the way Derrida flattens Kierkegaard's Abraham into a subject in this text is by resolving his undecidability, installing him and God as discrete and sovereign subjects, and converting faith in the absurd into "faith" in the economy of heaven. At every turn, Abraham has been divested of his anxiety (and, again, "without this anxiety, Abraham is not who he is") and made into an agent of good conscience. He has been stripped, in other words, of the very force that animates both de Silentio's book *and* Derrida's: *trembling*.

It is hardly as though Derrida ignores trembling; to the contrary, we heard him say a moment ago that the "who" of responsibility would be a who who trembles in secret. Earlier in the text, he suggests that trembling "tends to undo both seeing and knowing" (*Donner la mort*, 80/54). So trembling prevents the speculative "subject" from gathering itself together. What, then, is trembling? Opening with the words *mysterium tremendum,* the first few pages of the third chapter of *The Gift of Death* are devoted to investigating this movement. "Tremble. What does one do when one trembles? What is it that makes you tremble?" (*Donner la mort*, 79/53). And, interestingly enough, the movement of trembling eventually takes shape for Derrida as a double movement. Not quite de Silentio's double movement of faith, but also not quite *not*,[125] the strange repetition of trembling "ties an irrefutable past (a shock [*coup*] has taken place, a traumatism has already affected us) to a future that cannot be anticipated; anticipated but unpredictable; *apprehended*, but, and this is why there is a future, apprehended precisely *as* unforeseeable, unpredictable, approached *as* unapproachable" (*Donner la mort*, 80/54; translation altered slightly). In the double movement of trembling, which also begins to conjure Heideggerian *Verhaltenheit*, "we" are held simultaneously between a sudden disappearance of familiarity and a kind of hospitality to the *arrivant* for whose coming the shock has prepared: "we tremble first of all because we don't know from which direction the shock came, whence it was given (whether a good surprise or a bad shock, sometimes the good *as* bad); and we tremble from not knowing, in the form of a double secret, whether it is going to continue, start again, insist, be repeated: whether, how, or when. And why *this* shock" (*Donner la mort*, 80/54; translation altered). If the double movement of trembling marks the self as response, then trembling must accompany the decision. *Especially* in response to the call of the Fear of Isaac.[126] And yet, after its brief thematization in these few pages, trembling more or less disappears from this text. Could it be that Derrida's ultimate foreclosure of the decision—and of its heteronomous-singular "who"—has something to do with his foreclosure of trembling? What would provoke him to resolve Abraham's trembling in the first place, especially when the trembling of undecidability seems to be precisely what Derrida is trying to provoke for the sake of decision and responsibility?

At this point, let us reconsider Derrida's account of Patočka's genealogy of responsibility. We will recall that, for Patočka, the orgiastic or demonic mystery is incorporated by Platonic responsibility, and then this whole secret

bundle is repressed by the mysterium tremendum. This history of responsibility is, for Derrida as for Patočka, coextensive with the emergence of the
singular self, which exists in relation to its own death. Derrida tells us that
"responsibility" therefore relies upon two "disciplines": the continual repression of the orgiastic, on the one hand, and rehearsal for death (*meletê thanatou*), on the other. It is death, therefore, that ushers in philosophy, politics,
ethics, and all the sciences, for the very singular subject upon which they all
rely is the gift that death gives.

While death is the central theme of Patočka's fifth heretical essay, however, it is not nearly so central in the second and third, which offer a similar genealogy with a few crucial differences. Derrida's analysis relies almost
entirely upon the fifth, in which the most primordial stage is called "orgiastic"
or "demonic," and responsibility is obstructed primarily by unchecked material (particularly sexual) indulgence. It is only by practicing for death that the
philosophical self learns to detach itself from its own embodiment, a process
represented for Patočka in the ascent from the (feminine, bodily) cave to
the (masculine, philosophical) open. In both the second and third essays,
however, the most primordial stage is simply called "prehistoric," and it is
marked not by sexuality or even materiality per se, but rather by an utterly
unquestioned continuity of gods, mortals, animals, plants, life, and death.
Prehistoric humanity, leaving all understanding and all decision making to
the gods, does not think twice about its place in the universe, but rather lives
and works within a meaningful, if sometimes disappointing or even frightening, cosmic whole. There is no diabolical sexuality here; just an edenic
existence in which "the worth of the universe is in no way less because it
includes death, pain, and suffering, just as it is not disturbed by the perishing
of plants and animals or by everything being subject to the rhythm of generation and perishing."[127] As in the fifth essay, the entrance of history introduces
a transformed relationship to death: "historical" humanity will endeavor to
work out its immortality rather than just perish like plants and animals.

Yet the sudden arrival of history in the second and third essays is not
*primarily* characterized as the arrival of death, but rather as the arrival of
*mystery*, which the Patočka of these essays claims is utterly absent from the
first stage. This sudden onset of mystery in and as history—which is also to
say in and as philosophy, politics, and religion—is the most striking distinction between the schema of the second and third essays and the fifth, on
which Derrida focuses. In the second and third essays, the interruption of
history suddenly propels humanity from its "naïve certainty of meaning" into
*uncertainty*, totally invalidating the old ways of making sense: "Nothing of the
earlier life of acceptance remains in peace; all the pillars of the community,
traditions, and myths, are equally shaken, as are all the answers that once
preceded questions" (*Heretical Essays*, 39–40). History in this particular form

comes on the scene as the shocking disappearance of everything that had been familiar, which in turn gives way to an awe that anything could possibly *be* at all: "the primordial shaking of accepted meaning . . . is then linked to that explicit awe before beings as a whole, the aweful realization that the totality of being *is*, which, according to the ancient philosophers, is really the inmost pathos and origin of philosophy" (63). And because this awe responds to and *keeps open* the very uncertainty, difficulty, and questioning that make politics and philosophy possible, the practice of responsibility in this essay is not *meletê thanatou*, but rather thaumazein: "the renewal of life's meaning in the rise of political life bears within it the seed of philosophical life as well—if Plato and Aristotle are right in saying that *thauma archê tes sofias* ('wonder is the beginning of wisdom')" (40).

In the second and third heretical essays, Patočka characterizes the problem of both the metaphysical *and* the Christian traditions not in terms of their relationship to sexuality but rather as a progressive shutting down of the "awe-full" uncertainty that opens them in the first place. "Philosophy in its metaphysical form," he writes, "shed[s] that mystery which was the origin of the shock that gave rise to it." Philosophy turns itself from a wondrous questioning of all accepted meaning into one or another self-satisfied system—into "metaphysics in Plato and Democritus, into metaphysics in two modes, from above and from below, a metaphysics of the *logos* and the Idea on the one hand, a metaphysics of things in their sheer thinghood on the other, both pretending to a definitive clarity and a definitive explanation of things, both grounded in that model of clarity represented by the discovery of mathematics, that germ of the future transformation of philosophy into a science" (65). Christianity, for its part, all too frequently loses its (un-)foundation in the mysterium tremendum, explaining away every difficulty with reference to another, perfect world and thereby announcing itself as an even more "certain" framework than metaphysics: "Christians coming face to face with the human poverty of meaning, absolute and global, do not give up but assert their faith the more energetically, the more graphically that poverty is presented. Thus the question of meaning is resolved positively by dismissing philosophy and by countering skepticism with the word from an otherwise inaccessible 'true' world" (67). From *this* perspective then, Patočka's criticism of the "return of the orgiastic" or the eruption of irresponsibility within modern philosophy, politics, and religion is not a complaint about idolatry and sexual license, which is the way Derrida represents it in *Donner la mort*; it is rather a critique of the disappearance of mystery and uncertainty, of a resurgence of the propensity toward unreflective, "vegetative" complacency with respect to the (dis)order of things. Recalling the discipline of philosophy along *this* line of thought would mean recultivating the readiness to be shocked by the loss of meaning and to be astonished that, in the face of such meaninglessness, anything *is* at all.

And while it is true that the Patočka of the *fifth* essay frames the birth of philosophy, politics, and religion in terms of a relation to death rather than in terms of shock and awe, the two disciplines he ascribes to the philosopher are not, *pace* Derrida, the practice of death and simple repression, but rather the practice of death and the double movement of wonder. As we have seen, Patočka calls upon thaumazein as the primary philosophical response to the mysterium tremendum in the second and third essays. In the fifth essay, he describes philosophy not just as a response to the mysterious, but as a *conjuring* of it. Welcoming and warding off go(o)ds and monsters, philosophy itself becomes a *thauma-turgy*:

> As a result of this conception [the Good], in Neoplatonism the demonic—*Eros* is a great *daimon*—becomes a subservient realm in the eyes of the philosopher who has overcome all its temptations. Hence a somewhat unexpected outcome: the philosopher is at the same time a great *thaumaturge*. The Platonic philosopher is a magician—a Faustus. The Dutch historian of ideas, Gilles Quispel, derives from this one of the principle sources of the Faust legend and of Faustianism in general, that "endless striving" which makes Faust so dangerous but which ultimately can save him. (105)[128]

Attuned to the ghosts and daimons of philosophy, thaumaturgy is both exceedingly dangerous and potentially transformative. This is just what Socrates told Theaetetus and what Heidegger, Levinas, and Nancy have all confirmed: the wonder philosophy opens is both a curse and a blessing, exposing thinking to all manner of forces that exceed it. "But where danger is, grows / That which saves also."[129]

Patočka continues in a new paragraph, "Another important moment is that the Platonic philosopher overcame death fundamentally by not fleeing from it but by facing up to it. This philosophy was *meletê thanatou*, care for death" (105). It should be noted that in this passage Patočka names thaumaturgy first, relegating the rehearsal of death to the next paragraph and introducing it as "another important movement." Strangely enough, toward the very beginning of *Donner la mort*, Derrida quotes this passage in two parts, but then goes on to claim death as the sole giver of responsibility as singularity. He manages this, it seems, both by neglecting to connect thaumaturgy to thaumazein— which for Patočka is at the very least coeval with, if not anterior to, Thanatos— and by confining the practice of thaumaturgy to a simple repression of the orgiastic, in full service of the rehearsal for death. The eclipse of thaumaturgy and the absence of thaumazein here is so complete that, *immediately* after citing Patočka's reference to the philosopher as "a great thaumaturge . . .

namely, Faust," Derrida proceeds to comment not on thaumaturgy, but rather, once again, on the "concern for death." The Faustian practice of stirring up the most dangerous and most promising of spirits is collapsed for Derrida into an "awakening that keeps vigil over death." In the meantime, the art of conjuring is only helpful insofar as it represses all daimons in service of the philosopher's escape into the Good. And even this dessicated form of thaumaturgy eventually disappears during the course of Derrida's analysis.

I would like to suggest that the denial or repression of wonder's double movement throughout *The Gift of Death* has everything to do with the sudden disappearance of the double movement of trembling, as well as with the lack of any reference, critical or otherwise—in a book about *Fear and Trembling*—to the double movement of faith, which de Silentio calls "the one and only marvel." I would furthermore argue that this complex of repressions is what ultimately enables Derrida's installation of Abraham as a self-identical, "philosophical" subject,and his concomitant occlusion of decision. As we have seen by rereading Patočka, the history of responsibility provokes both "the awe-full realization that the totality of being *is*" *and* a kind of being-toward-death. Whether wonder is anterior to or equiprimordial with *meletê thanatou* is immaterial. What is crucial is that responsibility's *qui* not be assembled in relation to death-alone. For without the wonder (or faith, as de Silentio describes it, or trembling, as Derrida himself describes it) that would interrupt the "self"'s immediate relation to itself, death's gift of singularity collapses into a gift of autonomous subjectivity. Derrida elaborates upon this figure of being-toward-death thus: "the soul *only* distinguishes itself, separates itself, and assembles within itself in the experience of this *meletê tou thanatou*. It is nothing other than this concern for dying as a relation to self and an assembling of self. It only returns to itself, in both senses of assembling itself and waking itself, becoming conscious, in the sense of consciousness of self in general, through this concern for death" (*Donner la mort*, 31–32/14–15; emphasis added). Given by death-alone, Derrida's Abraham is, *just like his hedgehog*, ultimately a figure of being-toward-death without wonder's being-with. He is, in other words, singularity without heteronomy, doomed to certain flattening on the philosophical highway.

And yet, insofar as Derrida's analysis *points us* to precisely the trembling, infinitely interrupted "who" whom it itself cannot name, wonder is not so much *absent* from *The Gift of Death* as it is its spectral double, unsettling all firmly established selves and meaning, leaving its interlocutors astonished by the impossible isness of things. For this, of course, is precisely the way each of the Derridean texts that have been engaged here works—by *unworking* familiar concepts and practices to expose their impossibility and then by establishing that impossibility as their very possibility. What, then, might one call Derrida's tireless conjuring of the uncanny il y a, if not a kind of thaumaturgy? Could the double movement of wonder be thematized as the unnamed ethos of deconstruction? Might de-construction be one name for a thinking that would dwell in the haunted space of thaumazein?

As far as the majority of scholarly opinion goes, it would seem that deconstruction can make only the first movement of thaumazein—the shocking, shocked revelation of the groundlessness, inessentiality, and unfamiliarity at the very heart of the everyday. The "received" reading of deconstruction is more or less, as David Fryer has argued, for example, that it functions "only to expose."[130] In terms of the particular concept of decision under the microscope here, this would be to say, along with Laclau, Critchley, Kearney et al., that deconstruction can move thinking out to undecidability and loss of sovereignty, but cannot then move "back" from undecidability to the decision and its subject or object. What I have hoped to demonstrate in the course of this chapter, however, is that, far from leaving thinking "stranded" in aporia, Derrida's thought reveals the height of undecidability and nonself-identity *as* the moment of decision and identity itself. The decision is made, if it is made, in and through the very undecidability that divests me of all self-certainty. This realization—that a decision has taken place precisely there where decision was impossible—would constitute shock's simultaneous countermovement of awe. These two movements, which Derrida momentarily assembles under the experience of trembling, before abandoning them, would hold the self-as-other-as self between the unexpected and the unanticipatable, installing and interrupting responsibility as a radical hospitality toward the absurd possibility of the impossible. "Therefore as a stranger give it welcome."

One became great by expecting the possible, another by expecting the eternal; but he who expected the impossible became greatest of all.

—Søren Kierkegaard, *Fear and Trembling*

## POSTLUDE: Possibility

### The Opening of Closure

During the past fifteen years or so, and with increasing regularity, scholars across the disciplines have become fascinated with the proliferation between the fifteenth and seventeenth centuries of wonders, marvels, prodigies, automata, witches, wizards, and monsters, particularly as these figures served as foils for modern Europe's social, religious, political, and scientific self-becoming.[1] Although vastly different from one another, each of these recent studies demonstrates in one way or another that, thanks to the fantastic stories, amazing objects, and exotic bodies that flowed through newly established trade routes, early modern Europe was obsessed with wonders. John Onians, although he too claims that this era constituted "the period of wonder *par excellence*," has shown in his "short history of amazement" that it was hardly the first.[2] Onians defines wonder on a societal level as the product of "an upheaval, such as a move to a new breeding ground," and marks it as a broad cultural response to the introduction of "new phenomena" into a hegemonic cultural formation. He thus claims as "periods of wonder" New Kingdom Egypt, Assyria from the eleventh to the ninth centuries bce, the Hellenistic world, and the early Roman Empire as forerunners of the European age of curiosities ("We might not like to think of the Colosseum as a *Wunderkammer*, but it was").[3] Far from being confined to early modern Europe, the ethically repellent impulse toward collecting and showing off objects taken from other lands seems to Onians a biological imprint, for "each time new conquests brought people into contact with the unfamiliar they had to pause and wonder at it. Each time those conquests destroyed existing territorial rights and the existing pecking order the new dominant male re-established his rights and prestige by a ritual display."[4] It is Onian's contention, however, that while the wonder-drunk early modern period has had numerous ancestors, it will have no descendants, because seventeenth-century Europe eventually classified, recorded, and explained away every one of the strange beings, objects, and practices it was able to get its hands on. Wonder's consummation in this "period of wonder *par excellence*" was, in other words, its consummation in the Hegelian sense, for as the inquisitive approach to wonders grew more systematic and its scope grew literally global, the field of the inexplicable shrank to more or less negligible proportions, leaving wonder a weak sign of persistent ignorance or of some minute scientific incompletion. This was the difference between early modern Europe's amazement and that of its predecessors:

> In the case of Egypt and Assyria amazement at the new was followed by familiarity, but not by the establishment of a permanent and organized body of knowledge. The mechanisms people had for storing acquired expertise were limited. With the Greeks and Romans the situation started to change. Books now preserved knowledge and scientific instruments ensured its continued expansion. The impact of the later age of wonder was much greater. Not only were the tools for preserving and developing knowledge vastly improved, but as explorers traveled to all continents the limits of knowledge of this planet were being reached. In a sense the age of wonder of the sixteenth and seventeenth centuries brought wonder to an end.[5]

According to this narrative, once each of the world's wonders became the object of calculation and comprehension—even the favored daughter of Thaumas herself[6]—wonder became impossible.

During the course of this study, I have tried to argue that the will toward total mastery that periodically overtakes the dominant culture when it encounters something new, bizarre, different, and/or threatening is not wonder at all, but rather a retreat from wonder—a closure of the primordially open terrain of thaumazein. By locating a reopening of this originary attunement in the work of Martin Heidegger, I have therefore suggested that within the history of Western philosophy, at least, it was only after wonder had become impossible—its every object catalogued, calculated, bought, and sold—that wonder somehow became possible. Of course, this insight itself is indebted to Heidegger, who argues that the "closure of metaphysics" heralds the opening of a thinking of the unthinkable. If Heidegger claims being or beyng or *Ereignis* as the unthought condition of possibility of thinking, I have tried to trace wonder as thinking's unendured affect. Like being, wonder is domesticated and digested as the tradition comes to believe it has surpassed it: just as "beings" for Heidegger come to think themselves the source and origin of being itself, the modern European philosopher systematically fashions himself, by means of what he comprehends, into "the only miracle and wonder of the world."[7] And just as, for Heidegger, thinking being is a matter of recognizing being's progressive withdrawal from the beings it gives, dwelling in wonder is first and foremost a matter of recognizing the impossibility of doing so *now*—now when all miracles and wonders are subject to collection, dissection, and mass distribution; when the old European ways of making meaning have crumbled under the force of two disastrous world wars; when the elements that Civilization has conquered, disciplined, and poisoned threaten in turn to choke, drown, and burn it inexorably; and when the most astonishing lights in the sky are the bombs that one nation, having made itself into the world's only superpower ("Like God in a way"),[8] showers upon the people of Dresden or Hiroshima or Iraq or Afghanistan. The state of things is nothing short of *disastrous*, in Blanchot's sense of the word: "we" heirs to "the Greeks" are in the position not of our forefather Thales, who marveled at the stars, but rather of the child in *The Writing of the Disaster* who looks up to see the winter sky on an ordinary day suddenly turned black and starless.[9] Dis-*aster*: no heavenly lights that might ensure our safe sailing through the strange waters of the familiar. And so, again, the wonder that characterized (and caricatured) "our" first great philosopher is entirely inaccessible to us.

I have argued, however, that the Western tradition does not "expunge" wonder so much as it internalizes it and installs the transcendental subject as the sole source of the marvelous. To root this claim in its particular historical setting, there is perhaps no more ironic—or devastating—illustration of this self-deifying trend than the American military doctrine of "Shock and Awe." Outlined in a treatise in 1996 under the Clinton administration, Shock and Awe was first deployed in the inaptly named "Operation Iraqi Freedom" offensive that began in the spring of 2003.[10] Its authors theorize that if an enemy were sufficiently amazed by a display of overwhelming military power, "it" would abandon all hope of resistance, putting the aggressors in a state of complete physical and, more importantly, "psychological dominance." Psychological dominance, these authors explain,

> means the ability to destroy, defeat, and neuter the will of an adversary to resist; or convince the adversary to accept our terms and aims short of using force. The target is the adversary's will, perception, and understanding. The principal mechanism for achieving this dominance is through imposing sufficient conditions of 'Shock and Awe' on the adversary to convince or compel it to accept our strategic aims and military objectives.[11]

Such "sufficient conditions" include massive bombardment with conventional explosives (they suggest three to four hundred in a day), the destruction of military and civilian infrastructure (access to all power, roads, food, communication, and supplies), and the calculated circulation of "misinformation" or "disinformation."[12] Insofar as it achieves massive emotional and physical neutralization, Shock and Awe can be called "the non-nuclear equivalent of . . . Hiroshima and Nagasaki."[13] Without inflicting its attendant level of *physical* destruction, rapid dominance can inflict a nuclear "state of awe."[14]

This military imposition of wonder bespeaks a powerful will toward deification, which is confirmed by Ullman and Wade's comparison between the effects of Shock and Awe and those of the atomic bomb. As is well known, J. Robert Oppenheimer cited the Bhavagad Gita upon witnessing the test detonation of the atom bomb on July 16, 1945, in Jornada del Muerto, saying in astonishment, "If the radiance of one thousand suns were to burst into the sky, that would be like the splendor of the Mighty One" and, moments later, "I am become Death—the shatterer of worlds."[15] In response to the same sight, General Thomas Farrel reported hearing "an awesome roar which warned of doomsday and made us feel that we puny things were blasphemous to dare temper with the forces heretofore reserved for the Almighty."[16] Reading Ullman and Wade through Farrel's biblical invocation, one might say the idea behind Shock and Awe is to demonstrate in no uncertain terms that it would be as impossible to refuse to comply with the United States military as it would be to reject a divine commandment given in a pillar of cloud and fire. "The punishing air attacks rocked the Baghdad night Friday," one report put it, "with thunderous explosions that filled the skies with flames and huge clouds of smoke."[17] The point is precisely to provoke the kind of *yir'ah* that Moses experiences in the fiery cloud on Mount Sinai or that the Israelites finally express once the plagues have come, the sea has parted, and the Egyptians are dead on the shore: "Who is like thee, O Lord, among the gods? Who is like thee, majestic in holiness, terrible in glorious deeds, doing wonders?"[18] The attempt to *inflict* shock and awe, then, is thus an extreme and disastrous contemporary expression of the modern superpowerful ego's internalization of wonder, which, I have argued, stems from a refusal of all indeterminacy. Rather than undergo the awful uncertainty of wonder, the autonomous subject—or nation—masquerades as "the only miracle and wonder of the world,"[19] ultimately *imposing* wonder, in the most terrifying ways, upon the world it masters. "Achieving Shock and Awe rests in the ability to deter and overpower an adversary through the adversary's perception or fear of his vulnerability," write Ullman and Wade, "and our own invincibility."[20]

One might, justifiably, be led to argue with Descartes that insofar as the oscillation of shock and awe exposes its patients to good and evil, helpful and murderous forces alike, thinking should distance itself from its thauma-turgic ancestry as far as possible. One might even suggest that philosophy (not to mention militarism) ought to find itself a different mood altogether. But this, I would venture, is the problem, and ultimately the promise, of wonder's irreducible anteriority. It will not "just go away," and, much like the phenomenon of religion itself, the harder the West tries to expunge wonder, the more disastrously it asserts itself. If, then, wonder cannot be eradicated, but only either repressed and introjected or endured, might it be possible to imagine the task of thinking and being-in-the-world not as an exercise in imposing wonder upon others, but rather as continually undergoing, suffer-ing, the wonder that keeps existence vulnerable and unsure of itself? To be sure, opening itself to the wondrous, thinking opens itself to that which is most horrifying of all, but if it is truly the case that wonder opens thinking in the first place, then there is no other way to expose philosophy or politics or religion to the possibility of the transformative than to expose it at the same time to the possibility of the devastating.

And so, on the one hand, Heidegger's work not only allows but also *obliges* thinking to remain with thaumazein precisely where it seems to have become most impossible, that is to say, in the face of what Derrida in *Specters of Marx* calls the "plagues of the new world order."[21] Only wonder's attentiveness to the uncanniness of the everyday might stir us out of our unthinking partici-pation in the order of things and into the shocked recognition, ever renewed, that *"the time is out of joint.* The world is going badly."[22] So badly, in fact, that it is a wonder anything can be at all. And so in this book I have attempted to conjure the thaumazein that comes back to haunt philosophy in the midst of a horrifying century, tracing it as a double movement between a shock that attunes thinking to the strange or incomprehensible or downright awful state of things and an awe that things nevertheless are, when everything seems to prevent the being of anything. In Heidegger's unpublished work, this twofold attunement takes shape as Erschrecken at being's terrifying withdrawal and Scheu that this abandonment *gives* the very beings it abandons. These two moods are held together in *Verhaltenheit*, another of Heidegger's neologisms, which means something like restraint or reservedness, but also encodes *Ver-hältnis*, in the sense of both proportion and relationship. Verhaltenheit main-tains wonder's two movements in proportion to one another, and in relation to everyday beings, delivering Da-sein into and as concernful *In-sein*. Echoes of this double movement can be heard in Levinas's horror at the starkness of existence, which gives way to an aweful responsibility for those who suffer, and in Nancy's "violent shock" at the inessentiality of things, which opens onto a wonder that inessentiality gives beings as relational, interdependent, singular. Finally, there can be found in Derrida an oscillation between the impossibility of everyday concepts and practices (hospitality, forgiveness, friendship, decision) and the recognition that it is the impossibility of the most familiar that conditions its possibility in the first place.

On the other hand, however, we have seen even in these wonder-dwellers a tendency to shut down the space their own thought compels us to keep open. The over- and indeterminacy of wonder is often too much to bear. Like Socrates himself, who left out wonder's unpleasant half in his failure to mention Rainbow's hellish sisters and later ran from thaumazein's excessive uncertainty by taking refuge in the phantasmic pseudês doxa, Heidegger tries variously to confine the thaumazein he reawakens to metaphysics, to the "open," to thirteen bullet points, or to the prongs of a diagrammed doxazein. In subsequent chapters, we experienced similar flights from wonder in Levinas's repeated efforts to "put an end to the absurd rumbling of the *il y a*," in Nancy's momentary attempt to "avoid all ambiguity" by keeping politics pure of religion, and in Derrida's resolution of undecidability, most notably in *The Gift of Death*. In each of these cases, the evidence of thaumazein's foreclosure came in the form of two metaphysical remnants: a transcendental subject (whether in the form of a didactic, violent, or escapist liberator, a hypostatic ego, a self-in-everyone-else's-place, an excessively exalted Other, a simply given "religious" subject, a hedgehog, an "all-square" Abraham, or a voluntaristic God) and an "other" world that stands in stark opposition to "this" one (the open versus the cave, a good, spiritual infinity versus a bad, material infinity, the religious versus the political, the kingdom of heaven versus this world here, now). The denial of thaumazein, it seems, necessitates a reconstitution of the simple identity and pure self-presence of the subject, its objects, *that* world as opposed to *this* one, *our* nation as opposed to *theirs*, and *this* people as opposed to *those*. I would therefore suggest that all these thinkers—sometimes explicitly and sometimes quite inadvertently—have taught us that learning to dwell in wonder is a matter of unsettling the integrity of these formations and retying them differently, of welcoming the most troubling of houseguests into the structure of identity, of learning, to invoke Derrida, to live with ghosts.

### "Il n'y a qu'es spukt"

From the outset, the effort to think through the dynamic of wonder can be called a coming-to-terms with ghosts, if only because, to put it plainly, wonder itself *is* a ghost, haunting the entire tradition it engenders and, like some dead Freudian father, returning most powerfully once it has been most thoroughly excised. The moment it gets going, then, any thinking that conjures thaumazein is a thaumaturgy. On a more complicated level, remaining *with* this disruptive *arrivant* means leaving the house of philosophy wide open to the other specters thaumazein brings along with it: ghosts that trouble the specular integrity of all subjects, objects, spaces, and temporalities. Such specters render being and the world it is in devoid of all essence except existence itself, which is to say relation to innerworldly beings, only themselves as interrupted by a host of others that make them themselves. Thaumazein and its phantom friends thus prevent at all turns the consolidation of the transcendental ego and, at the same time, open all "other" worlds *through* (and only through) this one, revealing the Levinasian il y a as irreducibly haunted—the Heideggerian *es gibt* as *es spukt*.

*Es spukt*: this particular phrase captures Derrida's imagination most powerfully in *Specters of Marx*, where he establishes the structure-interrupting structure of haunting as anterior to the neat distinctions upon which all proper ontology relies. Specters, Derrida notes, refuse to be gathered into one side or another of the classic divides between presence and absence, me and you, us and them, the living and the dead, here and there, now and then, and past and future. A ghost arrives, in excess of this logic, as an other in the heart of the very self it constitutes nonidentically; a ghost emerges as a then and there (whether past, futural, or mythic) in the midst of the nonidentical here, now. For Derrida, then, the most fundamental state of things is that *es spukt*; it haunts; things are insofar as things are haunted. It is therefore possible to extend the insight gained alongside Jean-Luc Nancy in chapter 3 and proclaim that "il n'y a qu'es spukt."

Derrida focuses on the es spukt in his reading of Marx, who gets the phrase from the allegedly ghost-crazed Max Stirner, who avowed, "Ja, es spukt in der ganzen Welt."[23] Interestingly enough, however, a brief treatment of the es spukt can also be found in Rudolf Otto's *Idea of the Holy*, in which he announces the phrase *es spukt hier* as "a first vaguely intimated idea of a numinous something" and even "a *pure* expression of the emotion of uncanniness itself."[24] Otto goes on to vitiate the "purity" of this expression, however, saying that the feeling of being haunted is actually just a "debased" form of the "original awe."[25] He looks in vain through the German language for a "word less vulgar than '*spuken*,'" one that might capture "in an unperverted form" the true response to the awful, awesome nature of the holy. For, unlike "original awe," the es spukt attends to lowly ghosts and spirits—and what's worse, to demons as well—rather than to the truly transcendent, truly awesome, otherworldly Other. Yet one gets the sense from this passage that the es spukt is what "we" are left with, both linguistically and spiritually, here and now, and that if the genuinely aweful other were to break into our degraded spirit-scape, it would do so *through* this not-quite-religious awe:

> It is to be regretted that the German language possesses no general word less vulgar than "spuken," no word which, instead of pointing us aside, as this word does, to the domain of superstition and the impure offshoots of the numinous consciousness,

should retain its fundamental meaning in an unperverted form. But even so we can feel by an effort of imaginative introjection how akin the debased feeling of haunt- ing, given by this word, is to those primary numinous experiences by which long ago seers had experience of "aweful," "holy," numen-possessed places, discovering thereby the starting-points for local cults and the birth places of the "El" worshipped there. . . . Nor can we doubt that even to-day the finer awe that may steal over us in the stillness and half-gloom of our own present-day sanctuaries has ultimate kin- ship . . . with genuine "ghostly" emotions.[26]

One might therefore say that for Otto, *es spukt hier* is the expression of won- der in a time and place where proper, metaphysical wonder is impossible. By remaining with the kind of "debased" awe left to us, however, "we" might briefly catch some of the authentic awe of days gone by: of Moses and Abra- ham, the Psalms and the Vedas—all sites of authentic religious sentiment for Otto and all in the deep past.

What is different about the temporality of the trajectory this study has attempted to follow is that the orientation toward the primordial in Hei- degger's thought is always fundamentally *futural*. Because the "origin" has never *been* as such, it does not lie in wait for our regression to it, but rather always remains to come. This is certainly the case with the thinking of being: because the being that got thinking going has never been thought in the first place, Heidegger's step backward would propel thinking *forward* into an entirely different beginning. Consequently, the Scheu that might endure and wonder at the gift of being's terrifying withdrawal is always articulated in Heidegger's work as a mood of *expectation*.

Faced with the sudden withdrawal of everything it had thought to be familiar, awe understood along these lines remains attuned to the possibility of the impossible; that is, it waits for the arrival of that which *cannot* arrive. This expectation usually finds expression in Heidegger's *Contributions to Phi- losophy* as the anticipation of the passing or the staying away of "the last god," a controversial figure in his late and unpublished writings, to say the least, but also a herald of the arguably more palatable theme in Derrida's work of "the messianic." Distinguishing this hope from messianism, which expects something or someone in particular, Derrida characterizes messiani*city* as the profoundly uncertain, even absurd, expectation of the unforseeble as such:

Awaiting without horizon of the wait, awaiting what one does not expect yet or any longer, hospitality without reserve, welcoming salutation accorded in advance to the absolute surprise of the *arrivant* from whom or from which one will not ask anything in return and who or which will not be asked to commit to the domestic contracts of any welcoming power (family, State, nation, territory, native soil or blood, language, culture in general, even humanity), *just* opening which renounces any right to property, any right in general, messianic opening to what is coming, that is, to the event that cannot be awaited *as such*, or recognized in advance therefore, to the event as the foreigner itself, to her or to him for whom one must leave an empty place, always, in memory of the hope—and this is the very place of spectrality.[27]

Insofar as the unanticipatable can only be anticipated from the thick of impossibility, one might argue that this messianic hope constitutes the much anticipated countermovement to the shock of deconstructive unworking. Shock reveals the terrifying es spukt, and awe learns like Horatio how to speak to ghosts. But this in- and overdeterminate anticipation also sharpens the hazy understanding of Scheu one can garner from the *Contributions*. If shock reveals the impossibility of the possible, then awe, by revealing that the possible is possible by virtue of its impossibility, furthermore *awaits* the possibility of the impossible *as such*: of that which exceeds every horizon of expectation because it cannot be derived from the calculable field of the possible. Awe, along this understanding, would be the attunement to the impossible possibility of the transformative, whether it be in the form of a "new cosmopolitanism," an authentic scene of forgiveness, or genuine relations of care.

Again, because it must welcome that which it cannot foresee, this readiness not to be ready,[28] as Derrida puts it, leaves itself open to the most helpful and the most harmful of spirits. But, without this danger, thinking is condemned to an identical repetition of the safe, the possible, the Same, all reassuring and ultimately violent structures whose integrity is ensured by the twin edifices of the transcendental subject (whether human or divine) and a perfect world that hovers over this imperfect one. I have argued that the vertiginous double movement of wonder, precisely because it dismantles all subjective and otherworldly pretensions, reveals the ordinary as strange, contingent, and, in many cases, ethically insupportable. Wonder takes thinking out to a terrain of impossibility or unacceptability or outrage, where thinking might open itself to another way of doing things. In the absence of any subjective or otherworldly North Star by which it might stop and get its bearings, a thinking that tries to remain within the aboriginally futural opening of thaumazein here, now, must above all learn to watch for the impossible in the midst of a terrifying uncertainty, maintaining itself within what Levinas calls an "open-eyed ignorance."[29] Or, as Nancy puts it, thinking must keep its *"eyes wide open* to the absence of sense, to sense as absence of sense."[30]

### Nearer Than Hands and Feet

The physiognomy here is hardly accidental. Theodorus reports in the *Theaetetus* that both Socrates and the astonished/astonishing Theaetetus have "eyes that stick out" (143e). A moment later, Theodorus praises the boy for being "acute and keen and retentive" (144a), qualities that are ostensibly aided by his wide-open eyes, which seem furthermore to have something to do with his tendency to inspire and experience wonder. We can find these characteristics preliminarily tied together in Descartes' *Passions of the Soul*, wherein wonder takes shape as a "sudden surprise of the soul" that increases attentiveness and strengthens the impression made by its object. Descartes provides a cursory physiological explanation for this, saying that wonder is "by the motion of spirits disposed by this impression [of a wondrous object] to advance with great force upon the place in the brain where it is, to strengthen and preserve it there—as they are also disposed by it to flow from there into the muscles for keeping the sense organs in the same position that they are in, so that if it has been formed by them it will still be maintained by them."[31] Half a century after the publication of *The Passions of the Soul* (1649), the artist Charles Le Brun published his drawings of the emotions Descartes had described, seeking, as one scholar explains it, "to show the necessary connection between the movements of the passions described by Descartes and the movements of facial muscles, and to formulate the laws of facial expression."[32] And, in keeping with the physiognomy suggested in both Descartes and the *Theaetetus*, Le Brun depicts wonder, astonishment, and the more terrified admixtures thereof with abnormally wide eyes as well as dropped jaws and open mouths.[33]

It is upon these two characteristics that Darwin will focus in his *Expression of the Emotions in Humans and Animals*, saying that "the eyes and mouth being widely open is an expression universally recognized as one of surprise or astonishment."[34] As supporting evidence, Darwin cites not only the responses to a questionnaire he had distributed to "informants" around the globe but also Shakespeare, Le Brun, and a nineteenth-century psychologist named Duchenne de Boulogne who, a century and a half after Le Brun's studies, had obtained similar, if infinitely more troubling, results in the eye and mouth regions by stimulating the facial muscles of live human subjects with electrodes.[35] According to Darwin, the facial responses common to these drawings and photos are favorable adaptations, because both increase the animal's chances of surviving the astonishing encounter. The widening of the eyes increases the creature's field and acuity of vision and the opening of the mouth allows the astonished one to hear more acutely by silencing his own breathing (breath enters and exits the body more softly through the mouth than through the nose). Most importantly for Darwin, the wider the mouth is open in astonishment, the more air the animal can take into its body. Wonder, in other words, makes a living being breathe better.

It may seem strange, having gone to such lengths to dismantle so many self-identical constructions of subjectivity, that this study would use its last few breaths to call upon Darwin, whose work, however unwittingly, has in one way or another undergirded some of the most agonistic and egoistic social "ethics" of the last century. What does it mean with respect to the construction of autonomy, however, to breathe? To be sure, the intake and outlet of air constitutes, in perhaps the most elemental way of all, the life of a single organism. Humanly speaking, air makes the self most properly itself; insofar as I breathe, I am no one else but me. At the same time, however, breathing opens the self *essentially* onto every other, taking in and releasing others and self and others-in-self-as-other at each moment. With every inhalation, one is told in elementary school science class, one could well be breathing in a little bit of Einstein, a little bit of Eva Peron, a little bit of the Dalai Lama. With every exhalation, one sends oneself out into the lives of others, for better or worse. And so the same double movement that makes me myself divests me of myself, continually. Perhaps not surprisingly, after commending an "open-eyed ignorance," Levinas concludes *Otherwise Than Being* with a reflection on the astonishing fact "that the breathing by which entities seem to affirm themselves triumphantly in their vital space would be a consummation, a coring out of my substantiality, that in breathing I already open myself to my subjection to the whole of the invisible other." Then, seemingly out of nowhere, he concludes, "it is this wonder [*étonnement*] that has been the object of the book presented here."[36] So the breathing that wonder inspires, dispersing the very self it animates, is itself a wonder.

To recognize this is to recognize that *air itself* suddenly becomes strange when one goes about thinking through wonder. Air: the first element of any thought or being whatsoever and, on an ordinary day, the last thing one would ever think about. Luce Irigaray calls this element "the unthinkable that exceeds all declaration, all saying. Or posing, phenomenon, or form. While remaining the condition of possibility, the resource, the groundless ground." She adds that "to recall that air is at the groundless foundation of metaphysics amounts to ruining metaphysics through and through."[37] For what kind of Being, Idea, or Substance would air constitute? Wind-egg, phantom, vanity, abyss. And yet, what is the isness of anything if not air? And so the astonishing remembrance of air can be said to be twofold: there is on the one hand a shocked recognition that air *essentially* unworks me, installing all sorts of others in me and me in, and as, others, and on the other hand an awed recognition that this perpetual porousness is what—and all—"I" am. This take-and-give thus times itself as the double movement of inhalation, which disrupts all interiority, and exhalation, which affirms existence precisely by disrupting it. Terror and amazement, horror and admiration, anger and resolution, repulsion and fascination, distress and expectation: taking in and letting go. The wonderer wonders: jaw dropped in astonishment, incomprehension, anticipation, rage; ears trained on what calls for help, for justice, for thought; eyes wide open to the absence of sense, the limits of knowledge, the touch of all things that opens out possibility. Perhaps that is it, then: perhaps dwelling in wonder is merely a matter of learning to breathe.[38]

# NOTES

## INTRODUCTION

1. Plato, *Theaetetus*, ed. Williams and Burnyeat, trans. Levett, 144a–b. Other translations that will be cited occasionally are *Theaetetus*, trans. Harold North Fowler, in *Works*, 7:7–257; and *Theaetetus*, trans. F. M. Cornford, in *Plato*, 845–919. All internal citations refer to the Levett and Burnyeat translation with occasional slight modifications; references to other editions are noted.

2. From a Socratic perspective, this not-knowing is, of course, the height of human wisdom. See the *Apology*, in which Socrates explains to the jurors that his wisdom (*sophia*) is only greater than that of others "to this small extent, that I do not think I know what I do not know" (Plato, *Apology*, trans. G. M. A. Grube, in *Complete Works*).

3. Fowler opts for the more conservative "image" to translate *eidôlon*, but both Cornford and Levett/Burnyeat render it as "phantom," which Lidell and Scott list as the sense in which Homer and Aeschylus have used the word, in reference to the ghostly appearances of dead people. See *Lidell and Scott's Greek-English Lexicon*, 7th ed., s.v. "eidolôn."

4. "Kai nê tous theous ge, ô Sôkrates hyperphuôs ôs thaumazô ti pot esti tauta, kai eniote ôs alêthôs Blepôn eis auta skotodiniô." Plato, *Theaetetus*, trans. Fowler, 155c. Because of its retention of Theaetetus's invocation of the gods, as well as the sense of disorientation (rather than glee) that it conveys, the Fowler translation is prefer-

able, at least for these purposes, to Levett's and Burnyeat's, which reads, "Oh yes, indeed, Socrates, I often wonder like mad what these things can mean; sometimes when I'm looking at them I begin to feel quite giddy." Elizabeth Castelli has suggested that, insofar as *hyperphuôs* connotes that which is "monstrous, marvelous, or strange," an even more appropriate translation of the first phrase would be, "I wonder in marvelous excess" (private communication).

5.   Although *thaumazein* is an infinitive, the post-Platonic tradition has gone on to nominalize it into wonder, awe, astonishment, *admiratio, étonnement, Erstaunen,* etc. This study will use both the noun and the gerund forms: the latter more accurately retains the sense of the *activity* of this particular *pathos,* but the former is usually stylistically cleaner.

6.   Sallis, "A Wonder," 252–53.

7.   Plato, *Parmenides,* trans. Mary Louise Gill and Paul Ryan, in *Complete Works,* 129c.

8.   "Astounded at his wisdom as though he were a god": "ethaumazomen epi sophia hôsper theon."

9.   This is a swipe both at Protagoras's exorbitant tuition fees and at the Sophists, who push logic out to false paradox simply for the sake of gaining the reverence of their amazed interlocutors. Among such characters one might name Euthydemus and Dionysodorus, who manage to demonstrate to one of Socrates' pupils that it "is the ignorant who learn and not the wise" *and* that "it is the wise who learn and not the ignorant." Observing Socrates's distress and, as Socrates reports, "in order to confound us further [*mallon thaumaziomen auton*]," the pair of pseudo-teachers "would not let the boy go," continuing to hurdle impossible questions at him and whispering to Socrates, "All our questions are of this same inescapable sort" (Plato, *Euthydemus,* trans. Rosamond Kent Sprague, in *Complete Works,* 276d–e).

10.  See Heidegger, *Vom Wesen der Wahrheit,* 287/*The Essence of Truth,* 204. References to this and all other Heideggerian texts will be given with the German page numbers separated by a slash (/) from the English page numbers.

11.  Sarah Kofman confirms this doubling and also links it to the dynamic of *eros:* "From the beginning, the *Theaetetus* insists upon the corporal and spiritual resemblance of Theaetetus and Socrates: Socrates as the double of Theaetetus: older, favored double who permits Theaetetus, by virtue of the image he offers him, to attain to himself after being stripped of the opinions he falsely imagined to be his own. . . . Miming the erotic pursuit, philosophy is in the pursuit of a soul appropriated to one's own (Kofman, *Lectures de Derrida,* 176; translation mine).

12.  The physiognomy attributed to Socrates and Theaetetus here is important: Charles Darwin, citing Shakespeare, several recent psychological experiments, and ethnographies from five continents, declares that "the eyes and mouth being widely open is an expression universally recognized as one of surprise or astonishment." For Darwin, the wide eyes of the wonderer are a genetic adaptation that increases one's attentiveness by expanding the field of vision (Darwin, *The Expression of Emotions,* 278–82). This will find further elaboration in the postlude.

13.  These two strands can be seen respectively in the tonal difference between two recent explorations of scientific wonder. Charles Scott, a contemporary American

philosopher and ethicist, begins his exploration by considering the viewpoint that science and wonder are mutually exclusive, but ends up arguing that facts can actually *deepen* wonder, precisely by deepening the strangeness and impossibility of their subject matter. Thus the mechanism of the ear and the speed of light are actually more astonishing once our calculations of them reveal the extent to which they exceed our ability to grasp them. Literary critic Philip Fisher, on the other hand, claims that "scientific wonder" is only possible once the self has been secured noetically by a complete understanding of the matter at hand. Rather than revealing the familiar as strange, science for Fisher chases down the new and unfamiliar in order to assimilate it to the realm of the known, a pursuit that produces a calm, delightful "now I get it" experience that Fisher equates with wonder, despite Theaetetus's lostness and the limitations of Horatio's philosophy (both of which Fisher cites in the course of the study). I would argue that the distinction between these two scholars' conceptions of wonder can be roughly mapped onto the distinction between Platonic and Aristotelian wonder sketched below. See Scott, *The Lives of Things;* and Fisher, *Wonder, the Rainbow.*

14. Sallis, "A Wonder," 255.

15. Proudfoot, *Religious Experience,* 84. Particularly in response to Rudolph Otto, Proudfoot discusses the possibility of an emotion's exceeding the limits of rational explanation, venturing that the only reason such an account is plausible at all is that "the rules have been drawn up so as to preclude any naturalistic explanation" (ibid., 118). It should be emphasized in relation to this insight that pushing a pathos beyond the limits of thought for the sake of foreclosing analysis is different from trying to isolate the pathos that, even according to Aristotle, opens the possibility of conceptual analysis in the first place.

16. Beckett, *Happy Days,* 60.

17. Sallis, "A Wonder," 225.

18. See the linking of *wunde, wunt,* and *wond* in the *Mittelhochdeutsches Handwörterbuch von dr. Matthias Lexer* (Leipzig: Hirzel, 1872–78), s.v. *wunde, wunder.* See also Parsons, "A Philosophy of Wonder," 85.

19. *The Oxford English Dictionary* (Oxford: Oxford University Press, 2004), s.v. *wonder.*

20. Burke, *A Philosophical Enquiry,* 58. John Onians does take up the call and expand this etymology somewhat, calling upon the Sanskrit *stupa* and Scandanavian *wundar,* but does so primarily in the service of demonstrating wonder's "universality," rather than its ambivalence. See "'I Wonder . . . '" 11–12. For a treatment of the double meaning of *deinos,* particularly as it is thematized in *Antigone,* see Nussbaum, *The Fragility of Goodness,* 52–73. See David Bollert's connection of this passion to the double valence of the philosopher's thaumazein: "*deinos* can pertain at once to that which evokes an affirming wonder with respect to a human being *and* to that which is uncanny or even monstrous in humanity" (Bollert, "The Wonders," 16). In this study, Bollert distinguishes between the thaumazein of the *bios theoretikos,* which he argues leaves the philosopher in silence and solitude, and the thaumazein of the *bios politikos,* which takes place "amongst the hustle and bustle of active political life" (ibid., 87). While I have a number of reservations about this

separation, one of them is that the wonder of the *bios politikos* in Bollert's work loses the valence of the monstrous, the uncanny, the frightening, and becomes a calm pleasure akin to Philip Fisher's "now I get it" experience: an "of course!" feeling evoked most powerfully in tragedy and rhetoric (see 468). While Bollert acknowledges that "rhetoric and tragedy do not make for a complete political philosophy," they do seem for Bollert to cover the extent of wonder's reach into the political (479).

21. Psalm 33:8. Both the King James and Revised Standard Versions render *yare'* in this passage as "stand in awe"; the Jewish Publication Society version translates it as "dread."

22. Psalm 139:14. JPS translates *yare'* here as "awesomely," *palah* as "wondrously," and *pala'* as "wonderful."

23. Deuteronomy 4:34. JPS translates *mowpheth* as "portents, and *mowra'* (a derivative of *yare'*) as "awesome powers."

24. Exodus 14:31.

25. "Terra Sodomorum non fuit utique ut nunc est. . . . Ecce a conditiore naturarum natura eius in hand foedissimam diversitatem mirabili mutatione conversa est." Augustine, *City of God*, 21.8.1063.

26. Genesis 31:42 and 31:53. Like *yir'ah*, the word *pachad* is used throughout the Hebrew Bible to denote alarm, fright, terror, and dread; see, for example, Deuteronomy 11:25, Isaiah 24:17, and Lamentations 3:47.

27. Psalms 111:10, Proverbs 1:7; cf. Job 28:28. The word for wisdom in Hebrew is *chokmah*, which the Septuagint translates as *Sophia*. Abraham Joshua Heschel confirms this connection between Athens and Jerusalem in two chapters in *God in Search of Man*, where he suggests that "awareness of the divine begins in wonder," and that "the beginning of awe is wonder, and the beginning of wisdom is awe" (Heschel, *God in Search of Man*, 46, 74). "Awe," for Heschel, is wonder that has some understanding of its source; mature wonder, as it were. Heschel does note the ambivalence of the word with which he is working here: *yir'ah*, which "has two meanings: *fear* and *awe*." He goes on, however, to split these two meanings apart from one another, claiming that proper religious awe, "compatible with both love and joy," has no admixture of fear at all: "in a sense," Heschel concludes, "awe is the antithesis of fear," and should therefore render fear null and void (76–77). In the following pages, we will see many such reductions of wonder to a more manageable passion.

28. See Pascal, *Pensées*, 126–29/*Pensées*, 89–90; Burke, *A Philosophical Enquiry*, especially 57–87; Kant, *Kritik der Urteilskraft*/*The Critique of Judgement*, especially "The Analytic of the Sublime"; Otto, *Das Heilige*/*The Idea of the Holy*; Blanchot, *L'écriture du désastre*/*The Writing of the Disaster*; Lacan, *Ecrits*, especially 30–144; and Kristeva, *The Powers of Horror*; Kierkegaard, *Fear and Trembling*, 61.

29. Onians, "'I Wonder . . .'" 32.

30. Hesiod, *Theogony*, 68.

31. David Kravitz, "Harpies," in Kravitz, *Who's Who in Greek and Roman Mythology*, 111.

32. Aristotle, *Metaphysics*, in *The Complete Works of Aristotle*, 983a.

33. Ibid., 982b.

34. Ibid., 983a.

35. Cited in Fisher, *Wonder, the Rainbow*, 60. Over against the logic of a self-eclipsing thaumazein in the *Metaphysics*, David Bollert would posit the section of *On the Parts of Animals* that refers to Heraclitus's kitchen gods, saying that "every realm of nature is marvelous" (*On the Parts of Animals*, 546a15–23; see Bollert, "The Wonders," 398). This, however, is not the dominant strand of Aristotle's thought on wonder's relationship to philosophy and science, and ultimately, Bollert finds thaumazein most convincingly sustained in Aristotle's work on *poesis*, rather than *theoria*. Wonder, even sustained to the point of astonishment (*ekplexis*), is the telos of poetry for Aristotle, and Bollert is concerned throughout "The Wonders" to associate the rhetorical and the tragic with the sphere of the political (see 326, 478). It can therefore be said that there is a rift in Aristotle's work between a self-eclipsing (theoretical) wonder and a sustained (practical-poetic) wonder that, again, is confined to the pleasing, the pleasant, and the desirable (see notes 13 and 21, this chapter).

36. Adelard of Bath, *Die Quaestiones*, 58–59; trans. Daston and Park, *Wonders and the Order of Nature*, 109. Six hundred years later, Goethe will reverse the charge, accusing this investigative curiosity *itself* of childishness. Eckermann records his words thus: "The highest a man can attain . . . is wonder [*Erstaunen*], and when the primordial phenomenon makes him wonder he should be content; it can give him nothing higher, and he should not look for anything beyond it; here is the boundary. But the sight of a primordial phenomenon is not generally enough for men; they think there must be more in back of it, like children who, having looked into a mirror, turn it around to see what is on the other side" (Conversation of Wednesday, February 18, 1829, in Eckermann, *Gespräche mit Goethe*, 244/*Conversations with Goethe*, 147.

37. Albertus Magnus, *Opera Omnia*, tract 2, caput vi; trans. Cunningham, *Woe or Wonder*, 79–80.

38. See Guidon, "L'émerveillement." For a comparison of the overlapping conceptions of wonder between Thomas, Hugh of St. Victor, and Galbert of Bruges, see Rider, "'Wonder with Fresh Wonder.'"

39. "Admiramur enim aliquid cum, effectum videntes, causam ignoramus" (Aquinas, *Summa Theologiae* 1:Q105, A7.

40. "Illud ergo simpliciter mirum est habet causam simpliciter occultam: et hoc sonat nomen miraculi. . . . Causa autem simpliciter occulta omni homini est Deus." Ibid.

41. "Admiratio et stupor refugiunt difficultatem consderationis rei magnae et insolitae, sive sit bona sive male." Ibid., 2/1:Q41, A4.

42. With thanks (and apologies) to Denys Turner and Jeff Rider.

43. Kenseth, *The Age of the Marvelous*, 29.

44. See Weschler, *Mr. Wilson's Cabinet of Wonder*, especially 61; and Impey and MacGregor, *The Origins of Museums*.

45. Onians, "'I Wonder . . . '" 24.

46. Daston and Park, *Wonders and the Order of Nature*, 103.

47. Ibid., 107.
48. Bacon, *The Advancement of Learning*. Just as Aquinas left at least a nominal space for wonder in the category of *miracula*, however, it seems as though, for all his efforts to explain wonder away, Bacon was frequently struck by the possibility that, precisely because nothing was miraculous, everything was miraculous: the Eucharist, the magnet, the common fly, and "the bending of cut twigs toward each other" (Bacon, cited in Bynum, "Wonder," 9).
49. Descartes, *Les passions de l'âme* (Paris, J. Vrin, 1955), A70, A75.
50. Ibid., A73.
51. Ibid., A76. A modern articulation of this argument can be found in the work of Mark Silverman, an American scientist who argues that "wonder is the germinal seed of science" because it drives the scientist to look for causes and results. For that reason, it should be cultivated insofar as it leads to its own resolution in determinate knowledge. "But wonder, in the sense of the magical, miraculous, and incomprehensible is like a narcotic that destroys curiosity and anesthetizes the intellect into catatonic inactivity" (Silverman, "Two Sides of Wonder," 44). The American philosopher Marie I. George calls upon Silverman's thesis to insist that, properly experienced, "wonder is self-destructive" and should act only as a temporary provocation toward certain knowledge of increasingly complex ideas and phenomena: "both science and philosophy involve a chain of wonderings, but not about what has already been understood." While, for George, philosophy wonders at "the natures of things" and science at "their quantitative or particular aspects," both disciplines (at least in their "proper" instantiations) function by means of a progressive eradication of the "naïve" wonder that sparks them: "it is proper to science and philosophy to break matters down into questions which are resolvable" (George, "Wonder as Source," 98, 118, 122, 101). This view stands in stark contrast to Fisher's and Scott's construals of "scientific" or "intellectual" wonder, both of which, despite their prodigious differences, seem indebted to Gabriel Marcel's career-long insistence that "a philosopher remains a philosopher only so long as he retains the capacity for wonderment (*étonnement*) . . . despite everything . . . that tends to dispel it" (Marcel, *The Existential Background of Human Dignity*, 12). A similar argument has been made about good scientists by Charles Peirce, who argued that while second-rate thinkers might think they have overcome wonder, "the Faradays and Newtons seem to themselves like children who have picked up a few pretty pebbles upon the ocean beach" (Peirce, *Collected Papers of Charles Sanders Peirce*, 5:65). The persistence of wonder through scientific discourse particularly holds for quantum physicists, most famously Niels Bohr, who declared, "anyone who is not shocked by quantum theory has not understood it" (cited in Al-Khalili, *Quantum*). This shock has not abated in the decades since Bohr, Einstein, and Schrödinger: at a recent conference at the Massachusetts Institute of Technology, Anton Zeilinger, chair of experimental physics at the University of Vienna, announced, "My personal opinion is that the world is even weirder than what quantum physics tells us" (cited in Dennis Overbye, "Quantum Trickery: Testing Einstein's Strangest Theory," *New York Times*, December 27, 2005, F:1).

52.  Ibid., A152.

53.  Bacon, cited in Daston and Park, *Wonders and the Order of Nature*, 290.

54.  Augustine, *Confessions*, 5.3.5; emphasis added. This is not to say, of course, that a nod toward the divine source of all things would clear the controller, possessor, and/or spectator of marvels from charges of attempted mastery over others. See Elizabeth Castelli's critique of Sydney Parkinson's purported "innocent curiosity," particularly when it is rhetorically referred out to "the Great Superintendant of the universe" (Castelli, "Problems, Questions, and Curiosities").

55.  Augustine, *Confessions*, 5.4.4.

56.  Onians, "'I Wonder . . . '" 32.

57.  For the sake of consistency, and in the interest of not ascribing to Heidegger—at least not immediately—the very ontotheological impulse he was trying to avoid, *being* will be uncapitalized throughout this book, even when the original translator has chosen to render it *Being* to distinguish it from particular beings. No further indication of this change will be given, unless other elements of the translation have been revised as well.

58.  Heidegger, *Beiträge zur Philosophie*, 111/*Contributions to Philosophy*, 78. Emad and Maly render *Seyn* as *be-ing*. In order to retain the archaic resonance of the word, however, other translators prefer *beyng*, which I have also chosen to use throughout. No further indication of this change will be given, unless other elements of the translation have been revised as well.

59.  Heidegger, "Die Frage nach der Technik," in *Vorträge und Aufsätze*, 31; trans. William Lovitt and David Farrell Krell, "The Question Concerning Technology," in *Basic Writings*, 332.

60.  See Martin Heidegger, "Einleitung zu 'Was Ist Metaphysik?'" in *Wegmarken*, 365–83. Translated by Walter Kaufmann as "The Way Back Into the Ground of Metaphysics," in Kaufmann, *Existentialism from Dostoevsky to Sartre*, 206–21.

61.  Heidegger, *Der Satz vom Grund*, 5/*The Principle of Reason*, 5.

62.  Plato, *Sophist*, 244a, cited in the frontmatter of Heidegger, *Sein und Zeit/Being and Time*, xix.

63.  Heidegger, *Was heißt Denken?* 20/*What Is Called Thinking?* 17.

64.  The "joke" could easily be "applied" to Socrates as well, who famously stood still for a whole day in the middle of an active battlefield during the Peloponnesian War. See David Bollert's gloss on this image, as well as that of Socrates standing alone on the neighbor's porch in the middle of *The Symposium*, as prototypical illustrations of the wonder of the *bios theoretikos*. My disagreement with this conclusion will become clear in the following analysis, but Bollert's readings of this dialogue are careful and compelling (see Bollert, "The Wonders," 21–22, 79–86).

65.  Arendt, "Martin Heidegger ist achtzig Jahre alt"/"Martin Heidegger at Eighty."

66.  Arendt, "Philosophy and Politics," 97. Cf. Plato's Seventh Letter: "Acquaintance with [philosophy] must come rather after a long period of attendance on instruction in the subject itself and of close companionship, when, suddenly, like a blaze kindled by a leaping spark, it is generated in the soul and at once becomes self-sustaining" (Plato, *Seventh Letter*, trans. L.A. Post, in *Plato: The Collected Dialogues*, 341c).

67. Socrates himself spends the entirety of the discussion of *khôra* in the *Timaeus* in an attitude of thaumazein, professing a wondrous (*thaumasious*) acceptance of what Timaeus is about to say and allowing the rest of the unforeseeable dialogue to unfold by welcoming it from the beginning (*Timaeus*, 29d). This gesture has provoked some scholars to call Socrates himself a figure of khoric receptivity. See John Sallis, *Chorology: On Beginning in Plato's* Timaeus (Indianapolis: Indiana University Press, 1999), 56; and Derrida, *Khôra*, 61/"Khôra," 110.

68. Heidegger, *Vorträge und Aufsätze*, cited in Arendt, "Martin Heidegger ist achtzig Jahre alt," 240/299.

69. Ibid., 244/303.

70. Ibid., 243/302.

71. Arendt, "Philosophy and Politics," 97–100. On the silence and singularity of the knight of faith, see Søren Kierkegaard, "Problema III: Was It Ethically Defensible for Abraham to Conceal His Undertaking from Sarah, from Eliezer, and from Isaac?" in *Fear and Trembling*, 82–123. A strong reading of the Kierkegaardian self as antisocial and narcissistic can be found in Levinas, "Existence and Ethics," 36. What this interpretation misses, however, and what sets the knight of faith apart from Socrates's caricature of Thales, is the knight's ability to leap out of the world and back into it in the same instant. Along Kierkegaard's reading, faith is a constant double movement that delivers the "single individual" not into some other world but rather back into this one, transforming his relationship to the everyday.

72. Arendt, "Ideology and Terror," 603.

73. Arendt, "Philosophy and Politics," 80.

74. Plato, *Republic*, 514a–20d.

75. "Die grösste Dummheit." See Lacoue-Labarthe, *La fiction du politique*, 26/*Heidegger, Art, and Politics*, 12; see also Ronell, *Stupidity*, 41. It is not certain that Heidegger actually said that his Nazi affiliation was his *grösste Dummheit*; in fact, it is possible that a communal longing for such a statement somehow managed to produce it. Likewise, it has been rumored, but cannot be verified, that Heidegger once said, "Auschwitz is the absolute horror; it is what I fundamentally condemn." Derrida suggests it is not helpful to dwell on either of these as authentic Heideggerian utterances, insofar as verifying and clinging too closely to them risks bringing to a tidy resolution the prodigious difficulty of the relationship between Heidegger's thought and his political commitments. See Derrida, "Heideggers Schweigen," in Neske and Kettering, *Antwort*, 159–60/"Heidegger's Silence," in Neske and Kettering, *Martin Heidegger and National Socialism*, 147.

76. Arendt, "Ideology and Terror," 609

77. Ibid., 607. Cf. Sylviane Agacinski's insistence that "the putting-into-parentheses of experience, which is proper to the existence of foundations, is always at the same time a putting-into-parentheses of others" (Agacinski, *Critique de l'égocentrisme*, 31; translation mine).

## 1. REPETITION

1.  Martin Heidegger, "Überwindung der Metaphysik," in Heidegger, *Vorträge und Aufsätze*, 68/"Overcoming Metaphysics," in *The End of Philosophy*, 85.

2.  For an exploration of this fascination as a broad, and sinister, cultural trend, see Butler, *The Tyranny of Greece Over Germany*.

3.  "Wo aber Gefahr ist, wächst / Das Rettende auch"; Friedrich Hölderlin, "Patmos," cited in Heidegger, "Die Kehre," in *Die Technik und die Kehre*, trans. William Lovett as "The Turning," in *The Question Concerning Technology*, 41. Translation has been altered slightly. For the full text in German and English, see Hölderlin, "Patmos," in *Poems and Fragments*, 463–88.

4.  See Heidegger, "Die Metaphysik als Geschichte des Seins," 397–416/32–54.

5.  Heidegger, "Die Frage nach der Technik," 30/331.

6.  Ibid.

7.  *Die Neugier*; cf. the condemnation of *curiositas* in Augustine, *Confessions* 10.14.54–55.

8.  Heidegger, *Sein und Zeit*, 171/160.

9.  In the *Contributions to Philosophy*, Heidegger shows curiosity to be bound up with modernity's mania for *Berechnung* (calculation) and *Schnelligkeit* (acceleration); Heidegger, *Beiträge zur Philosophie*, 120–21/84.

10. The word for "not-staying" is *Unverweilen*. Heidegger, *Sein und Zeit*, 347/319. For a contemporary study of this impulse as a kind of broad cultural mania, see Gleick, *Faster*.

11. Heidegger, *Sein und Zeit*, 347/319.

12. Gottfried Wilhelm Leibniz, "An Odd Thought Concerning a New Sort of Exhibition," in *Selections*, 587–88.

13. Heidegger, *Sein und Zeit*, 172/161. For a discussion of the earliest appearance of wonder in Heidegger's work, see Bollert, "The Wonders," chapter 3, especially 391–400. Bollert works with Heidegger's 1924–25 lecture series at the University of Marburg in order to illustrate Heidegger's selective reading of Platonic/Aristotelian thaumazein; particularly the extent to which Heidegger neglects to address the *bios politikos* in either thinker (see also 288f).

14. On the relationship between *Angst* and thaumazein, see the discussion in the following section of this chapter.

15. Heidegger, *Grundfragen der Philosophie*, 156/136.

16. Ibid.

17. Ibid., 163/142.

18. "Der bestirnte Himmel über mir, und das moralische Gesetz in mir." Kant, *Kritik der praktischen Vernunft*, 300/*Critique of Practical Reason*, 203.

19. Kant, *Kritik der Urteilskraft*, 199/ *The Critique of Judgment*, 133.

20. Heidegger, *Grundfragen der Philosophie*, 166/144; translation altered slightly. Further citations will appear internally.

21. These deleted passages are appended to both the German and English volumes of the *Grundfragen*, 195–223/168–186.

22. See Safranski, *Martin Heidegger*, 320.

23. In the first decade of the twenty-first century, we might be quicker to associate the affective complex of *Erschrecken* and *Scheu* with the American military strategy of "Shock and Awe," a tactic that aims to achieve "rapid dominance" in war zone and occupied territories. See the postlude for a discussion of this tactic in relation to an internalized thaumazein.

24. This utterance, which Heidegger did, in fact, deliver in public, hails from his 1929–30 lecture series. Heidegger, *Die Grundbegriffe der Metaphysic*, 255/172.

25. Heidegger, *Beiträge zur Philosophie*, 21/16.

26. Ibid., 14/11. Emad and Maly render *Verhaltenheit* as "reservedness," *Erschrecken* as "startled dismay," and *Scheu* as "deep awe." For the sake of consistency, however, this study generally stays with Rojcwicz's and Schuwer's translations of *Erschrecken* and *Scheu* as "terror" and "awe"—"dismay" seems far too mild for what Heidegger has in mind, and there is no typically Heideggerian diacritical mark or spelling alteration in the German that would necessitate adding "deep" as a qualifier of "awe." Emad's and Maly's translation of *Schrecken* as "shock" (which Heidegger occasionally uses interchangeably with *Erschrecken*) will be retained.

27. Heidegger, "Was ist Metaphysik?" in *Wegmarken*, GA 9 (Frankfurt am Main: V. Klostermann, 1967), 19. Translated by David Farrell Krell as "What is Metaphysics?" in *Basic Writings*, 110.

28. Heidegger, *Sein und Zeit*, 189/176.

29. Heidegger, "Was ist Metaphysik?" 9/100.

30. Heidegger, "Nachwort zu 'Was ist Metaphysik?'" in *Wegmarken*, 103, trans. William McNeill as "Postscript to 'What Is Metaphysics?'" in *Pathmarks*, 234.

31. The verb "to marvel" is *admirer*; "to be terrified" is *s'effraier*. Pascal, *Pensées*, 127–128/89–90.

32. Ibid., 127–128/90.

33. Ibid., 125/88.

34. Heidegger, *Beiträge zur Philosophie*, 16/12.

35. Ibid., 487/343.

36. Ibid., 69/48.

37. Ibid., 16/12.

38. Heidegger, "Was ist Metaphysik?" 13/102.

39. Heidegger, *Beiträge zur Philosophie*, 16/12.

40. Ibid., 353/247.

41. Ibid., 36/25.

42. *Erstaunlichen Aufbau*. Heidegger, *Vom Wesen der Wahrheit*, 269/191; translation modified, emphasis added. Further references to this work appear parenthetically in text.

43. In the *Grundfragen*, Heidegger will say that *Staunen* is closer to amazement or stupefaction than it is to authentic wonder; see the discussion in "Wonder and the 'First Beginning,'" this chapter.

44. "Die volle Kraft des Überraschenden und zugleich des Verwunderlichen."

45. "The curious or marvelous [*das Wunderliche und Verwunderliche*] . . . arises from the desire for amazement [*das Sichwundern*], engages it, and sustains it . . . makes

the search for ever new things of this kind more ardent"; Heidegger, *Grundfragen*, 157/136.

46. Socrates asks, "But a man certainly doesn't think that things he knows are things he does not know, or again that things he doesn't know are things he knows." Theaetetus responds, "Teras gar estai" (Plato, *Theaetetus*, 188c), which Heidegger translates as "Wenn es so etwas gäbe, wäre das das reine Wunder": "If that were the case, it would be a miracle"; Heidegger, *Vom Wesen der Wahrheit*, 269/191; translation altered. The Levett and Burnyeat translation, "that would be a very odd thing" loses all sense of the miraculous, and Fowler's "that would be a monstrous absurdity" is a bit dramatic.

47. Some of the labels of the diagram have been modified to reflect the attributes Heidegger assigns to each stage.

48. Some of the labels of the diagram have been modified to reflect the attributes Heidegger assigns to each stage.

49. Plato, *Theaetetus*, 210c.

50. Heidegger, *Der Satz vom Grund*, 157/104–5.

51. Arendt, "Martin Heidegger ist achtzig Jahre alt," 240/"Martin Heidegger at Eighty," 299.

52. The first account of the cave can be found in Heidegger, *Vom Wesen der Wahrheit*, 1–147/1–106. The second account can be found in Heidegger, "Platons Lehre von der Wahrheit," in *Wegmarken*, 109–44, trans. Thomas Sheehan as "Plato's Doctrine of Truth," in *Pathmarks*, 155–82. On Heidegger's postwar censure, see Jaspers, "Letter to the Freiburg University Denazification Committee"; and Jaspers' request that the censure be lifted: "Letter to Gerd Tellenbach," 5 June 1949, in Neske and Kettering, *Martin Heidegger and National Socialism*, 239–40.

53. Platon, *Der Staat*, in *Sämtliche Werke in Zwei Bänden*, 2:92–394.

54. Plato, *Republic*, 514a–15c. Subsequent references will be cited internally.

55. Heidegger translates *alêthetera* as *das Wahrere* and *das Unverborgene*, and *mallon onta* as *seiender*.

56. Heidegger, "Platons Lehre von der Wahrheit," 121/165. Further references will appear internally.

57. Hume, *The Natural History of Religion*, in *Dialogues and Natural History of Religion*, 185.

58. Arendt, , "Martin Heidegger ist achtzig Jahre alt," 242/ "Martin Heidegger at Eighty," 300.

59. Caputo, "From the Primordiality of Absence," 196.

60. Heidegger, "German Students," November 3, 1938, trans. William S. Lewis, in Wolin, *The Heidegger Controversy*, 47.

61. Jaspers, *Philosophische Autobiographie*, 101, cited in Safranski, *Martin Heidegger*, 232.

62. Safranski, *Martin Heidegger*, 333.

63. See Otto Pöggeler, "Heidegger's Political Self-Understanding," trans. Steven Galt Crowell, in Wolin, *The Heidegger Controversy*, 228.

64. Heidegger, *Einführung in die Metaphysik*, 10/14.

65. Heidegger, "Nachwort zu 'Was ist Metaphysik?'" 102/233.

66. Heidegger, *Grunfragen der Philosophie*, 168/145.
67. Heidegger, *Sein und Zeit*, 267/247, 179/167.
68. Heidegger, *Beiträge zur Philosophie*, 417/293.

## 2. OPENNESS

1.  Heidegger, *Beiträge zur Philosophie*, 16/12.
2.  Aristophanes, *Clouds*, line 260.
3.  See Levinas, *De l'existence*, 19/4. References to this and all other texts by Levinas are given with the original page numbers separated by a slash (/) from the page numbers in translation. Perhaps following Derrida's playful suggestion in "Violence and Metaphysics" that Levinas might be "allergic" to Heidegger (Jacques Derrida, "Violence and Metaphysics: An Essay on the Thought of Emmanuel Levinas," trans. Alan Bass, in *Writing and Difference*), Levinas finally did admit to his inability to escape the problems and possibilities Heidegger had opened. See Levinas, *Ethique et infini*, 33–40/37–42.
4.  Levinas, *Autrement qu'être*, 81/48.
5.  Levinas, *Totalité et infini*, 45/15.
6.  Levinas, *Entre nous*, 23, 22/10, 9.
7.  Arendt, "Martin Heidegger ist achtzig Jahre alt," 242/ "Martin Heidegger at Eighty," 300.
8.  Levinas, *Entre nous* 17/5.
9.  Levinas, *Totalité et infini*, 17/47. Since Levinas capitalizes *being* in order to critique it as a totality, I have retained this choice in quotations from his work.
10. Ibid., 17/47, 22/51.
11. It was in 1943 that Heidegger wrote "being presumably prevails in its essence without beings," and in 1947 that he changed the "presumably" to "never." See chapter 1, "Rethinking Thaumazein."
12. Derrida, "Violence and Metaphysics," 136.
13. Heidegger, "Nachwort," 102/233.
14. Martin Heidegger, "Vom Wesen der Wahrheit," in *Wegmarken*, 84, trans. John Sallis as "On the Essence of Truth," in *Basic Writings*, 125; emphasis added.
15. See chapter 1, "Once Again to the Cave."
16. Especially in his earlier work, Levinas seems to reinstall a metaphysics of presence in his appeal to the face—a move he tries to correct in later interviews by characterizing the face as an "enigma" rather than a phenomenon, or a call rather than an appearance (See *Ethique et infini*, 89/95). Whether or not he is entirely successful is of little import to this study, for whose purposes Levinas's face would perhaps be better translated as "gaze"—the exposing and exposed trace of the strange in the familiar.
17. Levinas, *Hors Sujet*, 68/47; translation modified slightly.
18. Levinas, *De Dieu qui Vient à l'idée*, 114/69.
19. Although Levinas insists, contra Martin Buber and Gabriel Marcel, that "intersubjectivity" (what he will come to call the ethical/metaphysical relationship) must

remain nonreciprocal lest it dissolve into a self-interested totality, we see catch in this mutual exposure a glimpse of what Derrida calls a "strange symmetry" underlying the asymmetrical ethical relationship. See Derrida, "Violence and Metaphysics," 127.

20. Levinas, *Autrement qu'être*, 147/92, 218/139. See also Levinas's discussion of testimony and the biblical *hineni* in *Ethique et infini*, 113–121/106–113.

21. Levinas, *Les Noms Propres*, 62/43.

22. "Se noyaute le noyau du Moi" (Levinas, *Autrement qu'être*, 105/64; translation altered slightly).

23. Levinas, *De Dieu qui Vient à l'idée*, 120/73.

24. Ibid., 36/16.

25. Alphonso Lingis, "Introduction," in Derrida, *Otherwise Than Being*, xxxiii. The responsibility for one's own suffering continually troubles Levinas, but he nevertheless maintains its inescapability as the extreme logic of ethical passivity. See, for example, *Autrement qu'être*, 81/47, 121/75, *Entre nous*, 75/59, and *Ethique et infini*, 106/99.

26. Levinas, *Ethique et infini*, 61/60. This is Descartes' first of two major proofs of the existence of God, located in Meditation Three (Descartes, *Meditationes de Prima Philosophia/Méditations Métaphysiques*, 34–51/*Meditations on First Philosophy*, 69–81). The other proof, which seems directly to contradict the insight that the self cannot arrive at the idea of God through its own faculties, can be found in Meditation Five: "from the fact that I cannot think of God except as existing, it follows that existence is inseparable from God, and that for this reason he really exists" (ibid., 66/89).

27. Descartes, *Meditationes de Prima Philosophia*, 51/80.

28. Levinas, *De Dieu qui Vient à l'idée*, 104/62. Rigorous as this demonstration may be, the question whether the total rupture of the *res cogitans* is what Descartes had in mind when he set out to prove God's existence remains, at the very least, an open one.

29. Levinas, *Ethique et infini*, 96–97/91.

30. In other works, Levinas criticizes *anamnesis* more directly, charging it with egoism and uninterrupted interiority. *Totalité et infini*, in particular, is ridden with critiques of Socratic midwifery: see, for example, 14/44, 22/51, 155/180, and 178/203. Through to the end of his authorship, Levinas insisted that since Socratically speaking, I can "receive nothing of the other but what is in me," the idea of the infinite is refractory to all "Socratic" recollection (Levinas, *Noms propres*, 13/43; *De Dieu qui Vient à l'idée*, 107–8/64).

31. Strangely, one of Levinas's antimaieutic moments *immediately* follows a lengthy praise of the fourth delirium's unassimilable exteriority. See *Totalite et infini*, 22/51.

32. Plato, *Theaetetus*, trans. Cornford, 210b. Levinas seems to have been familiar with the *Theaetetus* (see *Totalité et infini*, 31/59), but does not discuss it in connection with the idea of the infinite.

33. Descartes, *Les passions de l'âme*, A73.

34. Descartes, *Meditationes de Prima Philosophia*, 51/80; emphasis added.

35. "This penetration of a total system into a partial one that cannot assimilate it is miracle [*miracle*]" (Levinas, *Entre nous*, 28/16). "Before being posed in the world and satisfied with responses, the question would be, by way of the demand or the prayer that it carries—by way of the wonder [*émerveillement*] in which it is opened—a relationship-to-God" (Levinas, *De Dieu qui Vient à l'idée*, 186/120). "What, in action, breaks forth as essential violence is the surplus of being over the thought that claims to contain it, the marvel [*merveille*] of the idea of infinity" (Levinas, *Totalité et infini*, xv/27). "What then is the intrigue of meaning, other than that . . . formed in the idea of the Infinite—in the monstrosity [*monstruosité*] of the Infinite *placed* in me—an idea which in its passivity beyond all receptivity is no longer an idea?" (Levinas, *De Dieu qui Vient à l'idée*, 110/66). "Through a third term . . . the shock [*choc*] of the encounter with the other is deadened" (Levinas, *Totalité et infini* 12/42); "a shock must be produced which . . .would furnish the *occasion* for a resumption of relations with exteriority" (ibid., 123/149; emphasis in text). "Subjectivity realizes these impossible exigencies—the astonishing feat [*le fait étonnant*] of containing more than it is possible to contain" (ibid., xv/27); "Discourse is thus the experience of something absolutely foreign, a *pure* 'knowledge' or 'experience,' a *traumatism of astonishment* [*traumatisme de l'étonnement*]" (ibid., 45–46/73; emphasis in text). "The Infinite . . . an order that slips into me like a thief, despite the taut weave of consciousness; a trauma that surprises me absolutely [*traumatisme qui me surprend absolument*] . . ." (Levinas, *De Dieu qui Vient à l'idée*, 123/75). "The breakup of the actuality of thought in the 'idea of God' is a passivity more passive than any passivity, like the passivity of a trauma [*traumatisme*] through which the idea of God would have been placed in us" (ibid., 106/64).

36. Levinas, *De Dieu qui Vient à l'idée*, 108/65. See also the interview with Philippe Nemo in which, in response to Nemo's "how does one begin thinking?" Levinas answers, "It probably begins through traumatisms or gropings to which one does not even know how to give a verbal form: a separation, a violent scene . . . initial shocks become questions and problems, giving one to think" (Levinas, *Ethique et infini*, 15/21).

37. Levinas, *Totalité et infini*, 45–46/73.

38. Levinas, *Entre nous*, 151/132.

39. Derrrida, "Violence and Metaphysics," 127.

40. See Levinas's exposure of the violence of theodicy in Levinas, "La souffrance inutile," in *Entre Nous*, 107–19/91–102, and "Transcendence et Mal," in *De Dieu qui Vient à l'idée*, 189–207/122–36.

41. Levinas, *Entre nous*, 109–10/93.

42. Levinas, *De Dieu qui Vient à l'idée*, 198/128.

43. Richard Bernstein, "Evil and Theodicy," in Critchley and Bernasconi, *The Cambridge Companion to Levinas*, 260.

44. Levinas, *De Dieu qui Vient à l'idée*, 203/131.

45. Ibid, 201/130; see also *Entre nous*, 118/100.

46. Levinas, *De Dieu qui Vient à l'idée*, 134/83.

47. "Monde cassé . . . monde bouleversé" (Levinas, *De l'existence*, 25/7).

48. Ibid., 44/80.

49. Levinas, *Le temps et l'autre*.

50. Levinas, *Ethique et infini*, 47/49.

51. Levinas, *De l'existence*, 112/63.

52. In the next sections, especially, I am indebted to Catherine Keller's work on the violent subjections and uninvited returns of preontological *tehom*, whose messy, feminine not-nothingness Christian orthodoxy in particular goes to such lengths to repress. Keller, *The Face of the Deep*.

53. Levinas insists that the il y a is neither personal nor a figure of donation. He thereby aligns himself ahead of time with Derrida's reading of Plato's *khôra*, which both generates and negates the subject, but which neither gives nor promises anything. Derrida, *Khôra*. See also John Caputo, "Khôra: Being Serious with Plato," in Derrida and Caputo, *Deconstruction in a Nutshell*, 71–105. As we will see in our reading of *Totality and Infinity*, however, it is hardly clear that the il y a is distinct from primordial donation.

54. See, for example, Levinas, *De l'existence*, 99–100/56 and *Ethique et infini*, 47/49. Levinas uses the word *experience* tentatively and only insofar as such an event is neither undergone nor assimilated by a self-identical "subject of experience."

55. For a thorough discussion of this question, see Brogan, "Nausea."

56. Levinas, *De l'existence*, 27–28/9.

57. Ibid., 98/54.

58. Ibid., 121/68, 102/58. For a consideration of the possible echo of Sartre's *huis clos* in Levinas's *sans-issus*, see Brogan, "Nausea," 148.

59. Levinas, *De l'existence*, 96/54.

60. Levinas, *Le temps et l'autre*, 21/40. This is the text of the first lecture at the Collège Philosophique, 1946–47, in which Levinas rejects Heidegger's primordial ontological relation primarily because, as "precomprehension," it allegedly reinscribes the self, others, and being within an epistemological totality. As Avital Ronell has argued, however, precomprehension does not comprehend much: "*Dasein*'s precomprehension of being is more or less dumbfounded. As [Jean-Luc] Nancy writes of Heidegger, 'It is perhaps possible to say, however, that it is a comprehension that is "entirely stupid"' (Ronell, *Stupidity*, 74). Such a relation, in other words, is closer to a primordial openness to being than it is to any epistemological grasp on being.

61. Levinas, *De l'existence*, 140–41/83.

62. The verse continues: "and here shall thy proud waves be stayed" (Job 38:11 [JPS]). The il y a will take on an even more explicitly elemental, especially watery, tone in *Totalité et infini*.

63. Levinas, *De l'existence*, 98/55, 122/69.

64. Hobbes, *Leviathan*, 2.17.13.

65. Ibid., 172–73/105.

66. *Le temps et l'autre*, 37/56.

67. Ibid., 39/58.

68. Levinas, *De l'existence*, 170/103.

69. Ibid., 159/96.

70. Levinas, *Ethique et infini*, 57–58/57.

71. Levinas, *Le temps et l'autre*, 28/49.

72. Ibid., 64/76.

73. Ibid., 58/71.

74. Ibid., 71/80.

75. See Levinas, *De l'existence*, 83–105/45–60, and "La réalité et son ombre," trans. Lingis as "Reality and Its Shadow." Perhaps needless to say, this is a disappointingly unnuanced reading of Heidegger, who is quite clear that, in accordance with his understanding of truth, the "opening" of art is not only a revealing but also a concealing: its world, as vertically suspended between sky and earth, a clearing that both illuminates and obscures. See Heidegger, *Der Ursprung des Kunstwerkes*, trans. Albert Hofstadter as "The Origin of the Work of Art," in *Basic Writings*, 143–212.

76. Levinas, *De l'existence*, 91–2/51; "La realité et son ombre," 777/5.

77. Levinas, "La realité et son sombre," 774/3, 776/4.

78. Gerald Bruns, "Concept of Art," in *The Cambridge Companion to Levinas*, 214.

79. Levinas, "La realité et son sombre," 784/10.

80. Ibid., 786/11.

81. Ibid., 787/12.

82. Ibid. It should be noted that along with Levinas's reduction of the il y a to the pleasing comes his reduction of art to "the beautiful," a move that excludes the horrifying, the astonishing, and the sublime, all in the same brush stroke.

83. Levinas, *Difficile liberté*, 375–76/293.

84. Levinas, *Totalité et infini*, 13/43.

85. "Here is the path taken by the author of this book: an analysis which feigns the disappearance of every existent—and even of the *cogito* which thinks it—is overrun by the chaotic rumbling of an anonymous 'to exist,' which is an existence without existents and which no negation manages to overcome. . . . Enlightenment and meaning dawn only with the existents rising up and establishing themselves in this horrible neutrality of the *there is*. They are on the path which leads from existence to the existent and from the existent to the Other, a path which delineates time itself" (Levinas, *Difficile liberté*, 375/292).

86. Levinas, *Totalité et infini*, 110/136. It should be noted, particularly as a qualification of the psychoanalytic connection we have opened here, that the calm, self-satisfied, need-driven *jouissance*—at least as *Levinas explicitly understands it* (and his thought may well betray him)—differs fundamentally from the insatiable desire and erotic excess for which a Lacan, Kristeva, or Bataille would reserve the term.

87. Ibid., 104/130–31. For a critique of woman's nonreciprocal role as "an *envelope*, a *container*, the starting point from which man limits his things," see Irigaray, *Ethique de la difference sexuelle/An Ethics of Sexual Difference*, 17–19/10–12.

88. Ibid., 108/135, 110/137, 114/141.

89. Ibid., 132/158–59.

90. The fragment in which Anaximander posits the *apeiron* has been preserved in Simplicius's *Commentary on Aristotle's Physics* as "ex ôn de ê genesis esti tois ousi kai tên phthoran eis tauta ginesthai kata to khreôn. didonai gar auta dikên kai tisin allêlois tês adikias kata tên tou khronou taxin." After a number of preparatory attempts, Heidegger finally translates the fragment, "But that from which things

arise also gives rise to their passing away, according to what is necessary; for things render justice and pay penalty to one another for their injustice, according to the ordinance of time" (Heidegger, "Der Spruch des Anaximander," in *Holzwege*, 303, trans. David Farrell Krell and Frank A. Capuzzi as "The Anaximander Fragment," in *Early Greek Thinking*, 20). It is Simplicius who clarifies that Anaximander's *aperion* is "the Infinite, [Anaximander] being the first to introduce this name for the material cause. He says it is neither water nor any other of the so-called elements, but a substance different from them, which is infinite, from which arise all the heavens and the worlds within them. And into that from which things take their rise they pass away once more" (*Philoctetes: textes anciennes*, s.v. "Anaximander," trans. John Bernet, [http://philoctetes.free.fr/Anaximander.html]).

91.   Levinas, *Totalité et infini*, 115/141, 132/159.

92.   Ibid., 116/143.

93.   Ibid., 121/147.

94.   Cf. Catherine Keller's reading of Marduk's slaying of Tiamat in the *Enuma Elish* (Keller, *The Face of the Deep*, 28–31).

95.   "The elements remain at the disposal of the I [*le moi*]—to take or leave. Labor will henceforth draw things from the elements and thus *discover* the world"; Levinas, *Totalité et infini*, 130/156. Cf. the introduction to Hegel's *Philosophy of History*, in which the dialectic is exemplified in the process of domesticating and excluding the very elements used to build a house. Hegel, *Introduction to the Philosophy of History*, 30.

96.   Levinas, *Totalité et infini*, 134/160; emphasis added; subsequent references will be cited internally.

97.   See the discussion in the section "Closing Down: From Existence to Existent," this chapter.

98.   See, in particular, Heidegger, "Nachwort zu 'Was ist Metaphysik?'"

99.   "L'étranger . . . trouble le chez soi."

100.   Again, this particular opposition depends upon a highly reductive reading of *anamnesis*; see the section "Infinity and Astonishment," this chapter.

101.   "Fear no more the heat o' the sun, / Nor the furious winter's rages; / Thou thy worldly task hast done, / Home art gone, and ta'en thy wages: / Golden lads and girls all must, / As chimney-sweepers, come to dust." William Shakespeare, *Cymbeline*, in *The Riverside Shakespeare*, 4.2.258–263. As Shakespeare demonstrates in this eulogy, the only other who could truly silence the elements would be *death*.

102.   This, at least, is the position Levinas most consistently espouses throughout the work. There are numerous moments in the text, however, that betray a certain reluctance to abandon the self-constituted self of his earlier work. Levinas argues, for example, that the pain of suffering for the other *must* be preceded (not equiprimordial) with the pleasure of enjoyment (*jouissance*): "one has to first enjoy one's bread, not in order to have the merit of giving it, but in order to give it with one's heart, to give oneself in giving it" (Levinas, *Autrement qu'être*, 116/72). Or: "Enjoyment in its ability to be complacent in itself, exempt from dialectical tensions, is the *condition* of the for-the-other involved in sensibility" (ibid., 119/74; emphasis added).

103. Ibid., 111/69.
104. Levinas, "Humanisme et An-archie," in *Humanisme de l'autre homme*, 81/137.
105. Ibid., 82/138.
106. Levinas, *Autrement qu'être*, 30/14.
107. Ibid., 181/115.
108. Levinas, *Le temps et l'autre*, 19/41.
109. Levinas, *Autrement qu'être*, 29/13; translation modified slightly.
110. Levinas, *Entre nous*, 133–4/115.
111. See Levinas, *Le temps et l'autre*, 28/49, and *Totalité et infini*, 60/31. See also the section "Closing Down: From Existence to Existent," this chapter.
112. Levinas, *De Dieu qui Vient à l'idée*, 115/69.
113. See the discussion of Descartes in the introduction, "The Death and Resurrection of Thaumazein."
114. Miller, *In the Throe of Wonder*, 7–8.
115. Peperzak, "Illeity According to Levinas," 43.
116. Ibid.
117. Ibid., emphasis added.
118. Kearney, *Strangers, Gods, and Monsters*, 77.
119. Ibid., 72.
120. Heidegger, *Was heißt denken?* 15/13.
121. Levinas, *Sur Maurice Blanchot*, 23/137.
122. Ibid., 22/136.
123. Augustine, *City of God*, 21.8.1063. See the discussion of Augustine in the introduction, "The Death and Resurrection of Thaumazein."
124. Levinas, *Sur Maurice Blanchot*, 25/139.
125. Levinas, *Difficile liberté*, 22/8; emphasis in last sentence added.
126. Levinas, *Autrement qu'être*, 246/158.
127. Levinas, *Hors sujet*, 52/35.
128. Levinas, *Autrement qu'être*, 137–8/86.
129. "I am I in the sole measure that I am responsible, a non-interchangeable I. I can substitute myself for everyone, but no one can substitute himself for me. Such is my inalienable identity of the subject" (Levinas, *Ethique et infini*, 108/101).
130. "With regard to its positive modes, concern [*Fürsorge*] has two extreme possibilities. It can, so to speak, take the other's 'care' [*Sorge*] away from him and put itself in his place in taking care [*besorgen*], it can *leap in* for him. Concern takes over what is to be taken care of for the other. *The other is thus displaced*, he steps back so that afterwards, when the matter has been attended to, he can take it over as something finished and available or disburden himself of it completely. In this concern, *the other can become one who is dependent and dominated* even if this domination is a tacit one and remains hidden from him" (Heidegger, *Sein und Zeit*, 122/114; emphasis added to last two sentences).
131. Levinas, *Entre nous*, 129/111.
132. Ibid., 49/35.
133. Deleuze, *Masochism*, 41, 75.
134. Levinas characterizes the passive subject as the one who is "vulnerable, that is,

sensible, to which—like the One of Plato's *Parmenides*—being cannot be attributed" (Levinas, *Autrement qu'être*, 91/54).

135. Again confirming our suspicion that universal place taking is not the task of mere mortals, Levinas writes that like the One, the subject can only "overflow with plenitude" from *beyond* being, "out of disinterestedness, out of signification, out of the one-for-the-other" (ibid., 152/95).

136. Ibid., 183/116. At this point, it has become highly doubtful whether the meaning of "subject" can, in fact, be divorced from its association with *substantia, hypokeimenon*, etc.

137. Ibid., 235/150; cf. 218/139.

138. See Avital Ronell's meditation on the tragedy of stupidity as answering a call that was never placed (in particular, the possibility that Abraham's "Here I am," in this sense, could have enacted the worst stupidity of all). Ronell, *Stupidity*, 306–19.

139. Isaiah 65:25 (JPS); emphasis added.

140. This conviction runs through the bulk of these thinkers' works, but for concise formulations of this argument, see for example Derrida, *Donner la mort*, especially the section surrounding Derrida's inscription of "tout autre est tout autre," 114–57/82–115; and Wyschogrod, "Language and Alterity."

141. Levinas, *Hors sujet*, 10/2; translation modified.

142. Levinas, *Autrement qu'être*, 181/115; translation modified.


## 3. RELATION

1. Dasein as Mitsein "has the primordial constitution of being of care (being-ahead-of-itself—already-being-in-a-world—as being together with innerworldly beings)" (Heidegger, *Sein und Zeit*, 202/188).

2. "This being-with-one-another dissolves one's own Dasein completely into the kind of being of 'the others' in such a way that the others, as distinguishable and explicit, disappear more and more. In this inconspicuousness and unascertainability, the they unfolds its true dictatorship. We enjoy ourselves and have fun the way *they* enjoy themselves. We read, see, and judge literature and art the way *they* see and judge. But we also withdraw from the 'great mass' the way *they* withdraw, we find 'shocking' what *they* find shocking. The they [*das Man*], which is nothing definite and which all are, though not as a sum, prescribes the kind of being of everydayness" (ibid., 126–27/119).

3. Ibid., 251/232. See also Heidegger's insistence that "the ownmost possibility is *nonrelational*. Anticipation lets Dasein understand that it has to take over solely from itself the potentiality-of-being in which it is concerned absolutely about its ownmost being" (ibid., 263/243).

4. While Heidegger writes that "a mere subject without a *world* 'is' not initially and is also never given," he does not extend this "never" in relation to other beings, implying, it seems, that while Dasein cannot escape the world, it can ultimately escape relations: "an isolated I without the others is in the end just as far from being given *initially*" (ibid,. 116/109).

5.   "Dasein is individuated, but *as* being-in-the-world. Being-in enters the existential 'mode' of *not-being-at-home*. The talk about "uncanniness" [*Unheimlichkeit*] means nothing other than this" (ibid., 189/176).

6.   Levinas, *Autrement qu'être*, 146/115.

7.   A similar line of thought forms part of Derrida's reading of Levinas in "Violence and Metaphysics." Derrida, "Violence and Metaphysics."

8.   Against the almost unbearable weight of the "received" reading of Heidegger, such interpretations have been explicitly developed by a number of scholars, perhaps foremost among them Jean-Luc Nancy. See also Alan Bass, *Difference and Disavowal: The Trauma of Eros* (Stanford: Stanford University Press, 2000); Carman, *Heidegger's Analytic*; Dreyfus, *Being in the World*; Fynsk, *Heidegger, Thought, and Historicity*; Raffoul, *A chaque fois mien/Heidegger and the Subject*; and Schürmann, *Heidegger on Being and Acting*. Although the interpretive possibility offered throughout this chapter is to a large extent dependent upon the work of these authors, it also diverges from their (already divergent) approaches to this question, most notably in its suggestion that something like a "repetition" takes place in the moment of authenticity.

9.   Heidegger, *Sein und Zeit*, 179/167.

10.  See for example ibid., 130/122, 297–98/274. Some of Heidegger's later works, including "On the Essence of Truth," "The Way Back into the Ground of Metaphysics," and the *Beiträge zur Philosophie*, are discussed in this chapter.

11.  Adorno, *Jargon der Eigentlichkeit*; Farías, *Heidegger et le nazisme*. See also the MIT edition of Wolin, *The Heidegger Controversy*, the editor's introduction to which sets forth the simplistic and, one senses, mean-spirited charge that "Deconstruction," as incorrigibly Heideggerian, is infected with Nazism. See also Jacques Derrida's responses to the variously scandalous "affairs" generated by such conversations in "Heidegger: L'enfer des philosophes," in *Points de suspension*, 193–202, trans. Peggy Kamuf as "Heidegger, the Philosopher's Hell," in *Points*, 181–90; see also Jacques Derrida, "The Work of Intellectuals and the Press (The Bad Example: How the *New York Review of Books* and Company Do Business)," in *Points*, 422–54. For a nuanced, reflective set of considerations of the relation between Heidegger's ontology and the political landscape of the early twentieth century, see Neske and Kettering, *Antwort*.

12.  Heidegger, *Sein und Zeit*, 263–64/243.

13.  Agamben, "La passion de la facticité," 74; translation mine.

14.  Heidegger, *Sein und Zeit*, 297–98/274.

15.  Ibid., 121/114.

16.  Ibid., 298/274.

17.  Jean-Luc Nancy, "L'amour en éclats," in *Une pensée finie*, 258, trans. Lisa Garbus and Simona Sawhney as "Shattered Love," in *The Inoperative Community*, 104; translation modified slightly.

18.  Jean-Luc Nancy, "La communauté désoeuvrée," in *La communauté désoeuvrée*, 40–41, trans. Peter Conor as "The Inoperative Community" in *The Inoperative Community*, 14.

19.  Both Nancy and Philippe Lacoue-Labarthe, with whom he has coauthored a num-

ber of major studies, seem suspicious a kind of melodrama inherent to the moods sketched in the *Beiträge zur Philosophie*, in particular, of the "last god" material, preferring, as they tend to with most explicitly theological considerations, to "leave the question in reserve" (Jean-Luc Nancy, "Gravity: Introductory Remarks," *The Gravity of Thought*, 2). Of the *Beiträge* as a whole, Lacoue-Labarthe has written that it was Heidegger's other *Dummheit*. See Lacoue-Labarthe, *La fiction du politique*, 26/*Heidegger, Art, and Politics*, 12, and Philippe Lacoue-Labarthe, "In the Name of . . . ," trans. Simon Sparks, in Philippe Lacoue-Labarthe and Jean-Luc Nancy, *Retreating the Political*, ed. Simon Sparks (New York: Routledge, 1997), 67.

20. Heidegger, *Beiträge zur Philosophie*, 17/13.

21. Ibid., 396/277.

22. Arendt, "Philosophy and Politics," 97–100.

23. Martin Heidegger, "Vom Wesen der Wahrheit," in *Wegmarken*, 91, 90, trans. John Sallis as "On the Essence of Truth," in *Basic Writings*, 132, 131.

24. Martin Heidegger, "Einleitung zu 'Was Ist Metaphysik?'" in *Wegmarken*, 203, trans. Walter Kaufmann as "The Way Back Into the Ground of Metaphysics," in Kaufmann, *Existentialism from Dostoevsky to Sartre*, 214.

25. Heidegger, *Beiträge zur Philosophie*, 217/151–52.

26. Ibid., 35/25.

27. Heidegger always maintained that *ethos* denoted "abode, dwelling place . . . the open region in which man dwells," an ontologico-existential in-stasis that distinguishes it from morality, codes of behavior, etc. Heidegger grounds his conviction that ethics means dwelling place in Heraclitus's fragment 119, translating *ethos anthropoi daimon* as "Man dwells, insofar as he is man, in the nearness of god," rather than "A man's character is his daimon." He goes on to cite (pseudo-) Aristotle's *De partibus animalium*, which tells the story of some strangers who were "astounded [*überrascht*]," upon paying a visit to Heraclitus, to find him doing nothing more ethereal than warming his hands at the stove in his kitchen. Heraclitus is reported to have told them to come in and join him, "For here too the gods are present" (Martin Heidegger, "Brief über den Humanismus,'" in *Wegmarken*, 185, trans. Frank A. Capuzzi in collaboration with J. Glenn Gray as "Letter on Humanism," in *Basic Writings*, 256).

28. Although she engages a Cartesian, rather than a Heideggerian, understanding of "the first passion," Luce Irigaray channels the post-*Kehre* Heidegger when she claims *l'admiration* as the only affect that *lets the other be* as radically other. And since the only radical difference for Irigaray is sexual difference, she argues that "to arrive at the constitution of an ethics of sexual difference, we must at least return to what is for Descartes the first passion: *wonder*. This passion has no opposite or contradiction and exists always as though for the first time. Thus man and woman, woman and man are always meeting as though for the first time because they cannot be substituted one for another. I will never be in a man's place, never will a man be in mine. . . . The other who is forever unknowable is the one who differs from me sexually. This feeling of surprise, astonishment, and wonder in the face of the unknowable ought to be returned to its locus: that of sexual

difference . . . wonder . . . beholds what it sees always as if for the first time, never taking hold of the other as object. It does not try to seize, possess, or reduce this object, but leaves it subjective, still free." Irigaray, *Ethique de la difference sexuelle*, 19–20/*An Ethics of Sexual Difference*, 12–13.

29. Heidegger, *Beiträge zur Philosophie*, 294/208.

30. "Man is . . . 'thrown' from Being itself into the truth of being, so that ek-sisting in this fashion he might guard the truth of being, in order that beings might appear in the light of being as the beings they are. Man does not decide whether and how beings appear. . . . Man is the shepherd of being" (Heidegger, "Brief über den 'Humanismus,'" 162/234). Although Heidegger is clear here to emphasize the "essential poverty of the shepherd" (ibid., 172/245), the relentlessly dialectical logic of the Christian inversion he evokes here (e.g., "the meek shall inherit the earth" or the sacrifice, resurrection, and ascension of the poorest of "shepherds") renders such "poverty" nothing if not *in*essential or, at the very least, sublatable.

31. Heidegger, *Beiträge zur Philosophie*, 397/278.

32. Ibid., 69/48.

33. See for example Nancy, *Etre singulier pluriel*, 105–6/82. References to this and other texts by Nancy will be given with the French page numbers separated by a slash (/) from the English page numbers.

34. Martin Heidegger, "Vom Wesen des Grundes," in *Wegmarken*, 35, 54, trans. William McNeill as "On the Essence of Ground," in *Pathmarks*, 109, 122.

35. Heidegger, *Beiträge zur Philosophie*, 481/339.

36. Nancy, *Etre singulier pluriel*, 46/26.

37. Ibid., 117/93.

38. Ibid., 29–30/11–12.

39. Ibid., 57/37.

40. This double valence is crucial for Nancy, insofar as that which existents hold in common prevents any of them from being itself-by-itself. For a consonant reflection on existence as fundamentally *partagée*, see Agacinski, *Critique de l'égocentrisme*, 11f.

41. Nancy, "Le Mythe Interrompu," in *La communauté désoeuvrée*, 146, trans. Peter Conor as "Myth Interrupted" in *The Inoperative Community*, 58.

42. Nancy, *Etre singulier pluriel*, 22/4.

43. Cited in *The Fundamental Wisdom of the Middle Way: Nagarjuna's Mulamadhyamikakarika*, ed. Jay L. Garfield (New York: Oxford University Press), 307, n. 20.

44. "The 'essence' of Dasein lies in its existence" (Heidegger, *Sein und Zeit*, 42/40). Heidegger repeats this sentence in the "Brief über den 'Humanismus,'" (176/248), altering the spelling of *existence* to *ek-sistence* in order to emphasize the "essential" openness of Dasein. On the scholastic evolution of the identity of essence and existence in God, see Burrell, *Knowing the Unknowable God*.

45. Nancy and Lacoue-Labarthe, *L'absolu littéraire*, 46, 44/*The Literary Absolute*, 32, 31.

46. Nancy, *Etre singulier pluriel*, 50/30; translation modified slightly.

47. Nancy, *Le sens du monde*, 53–54/31.

48. "Because sense is 'being-toward [*être-à*],' it is also 'being-toward-more-than-one,'

and this obtains even at the heart of solitude" (Nancy, *Le sens du monde*, 139/88). "The fact that being itself is finite means that it is neither substance nor subject, but its being (or its *sense*) consists only in being *offered in* existence and *to* existence" (Nancy, "Finite History," trans. Brian Holmes, in *The Birth to Presence*, 158). "'Whatever' [*Quelconque*] is the indeterminateness of being in what is posited and exposed within the strict, determined concretion of a singular thing, and the indeterminateness of its singular existence . . . it is common to all beings to be, and in this way, being is their whatever" (Jean-Luc Nancy, "Le coeur des choses," in *Une pensée finie*, 206, 220, trans. Brian Holmes and Rodney Trumble as "The Heart of Things," in *The Birth to Presence*, 174, 185). "Freedom [*la liberté*] . . . is the fact of existence as the essence of itself" (Nancy, *L'experience de la liberté*, 15/11). "'Sense' is the sharing of being [*le "sens" est le partage de l'être*]" (*Etre singulier pluriel*, 122/98). "Being 'itself' comes to be defined as relational, as non-absoluteness, and, if you will—in any case this is what I am trying to argue—as *community* [*communauté*]" (Nancy, "La communauté désoeuvrée," 22/6). "Finitude compears [*comparaît*], that is to say it is exposed [*exposée*]: such is the essence of community" (ibid., 73/29). "The world is nothing other than the touch [*l'attouchement*] of all things and wherever nothing is touching, wherever contact is severed, there is nothing; this is the absolute exposure of the world" (Jean-Luc Nancy, "Res ipsa et ultima," in *La pensée dérobée*, 184, trans. Steven Miller as "Res ipsa et ultima," in *A Finite Thinking*, 316. "Communication [*communication*] takes place on the limit, or on the common limits where we are exposed and where it exposes us" (Nancy, "La communauté désoeuvrée," 167–68/67). "The very fact of this existence is indistinguishable from its transcendence [*sa transcendence*]" (Nancy, *L'experience de la liberté*, 37/30).

49. "Being is each time [*jeweils*] the being of a being" (Heidegger, *Sein und Zeit*, 9/7); translation modified.

50. This plane has been most prominently figured by Gilles Deleuze. Even for Deleuze, however, one might argue that immanence is not actually "pure" at all by virtue of the infinite com-pli-cation of the figure of the fold. See Gilles Deleuze, *L'immanence/Pure Immanence*, and *Le Pli/The Fold*.

51. Nancy, "Finite History," 155.

52. "Une seule fois, celle-ci." Nancy, *L'experience de la liberté*, 91/66.

53. *Ereignis*, Heidegger often tells us, is also *Ent-eignis*. See, for example, Heidegger's conversation with Joan Stambaugh in Heidegger, *The End of Philosophy*, xi–xiv.

54. Jean-Luc Nancy, "Une pensée finie," in *Une pensée finie*, 23–24, trans. Edward Bullard, Jonathan Derbyshire, and Simon Sparks as "A Finite Thinking," in *A Finite Thinking*, 12.

55. Nancy, *Etre singulier pluriel*, 26–27/8.

56. One glaring exception to this list is the global market—and its information technologies—which makes and unmakes each of these "powers" in its relentless, nonidentical circulation. For all its inescapability, the capitalist nation-state is no more substantial than the subject. On the question of the market as a total system that nevertheless remains nonidentical, see Taylor, *Confidence Games*.

57. Nancy, "Mythe Interrompu," 132/52.

58.  "In fact, a pure identity would not only be inert, empty, colorless and flavorless (as those who lay claim to a pure identity often are), it would be an absurdity. A pure identity cancels itself out; it can no longer identify itself. Only what is identical to itself is identical to itself. As such, it turns in a circle and never makes it into existence" (Nancy, *Être singulier pluriel*, 178/153).

59.  Nancy, "La communauté désoeuvrée," 16/3. On the question of German identity, see Lacoue-Labarthe and Nancy, *Le mythe Nazi*.

60.  Nancy, *L'experience de la liberté*, 166/128.

61.  See the address given a week after September 11, 2001, in which the American president famously said, "Americans are asking, why do they hate us? They hate what we see right here in this chamber—a democratically elected government. Their leaders are self-appointed. They hate our freedoms—our freedom of religion, our freedom of speech, our freedom to vote and assemble and disagree with each other." George W. Bush, "Address to a Joint Session of Congress and the American People," September 20, 2001, http://www.whitehouse.gov/news/releases/2001/09/20010920-8.html.

62.  On the philo-ethico-political parallel of a body's turning against itself, see Jacques Derrida, "Foi et savoir: Les deux sources de la 'religion' aux limites de la simple raison," in Jacques Derrida and Gianni Vattimo, eds., *La religion* (Paris: Seuil, 1996), trans. Samuel Weber as "Faith and Knowledge: The Two Sources of 'Religion' at the Limits of Reason Alone," in *Acts of Religion*, 40–101. See also Jacques Derrida and Giovanni Borradori, "Autoimmunity: Real and Symbolic Suicides—A Dialogue with Jacques Derrida," in Borradori, *Philosophy in a Time of Terror*, 85–136.

63.  Nancy, *L'experience de la liberté*, 162/125.

64.  "This, then, is the paradox of thought: to want to discover something that thought itself cannot think" (Kierkegaard, *Philosophical Fragments*, 37). In public lectures and seminars, Derrida would frequently extend this logic out to every act of thought, saying that he could not for the life of him understand why one would spend any time at all thinking about the thinkable.

65.  Nancy, *Le sens du monde*, 225/148.

66.  Nancy, *Être singulier pluriel*, 39/20.

67.  On the distinction between *die Neugier* and *thaumazein*, see Heidegger, *Sein und Zeit*, 172/161 and the discussion in chapter 1, "Wonder and the 'First Beginning.'"

68.  Nancy, *Être singulier pluriel*, 107/83.

69.  Ibid., 39/20.

70.  Ibid., 39/20; translation modified slightly.

71.  *Désoeuvrement* and *désoeuvrée* have recently also been translated as "unoccupancy" and "unoccupied," respectively, by Amanda Macdonald, who justifies this choice in "Working Up, Working Out, Working Through." While this rendition has its merits, I have retained *unworking* and *unworked*, among other reasons, in the hopes of calling attention to the *practice of* désoeuvrement. *Unworking* retains a transitivity that *unoccupancy* cannot accommodate.

72.  See the mythic beginning of Nancy, "Le mythe interrompu," 109–10/43–44.

73.  Insofar as *sacrifice* attempts to name a certain annulment of finitude through an act of violence that will be sublated by and into the sacred, the meaninglessness

of what has perversely been named "the Holocaust" reveals nothing if not that "we need to concede once and for all that the economy of Western sacrifice is finished, that it ends in the decomposition of the sacrificial operation itself, this bloody transgression that overcame and infinitely appropriated the 'moment of the finite'" (Nancy, *Une pensée finie*, 101/73–74).

74. Nancy, "La communauté désoeuvrée," 83/35.

75. Jean-Luc Nancy, "You Ask Me What It Means Today . . . " *Paragraph* 16, no. 2 (July 1993): 108, special issue, *On the Work of Jean-Luc Nancy*.

76. Jean-Luc Nancy, "L'Indestructible," *Cahiers Intersignes* 4–5 (Autumn 1992): 237, trans. James Gilbert-Walsh as "The Indestructible," in *A Finite Thinking*, 78.

77. Nancy, "You Ask Me," 108.

78. Nancy, *Le sens du monde*, 11/2.

79. Nancy, *L'oubli de la philosophie*, 15/13.

80. Nancy, "You Ask Me," 109.

81. Ibid., 109. See also Nancy, *Le sens du monde*, 19/8–9.

82. Nancy, "La communauté désoeuvrée," 42/15.

83. Ibid., 153/61.

84. Jean-Luc Nancy, "L'éthique originaire' de Heidegger," 109, trans. Duncan Large as "Originary Ethics," in *A Finite Thinking*, 192.

85. Nancy, *Le sens du monde*, 173/111.

86. Ibid., 175/112.

87. Ibid. Georgio Agamben similarly hails the coming of a "politics of whatever singularity, that is, of a being whose community is mediated not by any condition of belonging (being red, being Italian, being Communist) nor by the simple absence of conditions (a negative community, such as that recently proposed in France by M. Blanchot), but by belonging itself." Agamben ventures that only a nonidentity politics holds out the possibility for genuine transformation, for while the state can reappropriate any special interest group that names and presents itself, "what the State cannot tolerate in any way . . . is that the singularities form a community without affirming an identity, that humans co-belong without any representable condition of belonging . . . the possibility of the *whatever* itself being taken up without an identity is a threat the State cannot come to terms with." Agamben, *The Coming Community*, 84–86.

88. C.f. Taylor, *Disfiguring*; and Mark C. Taylor, *nOts* (Chicago: University of Chicago Press, 1993).

89. Nancy, *Le sens du monde*, 173–4, n. 2/192, n. 119; translation modified.

90. C.f. Nancy, *Le poids d'une pensée*, 15/84, *Etre singulier pluriel*, *Le sens du monde*, and "Euryopa."

91. See Nancy, "The Deconstruction of Christianity," "Deconstruction of Monotheism," and "The War of Monotheism."

92. Nancy distinguishes between God (the question of whom must be more or less infinitely interrupted and deferred for God's sake and our own) and "God," the superego in the sky whose existence is no more sustainable than that of the self-identical subject. "Being-*essentia* that has its end in itself—and that, in this sense, is finished, achieved, accomplished, and perfect, infinitely perfect—is at most pure

truth, but truth deprived of sense: and it is exactly due to this that God, as such a being, is dead" (Nancy, *Le sens du monde*, 55/32). Insofar as God is not "such a being"—that is, not "God,"—God would be (if we were talking about God) something like "the togetherness or being-together of all that is" (Nancy, *Être singulier pluriel*, 81/60). It is by raging against such togetherness, then, that positing the "self" and/as "God" against the il y a kills God, filling in the space and spacing of God with an existential "foundation."

93.  Nancy, *Le sens du monde*, 96/58.
94.  Levinas, *Totalité et infini*, 239/261.
95.  Nancy, "L'indestructible," 245–46/85.
96.  Ibid., 248/88.
97.  Nancy, "Res ipsa et ultima," 184/316.
98.  Nancy, *La communauté désoeuvrée*, 159/63, 159/64.
99.  Ibid., 179/72.
100. Nancy, "L'éthique originaire,'" 111/194.
101. Nancy, *Le sens du monde*, 91/55. The infinite task of unworking Christianity, which I am not (at least in any explicit manner) taking up here, would do well on this point to revisit Dietrich Bonhoeffer's reading of the incarnation as the "beyond in the midst of our life" [*mitten in unserm Leben jenseitig*], by virtue of which worldly beings must refrain from positing God as an extramundane deus ex machina and turn instead toward one another in accordance with the transimmanent spacing between and within them, living "before God and with God . . . without God [*vor und mit Gott leben wir ohne Gott*]." Dietrich Bonhoeffer, *Widerstand und Ergebung: Briefe und Aufzeichnungen aus der Haft* (Bielefeld: Gütersloher, 2002), 142, 192, ed. Eberhard Bethge, trans. Regina Fuller, Frank Clark et al. as *Letters and Papers from Prison*, enlarged ed. (New York: Simon and Schuster, 1997), 282, 360.
102. Nancy, *Le sens du monde*, 240/159.
103. Wittgenstein, "Lecture on Ethics," 12. On the question of Wittgenstein's understanding of wonder, see John, "Wittgenstein's 'Wonderful Life.'"
104. Nancy, *L'oubli de la philosophie*, 14/10; translation modified slightly. It should be noted that here Nancy chooses *l'étonnement*, rather than *l'admiration*, to translate *thaumazein*, indicating perhaps that, properly speaking, there is no distinction between wonder and an excess of wonder and that Descartes' prohibition against astonishment is really a prohibition against wonder *tout court*.
105. Wittgenstein, *Tractatus Logico-Philosophicus*, 6.44–6.45.
106. Wittgenstein, *Notebooks*, 86/86e; translation modified slightly, emphasis added.
107. Wittgenstein, *Culture and Value*, 5/5e.
108. Nancy, *Être singulier pluriel*, 28/10.
109. Nancy, *Le poids d'une pensée*, 15/84.
110. See the discussion in the introduction, "Wonder and the Births of Philosophy."
111. Nancy, *L'oubli de la philosophie*, 102/66.
112. Ibid., 103/67.
113. The denigration of a certain kind of wonder and fascination can be found, respectively, in *Être singulier pluriel*, 191/165, and throughout "L'insacrifiable." The last

allegation is mere conjecture; as far as I can tell, Nancy does not mention the contours wonder takes on in Wittgenstein's writings.

114. Nancy, *L'oubli de la philosophie* 104/67.

115. Ibid., 102/66; translation modified slightly.

116. As we saw in chapter 1, although *Erstaunen* wonders at the extraordinary nature of the most ordinary, Heidegger ultimately confines this term in his 1937–38 lectures to describe a metaphysical wonder that wonders at what-ness (see the discussion in chapter 1, "Wonder and the 'First Beginning'"). In the postscript to *What Is Metaphysics*, he extends the wonder of *Wunder* out to that-ness, albeit the that-ness of beings, saying that "of all beings, only the human being, called upon by the voice of being, experiences the wonder of all wonders: that beings are." Martin Heidegger, "Nachwort zu 'Was ist Metaphysik?" in *Wegmarken*, 103, trans. William McNeill as "Postscript to 'What Is Metaphysics?'" in *Pathmarks*, 234.

117. Nancy, "Gravity," 2.

118. This is not to say that existence is never awaited; to the contrary, a thinking that de-constructs, gets in touch, and lets-be must in a sense anticipate the event for which it is continually clearing space. But the recognition that being is not substance, and furthermore the realization that being takes place *in and as the spacing that unsettles all essence*, surprises thinking each time. Nancy thus compares the (un)work of thinking to being in labor: *what* happens after nine months of waiting for a child to be born is no surprise, but *that* it happens is amazing. It is the same with death, which for Nancy, and contra a certain reading of Heidegger, does not "individualize Dasein down to itself," but rather discloses Dasein's absolute finitude—thus its heteronomy, relationality, and interdependence. Both birth and death reveal a nonself-sufficiency at the absolute limits of thinking, and, in this way, they are paradigmatic events of the shock of existence (See *L'experience de la liberté*, 123/95, *Etre singulier pluriel*, 112–13/89, and "La communauté désoeuvrée, 39–44/14–16, 68/26. Cf. Hubert Dreyfus, who argues that death reveals Dasein's inability to ground itself as a stable identity (Dreyfus, *Being in the World*, esp. 311–13).

119. Nancy, *Etre singulier pluriel*, 185/159.

120. Ibid., 192/166.

121. Alphonso Lingis, "Anger," in Sheppard, Sparks, and Thomas, *On Jean-Luc Nancy*, 213, 209. For a critique of the frequently mixed motivations and limited usefulness of the witnessing of suffering, particularly as filtered through a popularized "politics of pity," see Boltanski, *Distant Suffering*. A resonant argument, which focuses on the problem of saturation—that is, the limits of sympathy for those who suffer when images and stories of innumerable sites of atrocity are heaped on top of one another by means of printed and visual media—can be found in Cohen, *States of Denial*.

122. Nancy, cited in Lingis, "Anger," 212.

123. Nancy, *L'oubli de la philosophie*, 103/67.

124. Ibid., 99–100/65.

125. This last pairing is the distinction Nancy draws between truth and sense (Nancy, *Le sens du monde*, 25–30/12–15).

126. Nancy, "Euryopa," 92; translation mine.
127. Derrida, "Violence and Metaphysics," 80.
128. Nancy, "Le cœur des choses," in *Une pensée finie*, 218–19/184.
129. Insofar as being-in-common does not permit common substance or "beings that are utterly distinct," Nancy calls it a very "scant being" indeed. "But this scant being is our whole reality, our most concrete, most existing, most 'in the world' reality. We are in the world thanks to this scant being" (Jean-Luc Nancy and Ann Smock, "Speaking Without Being Able To," in *The Birth to Presence*, 318).
130. Nancy, *L'experience de la liberté*, 180/140.
131. Ibid., 181/141.

## 4. DECISION

1. *Theaetetus*, trans. Cornford, 210b.
2. *Beschlossen* versus *ent-schlossen*. Heidegger, *Der Ursprung des Kunstwerkes* 54/180; *Beiträge zur Philosophie*, 69/101.
3. Levinas, *Autrement qu'être*, 191/120.
4. Nancy, *L'experience de la liberté*, 183–84/142; translation modified slightly.
5. See Patočka, *Heretical Essays*, 61.
6. Derrida, *Donner la mort*, 17/3. References to this and all other Derridean texts are given with the original page numbers separated by a slash (/) from the page numbers in translation.
7. Patočka, *Heretical Essays*, 104; also cited in Derrida, *Donner la mort*, 27–28/11. See Fink, *Metaphysik der Erziehung*. Since the English translation of the *Heretical Essays* had not yet emerged at the time, David Wills translated Derrida's citations of Patočka from the French edition of the text, *Essais hérétiques sur la philosophie de l'histoire*. All citations of Patočka in this chapter refer to Kohák's English translation, although significant differences (at least for our purposes) between this text and the French version will be noted. On the thoroughly sexed nature of this movement away from the maternal and into the world of the father, see Luce Irigaray, "Plato's Hystera," trans. Gillian C. Gill in *Speculum of the Other Woman*, 243–364.
8. Derrida, *Donner la mort*, 29/12.
9. Patočka, *Heretical Esssays*, 106; also cited in Derrida, *Donner la mort*, 52/31.
10. Ibid., 38/20.
11. Ibid.
12. Derrida, *Adieu*, 201/117. This conviction echoes Hannah Arendt's exposure of the relentless and watertight logic of totalitarianism; see the discussion of the introduction, "The Thales Dilemma."
13. The word for "test" here is *l'epreuve*, which also has the sense of "ordeal." Derrida, *L'autre cap*, 78, 43/80, 41; and Derrida, *Force de loi*, 53/252; translation modified slightly.
14. Jacques Derrida, "Afterword: Toward an Ethic of Discussion," trans. Samuel Weber, in *Limited Inc.*, 116.

15. On Derrida's response to Fukuyama's infamous claim, see Derrida, *Spectres de Marx*, 97/56f.

16. See in particular *L'autre cap* and *Spectres de Marx*. Certainly, it has become especially difficult to maintain the mutual exclusivity of deconstruction and concrete political engagement ever since the publication of "The Force of Law," a lecture given in October 1989 at the Benjamin Cardozo School of Law at New York University, in which Derrida stated (to the surprise of not a few audience members) that the act of deconstruction is always and only motivated by a concern for a justice to-come [*à-venir*]. Justice, Derrida argues, only *is* as to-come, as not-yet, as the impossible. And insofar as deconstruction is always and only concerned to provoke the advent of the impossible, Derrida goes so far as to say that "*Deconstruction is justice*" (Derrida, *Force de loi*, 35/243).

17. On forgiveness, see Derrida, "On Forgiveness," "What Is a 'Relevant' Translation?"; and Jacques Derrida, "To Forgive: The Unforgivable and the Imprescriptible," trans. Elizabeth Rottenberg, in Caputo, Dooley, and Scanlon, *Questioning God*, 21–51. On hospitality, see *Cosmopolites de tous les pays*; *De l'hospitalité*; and Jacques Derrida, "Hostipitality," trans. Gil Anidjar, in *Acts of Religion*, 356–420. On friendship, see *Les politiques de l'amitié*. Finally, on the gift, see *Donner le temps*.

18. Derrida, "To Forgive," 22.

19. Derrida, "Apories," 315–16/19–20.

20. Derrida, "Hostipitality," 387.

21. Derrida, *De l'hospitalité*, 29/25.

22. Jacques Derrida and Giovanni Borradori, "A Dialogue with Jacques Derrida," in Borradori, *Philosophy in a Time of Terror*, 127.

23. Derrida, *Cosmopolites de tous les pays*, 46/18.

24. Derrida, *Adieu*, 85/45; translation modified slightly.

25. Derrida, *De l'hospitalité*, 72–73/77.

26. *S'il y en a* is a more or less constant refrain whenever Derrida mentions the "pure" concepts of the gift, forgiveness, friendship, decision, etc.

27. Derrida, "On Forgiveness," 56.

28. Jacques Derrida and Giovanni Borradori, "Autoimmunity: Real and Symbolic Suicides—A Dialogue with Jacques Derrida," in Borradori, *Philosophy in a Time of Terror*, 85–136; 129.

29. See Derrida's distinction between his "quasi-transcendentals" and the Kantian "regulative ideals" they both recall and shatter in *Spectres de Marx*, 142–43/86–87; "On Forgiveness: A Roundtable Discussion with Jacques Derrida," in Caputo, Dooley, and Scanlon, *Questioning God*, 66, henceforth abbreviated as "Roundtable" to avoid confusion with the essay in *On Cosmopolitanism and Forgiveness*; and "Autoimmunity," 134–35.

30. Derrida, *De l'hospitalité*, 75/79.

31. Derrida, "On Forgiveness," 44.

32. Derrida, *De l'hospitalité*, 73/77, 75/81; "On Forgiveness," 45; *De l'hospitalité*, 71/75.

33. Derrida, *Cosmopolites de tous les pays*, 56–57/22–3.

34. Derrida, "Roundtable," 58.

35. Derrida, *Spectres de Marx*, 144/87.

36. Derrida, *Adieu*, 194/112.

37. Jacques Derrida, "Hospitality, Justice, and Responsibility: A Dialogue with Jacques Derrida," in Kearney and Dooley, *Questioning Ethics*, 70.

38. Kearney, *Strangers, Gods, and Monsters*, 72.

39. Derrida, "Hospitality, Justice, and Responsibility," 66.

40. Kearney, *Strangers, Gods and Monsters*, 72.

41. Derrida, *Force de loi*, 52/252.

42. Derrida, *Adieu*, 119–20/116.

43. Derrida, *Les politiques de l'amitié*, 88/69. See also Derrida's interview with Jean-Luc Nancy, in which he states that "there has to be some calculation, and this is why I have never held against calculation that condescending reticence of 'Heideggerian' haughtiness. Still, calculation is calculation. And if I speak so often of the incalculable and the undecidable it's not out of a simple predilection for play nor in order to neutralize decision: on the contrary, I believe there is no responsibility, no ethico-political decision, that must not pass through the proofs of the incalculable or the undecidable. Otherwise everything would be reducible to calculation, program, causality, and, at best, 'hypothetical imperative.'" Jacques Derrida, "'Il faut bien manger,' ou le calcul du sujet," in *Points de suspension*, 28, trans. Peter Connor and Avital Ronell as "'Eating Well,' or the Calculation of the Subject," in *Points*, 272–73.

44. Graham Ward in Derrida, "Roundtable," 61. See also Ward's more sustained suggestion that undecidability might be productively supplemented by a Joban and/or Augustinian theology of questioning, Graham Ward, "Questioning God," in Caputo, Dooley, and Scanlon, *Questioning God*, 274–90.

45. Derrida in "Roundtable," 62.

46. Derrida, "On Forgiveness," 51.

47. Derrida, *Force de loi*, 57–58/255.

48. Derrida, "Hospitality, Justice and Responsibility," 77.

49. Cited in Derrida, *Donner la mort*, 94/65.

50. Jacques Derrida, "Une 'folie' doit veiller sur la pensée," in Derrida, *Points de Suspension*, 374, trans. Peggy Kamuf as "A 'Madness' Must Watch Over Thinking," in *Points*, 363.

51. With thanks and apologies to Emily Dickinson: "Much Madness is divinest Sense —/ To a discerning Eye — / Much Sense — the starkest Madness — / 'Tis the Majority / In this, as All, prevail — / Assent — and you are sane — / Demur — you're straightway dangerous — / And handled with a Chain — " Dickinson, *The Complete Poems*, 209; and to Jean-Luc Nancy, whose question to a number of contemporary French thinkers has produced the volume, *Who Comes After the Subject?* ed. Eduardo Cadava, Peter Connor, and Jean-Luc Nancy (New York: Routledge, 1991).

52. Derrida, *Force de loi*, 53/253. C.f. Derrida's declaration that "undoubtedly the subjectivity of a subject, already, never decides anything; its identity in itself and its calculable permanence make every decision an accident which leaves the subject unchanged and indifferent. *A theory of the subject is incapable of accounting for the slightest decision*" (*Les politiques de l'amitié*, 87/68).

53. See in particular Laclau and Mouffe, *Hegemony and Socialist Strategy*.

54. Ernesto Laclau, "Deconstruction, Pragmatism, Hegemony," in Mouffe, *Deconstruction and Pragmatism*, 48.

55. Ibid., 53.

56. Ibid., 59.

57. Ernesto Laclau, "New Reflections on the Revolution of Our Time," in *New Reflections on the Revolution of Our Time*, 3–85.

58. Laclau, "Deconstruction, Pragmatism, Hegemony," 54–55.

59. Ibid., 56.

60. Ibid., 55.

61. Jacques Derrida, "Remarks on Deconstruction and Pragmatism," trans. Simon Critchley, in Mouffe, *Deconstruction and Pragmatism*, 83.

62. Ibid., 83–84; emphasis added.

63. Ibid., 84. To justify this mostly intuited reference to Levinas, I refer the reader to Derrida's 1997 lecture notes, which rely entirely on the shift between the self-as-host and self-as-hostage in Levinas's work, and in which Derrida claims that, insofar as it is possible only as impossible, forgiveness (and thus hospitality, the decision, etc.) "is the chaos at the origin of the world" (Derrida, "Hostipitality," 400).

64. Derrida, "Remarks on Deconstruction and Pragmatism," 84.

65. Critchley, "Deconstruction and Pragmatism," 35.

66. In this piece, Critchley, having established that "hegemony is a theory of decisions taken in the undecidable terrain opened by deconstruction," asks Derrida precisely how he might go about "hegemonizing" the "New International" anticipated in *Spectres de Marx* (Critchley, "On Derrida's *Specters of Marx*," 21, 24).

67. Derrida, *Adieu*, 52/23.

68. Levinas, *Autrement qu'être*, 81/48.

69. Derrida, *Les politiques de l'amitié*, 87–88/68–69.

70. In a discussion with André Jacob, Derrida responds to a question about the viability of Levinas's thought by saying, "I don't know. . . . Faced with a thinking like that of Levinas, I never have an objection. I am ready to subscribe to everything that he says. This does not mean that I think the same thing in the same way, but in this respect the differences are very difficult to determine." Derrida, *Altérités* (Paris: Osiris, 1986), 74; cited in Critchley, *The Ethics of Deconstruction*, 9.

71. Agacinski, *Critique de l'égocentrisme*, 14; translation mine.

72. This particular avoidance amounts, as far as Richard Rorty is concerned, to an avoidance of philosophy *tout court*. Insisting with Ernst Tugendhat that philosophical arguments *must* be propositional, Rorty denies not only the political but also the philosophical usefulness of Derrida's work, preferring to refer to it (or, at least, the part of it that Rorty prefers) as that of a "private ironist" or an "oracular world-discloser." He thus classes Derrida against Aristotle and Bertrand Russell (or "people good at rendering public accounts") and *with* Plato and Hegel (or "people good at leaping in the dark"). Rorty, "Is Derrida a Transcendental Philosopher?" 239. See also Rorty's somewhat contentious claim that "Derrideans tend to think that the more questioning, problematizing, and *mettant-en-abîme* you can squeeze into the day's work, the better . . . [but] if you want to do some political work,

deconstructing texts is not a very efficient way to do it. Getting rid of phallogocentrism, metaphysics and all that is an admirable long-term cultural goal, but there is still a difference between such goals and the relatively short-term goals served by political deliberation and decision" (Richard Rorty, "Response to Simon Critchley," in Mouffe, *Deconstruction and Pragmatism*, 44–45).

73. Derrida, "Il faut bien manger," 270/255.

74. Ibid., 179–80/265. As far as Derrida is concerned, the most notable exception to the lineage of Western philosophers as theorists of the subject is Baruch Spinoza, whose rationalism alone "does not rest on the principle of reason. . . . Spinoza's substantialist rationalism is a critique of both finalism and the (Cartesian) representative determination of the idea; it is not a metaphysics of the cogito or of absolute subjectivity" (ibid., 280/265).

75. Derrida, "Les fins de l'homme," in *Marges de la philosophie* (Paris: Minuit, 1972), 143, trans. Alan Bass as "The Ends of Man," in *Margins of Philosophy*, 121.

76. Derrida, "Il faut bien manger," 287–88/273.

77. *L'autre cap*, 16/9.

78. Jacques Derrida, "The Villanova Roundtable: A Conversation with Jacques Derrida," in Derrida and Caputo, *Deconstruction in a Nutshell*, 14.

79. Derrida, *Spectres de Marx*, 212/133.

80. Derrida, "Che cos'è la poesia," in Derrida, *Points de suspension*, 307/297. The French text can also be found on facing pages of the English edition.

81. Ibid., 306–7/297.

82. Ibid., 307/297.

83. Goicoechea, "The Moment of Responsibility," 211.

84. Ibid., 212.

85. Jacques Derrida, "*Istrice* 2: *Ich bünn all hier*," in Derrida, *Points de suspension*, 321/311.

86. The whole work is concerned with the fragment, but perhaps the most condensed treatment of this trope can be found in the chapter entitled "Le Fragment: Exigence Fragmentaire." See Lacoue-Labarthe and Nancy, *L'absolu littéraire*, 57–80/39–58.

87. Ibid., 58/40. As Lacoue-Labarthe and Nancy argue, the fragment both prepares the way for and renders perpetually incomplete (thereby keeping in motion) the Hegelian system that "fragmentation" might seem simply to resist. What is striking, they argue, is that "the fragment does not exclude systematic exposition. . . . The co-presence of the fragment and the systematic has a double and decisive significance: it implies that both the one and the other are established in Jena within the same horizon and that this horizon is the very horizon of the System, whose exigency is inherited and revived by romanticism." Later, they explain that "the fragment combines completion and incompletion within itself, or one may say, in an even more complex manner, it both completes and incompletes the dialectic of completion and incompletion"; ibid., 60/42, 71/50.

88. Schlegel cited ibid., 63/43. Derrida cites this fragment in the "*Istrice* 2" interview as well (311/302).

89. Lacoue-Labarthe and Nancy, *L'absolu littéraire*, 64/44.

90. Ibid., 68/48.

91. Schlegel cited in ibid., 191/67.
92. Ibid., 74/52. Of this Subject-Author-Creator, Lacoue-Labarthe and Nancy write, "He *is* the Subject itself, in the possibility of its own infinitization or absolutization. The subject, as we shall see, insofar as it is equated with the divine. Thus, the artist is . . . that absolute mediator who 'perceives the divinity within himself'—who perceives himself as divine or as 'the God within us'" (ibid., 194–95/70).
93. Derrida, "Istrice 2," 311/301. According to Plato, this story can be attributed to Archileochus of Paros (c. 756–716 bce). See Plato, *Republic*, 365c.
94. Derrida, "Istrice 2," 311/301–2. Further references will appear internally.
95. The translation of "l'être-pour-la-mort" in these citations has been modified from "being-for-death" to "being-toward-death" for the sake of consistency with most standard English translations of Heidegger.
96. Jacques Derrida, "Dialangues," in Derrida, *Points de suspension*, 157, trans. Peggy Kamuf as "Dialanguages," in *Points*, 147.
97. Ibid., 155–56/146.
98. Ibid., 157/147.
99. Ibid., 157/148; emphasis added.
100. Derrida, "Remarks on Deconstruction and Pragmatism," 84.
101. Derrida, "Dialangues," 158/148.
102. Ibid., 159/149.
103. *Akedah* in Hebrew means "binding," and we will be particularly attentive in our journey to the question of "who" is bound, and how, in the instant of decision; *korban*, the word used to refer to the offering or sacrifice of an animal, literally means "to come close to." Derrida mentions this derivation in *Donner la mort*, 85/58.
104. See Kierkegaard, *Fear and Trembling*, especially "Problema I: Is There a Teleological Suspension of the Ethical?" 54–67.
105. Derrida, *Donner la mort*, 88–89/61. Further citations appear parenthetically in text.
106. Derrida, *Apories*, 315/19. The instances of Derrida's railing against good conscience as absolutely inimical to ethics are too numerous to list here, but some of them can be found in "Roundtable," 62, *Spectres de Marx*, 11/xv, and *Donner la mort*, 117–120/84–86. In fact, the dictum around which the text at hand continually circles, "tout autre est tout autre," says nothing if not that any ethics must be perpetually animated by bad conscience, for "I am responsible to any one (that is to say to any other) only by failing in my responsibilities to all the others, to the ethical or political generality"; Derrida, *Donner la mort*, 101/70.
107. Cf. "I would not claim that I am sure that there is such a thing as decision. The sentence 'I decide' or 'I make a good decision' or 'I assume responsibility' is a scandal; it's just good conscience"; Derrida, "Hospitality, Justice, and Responsibility," 67.
108. Derrida, "Remarks on Deconstruction and Pragmatism," 84.
109. Kierkegaard, *Fear and Trembling*, 115.
110. Ibid., 37, 59.
111. Agacinski, *Critique de légocentrisme*, 111; translation mine.
112. Ibid., 65.

113. Taylor, *Altarity*, 350. See Kierkegaard, *The Sickness Unto Death*, 38–39.

114. Matthew 6:18–21 (RSV); parts of this chapter are cited throughout *Donner la mort*, 131–35/95–99.

115. This is not to say that Kierkegaard does not Christianize Abraham at all; the sheer fact of his having named this text after the most famous of Paul's injunctions (Philippians 2:12) renders this portrait "Christian" in a certain sense; it is simply not the kind of "Christian," I would argue, that capitulates to the facile logic of redemption Derrida seems to be attributing to Kierkegaard. Moreover, one should perhaps not put too much stock in titles; see Mark C. Taylor's unearthing of another title Kierkegaard had thought to give the work, when "Fear and Trembling" was just a marginal note: *Mellemhverandere* [sic]. "To form this improper word," Taylor explains, "Kierkegaard joins *mellem*, between, and *hverandre*, each other or one another. The title Kierkegaard leaves out of his published work could be translated 'Between Each Other.'" As Taylor points out, this means that both these titles render one another in a sense marginal, and "in this way, the title remains *mellemhverandre*" (Taylor, *Altarity*, 324). Taylor's discovery also reinforces the notion that the "selfhood" constructed in this text is only itself as infinitely divided from itself—as shot through with *each other*.

116. Kierkegaard, *Fear and Trembling*, 20. Cf. "Abraham had faith. He did not have faith that he would be blessed in a future life but that he would be blessed here in the world. . . . He had faith by virtue of the absurd, for all human calculation ceased long ago"; ibid., 36.

117. Ibid., 30; emphasis added.

118. Ibid., 74.

119. Kierkegaard, *Fear and Trembling*, 49. Further citations will appear internally.

120. Derrida does open the way toward a psychosomatic connection between *transir* and *trembler*, at one point asking, "Why does terror make us tremble, since one can also tremble with cold, and such analogous physiological manifestations translate experiences and sentiments that appear, at least, not to have anything in common? This symptomatology is as enigmatic as tears. . . . What does *the body mean to say* by trembling or crying, presuming one can speak here of the body, or of saying, of meaning, and of rhetoric?" Derrida, *Donner la mort*, 81–82/55.

121. I have treated the question of Abraham's nonself-identity at greater length elsewhere: see Rubenstein, "Kierkegaard's Socrates," especially 464–69.

122. This relation is possible by virtue of a conception of God on Kierkegaard's part that looks very little like the "God of the Philosophers" reinscribed here. See Pat Bigelow's explanation that "whereas God is understood within the 'metaphysics of presence' as the name and element of that which makes possible an absolutely pure and absolutely self-present self-knowledge, for Kierkegaard the divine is a furtive etching on the far side of self-presence, an etching, fugitive and fleeting, of ambiguity and paradox imprinted into the experience of self-presence from the other side of self-presence"; Pat Bigelow, *Kierkegaard and the Problem of Writing* (Tallahassee: University Press of Florida, 1987), 99. What Bigelow does not quite make clear here is that insofar as this furtively etched God could be imprinted into experience, all self-presence would be radically interrupted: the "subject" itself

rendered just as fleeting, fugitive, ambiguous, and paradoxical as the God in relation to whom it emerges. As Sylviane Agacinski reflects, "Kierkegaardian subjectivity is therefore never an absolute; it is always severed from itself"; *Critique de
l'égocentrisme*, 14; translation mine.

123. Again, the key here for Derrida is to *recognize* the infinity of one's responsibility, so as to expand the limits of the beings to and for whom one is responsible.
Thus, when John Milbank asked him at a conference whether it is not more
sound (not to mention more realistic) to side with the preferential love commended, for example, in Thomas Aquinas, Derrida responded, "I, of course,
have preferences. I am one of the common people who prefer their cat to their
neighbor's cat and my family to others. But I do not have a good conscience
about that. I know that if I transform this into a general rule it would be the
ruin of ethics. If I put as a principle that I will feed first of all my cat, my family, my nation, that would be the end of any ethical politics. So when I give a
preference to my cat, which I do, that will not prevent me from having some
remorse for the cat dying or starving next door, or, to change the example, for all
the people on earth who are starving and dying today. So you cannot prevent me
from having a bad conscience, and that is the main motivation of my ethics and
my politics. . . . It is not because I am indifferent, but because I am not indifferent, that I try not to make a difference, not to make a difference ethically and
politically, between my family and his family and your family. I confess that it is
not easy. I know that practically I grant a privilege to kinship, to my language,
to France, to my family, and so on. But I do not have a good conscience about
that"; Derrida, "Roundtable," 69.

124. Elsewhere, I have criticized this dictum from a more theological and early Heideggerian perspective, inasmuch as it seems immediately to shut down the ontological difference; see Rubenstein, "Relationality." In the study at hand, however,
my concern is far less ontological and more explicitly political. In the earlier
piece, I was concerned to establish that every other *is* neither equivalent to every
other other nor as "secret and transcendent as Yahweh," a position to which I
would still adhere. In this context, however, I am more concerned to consider the
concrete possibilities opened by a practice of *thinking* of the other as completely
other; that is, of acknowledging the inexhaustibility of one's obligations to every
other in the hopes of expanding the limits of ordinary responsibility, hospitality,
justice, etc.

125. The double movement of Kierkegaardian faith is, strangely, never mentioned in
*The Gift of Death*.

126. See the introduction's discussion, "The Wound of Wonder."

127. Patočka, *Heretical Essays*, 61. Further citations will appear internally.

128. This passage is also cited in Derrida, *Donner la mort*, 32–33/15–16.

129. Friedrich Hölderlin, "Patmos," in *Poems and Fragments*, bilingual edition, trans.
Michael Hamburger (Cambridge: Cambridge University Press, 1980). See the discussion in chapter 1, "Metaphysics' Small Difficulty."

130. Fryer, "Of Spirit," 21.

## POSTLUDE

1.  Some of these include Burnett, *Constructing "Monsters" in Shakespearean Drama*; Clark, *Thinking with Demons*; Findlen, *Possessing Nature*; Fudge, *Renaissance Beasts*; Greenblatt, *Marvelous Possessions*; Kaufmann, *The Mastery of Nature*; Knoppers and Landes, *Monstrous Bodies*; Mitter, *Much Maligned Monsters*; Pare and Pallister, *On Monsters and Marvels*; Platt, *Wonders, Marvels, and Monsters*; Pomian, *Collectors and Curiosities*; Roper, *Witch Craze*; Styers, *Making Magic*; Weschler, *Mr. Wilson's Cabinet of Wonders*.

2.  Onians, "I Wonder . . . ," 16. For differing, but compatible, accounts of the profound scientific, theological, political, philosophical, and exploratory shifts during the preceding four centuries that engendered this explosion of wonders, see Daston and Park, *Wonders and the Order of Nature*; and Peters, "The Desire to Know."

3.  Onians, "I Wonder . . . ," 31, 26. In a hypothetical conversation between the two scholars, Edward Peters would likely suggest that Onians add to his list the period during and after the crusades, which prefigured not only the onslaught of curious objects that Columbus's voyages would provoke but also the early modern period's scientific response to them. Peters writes, "especially in the aftermath of the Fourth Crusade, some of these wonders became Europeans' first 'marvelous possessions'—the relics that flooded western Europe after 1099 and especially after 1204. In this sense many aspects of wonder, including distant wonder, may be said to have been domesticated in and appropriated by the European imagination during the eleventh and twelfth-centuries" (Peters, "The Desire to Know," 600).

4.  Onians, "I Wonder . . . ," 31.

5.  Ibid., 32.

6.  Because it "unweaves the rainbow" (with apologies to Richard Dawkins), the advent of Newton's optical science signals, for Onians at least, the end of wonder: "The colours of the rainbow were for thousands of years a testimony to the divine, a manifestation which surpassed understanding. In the seventeenth century all that changed. Newton's experiments with a glass prism broke it down into the spectrum and robbed it of its mystery. The prism was an optical device such as might be housed in any Cabinet of Curiosities. In the *Wunderkammer* was kept the instrument with which the first-born daughter of Wonder would be killed"; Onians, "I Wonder" . . . , 32. See also Fisher, *Wonder, the Rainbow*, 33–56, and Dawkins, *Unweaving the Rainbow*. The *un*-favored daughters of Thaumas, of course, neglected by Socrates and Onians alike, are the Harpies.

7.  Francis Bacon in Daston and Park, *Wonders and the Order of Nature*, 290.

8.  Descartes, *The Passions of the Soul*, A152.

9.  Blanchot, *L'écriture du désastre/The Writing of the Disaster* 117/72.

10. Harlan Ullman, one of the chief architects of the doctrine, has since argued that, considering the number of United States troops mobilized, the long duration of the war in Iraq and the number of civilian "casualties" (none of which he condemns as such), this particular military action was not what he and his colleagues had envisioned; see Ullman, "Shock and Awe Lite," in *Shock and Awe*, 96–98. See also

Sperry, "No Shock, No Awe"; Peterson, "U.S. Mulls Air Strategies in Iraq"; and Blakesley, *Shock and Awe*.

11. Ullman and Wade, *Shock and Awe*, http://purl.access.gpo.gov/GPO/LPS29021, "Introduction to Rapid Dominance"; see also Ullman and Wade, *Rapid Dominance*.

12. Ullman and Wade, *Shock and Awe*, "Introduction to Rapid Dominance."

13. The passage goes on to say, "The Japanese were prepared for suicidal resistance until both nuclear bombs were used. The impact of these weapons was sufficient to transform both the mindset of the average Japanese citizen and the outlook of the leadership through this condition of Shock and Awe. The Japanese simply could not comprehend the destructive power carried by a single airplane. This incomprehension produced a state of awe"; ibid.

14. Ibid., "Appendix A, Introduction."

15. These are Krishna's words in the *Gita* as he reveals himself as Shiva. Cited in "J. Robert Oppenheimer."

16. Cited in Beal, *Religion and Its Monsters*, 159. It is interesting to compare Farrel's troubled reflection on this human usurpation of divine right with an awestruck report on the same event by *New York Times* staff writer William L. Laurence, who wrote, "It was as though the earth had opened and the skies had split. One felt as though he had been privileged to witness the Birth of the World—to be present at the moment of Creation when the Lord said: Let there be Light." This awe gives way to a certain giddiness as Laurence describes the moment of detonation: "A loud cry filled the air. The little groups that hitherto had stood rooted to the earth like desert plants broke into a dance, the rhythm of primitive man dancing at one of his fire festivals at the coming of spring. They clapped their hands as they leaped from the ground—earth-bound man symbolizing a new birth in freedom—the birth of a new force that for the first time gives man means to free himself from the gravitational pull of the earth that holds him down"; Laurence, "Drama of the Atomic Bomb."

17. "Massive Firestorm Targets Iraqi Leadership," *CNN.com*, 21 March 2003.

18. Exodus 15:11 (RSV/JPS).

19. See the discussion in the introduction, "The Death and Resurrection of Thaumazein."

20. Ullman and Wade, *Shock and Awe*, chapter 2.

21. In this text, Derrida chooses to list ten: unemployment; homelessness; the "economic war" between and among Western Europe, Eastern Europe, America, and Japan; the oxymoron of a "free market"; international debt; the cancerous arms industry; nuclear proliferation; "inter-ethnic wars"; the "phantom states" of "the mafia and the drug cartels"; and the fragility of international law in the face of the rupture of the European ideal of the State (Derrida, *Spectres de Marx*, 134–39/ *Specters of Marx*, 81–84).

22. Ibid., 129/77.

23. Cited ibid., 216/315. One might translate this utterance as something like, "Indeed, the whole world is haunted." Derrida's version reads "Oui, le monde tout entier est peuplé de fantômes," and the translation of Marx that Peggy Kamuf cites is, "Yes, ghosts are teeming in the whole world." A shortcoming of both these versions is

that they re-introduce the very subject that the *es spukt* deconstructs, prompting Derrida to say that "translations are obliged to circumvent" this little phrase, which he usually renders as "it haunts [*ça hante*]," "it ghosts [*ça revenante*]," or "it specters [*ça spectre*]." Kamuf also translates *ça hante* as "it spooks."

24. Otto, *Das Heilige*, 147/ *The Idea of the Holy*, 127; emphasis added.

25. *Der ursprünglich Schauer*. Otto uses the noun *Scheu* interchangeably with *Schauer* throughout this text.

26. Otto, *Das Heilige*, 147–48/*The Idea of the Holy*, 127–8.

27. Derrida, *Spectres de Marx*, 111/*Specters of Marx*, 65.

28. Derrida, "Hostipitality," 361.

29. Levinas, *Autrement qu'être*, 272/*Otherwise Than Being*, 177.

30. Nancy, "You Ask," 109; emphasis added.

31. Descartes, *Les passions de l'âme*, A70.

32. Montagu, *The Expression of the Passions*, 7.

33. See ibid., especially 128–32, 145–46.

34. Darwin, *The Expression of the Emotions in Humans and Animals*, 279.

35. See Duchenne de Boulogne, *The Mechanism of Human Facial Expression*, especially 183, 187, 244.

36. Levinas, *Autrement qu'être*, 228/ *Otherwise Than Being*, 181.

37. Irigaray, *L'oubli de l'air chez Martin Heidegger*, 12–13/*The Forgetting of Air in Martin Heidegger*, 5.

38. And perhaps this is what Heidegger was hinting at when he wrote that "only when there is the perilousness of being seized by terror do we find the bliss of wonder—being torn away in that wakeful manner that is *the breath of all philosophizing*" (Heidegger, *Grundbegriffe zur Metaphysik* 531/366; translation modified slightly; emphasis added).

# BIBLIOGRAPHY

Adelard of Bath. *Die Quaestiones naturals des Adelardus von Bath.* Ed. Martin Müller. Münster: Aschendorff, 1934.

Adorno, Theodor W. *Jargon der Eigentlichkeit: Zur deutschen Ideologie.* Frankfurt: Suhrkamp, 1969. Trans. Knut Tarnowski and Frederic Will as *The Jargon of Authenticity.* Evanston, IL: Northwestern University Press, 1973.

Agacinski, Sylviane. *Critique de l'égocentrisme: L'événement de l'autre.* Paris: Galilée, 1996.

Agamben, Georgio. *The Coming Community.* Trans. Michael Hardt. Minneapolis: University of Minnesota Press, 1993.

———. "La passion de la facticité." Trans. Georgio Agamben and Charles Alunni. In Eliane Escoubas, ed., *Heidegger: Questions ouvertes,* 63–81. Paris: Osiris, 1988.

Albertus Magnus. *Opera Omnia.* Ed. Augustus Barnet. 20 vols. Paris: Ludovicus Vives, 1890.

Aquinas, Thomas. *Summa Theologiae.* 4 vols. Taurini: Marietti, 1948. Trans. English Dominican Fathers as *Summa Theologiae.* 2 vols. Chicago: Encyclopaedia Brittanica, 1988.

Arendt, Hannah. "Ideology and Terror: A Novel Form of Government." In *The Origins of Totalitarianism,* 593–616. New York: Schocken, 2004.

———. "Martin Heidegger ist achtzig Jahre alt." In Günther Neske and Emil Kettering, eds., *Antwort—Martin Heidegger im Gespräch,* 232–46. Pfullingen: Neske, 1988. Trans. Albert Hofstadter as "Martin Heidegger at Eighty." In Michael Murray, ed., *Heidegger and Modern Philosophy,* 293–303. New Haven: Yale University Press, 1978.

————. "Philosophy and Politics." *Social Research,* 57, no. 1 (Spring 1990): 73–103.

Aristotle. *The Complete Works of Aristotle: Revised Oxford Translation*. Ed. Jonathan Barnes. 2 vols. Princeton: Princeton University Press, 1984.

Aristophanes. *Clouds*. Trans. Peter Meineck. Indianapolis: Hackett, 2000.

Augustine of Hippo. *City of God Against the Pagans*. Ed. and trans. Robert Dyson, Raymond Geuss, and Quentin Skinner. Cambridge: Cambridge University Press, 1998.

————. *Confessions*. Trans. Henry Owen Chadwick. Oxford: Oxford University Press, 1998.

Bacon, Francis. *The Advancement of Learning*. Ed. Michael Kiernan. Oxford: Clarendon, 2000.

Bailly, Jean-Christophe, and Jean-Luc Nancy. *La comparution: Politique à venir*. Paris: Bourgois, 1991.

Bass, Alan. *Difference and Disavowal: The Trauma of Eros*. Stanford: Stanford University Press, 2000.

Beal, Timothy. *Religion and Its Monsters*. London: Routledge, 2001.

Beaufret, J., Richard Kearney, and Joseph Stephen O'Leary, eds. *Heidegger et la question de Dieu*. Paris: Grasset, 1980.

Beckett, Samuel. *Happy Days: A Play in Two Acts*. New York: Grove, 1961.

Benveniste, Emil. *Le vocabulaire des institutions indo-européenes*. Paris: Minuit, 1969.

Bigelow, Pat. *Kierkegaard and the Problem of Writing*. Tallahassee: University Press of Florida, 1987.

Blakesley, P. J. *Shock and Awe: A Widely Misunderstood Effect*. Fort Leavensworth, KS: United States Army Command and General Staff College, 2004.

Blanchot, Maurice. *L'écriture du désastre*. Paris: Gallimard, 1980. Trans. Ann Smock as *The Writing of the Disaster*. Lincoln: University of Nebraska Press, 1995.

Bollert, David. "The Wonders of the Philosopher and the Citizen: Plato, Aristotle, and Heidegger." Ph.D. thesis, Boston College, 2005.

Boltanski, Luc. *Distant Suffering: Morality, Media, and Politics*. Trans. Graham Burchell. Cambridge: Cambridge University Press, 1999.

Bonhoeffer, Dietrich. *Widerstand und Ergebung: Briefe und Aufzeichnungen aus der Haft* (Bielefeld: Gütersloher, 2002). Ed. Eberhard Bethge, trans. Regina Fuller, Frank Clark et al. as *Letters and Papers from Prison*, enlarged ed. New York: Simon and Schuster, 1997.

Borradori, Giovanni. *Philosophy in a Time of Terror: Dialogues with Jürgen Habermas and Jacques Derrida*. Chicago: University of Chicago Press, 2003.

Brogan, Michael J. "Nausea and the Experience of the 'Il y a': Sartre and Levinas on Brute Existence." *Philosophy Today* 45, no. 2 (Summer 2001): 144–53.

Bulkeley, Kelly. *The Wondering Brain: Thinking About Religion with and Beyond Cognitive Neuroscience*. New York: Routledge, 2005.

Burke, Edmund. *A Philosophical Enquiry Into the Origin of Our Ideas of the Sublime and Beautiful*. Ed. J. T. Boulton. London: Routledge and Paul, 1958.

Burnett, Mark. *Constructing "Monsters" in Shakespearean Drama and Early Modern Culture*. New York: Palgrave Macmillan, 2002.

Burrell, David B. *Knowing the Unknowable God: Ibn-Sina, Maimonides, Aquinas*. Notre Dame, IN: University of Notre Dame Press, 1992.

Bush, George W. "Address to a Joint Session of Congress and the American People." September, 20, 2001. http://www.whitehouse.gov/news/releases/2001/09/20010920–8.html.

Butler, Eliza Marian. *The Tyranny of Greece Over Germany: A Study of the Influence Exercised by Greek Art and Poetry Over the Great German Writers of the Eighteenth, Nineteenth, and Twentieth Centuries.* Boston: Beacon, 1958.

Bynum, Caroline Walker. "Wonder." *American Historical Review* 102 (February 1997): 1–26.

Cadava, Eduardo, Peter Connor, and Jean Luc Nancy, eds. *Who Comes After the Subject?* New York: Routledge, 1991.

Caputo, John. "From the Primordiality of Absence to the Absence of Primordiality: Heidegger's Critique of Derrida." In Don Ihde and Hugh J. Silverman, ed., *Hermeneutics and Deconstruction,* 196. Albany: State University of New York Press, 1985.

——. *The Prayes and Tears of Jacques Derrida: Religion Without Religion.* Bloomington: Indiana University Press, 1997.

Caputo, John D., Mark Dooley, and Michael J. Scanlon, eds. *Questioning God.* Bloomington: Indiana University Press, 2001.

Carlson, David Grey, Drucilla Cornell, and Michel Rosenfeld, eds. *Deconstruction and the Possibility of Justice.* New York: Routledge, 1992.

Carman, Taylor. *Heidegger's Analytic: Interpretation, Discourse, and Authenticity in Being and Time.* Cambridge: Cambridge University Press, 2003.

Castelli, Elizabeth. "Problems, Questions, and Curiosities: A Response to Ivan Strenski." In Slavica Jakelic and Lori Pearson, ed., *The Future of the Study of Religion: Proceedings of Congress 2000,* 173–88. Boston: Brill, 2004.

Casti, John. *Complexification: Explaining a Paradoxical World Through the Science of Surprise.* New York: HarperCollins, 1994.

Clark, Stewart. *Thinking with Demons: The Idea of Witchcraft in Early Modern Europe.* Oxford: Oxford University Press, 1999.

Cohen, Stanley. *States of Denial: Knowing About Atrocities and Suffering.* Malden, MA: Blackwell, 2001.

Critchley, Simon. "Deconstruction and Pragmatism—Is Derrida a Private Ironist or a Public Liberal?" In Chantal Mouffe, ed., *Deconstruction and Pragmatism: Critchley, Derrida, Laclau, and Rorty,* 19–40. New York: Routledge, 1996.

——. *The Ethics of Deconstruction.* West Lafayette, IN: Purdue University Press, 1999.

——. "On Derrida's *Specters of Marx.*" *Philosophy and Social Criticism* 21, no. 3 (May 1995): 1–30.

Critchley, Simon, and Robert Bernasconi, eds. *The Cambridge Companion to Levinas.* Cambridge: Cambridge University Press, 2002.

Cunningham, J. V. *Woe or Wonder: The Passional Effect of Shakespearean Tragedy.* Denver: University of Denver Press, 1951.

Darwin, Charles. *The Expression of the Emotions in Man and Animals.* In *The Works of Charles Darwin,* vol. 10. New York: Appleton, 1986.

Daston, Lorraine, and Katharine Park. *Wonders and the Order of Nature, 1150–1750.* New York: Zone, 2001.

Dawkins, Richard. *Unweaving the Rainbow: Science, Delusion, and the Appetite for Wonder.* New York: Houghton Mifflin, 1998.

Deleuze, Gilles. *L'immanence: Une vie.* Paris: Minuit, 1995. Trans. Anne Boyman as *Pure Immanence: Essays on a Life.* New York: Zone, 2001.

———. *Masochism: Coldness and Cruelty.* New York: Zone, 1989.

———. *Le Pli: Leibniz et le baroque.* Paris: Minuit, 1988. Trans. Tom Conley as *The Fold: Leibniz and the Baroque.* Minneapolis: University of Minnesota Press, 1992.

Derrida, Jacques. *Acts of Religion.* Ed. Gil Anidjar. New York: Routledge, 2002.

———. *Adieu à Emmanuel Levinas.* Paris: Galilée, 1997. Trans. Pascalle-Anne Brault and Michael Naas as *Adieu to Emmanuel Levinas.* Stanford: Stanford University Press, 1999.

———. "Apories: Mourir-s'attendre aux limites de la vérité." In Marie-Louise Mallet, ed., *Le passage des frontières: Autour du travail de Jacques Derrida,* 309–38. Paris: Galilée, 1994. Trans. Thomas Dutoit as *Aporias.* Stanford: Stanford University Press, 1993.

———. *L'autre cap.* Paris: Minuit, 1991. Trans. Pascale-Anne Brault and Michael B. Naas as *The Other Heading: Reflections on Today's Europe.* Bloomington: Indiana University Press, 1992.

———. *La carte postale: De Socrate à Freud et au-delà.* Paris: Flammarion, 1980. Trans. Alan Bass as *The Post Card: From Socrates to Freud and Beyond.* Chicago: University of Chicago Press, 1987.

———. *Cosmopolites de tous les pays, encore un effort!* Paris: Galilée, 1997. Trans. Mark Dooley as "On Cosmopolitanism." In Simon Critchley and Richard Kearney, eds., *On Cosmopolitanism and Forgiveness,* 3–24. New York: Routledge, 2001.

———. *De l'esprit: Heidegger et la question.* Paris: Galilée, 1987. Trans. Geoffrey Bennington and Rachel Bowlby as *Of Spirit: Heidegger and the Question.* Chicago: University of Chicago Press, 1989.

———. *De l'hospitalité: Anne Dufourmantelle invite Jacques Derrida à répondre.* Paris: Calmann-Lévy, 1997. Trans. Rachel Bowlby as *Of Hospitality: Anne Dufourmantelle Invites Jacques Derrida to Respond.* Stanford: Stanford University Press, 2000.

———. *Donner la mort.* Paris: Galilée, 1999. Trans. David Wills as *The Gift of Death.* Chicago: University of Chicago Press, 1995.

———. *Donner le Temps: La fausse monnaie.* Paris: Galilée, 1991. Trans. Peggy Kamuf as *Given Time,* part 1: *Counterfeit Money.* Chicago: University of Chicago Press, 1992.

———. *Ecriture et différance.* Paris: Seuil, 1969. Trans. Alan Bass as *Writing and Difference.* Chicago: University of Chicago Press, 1978.

———. *Force de loi: Le "fondement mystique de l'autorité."* Paris: Galilée, 1994. Trans. Mary Quaintance as "Force of Law: The 'Mystical Foundation of Authority.'" In *Acts of Religion.* Ed. Gil Anidjar. New York: Routledge, 2002.

———. *Khôra.* Paris: Galilée, 1993. Trans. Ian McLeod as "Khôra." In Thomas Dutoit, ed., *On the Name,* 87–127. Stanford: Stanford University Press, 1995.

———. *Limited Inc.* Ed. Gerald Graff. Trans. Jeffrey Mehlman and Samuel Weber. Chicago: Northwestern University Press, 1988.

———. *Mal d'archive: Une impression freudienne.* Paris: Galilée, 1995. Trans. Eric Prenowitz as *Archive Fever: A Freudian Impression.* Chicago: University of Chicago Press, 1995.

———. *Marges de la philosophie*. Paris: Minuit, 1972. Trans. Alan Bass as *Margins of Philosophy*. Chicago: University of Chicago Press, 1982.

———. *Negotiations: Interventions and Interviews, 1971–2001*. Trans. Elizabeth Rottenberg. Stanford: Stanford University Press, 2002.

———. "On Forgiveness." Trans. Michael Hughes. In Simon Critchley and Richard Kearney, ed., *On Cosmopolitanism and Forgiveness*, 27–60. London: Routledge, 2001.

———. "Parti pris pour l'Algérie." *Les temps modernes* 580 (January-February 1995): 233–41.

———. *Passions*. Paris: Galilée, 1993. Trans. Thomas Dutoit as "Passions: 'An Oblique Offering.'" In Thomas Dutoit, ed., *On the Name*, 1–31. Stanford: Stanford University Press, 1995.

———. *Points de suspension: Entretiens*. Ed. Elisabeth Weber. Paris: Galilée, 1992. Trans. Peggy Kamuf as *Points . . . Interviews, 1974–1994*. Stanford: Stanford University Press, 1995.

———. *Les Politiques de l'amitié: Suivi de l'oreille d'Heidegger*. Paris: Galilée, 1994. Trans. George Collins as *The Politics of Friendship*. London: Verso, 1997.

———. *Psyché: Inventions de l'autre*. Paris: Galilée, 1987.

———. "Racism's Last Word." Trans. Peggy Kamuf. *Critical Inquiry* 12 (Autumn 1985): 290–99.

———. *Sauf le nom*. Paris: Galilée, 1993. Trans. John P. Leavey Jr. as "Sauf le nom (Post-Scriptum)." In Thomas Dutoit, ed., *On the Name*, 33–85. Stanford: Stanford University Press, 1995.

———. *Spectres de Marx: L'Etat de la dette, le travail du deuil et la nouvelle internationale*. Paris: Galilée, 1993. Trans. Peggy Kamuf as *Specters of Marx: The State of the Debt, the Work of Mourning, and the New International*. London: Routledge, 1994.

———. *Le toucher, Jean-Luc Nancy*. Paris: Galilée, 2000. Trans. Christine Irizarry as *On Touching—Jean-Luc Nancy*. Stanford: Stanford University Press, 2005.

———. *Verité en peinture*. Paris: Flammarion, 1978. Trans. Geoffrey Bennington and Ian McLeod as *The Truth in Painting*. Chicago: University of Chicago Press, 1987.

———. "Violence and Metaphysics: An Essay on the Thought of Emmanuel Levinas." Trans. Alan Bass. In *Writing and Difference*, 79–153. Chicago: University of Chicago Press, 1978.

———. "What Is a 'Relevant' Translation?" *Critical Inquiry* 27, no. 2 (Winter 2001): 174–200.

———. *The Work of Mourning*. Ed. Pascale-Anne Brault and Michael Naas. Chicago: University of Chicago Press, 2001.

Derrida, Jacques, and John Caputo, *Deconstruction in a Nutshell: A Conversation with Jacques Derrida*. New York: Fordham University Press, 1997.

Descartes, René. *Meditationes de Prima Philosophia/Méditations Métaphysiques*. French trans. Duc de Luynes. Ed. Geneviève Rodis-Lewis. Paris: Vrin, 1960. Trans. Donald A. Cress as *Meditations on First Philosophy*. In *Discourse on Method and Meditations on First Philosophy*. 4th ed. Indianapolis: Hackett, 1998.

———. *Les passions de l'âme*. Paris: Vrin, 1955. Trans. Stephen H. Voss as *The Passions of the Soul*. Bloomington: Hackett, 1989.

Desmond, William. *Being and the Between*. Albany: State University of New York Press, 1995.

Dickinson, Emily. *The Complete Poems*. Ed. Thomas H. Johnson. New York: Little, Brown, 1960.

Dreyfus, Hubert. *Being in the World: A Commentary on Heidegger's* Being and Time, Division 1. Cambridge: MIT Press, 1990.

Duchenne de Boulogne, G. B. *The Mechanism of Human Facial Expression*. Ed. and trans. R. Andrew Cuthbertson. Cambridge: Cambridge University Press, 1990.

Eckermann, Johann Peter. *Gespräche mit Goethe: In den letzten jahren seines lebens*. Ed. H. H. Houben. Weisbaden: Brockhaus, 1959. Trans. Gisela C. O'Brien as *Conversations with Goethe*. Ed. Hans Kohn. New York: Ungar, 1964.

Escoubas, Eliane. *Heidegger. Questions ouvertes*. Paris: Osiris, 1988.

Farías, Victor. *Heidegger et le nazisme*. Paris: Verdier, 1987. Trans. Paul Burrell, Dominic di Bernardi, and Gabriel R. Ricci as *Heidegger and Nazism*. Ed. Joseph Margolis and Tom Rockmore. Philadelphia: Temple University Press, 1991.

Findlen, Paula. *Possessing Nature: Museums, Collecting, and Scientific Culture in Early Modern Italy*. Berkeley: University of California Press, 1994.

Fink, Eugen. *Metaphysik der Erziehung im Weltverständnis von Plato und Aristoteles*. Frankfurt: Klostermann, 1970.

Fisher, Philip. *Wonder, the Rainbow, and the Aesthetics of Rare Experiences*. Cambridge: Harvard University Press, 1998.

Freud, Sigmund. "Das Unheimliche." In *Gesammelte Schriften*, 1:99–138. Leipzig: Internationaler psychoanalytischer Verlag: 1934. Trans. David McClintock as "The Uncanny." In *The Uncanny*, 123–62. New York: Penguin, 2003.

Fryer, David Ross. "Of Spirit: Heidegger and Derrida on Metaphysics, Ethics, and National Socialism." *Inquiry: An Interdisciplinary Journal of Philosophy* 39, no. 1 (March 1996): 21–44.

Fudge, Erica, ed. *Renaissance Beasts: Of Animals, Humans, and Other Wonderful Creatures*. Urbana: University of Illinois Press, 2004.

Fuller, Robert. *Wonder: From Emotion to Spirituality*. Chapel Hill: University of North Carolina Press, 2006.

Fynsk, Christopher. *Heidegger, Thought and Historicity*. Ithaca: Cornell University Press, 1993.

George, Marie I. "Wonder as Source of Philosophy and of Science: A Comparison." *Philosophy in Science* 6 (1995): 97–128.

Gleick, James. *Faster: The Acceleration of Just About Everything*. New York: Pantheon, 1999.

Goicoechea, David. "The Moment of Responsibility (Derrida and Kierkegaard)." *Philosophy Today* 43, no. 3 (Fall 1999): 211–25.

Greenblatt, Stephen. *Marvelous Possessions: The Wonder of the New World*. Chicago: University of Chicago Press, 1991.

———. "Resonance and Wonder." In I. Karp and S. D. Lavine, ed., *Exhibiting Cultures: The Poetics and Politics of Museum Display*, 42–56. Washington, D.C., 1991.

Guindon, André. "L'émerveillement: Etude du vocabulaire de l'admiratio chez Thomas d'Aquin." *Eglise et Théologie* 1 (1976): 61-97.

Hardon, John. "The Concept of Miracle from St. Augustine to Modern Apologetics." *Theological Studies* 15 (June 1954): 229–57.

Hegel, G. W. F. *Introduction to the Philosophy of History.* Trans. Leo Rauch. Indianapolis: Hackett, 1988.

Heidegger, Martin. *Aus der Erfahrung des Denkens.* Gesamtausgabe 13. Frankfurt: Klostermann, 1983.

———. *Basic Writings: Martin Heidegger.* Ed. David Farrell Krell, 343–64. London: Routledge, 2000.

———. *Besinnung.* Gesamtausgabe 66. Frankfurt: Klostermann, 1997.

———. *Beiträge zur Philosophie (Vom Ereignis).* Gesamtausgabe 65. Frankfurt: Klostermann, 1989. Trans. Parvis Emad and Kenneth Maly as *Contributions to Philosophy (from Enowning).* Bloomington: Indiana University Press, 1995.

———. *Discourse on Thinking.* Trans. John M. Anderson and E. Hans Freud. New York: Harper and Row, 1966.

———. *Early Greek Thinking.* Trans. D. F. Krell and F. A. Capuzzi. New York: Harper and Row, 1975.

———. *Einführung in Die Metaphysik.* Gesamtausgabe 40. Frankfurt: Klostermann, 1983. Trans. Gregory Fried and Richard Polt as *Introduction to Metaphysics.* New Haven: Yale University Press, 2000.

———. *The End of Philosophy.* Ed. and trans. Joan Stambaugh. Chicago: University of Chicago Press, 2003.

———. *Erläuterungen zu Hölderlins Dichtung.* Gesamtausgabe 4. Frankfurt: Klostermann, 1981. Trans. Keith Hoeller as *Elucidations of Hölderlin's Poetry.* Amherst, NY: Humanity, 2000.

———. *Feldweg Gespräche.* Gesamtausgabe 77. Frankfurt: Klostermann, 1995.

———. *Die Frage nach dem Ding: Zu Kants Lehre von den transzentdentalen Grundsätze.* Gesamtausgabe 41. Frankfurt: Klostermann, 1984. Trans. W. B. Barton, Jr. and Vera Deutsch as *What Is a Thing?* Chicago: Regnery, 1967.

———. *Gelassenheit.* Pfullingen: Neske, 1959.

———. *Die Geschichte des Seyns.* Gesamtausgabe 69. Frankfurt: Klostermann, 1998.

———. *Grundbegriffe.* Gesamtausgabe 51. Frankfurt: Klostermann, 1991. Trans. Gary E. Aylesworth as *Basic Concepts.* Bloomington: Indiana University Press, 1988.

———. *Die Grundbegriffe der Metaphysik: Welt—Endlichkeit—Einsamkeit.* Gesamtausgabe 29/30. Frankfurt: Klostermann, 1992. Trans. William McNeill and Nicholas Walker as *Metaphysics: World, Finitude, Solitude.* Bloomington: Indiana University Press, 1995.

———. *Grundfragen der Philosophie: Ausgewählte "Probleme" der "Logik."* Gesamtausgabe 45. Frankfurt: Klostermann, 2001. Trans. Richard Rojcewicz and André Schuwer as *Basic Questions of Philosophy: Selected "Problems" of "Logic."* Bloomington: Indiana University Press, 1994.

———. *Holzwege.* Gesamtausgabe 5. Frankfurt: Klostermann, 2003.

———. *Identität und Differenz.* Pfullingen: Neske, 1957. Trans. Joan Stambaugh as *Identity and Difference.* Chicago: University of Chicago Press, 2002.

———. *Nietzsche II.* Gesamtausgabe 6.2. Frankfurt: Klostermann, 1997.

———. *Pathmarks.* Ed. William McNeill. Cambridge: Cambridge University Press, 1998.

————. *The Piety of Thinking: Essays.* Ed. and trans. James G. Hart and John C. Maraldo. Bloomington: Indiana University Press, 1976.

————. *Platon: Sophistes.* Gesamtausgabe 19. Frankfurt: Klostermann, 1992. Trans. Richard Rojcewicz and André Schuwer as *Plato's Sophist.* Bloomington: Indiana University Press, 1997.

————. *Poetry, Language, and Thought.* Trans. A. Hofstadter. New York: Harper and Row, 1975.

————. *The Question Concerning Technology and Other Essays.* Ed. William Lovett. New York: Harper and Row, 1977.

————. *Der Satz vom Grund.* Gesamtausgabe 10. Frankfurt: Klostermann, 1997. Trans. Reginald Lilly as *The Principle of Reason.* Bloomington: Indiana University Press, 1991.

————. *Sein und Zeit.* Gesamtausgabe 2. Frankfurt: Klostermann, 1977. Trans. Joan Stambaugh as *Being and Time.* Albany: State University of New York Press, 1996.

————. *Die Technik und die Kehre.* Pfullingen: Neske, 1962.

————. *Unterwegs zur Sprache.* Gesamtausgabe 12. Frankfurt: Klostermann, 1985. Trans. Peter Hertz as *On the Way to Language.* New York: Harper and Row, 1971.

————. *Der Ursprung des Kunstwerkes.* Ed. H. G. Gadamer. Stuttgart: Reclam, 1960.

————. *Vom Wesen des Grundes.* Frankfurt: Klostermann, 1995. Trans. Terrence Malick as *Essence of Reasons.* Evanston: Northwestern University Press, 1969.

————. *Vom Wesen der Wahrheit: Zu Platons Höhlen gleichnis und Theätet.* Gesamtausgabe 34. Frankfurt: Klostermann, 1988. Trans. Ted Sadler as *Essence of Truth: On Plato's Cave Allegory and Theaetetus.* London: Continuum, 2002.

————. *Vorträge und Aufsätz.* Gesamtausgabe 7. Frankfurt: Klostermann, 2000.

————. *Was heißt Denken?* Gesamtausgabe 8. Frankfurt: Klostermann, 2002. Trans. Fred D. Wieck and J. Glenn Gray as *What Is Called Thinking?* New York: Harper and Row, 1968.

————. *Was ist das die Philosophie?* Pfullingen: Neske, 1956. Trans. W. Kluback and Jean T. Wilde as *What Is Philosophy?* London: Vision, 1989.

————. *Wegmarken.* Gesamtausgabe 9. Frankfurt: Klostermann, 1976.

————. *Zur Sache des Denkens.* Tübingen: Niemeyer, 1969. Trans. Joan Stambaugh as *On Time and Being.* Chicago: University of Chicago Press, 2002.

Hepburn, Ronald W. *Wonder and Other Essays: Eight Studies in Aesthetics and Neighboring Fields.* Edinburgh: Edinburgh University Press, 1984.

Heschel, Abraham Joshua. *God in Search of Man: A Philosophy of Judaism.* New York: Meridian and the Jewish Publication Society of America, 1959.

Hesiod. *Theogony.* Ed. and trans. M. L. West. Oxford: Clarendon, 1997.

Hobbes, Thomas. *Leviathan.* Oxford: Oxford University Press, 1998.

Hölderlin, Friedrich. *Poems and Fragments.* Trans. Michael Hamburger. Cambridge: Cambridge University Press, 1980.

Hume, David. *Dialogues and Natural History of Religion.* Ed. J.C.A. Gaskin. Oxford: Oxford University Press, 1998.

Husserl, Edmund. *Cartesian Meditations: An Introduction to Phenomenonlogy.* Trans. Dorion Cairns. The Hague: Nijhoff, 1967.

———. "Vienna Lecture." In *The Crisis of European Sciences and Transcendental Phenomenology*, 269–99. Trans. David Carr. Evanston: Northwestern University Press, 1970.

Ihde, Don, and Hugh J. Silverman, eds. *Hermeneutics and Deconstruction*. Albany: State University of New York Press, 1985.

Impey, Oliver, and Arthur MacGregor, eds. *The Origins of Museums: The Cabinet of Curiosities in Sixteenth- and Seventeenth-Century Europe*. New York: Oxford University Press, 1985.

Irigaray, Luce. *Ethique de la différence sexuelle*. Paris: Minuit, 1984. Trans. Carolyn Burke and Gillian C. Gill as *An Ethics of Sexual Difference*. Ithaca: Cornell University Press, 1993.

———. *L'oubli de l'air chez Martin Heidegger*. Paris: Editions de Minuit, 1983. Trans. Mary Beth Mader as *The Forgetting of Air in Martin Heidegger*. Austin: University of Texas Press, 1999.

———. *Speculum de l'autre femme*. Paris: Editions de Minuit, 1974. Trans. Carolyn Burke and Gillian C. Gill as *Speculum of the Other Woman*. Ithaca: Cornell University Press, 1995.

"J. Robert Oppenheimer, Atom Bomb Pioneer, Dies." *New York Times*, 19 February 1967.

Jaspers, Karl. "Letter to the Freiburg University Denazification Committee," 22 December 1945. Trans. Richard Wolin. In Richard Wolin, ed., *The Heidegger Controversy: A Critical Reader*, 144–51. Cambridge: MIT Press, 1993.

———. *Philosophische Autobiographie*. Munich: Piper, 1977.

John, Peter C. "Wittgenstein's 'Wonderful Life.'" *Journal of the History of Ideas* 49, no. 3 (July–September 1988): 495–510.

Kant, Immanuel. *Kritik der praktischen Vernunft*. In Wilhelm Weischedel, ed., *Immanuel Kant: Kritik der praktischen Vernunft/Grundlegung zur Metaphysik der Sitten*, 123–302. Frankfurt: Suhrkamp Taschenbuch Wissenschaft, 1974. Trans. Werner S. Pluhar as *The Critique of Practical Reason*. Indianapolis: Hackett, 2002.

———. *Kritik der Urteilskraft*. Edited by Wilhelm Weischedel. Frankfurt: Suhrkamp Taschenbuch Wissenschaft, 1974. Trans. Werner S. Pluhar as *The Critique of Judgment*. Indianapolis: Hackett, 1987.

Kaufmann, Thomas DaCosta. *The Mastery of Nature: Aspects of Art, Science, and Humanism in the Renaissance*. Princeton: Princeton University Press, 1993.

Kaufmann, Walter, ed. *Existentialism from Dostoevsky to Sartre*. New York: Meridian, 1956.

Kearney, Richard. *Strangers, Gods and Monsters: Interpreting Otherness*. New York: Routledge, 2003.

Kearney, Richard, and Mark Dooley, eds. *Questioning Ethics*. London: Routledge, 1999.

Keats, John. *John Keats: The Complete Works*. New York: Penguin, 1988.

Keller, Catherine. *The Face of the Deep*. London: Routledge, 2003.

Kenseth, Joy, ed. *The Age of the Marvelous*. Hanover: Hood Museum of Art, Dartmouth College, 1991.

Al-Khalili, Jim. *Quantum: A Guide for the Perplexed*. London: Weidenfeld and Nicolson, 2003.

Kierkegaard, Søren (Johannes de Silentio, pseud.). *Fear and Trembling*. Ed. and trans. Howard V. Hong and Edna H. Hong. Princeton: Princeton University Press, 1983.

———— (Johannes Climacus, pseud.). *Philosophical Fragments*. Ed. and trans. Howard V. Hong and Edna H. Hong. Princeton: Princeton University Press, 1985.

———— (Johannes Anti-Climacus, pseud.). *The Sickness Unto Death: A Christian Psychological Exposition for Upbuilding and Awakening*. Ed. and trans. Howard V. Hong and Edna H. Hong. Princeton: Princeton University Press, 1980.

Klossowski, Pierre. *Les lois de l'hospitalité*. Paris: Gallimard, 1965.

Knoppers, Laura Lunger, and Joan B. Landes, eds. *Monstrous Bodies/Political Monstrosities in Early Modern Europe*. Ithaca: Cornell University Press, 2004.

Kofman, Sarah. *Comment s'en sortir?* Paris: Galilée, 1983.

————. *Lectures de Derrida*. Paris: Galilée, 1984.

Kravitz, David. *Who's Who in Greek and Roman Mythology*. New York: Crown, 1975.

Kristeva, Julia. *The Powers of Horror*. Trans. Leon S. Roudiez. New York: Columbia University Press, 1982.

Lacan, Jacques. *Ecrits: A Selection*. Trans. Alan Sheridan. New York: Norton, 1977.

Laclau, Ernesto. *New Reflections on the Revolution of Our Time*. London: Verso, 1990.

Laclau, Ernesto, and Chantal Mouffe, *Hegemony and Socialist Strategy: Toward a Radical Democratic Politics*. London: Verso, 1985.

Lacoue-Labarthe, Philippe. *La fiction du politique: Heidegger, l'art et la politique*. Paris: Christian Borgois, 1987. Trans. Chris Turner as *Heidegger, Art, and Politics*. Oxford: Blackwell, 1990.

Lacoue-Labarthe, Philippe, and Jean-Luc Nancy. *Absolu Littéraire: théorie de la littérature du romantisme allemand*. Paris: Seuil, 1978. Trans. Philip Barnard and Cheryl Lester as *The Literary Absolute: The Theory of Literature in German Romanticism*. Albany: State University of New York Press, 1988.

————. *Le Mythe Nazi*. Paris: Editions de l'Aube, 1991. Trans. Brian Holmes as "The Nazi Myth." *Critical Inquiry* 16, no. 2 (Winter 1990): 291–312.

————. *Retreating the Political*, ed. Simon Sparks. London: Routledge, 1997.

Laufer, Peter, ed. *Shock and Awe: Responses to War*. Berkeley: Creative Arts, 2003.

Laurence, William L. "Drama of the Atomic Bomb Found Climax in July 16 Test." *New York Times*, 26 September 1945.

Leibniz, Gottfried Wilhelm. *Selections*. Ed. and trans. Philip Wiener. New York: Scribner's, 1951.

Levinas, Emmanuel. *Altérité et transcendence*. Saint Clement: Fata Morgana, 1995. Trans. Michael B. Smith as *Alterity and Transcendence*. New York: Columbia University Press, 1999.

————. *L'au-delà du verset: Lectures et cours talmudiques*. Paris: Minuit, 1982. Trans. Gary D. Mole as *Beyond the Verse: Talmudic Readings and Lectures*. Bloomington: Indiana University Press, 1994.

————. *Autrement qu'être: Ou au-delà de l'essence*. Dordrecht: Kluwer Academic, 1978. Trans. Alphonso Lingis as *Otherwise Than Being: Or, Beyond Essence*. Pittsburgh: Duquesne University Press, 2002.

————. *Basic Philosophical Writings*. Ed. Adriaan Peperzak, Simon Critchley, and Robert Bernasconi. Bloomington: Indiana University Press, 1996.

———. *Collected Philosophical Papers*. Trans. Alphonso Lingis. Pittsburgh: Duquesne University Press, 1998.

———. *De Dieu qui Vient à l'idée*. Paris: Vrin, 1982. Trans. Bettina Bergo as *Of God Who Comes to Mind*. Stanford: Stanford University Press, 1998.

———. "De l'évasion." *Recherches philosophiques* 5 (1935–36): 373–92.

———. *De l'existence à l'existant*. Paris: Vrin, 1998. Trans. Alphonso Lingis as *Existence and Existents*. Boston: Kluwer Academic, 1995.

———. *Difficile liberté: Presences du Judaïsme*. Paris: Albin Michel, 1976. Trans. Seán Hand as *Difficult Freedom: Essays on Judaism*. London: Althlone, 1990.

———. *Entre nous: Essais sur la pensée à l'autre*. Paris: Grasset, 1991. Trans. Michael B. Smith and Barbara Harshav as *Entre Nous: On Thinking-of-the-Other*. New York: Columbia University Press, 1998.

———. *Ethique et infini: Dialogues avec Philippe Nemo*. Paris: Fayard, 1982. Trans. Richard A. Cohen as *Ethics and Infinity: Conversations with Philippe Nemo*. Pittsburgh: Duquesne University Press, 1994.

———. "Existence and Ethics." Trans. Jonathan Rée. In Jonathan Rée and Jane Chamberlain, ed., *Kierkegaard: A Critical Reader*, 26–38. Oxford: Blackwell, 1998.

———. *Hors Sujet*. Saint Clement: Fata Morgana, 1987. Trans. Michael B. Smith as *Outside the Subject*. Stanford: Stanford University Press, 1993.

———. *Humanisme de l'autre homme*. Montpellier: Fata Morgana, 1972. Trans. Alphonso Lingis as "Language and Proximity," "Humanism and An-Archy," and "No Identity" in *Emmanuel Levinas: Collected Philosophical Papers*, 75–107, 127–139, 141–151. Boston: Nijhoff, 1987.

———. *The Levinas Reader*. Ed. Seán Hand. Cambridge: Blackwell, 1989.

———. "Martin Heidegger et l'ontologie." *Revue Philosophique de la France et de l'étranger* 63 (1932): 395–431. Trans. the Committee of Public Safety as "Martin Heidegger and Ontology." *Diacritics* 26, no. 1 (1966): 11–32.

———. *Les noms propres*. Saint Clement: Fata Morgana, 1987. Trans. Michael B. Smith as *Proper Names*. Stanford: Stanford University Press, 1996.

———. "Quelques réflexions sur la philosophie de l'hitlérisme." *Esprit* 2 (1934): 199–208. Trans. Seán Hand as "Reflections on the Philosophy of Hitlerism." *Critical Inquiry* 17 (1990): 62–71.

———. "La réalité et son ombre." *Les Temps Modernes* 38 (1948): 771–89. Trans. Alphonso Lingis as "Reality and Its Shadow." In *Collected Philosophical Papers*, 1–13. Pittsburgh: Duquesne University Press, 1998.

———. *Sur Maurice Blanchot*. Montpellier: Fata Morgana, 1975. Trans. Michael B. Smith as "On Maurice Blanchot" in *Proper Names*, 125–70. Stanford: Stanford University Press, 1996.

———. *Le temps et l'autre*. Montpellier: Fata Morgana, 1979. Trans. Richard A. Cohen as *Time and the Other*. Pittsburgh: Duquesne University Press, 1987.

———. *Totalité et infini: Essai sur l'extériorité*. The Hague: Nijhoff, 1961. Trans. Alphonso Lingis as *Totality and Infinity: An Essay on Exteriority*. Pittsburgh: Duquesne University Press, 2003.

Llewelyn, John. "On the Saying that Philosophy Begins in *Thaumazein*." In Andrew Benjamin, ed., *Post-Structuralist Classics*, 173–91. New York: Routledge, 1988.

Longinus. *On the Sublime*. Trans. James A. Arieti and John M. Crossett. New York: Mellen, 1985.

Lyotard, Jean-François. *Heidegger and "The Jews."* Minneapolis: University of Minnesota Press, 1990.

———. *The Inhuman*. Trans. Geoffrey Bennington and Rachel Bowlby. Stanford: Stanford University Press, 2000.

Macdonald, Amanda. "Working up, Working out, Working through: Translator's Notes on the Dimensions of Jean-Luc Nancy's Thought." *Postcolonial Studies* 6, no. 1 (April 2003): 11–21.

Marcel, Gabriel. *The Existential Background of Human Dignity*. Oxford: Oxford University Press, 1963.

Miller, Jerome A. *In the Throe of Wonder: Intimations of the Sacred in a Post-Modern World*. Albany: State University of New York Press, 1992.

Mitter, Partha. *Much Maligned Monsters: A History of European Reactions to Indian Art*. Chicago: University of Chicago Press, 1992.

Montagu, Jennifer. *The Expression of the Passions: The Origin and Influence of Charles Le Brun's* Conférence sur l'expression générale et particulière. New Haven: Yale University Press, 1994.

Mouffe, Chantal, ed. *Deconstruction and Pragmatism: Critchley, Derrida, Laclau, and Rorty*. New York: Routledge, 1996.

Nancy, Jean-Luc. *La communauté désoeuvrée*. Paris: C. Bourgois, 1986. Trans. Peter Connor, Lisa Garbus, Michael Holland, and Simona Sawhney as *The Inoperative Community*. Minneapolis: University of Minnesota Press, 1991.

———. "The Confronted Community." Trans. Amanda Macdonald. *Postcolonial Studies* 6, no. 1 (April 2003), 23–36.

———. "Consecration and Massacre." Trans. Amanda Macdonald. *Postcolonial Studies* 6, no. 1 (2003): 47–50.

———. "The Deconstruction of Christianity." Trans. Simon Sparks. In Hent DeVries, ed., *Religion and Media*, 112–30. Stanford: Stanford University Press, 2001.

———. "Deconstruction of monotheism." Trans. Amanda Macdonald. In *Postcolonial Studies* 6, no. 1 (April 2003): 37–46.

———. *Ego Sum*. Paris: Flammarion, 1979.

———. *Être singulier pluriel*. Paris: Galilée, 1996. Trans. Robert D. Richardson and Anne E. O'Byrne as *Being Singular Plural*. Stanford: Stanford University Press, 2000.

———. "Euryopa: Le regard au loin." *Cahiers d'Europe* 2 (Spring/Summer 1997): 82–94.

———. *L'expérience de la liberté*. Paris: Galilée, 1988. Trans. Bridget McDonald as *The Experience of Freedom*. Stanford: Stanford University Press, 1993.

———. *The Gravity of Thought*. Trans. François Raffoul and Gregory Recco. Amherst, NY: Humanity, 1997.

———. *Impératif catégorique*. Paris: Flammarion, 1983.

———. "L'insacrifiable." In *Une pensée finie*, 83–90. Paris, Galilée, 1990. Trans. Simon Sparks as "The Unsacrificable." In *A Finite Thinking*, 51–77. Stanford, CA: Stanford University Press, 2003.

———. "Manque de rien." In N. Avtonomova, ed., *Lacan avec les philosophes*, 201–6. Paris: Albin Michel, 1991.

———. *Muses*. Paris: Galilée, 1994. Trans. Peggy Kamuf as *Muses*. Stanford: Stanford University Press, 1996.

———. *La naissance à presence*. Trans. Brian Holmes et al. as *The Birth to Presence*. Stanford: Stanford University Press, 1993.

———. *L'oubli de la Philosophie*. Paris: Galilée, 1986. Trans. François Raffoul and Gregory Recco as "The Forgetting of Philosophy." In *The Gravity of Thought*, 7–74. Amherst, NY: Humanity, 1997.

———. *La pensée dérobée*. Paris: Galilée, 2001.

———. *Une pensée finie*. Paris: Galilée, 1990. Trans. and ed. Simon Sparks as *A Finite Thinking*. Stanford: Stanford University Press, 2003.

———. *Le poids d'une pensée*. Paris: Griffon d'argile and Presses Universitaires de Grenoble, 1991. Trans. François Raffoul and Gregory Recco as "The Weight of a Thought." In *The Gravity of Thought*, 75–84. Amherst, NY: Humanity, 1997.

———. *La remarque spéculative (un bon mot de Hegel)*. Paris: Galilée, 1973. Trans. Céline Surprenant as *The Speculative Remark (one of Hegel's bons mots)*. Stanford: Stanford University Press, 2001.

———. *Le sens du Monde*. Paris: Galilée, 1993. Trans. Jeffrey S. Librett as *The Sense of the World*. Minneapolis: University of Minnesota Press, 1997.

———. "The War of Monotheism." Trans. Amanda Macdonald. *Postcolonial Studies* 6, no. 1 (April 2003): 51–3.

Neske, Günther, and Emil Kettering, eds. *Antwort—Martin Heidegger im Gesprach*. Pfullingen: Neske, 1988. Trans. Lisa Harries and Joachim Neugroschel as *Martin Heidegger and National Socialism: Questions and Answers*. New York: Paragon House, 1990.

Nussbaum, Martha. *The Fragility of Goodness: Luck and Ethics in Greek Tragedy and Philosophy*. Cambridge: Cambridge University Press, 1986.

Onians, John. "'I Wonder . . . ': A Short History of Amazement." In John Onians, ed., *Sight and Insight: Essays on Art and Culture in Honour of E. H. Gombrich at 85*, 11–34. London: Phaidon, 1994.

Otto, Rudolf. *Das Heilige: Über das Irrationale in der Idee des Göttlichen und sein Verhältnis zum Rationalen*. Munich: Biederstein, 1947. Trans. John W. Harvey as *The Idea of the Holy: An Inquiry Into the Non-rational Factor in the Idea of the Divine and Its Relation to the Rational*. New York: Oxford University Press, 1970.

Pare, Ambroise, and Janis L. Pallister. *On Monsters and Marvels*. Chicago: University of Chicago Press, 1995.

Parsons, Howard L. "A Philosophy of Wonder." *Philosophy and Phenomenological Research* 30, no. 1 (September 1969): 84–101.

Pascal, Blaise. *Pensées*. Paris: Mercure de France, 1976. Trans. A. J. Krailsheimer as *Pensées*. New York: Penguin, 1966.

Patocka, Jan. *Heretical Essays in the Philosophy of History*. Ed. James Dodd. Trans. Erazim Kohák. Chicago: Open Court, 1996. Trans. Erika Abrams as *Essais hérétiques sur la philosophie de l'histoire*. Paris: Verdier, 1981.

Peperzak, Adriaan. "Illeity According to Levinas." *Philosophy Today* 42 (Supp. 1998): 41–46.

Peters, Edward. "The Desire to Know the Secrets of the World." *Journal of the History of Ideas* 62, no. 1 (October 2001): 593–610.

Peterson, Scott. "U.S. Mulls Air Strategies in Iraq." *Christian Science Monitor*, 30 January 2003.

Peirce, Charles S. *Collected Papers of Charles Sanders Peirce*. Cambridge: Harvard University Press, 1935.

Plato. *Complete Works*. Ed. John M. Cooper, with D. S. Hutchinson. Indianapolis: Hackett, 1997.

———. *Plato: The Collected Dialogues*. Ed. Edith Hamilton and Huntington Cairns. Princeton: Princeton University Press, 1989.

———. *The Republic*. Ed. C. D.C. Reeve. Trans. G. M.A. Grube. Indianapolis: Hackett, 1992. Trans. Friedrich Schleiermacher as *Der Staat*. In *Sämtliche Werke in Zwei Bänden*, 2:92–394. Vienna: Phaidon, 1925.

———. *Sämtliche Werke in Zwei Bänden*. Trans. Friedrich Schleiermacher. Vienna: Phaidon, 1925.

———. *Theaetetus*. Ed. Bernard Williams, revised by Myles Burnyeat. Trans. M. J. Levett. Indianapolis: Hackett, 1992.

———. *Works: Plato, with an English Translation*. Loeb Classical Library. 12 vols. Cambridge: Harvard University Press, 1914–1935.

Platt, Peter G. *Wonders, Marvels, and Monsters in Early Modern Culture*. Newark: University of Delaware Press, 2000.

Pomian, Krzysztof. *Collectors and Curiosities: Paris and Venice, 1500–1800*. Trans. Elizabeth Wiles-Portier. Cambridge: Polity, 1990.

Proudfoot, Wayne. *Religious Experience*. Berkeley: University of California Press, 1985.

Raffoul, François. *Heidegger and the Subject*. Trans. David Pettigrew and Gregory Recco. Atlantic Highlands, NJ: Humanities, 1999.

Ricoeur, Paul. *Autrement: Lecture d'autrement qu'être ou au-delà de l'essence d'Emmanuel Levinas*. Paris: Presses Universitaires de France, 1997.

———. *Soi-même comme un autre*. Paris: Seuil, 1990. Trans. Kathleen Blamey as *Oneself as Another*. Chicago: University of Chicago Press, 1992.

Rider, Jeff. "'Wonder with Fresh Wonder': Galbert the Writer and the Genesis of the *De Multro*." In Alan V. Murray and Jeff Rider, eds., *Galbert of Bruges and the Historiography of Medieval Flanders*. Washington, DC: Catholic University of America Press, 2009.

Ronell, Avital. *Stupidity*. Urbana: University of Illinois Press, 2002.

Roper, Lyndal. *Witch Craze: Terror and Fantasy in Baroque Germany*. New Haven: Yale University Press, 2004.

Rorty, Richard. *Contingency, Irony, and Solidarity*. Cambridge: Cambridge University Press, 1989.

———. "Derrida on Language, Being, and Abnormal Philosophy." *Journal of Philosophy* 74, no. 11 (November 1977): 676–77.

———. "Is Derrida a Transcendental Philosopher?" In David Wood, ed., *Derrida: A Critical Reader*, 235–46. Oxford: Blackwell, 1992.

Rubenstein, Mary-Jane. "Kierkegaard's Socrates: A Venture in Evolutionary Theory." *Modern Theology* 17, no. 4 (October 2001): 441–73.

————. "Relationality: The Gift After Ontotheology." *Telos* 123 (Spring 2002): 65–80.

Safranski, Rüdiger. *Martin Heidegger: Between Good and Evil.* Trans. Ewald Osers. Cambridge: Harvard University Press, 1998.

Sallis, John. *Delimitations: Phenomenology and the End of Metaphysics.* Bloomington: Indiana University Press, 1986.

————. *Force of Imagination: The Sense of the Elemental.* Indianapolis: Indiana University Press, 2004.

————. "A Wonder That One Could Never Aspire to Surpass . . ." In Kenneth Maly, ed., *The Path of Archaic Thinking,* 243–74. Albany: State University of New York, 1995.

Sartre, Jean-Paul. *Etre et le néant.* Paris: Gallimard, 1966. Trans. Hazel E. Barnes as *Being and Nothingness: A Phenomenological Essay on Ontology.* New York: Washington Square Press, 1992.

————. *La nausée.* Paris: Gallimard, 1982. Trans. Lloyd Alexander as *Nausea.* New York: New Directions, 1969.

Schleiermacher, Friedrich. *On Religion: Speeches to Its Cultured Despisers.* Ed. and trans. Richard Crouter. Cambridge: Cambridge University Press, 2000.

Schürmann, Reiner. *Heidegger on Being and Acting: From Principles to Anarchy.* Trans. Christine-Marie Gros in collaboration with the author. Bloomington: Indiana University Press, 1987.

Scott, Charles E. *The Lives of Things.* Bloomington: University of Indiana Press, 2004.

Shakespeare, William. *The Riverside Shakespeare.* Ed. G. Blakemore Evans. Boston: Houghton Mifflin, 1974.

Sheehan, James J., and Morton Sosna, eds. *The Boundaries of Humanity: Humans, Animals, Machines.* Berkeley: University of California Press, 1991.

Sheppard, Darren, Simon Sparks, and Colin Thomas, eds. *On Jean-Luc Nancy: The Sense of Philosophy.* New York: Routledge, 1997.

Silverman, Mark P. "Two Sides of Wonder: Philosophical Keys to the Motivation of Science Learning." *Synthèse* 80, no. 1 (July 1989): 43–61.

Solnit, Rebecca. "Three from Out of the Blue: Surprises of 2005." *TomDispatch.com,* 11 October 2005.

Sperry, Paul. "No Shock, No Awe, It Never Happened." *World Net Daily,* 3 April 2003.

Stein, Gertrude. "Galleries Lafayettes." In *Portraits and Prayers,* 169–172. New York: Random House, 1934.

Strenski, Ivan. "The Proper Object of the Study of Religion: Why It Is Better to Know Some of the Questions Than All of the Answers." In Slavica Jakelic and Lori Pearson, ed., *The Future of the Study of Religion: Proceedings of Congress 2000,* 145–71. Boston: Brill, 2004.

Styers, Randall. *Making Magic: Religion, Magic, and Science in the Modern World.* Oxford: Oxford University Press, 2003.

Taminiaux, Jacques. *The Thracian Maid and the Professional Thinker: Arendt and Heidegger.* Albany: State University of New York, 1997.

Taylor, Mark C. *Altarity.* Chicago: University of Chicago Press, 1987.

————. *Confidence Games: Money and Markets in a World Without Redemption.* Chicago: University of Chicago Press, 2004.

———. *Disfiguring: Art, Architecture, Religion*. Chicago: University of Chicago Press, 1992.

———. *Nots*. Chicago: University of Chicago Press, 1993.

Ullman, Harlan K., and James P. Wade. *Rapid Dominance—a Force for all Seasons: Technologies and Systems for Achieving Shock and Awe, a Real Revolution in Military Affairs*. London: Royal United Services Institute for Defence Studies, 1998.

———. *Shock and Awe: Achieving Rapid Dominance*. Washington, DC: Center for Advanced Concepts and Technology, 1996.

Ward, Benedicta. *Miracles and the Medieval Mind: Theory, Record, and Event, 1000–1215*. Philadelphia: University of Pennsylvania Press, 1987.

Weber, Samuel. *Targets of Opportunity: On the Militarization of Thinking*. New York: Fordham University Press, 2005.

Weschler, Lawrence. *Mr. Wilson's Cabinet of Wonders: Pronged Ants, Horned Humans, Mice on Toast, and Other Marvels of Jurassic Technology*. New York: Vintage, 1996.

Williams, David. *Deformed Discourse: The Function of the Monster in Medieval Thought and Literature*. Montreal: McGill-Queen's University Press, 1996.

Wittgenstein, Ludwig. *Culture and Value: A Selection from the Posthumous Remains*. Trans. Peter Winch. Oxford: Blackwell, 1998.

———. "Lecture on Ethics." *Philosophical Review* 74 (January 1965): 3–12.

———. *Notebooks, 1914–1916*. Ed. G. H. von Wright and G. E. M. Anscombe. New York: Harper, 1961.

———. *Tractatus Logico-Philosophicus*. Trans. D. F. Pears and B. F. McGuinness. New York: Routledge, 2001.

Wolin, Richard, ed. *The Heidegger Controversy*. Cambridge: MIT Press, 1993.

Wood, David, ed. *Derrida: A Critical Reader*. Oxford: Blackwell, 1992.

Wyschogrod, Edith. "Language and Alterity in the Thought of Levinas," in *The Cambridge Companion to Levinas*, 193. Cambridge: Cambridge University Press, 2002.

Young, Iris Marion. "Asymmetrical Reciprocity: On Moral Respect, Wonder, and Enlarged Thought." In *Intersecting Voices: Dilemmas of Gender, Political Philosophy, and Policy*, 38–59. Princeton: Princeton University Press, 1997.

# INDEX